"What an imaginative book—professors of communication theory writing about theology—and not just writing, but making quite illuminating remarks about theology and its communication."

—**Stanley Hauerwas, Gilbert T. Rowe Professor Emeritus of Divinity and Law, Duke University Divinity School**

"This volume announces the power of witnesses offering testimony for a faith narrative engaged in action. People embedded in a story of faith significance provide vivid markers that witness to the fact that God's world still has moments of revelatory change and genesis moments that transform lives."

—**Ronald C. Arnett, author of *Levinas's Rhetorical Demand: The Unending Obligation of Communication Ethics***

"*Words and Witnesses* provides long-needed explorations of the ways in which communication concerns, as well as theories of communication, run throughout the Christian tradition. Impelled by Christ's command to 'go, teach all nations,' and born in the era of Greco-Roman rhetoric, Christianity consistently engaged communication, laying an often-forgotten groundwork for contemporary communication study. *Words and Witnesses* wonderfully reintroduces those connections for a current generation of communication scholarship."

—**Paul A. Soukup, SJ, Pedro Arrupe Professor of Communication, Santa Clara University**

"*Words and Witnesses* is a beautiful book, cover to cover. Conceptually an original idea, it has collected communicative wisdom that has inspired the ages worldwide, and put it in a contemporary setting. Woods and Wood have given the academic fields of communications studies and theology a fundamental text."

—**Mark Fackler, Professor of Communications Emeritus, Calvin College**

"One of the most engaging compilations of cogent thought on religious communication. The collected forty-seven scholars have delved into relevant texts, contexts, and applications from seminal thinkers of theological communication. They have gleaned salient principles that not only inform our contemporary understanding of communication processes, but refresh and revitalize them. In the past God spoke to our ancestors through the prophets at many times and in various ways, and now speaks to us through communication scholars who have opened up tradition for us."

—**Terry Lindvall, Professor of Communication, Virginia Wesleyan University; author of *God Mocks: A History of Religious Satire from the Hebrew Prophets to Stephen Colbert***

"After thirty years in broadcasting, writing, speaking, and maintaining a personal library of over thirty thousand books, I assumed I had seen all that the publishing world had to offer. Never, I thought, could I describe any bound volume as 'unprecedented' or 'unique.' But *Words and Witnesses* exploded my lackadaisical assumptions. Never have I seen such an astute collection of essays analyzing the rhetorical styles, communications schemas, or dialogical strategies of so many different vendors of Christian words from so many different eras and from so many different Christian traditions. Of course, one would expect Augustine, Luther, Calvin, Kierkegaard, Newman, Merton, Ellul, Hauerwas, and C. S. Lewis, but you'll be delighted with Chiara Lubich, James Cone, Margaret Fell, Desmond Tutu, Saint Angela of Foligno, Peter Kreeft, Hans Urs von Balthasar, and dozens of others. Since we worship a Savior who warns that we will be judged by every word spoken, it does us wise to ask our elders and betters how they have dared to speak the Word through many, many words. Thank you for this extraordinary guide."

**—Al Kresta, President/CEO Ave Maria Communications
and Host of *Kresta in the Afternoon***

Words and Witnesses

Communication Studies in Christian Thought from Athanasius to Desmond Tutu

Edited by Robert H. Woods Jr. & Naaman K. Wood

HENDRICKSON
PUBLISHERS

Words and Witnesses: Communication Studies in Christian Thought from Athanasius to Desmond Tutu

Cover Design: Bradford Rusick

Printed in the United States of America

First Printing—September 2018

Library of Congress Cataloging-in-Publication

Names: Woods, Robert, 1970- editor.
Title: Words and witnesses : communication studies in Christian thought from
    Athanasius to Desmond Tutu / edited by Robert H. Woods Jr. and Naaman K. Wood.
Description: Peabody, MA : Hendrickson Publishers, 2018. | Includes bibliographical
    references and index.
Identifiers: LCCN 2018022891 | ISBN 9781683071730 (alk. paper)
Subjects: LCSH: Theology. | Communication--Religious aspects--Christianity.
Classification: LCC BR118 .W665 2018 | DDC 261.5/2--dc23
    LC record available at https://lccn.loc.gov/2018022891

Contents

PART TWO: Renaissance, Reformation, and Early Modern Christian Thinkers and Theologians

PART THREE: Modern and Contemporary
Christian Thinkers and Theologians

ACKNOWLEDGMENTS

Most books are labors of love, and this collection is no exception. We owe a debt of gratitude to several individuals and groups of people who supported us during the past three years as we worked to bring this project to publication.

To begin, we were blessed with a group of lovely, gifted, and sensitive writers, all brave enough in many cases to cross disciplinary borders into a territory not of their own. Instead of acting like colonists, they behaved liked guests. Their willingness to revise their work in ways that served our audience with distinction inspired us. We are extremely grateful to each author.

While the genesis of the book happened for us as graduate students, the desire to press more deeply into our shared Christian history emerged from a host of influences. Colleagues like Paul Patton and Kristen Sanders encouraged us to read Abraham Joshua Heschel. Conference presentations, conversations, and lifelong mentors loomed large over this project. Wise people (in alphabetical order) such as Ronald C. Arnett, Ken Chase, Cliff G. Christians, Mark Fackler, Benson Fraser, Janie Harden Fritz, Robert Fortner, Darlene Graves, Michael Graves, Em Griffin, Jack Keeler, Terry Lindvall, Martin Marty, Wally Metts, Robert Schihl, Quentin J. Schultze, Lynn Reynolds, Rodney Reynolds, Paul Soukup, Mark Allen Steiner, Bill Strom, Helen Sterk, Douglas Tarpley, Calvin Troup, Annalee Ward, and Mark Williams have all spoken with conviction and nuance about thinking Christianly in challenging times. And even though all of them could not contribute chapters to this collection, all of them had a hand in this work.

As we were in the final stages of editing, we heard that theologian Rev. Dr. James H. Cone had passed. We were fortunate that Cone reviewed Kevin Miller's essay in this volume. We found Dr. Cone to be a careful and gracious reviewer. At the end of his review, he made a request that took us aback. He asked that we let him know when the volume was published, so that he might use the essay in his courses. This request speaks not only of Miller's excellent reading of Cone, but also Cone's humility. Without a doubt, Cone is a towering figure in theological studies. He had little reason to care what communication scholars thought of his work. However, his willingness to let other voices have a say in how his students see his work is, to say the least, honoring to us and speaks to his commitment to hear voices that are not heard.

Additionally, many conversation partners and co-laborers helped to sustain the work in important ways. While the majority of the work occurred electronically, the generous support of Spring Arbor University's Forum 4:15 Conference and the Christianity and Communication Studies Network (www.theccsn.com) allowed us to interact personally with many of the authors. There is nothing like pondering over a problem together in silence, struggling toward a solution together, all the while looking someone in the eye.

Marsha Daigle-Williamson served as our primary copyeditor on this project, providing far more than basic copyediting skills. Marsha's command of Christian history and theology, her mastery of languages, and her keen nose for sniffing out inaccuracies, generalizations, and other misstatements added a layer of accountability that we would not otherwise have experienced. In the end, she did not agree with some analyses and statements in this book.

John Muether provided careful and outstanding work indexing this volume. His attention to detail throughout helps us to serve our readers better.

Spring Arbor University's (SAU) library staff (Robbie Bolton, Elizabeth Walker-Papke, Karen Parsons, Kami Moyer, and Susan Panak) provided research support that allowed us to stay on schedule. SAU also granted one of us (Robert) a sabbatical during fall 2017 to help complete this project. Redeemer University College colleagues Ray Louter and Deanne van Tol challenged and encouraged one of us (Naaman) during his transition from North Carolina to Canada. And Redeemer University's Office of Research generously awarded us a grant in support of publication.

We are grateful for Hendrickson Publishers and gifted editors like Carl Nellis who recognized the timeliness and significance of this project and offered invaluable feedback early on that focused our scope and tightened our arguments. Carl's advocacy and insights throughout the project made this work stronger.

Finally, we are extremely grateful for our spouses who provided encouragement during long editorial sessions. They provided time and space for us to miss dinners, weekend getaways, and normal household duties. Without their support this project would still be "in process."

We absolve all our friends and colleagues of any responsibility for any weaknesses that remain.

Contributors

Donald H. Alban Jr., PhD, Professor of Communication Studies, Liberty University.

Diane M. Badzinski, PhD, Professor and Chair of the Department of Communication, Colorado Christian University.

Kenneth Baillie, retired Salvation Army, former chief administrator of the Salvation Army's Central Territory.

Steven A. Beebe, PhD, Regents' and University Distinguished Professor of Communication Studies, Texas State University.

Stephanie Bennett, PhD, Fellow for Student Engagement and Professor of Communication and Media Ecology, Palm Beach Atlantic University.

William J. Brown, PhD, Professor and Research Fellow in the School of Communication and the Arts, Regent University.

Kathy Bruner, MFA, Assistant Professor of Film and Media Production, Taylor University.

Dennis D. Cali, PhD, Professor and Chair of the Department of Communication, University of Texas at Tyler.

Thomas J. Carmody, PhD, Professor of Communication Studies, Vanguard University.

Kenneth R. Chase, PhD, Associate Professor and Chair of the Department of Communication, Wheaton College.

Clifford G. Christians, PhD, Research Professor Emeritus of Communications; Professor Emeritus of Media Studies; Professor Emeritus of Journalism, University of Illinois at Urbana-Champaign.

Terri Lynn Cornwell, PhD, Associate Professor of Communication Studies, Lynchburg College.

Paul A. Creasman, PhD, Professor of Communication and Chair of the Department of Communication and English, Arizona Christian University.

Mary Albert Darling, MA, Associate Professor of Communication, Spring Arbor University.

Benson P. Fraser, PhD, Westminster Canterbury Fellow for Religious Studies and Lifelong Learning, Virginia Wesleyan University.

Janie Marie Harden Fritz, PhD, Professor of Communication and Rhetorical Studies, Duquesne University.

Frank Fuentes, BA in History, Texas Tech University.

Brian Gilchrist, PhD, Assistant Professor of Communication, Mount St. Mary's University.

Mark A. Gring, PhD, Associate Professor of Communication and Assistant Graduate Director, Texas Tech University.

Tom Holsinger-Friesen, PhD, Associate Professor of Theology, Spring Arbor University.

Russell P. Johnson, PhD candidate in Philosophy of Religions, University of Chicago Divinity School.

Jennifer Jones, PhD, Associate Professor of Communication, Seton Hill University.

John R. Katsion, PhD, Associate Professor of Communication, Northwest Missouri State University.

Thomas M. Lessl, PhD, Professor of Communication Studies, University of Georgia.

Christina Littlefield, PhD, Assistant Professor of Journalism and Religion, Pepperdine University.

Michael A. Longinow, Professor of Journalism, Biola University.

Craig T. Maier, PhD, Assistant Professor of Communication and Rhetorical Studies, Duquesne University.

Gerald J. Mast, PhD, Professor of Communication, Bluffton University.

Elizabeth W. McLaughlin, PhD, Associate Professor of Communication, Bethel College.

Kevin D. Miller, PhD, Professor of Communication, Huntington University.

Julie W. Morgan, EdD, Professor of Communication Studies, Eastern University.

Timothy M. Muehlhoff, PhD, Professor of Communication, Biola University.

Margaret M. Mullan, PhD, Assistant Professor of Communication, East Stroudsburg University of Pennsylvania.

Blake J. Neff, PhD, Lecturer in Communication, Indiana Wesleyan University.

Richard K. Olson, PhD, Associate Professor and Chair of the Department of Communication Studies, University of North Carolina at Wilmington.

Joy E. A. Qualls, PhD, Associate Professor and Chair of the Department of Communication Studies, Biola University.

Quentin J. Schultze, PhD, Professor Emeritus, Communication Arts and Sciences, Calvin College.

Asbjørn Simonnes, DMin, PhD, Professor of Humanities and Teacher Training, Volda University College, Norway.

Kathleen Osbeck Sindorf, MA, Associate Professor of Communication, Cornerstone University.

Michael Ray Smith, PhD, Professor of Public Relations, Lee University.

Barbara S. Spies, OFS, PhD, Professor of Communication Arts, Cardinal Stritch University.

Mark Allan Steiner, PhD, Associate Professor of Communication, Christopher Newport University.

Bill Strom, PhD, Professor of Media and Communication, Trinity Western University.

Calvin L. Troup, PhD, President, Geneva College.

Mark L. Ward Sr., PhD, Associate Professor of Communication, University of Houston-Victoria.

Kenneth E. Waters, PhD, Professor of Journalism, Pepperdine University.

Mark A. E. Williams, PhD, Associate Professor of Communication Studies, California State University, Sacramento.

Naaman K. Wood, PhD, Assistant Professor of Media and Communication Studies, Redeemer University College.

FOREWORD

Clifford G. Christians

Communication is a world of ideas. As is true of all academic disciplines, it is created of concepts, emic categories, and scientific models. Higher education is our home for communication studies, and the centerpiece of this field is the ideas needed for critical thinking and knowledge creation.

Communications is also a complex technological regime, the crux of the digital phenomenon that is revolutionizing the planet. But communication tools are a surface reality. The field's intellectual substance will determine whether communications is equipped for the globalized twenty-first century. The crucial issue is whether our theorizing is adequate, what foundations undergird our enterprise. Our trajectory now and in the future is conceptual.

If we understand communications as a world of ideas, our primary task is credible theory. The long-term future of the field depends on the common language of theory to assist us in thinking systematically about the issues that matter. In the absence of the continual clarification that active theorizing provides, communication studies will tend to deal with the secondary and the one-dimensional.

For those who understand communication as an intellectual network of ideas, this book is a gold mine. It is an electrifying compilation of theologians and the theologically minded across history and geography, luminaries who worked productively with concepts and were and are at home with the ideational. Through the erudite hand of the authors, the theistic worldview of key figures in intellectual history enriches our understanding of communication studies and enables readers to think Christianly about communication theory and practice.

This book is right about tradition, claiming that it is not a contract of "outdated rules and obsolete faith." Tradition is considered instead a dynamic resource of accumulated wisdom that challenges our scholarship today. The argument of *Words and Witnesses* is transparent: Christians ought to engage in thoughtful and meaningful recovery of their own legacy, "applying it to the present moment and preserving it for the next generation." This Woods-Wood volume accomplishes its purpose. It puts prominent concepts in communication studies and influential Christian thought in conversation. The chapters show communication scholars of faith how to interpret and apply wisdom from the past to the perplexities of today.

As an academic of faith, I resonate personally with its intelligence. The forty-three chapters have gravitas and are instructive. I'm committed to faith-based scholarship and its core beliefs about the created order, epistemology, the nature of the human, and axiology. In this book's knowledge abundance, the value of faith-based scholarship for communication theory became obvious in my reading. Theory is the substantive issue for our field, and in this book it is likewise *sine qua non*. As Mohandas Gandhi proved to the world, "without theory there is no revolution." In an ironic twist on conventional skepticism, theoretical claims are not a medieval remnant but the catalyst for innovation. Without theories that capture our minds and way of being, we cannot finally avoid agnosticism except on the arbitrary grounds of personal preference. Rigor in and agreement on borderless theory will enable us to work fruitfully in the international mode.

I develop the theory argument in this foreword, concentrating on the structure of theory itself. Specific theories are included below in this massive text; some of the earliest communication theories can be identified in Justin Martyr, Saint Augustine of Hippo, Saint Anselm of Canterbury, and Saint Ignatius of Loyola. They are informative, but this foreword presents a larger perspective on the nature of theorizing. Three arguments about theory are inescapable in these chapters: theories are presuppositional; theories produce parsimonious concepts; and theories are symbolic constructs. As I elaborate on this wider context, I invite those interested in the philosophy of communication to read this book with the current state of our theorizing in mind and come to grips with the density that these chapters contribute.

In the social scientific modality that dominates communications theory, theorizing is an examination of external events. Theories are neutral, the redactions of artificially fixed hypotheses. The Greek tradition of rational universals and the Enlightenment commitment to Cartesian noncontingency presume that theories have an ahistorical foundation derived from disembodied reason. In this theoretical formalism, an apparatus of neutral concepts is constructed in terms of objectivism. The social scientific modality entails a set of agreed-upon validity rules that ensures nonalignment. This is a proceduralism with a neutrality presumption.

Thomas Kuhn's *The Structure of Scientific Revolutions* is a classic in questioning the value-free character of theory formation. For Kuhn, theorizing is paradigm construction, rather than the normal science of verifying that propositions are externally and internally valid.[1] Theories are a complex mixture of politics, creativity, intuition, and beliefs. The forty-seven thinkers of this book represent theory in these terms. They are schooled in the humanities where theories are postulates about reality. For them, theories elucidate our fundamental beliefs about the world.

Theories for this book are not *ex nihilo,* arising out of nothing and non-contingent. Theorists identify niches and inconsistencies and conundrums over against existing conventions and calculate how to start over intellectually. Theories are not abstract theorems of statistical precision, but theorizing is redefined as the power of the imagination to give us an inside perspective on reality.

In the humanities, represented by the thinkers of this book, theory is grounded in presuppositions. From this perspective, questions of method are secondary to the basic belief system that guides the theoretician in epistemologically fundamental ways. Communication theory, in its semantic derivations, requires the mutually known and is therefore value-conditioned.

The theorizing of this book contradicts the scientific naturalism appropriated by the social sciences generally and communications specifically—naturalism which presumes that objects and events situated in space-time contain all the facts there are. The theistic worldview contradicts this structure of knowing. In this humanities version of theoretical modeling, the aim is not technical explanation but understanding and meaningful action. In worldview epistemology, the empirical remains embedded in human experience rather than becoming a statistical and abstract empiricism. It does not fall prey to the fallacy of naturalistic theorizing, where reason determines both the genesis and the conclusion. Faith-based scholarship challenges social scientific research to take seriously the humanities' portentous agenda.

Parsimonious generalization is the second important dimension of humanities-based theorizing. In the standard literature, these conclusions from theory are called "sensitized concepts."[2] This terminology is Herbert Blumer's influential distinction between sensitizing and definitive concepts. Quantitative methodologies typically produce definitive abstractions through fixed procedures that isolate concepts from the language of those being studied. IQ, for example, becomes the definition of intelligence. Sensitized concepts comprise a different framework for ordering knowledge. They are formed from within the intellectual arena being studied. They get at the essence, the meaning, of events or problematics. They are short of formalistic inelasticity, yet apropos to engage the scholar's mind and provoke activism.

Sensitizing concepts, here called parsimonious generalizations, integrate multiple levels of meaning accumulation. Through them, theorists of the humanities unveil meaningful portraits of the human condition. Examples of these parsimonious concepts are found in virtually every one of the forty-three essays, such as faithful witness, hostile audiences, institutional oppression, incarnate communication, realistic rhetoric, knowledge gaps, divine accommodation, attentive silence, embodied action, pacifism and abolition, blurring boundaries, relational messages, soul *agape*, hospitable resistance, prophetic imagination, perspective-taking, and moral reasoning.

The hermeneutics of humanitistic theorizing opposes causal explanations that formally stipulate the aegis of prediction and control. Parsimonious generalizations result when scholars know enough to identify the determinative aspects of the event being studied and to distinguish these main features from digressions and parentheses. When true interiority has occurred, the concepts are valid even though they are not based on randomization, controlled observation, and mathematical measurement.

As this book demonstrates, parsimonious generalizations are a claim for realism. In this knowledge production, conceptual properties do exist independently of the mind. In philosophical realism, there are entities that obtain in their own terms; humans do not invent them but discover their features. For realists, the external world contains a vast number of objects and properties independent of the human mind that need to be symbolized for us to recognize their exisence.

Social constructionism is the dominant pattern in today's social science, according to Robert Miner.[3] In constructivist theorizing, both problems and their solutions are fabricated. Bertrand Russell's epistemology, Rudolf Carnap's logical positivism, Claude Shannon and Warren Weaver's mathematical theory of communication, and Émile Durkheim's functionalism are models of constructivism. For the social science methodology of our field, humans as constructors and desconstructors are typically presumed. Theories in the humanities represent a realist perspective instead in which truths about the world that exist within it are discovered. Those conclusions that meet the test of parsimony are an antidote to relativism.

Third, the theorists of *Words and Witnesses* make interpretation indispensable in theory formation. Their argument, based on the nature of language, therefore, has special appeal for communication studies. From the theological theorists and their elaborations, *ars interpretandi* is the lifeblood of the theoretical genre. While this argument from the humanities scholars at work in this book does not in itself discount algorithmic modeling, it makes theories from the humanities indispensable for communication studies as an academic schema.

The humanities are based on the idea that through the study of language the fundamental conditions of our humanness are disclosed. Communication is not external to human life but constitutive of it. As Hans-Georg Gadamer puts it, "That language is originally human means at the same time that man's being-in-the-world is primordially linguistic."[4] With language situating us in reality, the mind is understood as reconstruing experience and representing it symbolically. The meaning of theoretical statements derives from the interpretive context that human culture symbolizes, according to Susanne K. Langer.[5]

Symbolic action as a distinctive feature of the human species comes into its own in our theory-making.

Humans live by interpretations. Systems of meaning and value are produced as a creative process. We are born into an intelligible and interpreted universe. As the book's chapters demonstrate profoundly, interpretation is dialogue with human existence past and present. We understand ourselves as subjects only through an interpretation of symbolic meanings we construct. Humans live by interpreting experience through the agency of culture.

In William Urban's celebrated dispute with Paul Tillich over his totally symbolic system, Tillich was convinced that all knowledge and experience cannot be of a symbolic character.[6] The symbolic realm must be limited by something nonsymbolic. Every theorist in this book insists on such a nonnegotiable ultimate that establishes for him or her the possibility of interpreting the world meaningfully. *Words and Witnesses* represents uniformly the nonsymbolic ground of being. People shape their own view of reality, but this fact does not presume that reality as a whole is inherently nonstructured until it is ordered by human language. In the theistic worldview, reality is not merely raw material, but a coherent whole, an intelligible order that makes theorizing intelligible.

This book offers a comprehensive review of humanities theory and, in so doing, teaches its readers the character of theoretical perspectives. Its keen execution helps communications in these turbulent days fulfill its promise of healing.

COMMUNICATION STUDIES AND CHRISTIAN THOUGHT IN CONVERSATION: FROM PAST TO PRESENT

Robert H. Woods Jr. and Naaman K. Wood

The Background

The seeds for this book were planted by our experiences in graduate school some twenty years ago and have been nurtured in subsequent conversations with colleagues and students since that time.

In graduate school, committed professors helped us to understand better how theology functioned as a lens for thinking Christianly about communication, and how some of the earliest communication theories actually could be identified in the writings and deeds of Origen, Saint Thomas Aquinas, and Saint Ignatius of Loyola, to name several. Since then, conferences and writing projects provided further opportunities to explore how John Calvin's, Karl Barth's, or C. S. Lewis's theology offered fresh understanding of a current event or popular artifact. More recently, our students' questions about faithful Christian living in a digital culture characterized by ideological division, incivility, and nationalism had us turning for wisdom to the works of Saint Irenaeus of Lyon, Jeanne-Marie Bouvier de la Motte-Guyon, Jacques Ellul, and Archbishop Desmond Tutu.

Most of the books we found in our "ancient-future"[1] quest, however, did not turn to key figures in the Christian tradition as a resource for tackling contemporary issues in communication studies. Although we did find a few, those books tended to be longer reflections and were written for smaller scholarly audiences.[2] Several sources we located drew on multiple Christian theologians and thinkers to address specific issues in an area such as interpersonal communication or public speaking.[3] We found all of these works extremely helpful, but none covered a broader array of theologians and topics aimed at a broader audience, from laypersons and pastors to undergraduate and graduate students. Enter this book.

Our goal is to provide an accessible guide that explores the works of a range of influential Christians throughout history to bring their wisdom and practical insights to communicative problems of everyday life and to expand our conversations with communication studies and faith. Our hope is that the forty-three chapters in this collection demonstrate how Christian thought encourages readers to reflect on communication theory and practice in not just distinctly Christian but also deeply Christian ways.

The "So What?" and "Why Now?"

In *Technopoly: The Surrender of Culture to Technology* (1992), communication theorist and cultural critic Neil Postman lamented that technological society's most insidious accomplishment was to convince people that the future does not need any connection to the past. Postman's main concern was that our culture's technological optimism equated information with wisdom, promoted individuality over community, and cut off people from the past, namely from *tradition*. In such a society, technology not only shapes reality but also becomes the standard by which the self and institutions, whether in the church, education, or politics, are ultimately measured.[4]

Note what we mean by the word "tradition." We do not mean that tradition is comprised of outdated rules or puritanical moralisms that support tyrannical power structures. Tradition is not the dead, lifeless, obsolete faith of the living. Nor is it the vain repetition of a fictional and homogenous past where Christians are thought to have said and believed the exact same thing. To the contrary, tradition is the "accumulated wisdom and the resulting disciplines, customs, and beliefs that a people carries from person to person through generational time—all of it nurtured as a living dialogue that includes the remembered 'voices' of the past."[5] And as tradition thrives on a deep engagement with the past, it also wisely discerns the needs and issues of the present moment. For those Christian communities who take seriously their conversations with remembered voices, the burden is on them to decide where the conversation needs to go next. Tradition is thus an active and dynamic event in the life of a community, because living communities are responsible for remembering what is passed down and for engaging it, interpreting it, applying it to the present moment, and preserving it for the next generation.

While nearly three decades have passed since Postman's prophetic utterance, many mainstream and religious communication scholars agree on at least one thing: our digital age fully embraces and determinedly perpetuates a "religion of technological optimism."[6] Technological optimism champions "the collection and dissemination of information as a route to social progress and personal happiness."[7] The end goal of personal happiness inadvertently places the individual human as the most important force in defining reality. It is the individual who defines all things, including the past, present, and future. In straining toward personal happiness, technological optimism denies any tradition that calls individuals to live in community, to reflect on the past, and to cultivate memory. After all, it is a communal and traditional memory that works against technological optimism by rightfully decentering the individual in his or her persistent and unfettered pursuit of self-interest and immediate gratification. Put another way, the Christian tradition utters a prophetic "no" to the individualism and unwarranted optimism at the core of our culture's dominant technological framing-story.

More insidiously, perhaps, technological optimism finds it roots in an older dominant framing story, the story of Enlightenment modernity. Similar to technological optimism, modernity is a thought system that self-consciously cuts itself off from tradition and makes so-called objective reason and science the supreme *epistemology* or way of determining what we believe.[8] Taken together, modernity's rejection of tradition and its "valorization of scientific facts end up reducing Christianity to just another collection of propositions."[9] As Calvin College philosopher and author James K. A. Smith observes, "Modern Christianity tends to think of the church either as a place where individuals come to find answers to their questions or as one more stop where individuals can try to satisfy their consumerists' desires. As such, Christianity becomes intellectualized rather than incarnate, commodified rather than the site of genuine community."[10] And if Christianity as a system of thought becomes just another commodity in the marketplace of ideas, it can quickly cease to have a vibrant life of communal memory embodied in peoples across time who converse and discern what it means to live out the gospel.

In short, without a recovery of the Christian tradition in all areas of life and study, modernity's influence on our communication may continue to weaken the efficacy of Christian witness. Ironically, many Christians have unknowingly exchanged the richness of community for a modernist world-and-life view, cutting themselves off from the Christian tradition and succumbing to the overemphasis on the values of progress, efficiency, propositions, consumerism, and individuality. In order to resist such values, it is vital that Christians engage in thoughtful and meaningful recovery of the Christian tradition.[11]

In this book, we hope to recover tradition with two activities. First, as explained in greater detail in the section below ("The Approach"), we asked our authors to engage in a strategic return, a rereading, and therefore an embodied remembering, of many influential Christian voices who have come before us. Second, a mere remembering of past Christian voices is not enough. Rather, Christians—and more specifically for this volume, communication scholars of faith—must interpret, contextualize, and apply wisdom from the past to contemporary issues of today.

The Approach

For many Christian communication scholars, engaging historical reflections of the church is somewhat uncharted territory. Although there are a handful of scholars who have led the way, many of us have not made a concerted effort to turn toward theological thinkers. Part of this hesitation makes perfect sense: communication scholars are not historical theologians. We have not been taught to read through the thick, beautiful, and sometimes troubling sea of Christian voices—from the apostolic church father Saint Irenaeus of Lyon to the medieval mystic St. Angela of Foligno to black theologian James Cone. Because many of us are in uncharted territory, this volume serves as a first step in what recovery of the Christian tradition for communication and media studies might look like.

Rather than provide an encyclopedic overview of a particular Christian thinker's writings, each author offers a tight, focused close reading of a single work (or smaller portions from a single or multiple works). While there is great merit in providing a broad picture of a Christian thinker's work, this collection is unique in that it emphasizes the depth of insight that a single work can offer to us today. Furthermore, the focus on a single or smaller portions of a text helps us to recognize that primary sources are vital to the process of recovering tradition, and that recovery is not a simple process. It proceeds slowly in a lifelong journey of returning, rereading, and remembering. Many of us, both authors and readers, are just at the beginning of this process.

Additionally, as part of their close reading, authors placed the text or texts into historical context, explaining why Christian thinkers wrote what they wrote, pressing more deeply into historical thinking. As they do, each Christian thinker's work becomes more illuminating, vibrant, and urgent. Instead of asking only, "*What* did Saint Augustine or John Calvin or Reinhold Niebuhr say here?" our authors also asked, "*Why* did Saint Augustine, John Calvin, or Reinhold Niebuhr say this at this particular moment?" These chapters therefore document the reality that Christians before us took seriously events on the ground of their lived experiences and responded seriously and theologically to those events. Their truths may be timeless, but the riches of their truths become increasingly profound and poignant the more clearly they are embedded in key contextual landmarks.

Finally, each chapter concludes with a practical application or a way that the wisdom of the Christian tradition can shed light on communicative issues facing the church and communication studies today. At times, authors focus on challenges of the digital age, the political tensions of the early days of the Trump Administration, historical and present social injustices, the witness of Christians to the wider world, the refinement of Communication Theory, or a host of related topics. There is a broad range of ideas in the applications that not all readers (just as not all of this collection's editors) may agree with, but this too shows the variety included in this volume. To this extent, this volume assists any Christian as she or he attempts to live faithfully in the present moment. For example, although Christians like Saint Augustine or Jeanne-Marie Bouvier de la Motte-Guyon could not have anticipated a world with digital messaging, their views of embodiment offer constructive points of reflection for living faithfully in a digital age. Or, similarly, although Saint Ignatius of Loyola and Thomas Cranmer could not have known about the almost overwhelming political divisiveness in twenty-first-century North America, their reflections on language help us recover a sense of public civility.

Similarly, the wisdom of theological thinkers can also offer insights into communication studies. For example, interpersonal communication scholar Diane M. Badzinski reflects on how *The Rule of St. Benedict* might help Relational Dialectic Theory nuance its understanding of the very nature of a dialectic. Journalist and communication professor Kathy Sindorf suggests that Archbishop Desmond Tutu's focus on the African concept of *ubuntu* offers a productive emphasis in the way communication scholars theorize and research forgiveness. Media scholar Dennis Cali argues that the spiritual reflections of Chiara Lubich assist media ecologists in heading off potential problems in the application of their work. These writings are, of course, opening statements in a fertile conversation between historical Christian thinking, communication studies, and the church.

In brief, individual chapters across the collection center around one or more of the following intersections between communication and theology:

- How contemporary communication scholars might turn to influential Christian theologians or thinkers as resources for addressing specific problems, controversies, or crises in communication today.

- How particular theologies (doctrines, church practices, biblical texts, etc.) articulated by influential Christian theologians or thinkers might help redescribe specific issues in communication in ways otherwise unavailable to mainstream communication scholars.

- How a particular text, communication theory, scholar, or phenomenon might offer a real critique of the church in a way that fairly exposes the church's specific ethical, communicative, or social failures.

- How traditions, ideas, or texts in communication studies might help solve a specific problem or oversight in the church as articulated by influential Christian theologians and thinkers.

The Theologians and Thinkers

Our use of the term "theological thinker" in addition to "theologian" seeks to open the breadth of the Christian tradition to include those who were not traditionally considered theologians. There are certainly the usual suspects of well-known theologians in this collection, including Saint Augustine, Saint Anselm of Canterbury, Martin Luther, Walter Rauschenbusch, Hans Urs von Balthasar, and Stanley Hauerwas. But we have also included other figures who are not traditionally considered theologians, such as the mystic Saint Thérèse of Lisieux, Salvation Army cofounder Catherine Booth, the mother of Quakerism Margaret Fell, French sociologist Jacques Ellul, and Catholic apologist Frank Sheed.

No doubt some will wonder how we chose the forty-three theologians and thinkers in this collection. To be clear, we consider all forty-three figures in this volume to be sages who said something significant, timely, and relevant for us today. We do not, however, wish to make the claim they are the *most* remembered or influential figures. In fact, the recovery of tradition means that we would do well to remember some voices that have been minimized or overlooked, as we have done in this collection with Norwegian revivalist Hans Nielsen Hauge and Franciscan mystic Saint Angela of Foligno, to name just two. Therefore, instead of starting with a predetermined list of theologians or thinkers, we turned to the wisdom, memory, and concerns of our authors. We knew several colleagues who had done work on a particular theologian or thinker and asked them to contribute. In some cases, they recommended other authors for us to invite. We also performed a review of literature in communication studies to see which theologians had been written about over the years and found several theological thinkers who had not been on our radar.

Furthermore, finding authors for a project like this was a bit of a challenge. We needed writers who could engage both theology and communication theory, and who could write with one foot firmly planted in each camp. At one point, we had over seventy theologians and nearly as many authors on board for what started out as a multivolume collection. But as projects like this tend to go, we lost several authors over the three-year span required to prepare this volume for publication. Ultimately, we decided that a single volume was the best way to get the conversation started.

Throughout, we made a point to include Catholics, Protestants, women, men, and theologians and thinkers of color in the collection, but our approach to selecting contributors along with the typical kind of author attrition on projects like this determined the final list of historical figures. While not reflecting the full diversity of the Christian tradition, we believe this collection is headed in the right direction. Quite frankly, losing chapters on Saint Thomas Aquinas, Origen, Saint Bonaventure, Hildegard of Bingen, Saint Catherine of Siena,

George Fox, Karl Barth, Dietrich Bonhoeffer, Pope Benedict XVI, and Cornel West, to name several, was painful, but as our colleagues reminded us, that is what additional volumes are for.

In conclusion, the voices throughout this volume beg for an "alternative consciousness"—a popular phrase we borrow from Old Testament theologian and author Walter Brueggemann—that is "devoted to the pathos and passion of covenanting."[12] This passion finds significant and consistent historical footing in the Christian assertion that individual identity is understood only within the context of communal identity as evidenced by tradition. It further recognizes the church as a nurturing community that provides a context for discipleship, education, and wisdom. Christians believe that throughout history God speaks to and through both individuals and the church. Many of the communication problems and crises they faced are ones we currently face. Their courage and devotion to interpretive reflection on the original deposit of faith in Scripture are sources of encouragement and instruction for living well and communicating wisely today.

So let the conversations begin, and may they bear much fruit.

PART ONE

EARLY CHURCH AND MEDIEVAL CHRISTIAN THINKERS AND THEOLOGIANS

CHAPTER 1

Justin Martyr: Articulating a "Faithful Witness" in Public and Political Life

Mark Allan Steiner

Abstract: Justin Martyr (c.100–165), a second-century apologist and martyr, articulates a compelling "faithful witness" stance in drawing upon his Christian faith to engage in the public and political life of the Roman Empire of his day. His ideas showcase and model for us today both the need for a compelling communal identity, and a combination of rhetorical skill and careful listening that finds and cultivates common ground.

Introduction

Justin Martyr, a second-century Christian apologist and theologian, is known in history by this name because of his faithfulness in sacrificing his life to declare ultimate allegiance to Christ rather than to the sensibilities and demands of the Roman Empire. He became a Christian after watching several other Christians brutally executed by the Roman authorities.[1] This uncompromising conviction marked Justin's life, which exhibited "a streak of the unquiet rebel" who "was not about to abandon his radicalism."[2]

Justin died exceedingly well, but that has tended to obscure the fact that Justin also lived exceedingly well. He was "a pioneer type of Greek apologist, show[ing] that philosophy is truth, reason a spiritual power and Christianity the fulness of both."[3] Justin engaged well and faithfully in the public and political spheres in which he lived, in the exacting crucible of Roman persecution and cultural hostility. While Christians living in twenty-first-century America are not called to die well in the specific way that Justin did, they do face many of the same challenges in living well and dying for their faith daily in a political and cultural landscape characterized by ideological division, incivility, scapegoating, and demonizing.

In this chapter, I explore how Justin serves as a positive example of how twenty-first-century Christians can engage culture and public life in authentic, faithful, and God-honoring ways. Our present sociopolitical climate is both strange and eerily hostile to the values and visions of Christian flourishing. More specifically, Justin's notion of the Logos, as it appears in his *First Apology* and *Second Apology*, is much more justifiably seen as a rhetorical innovation than as a theological one. As such, Justin exemplifies what an authentic "faithful witness" stance looked like in the theological uncertainty and the sociopolitical hostility of his day, and what that authentic "faithful witness" stance can look like in ours today.[4]

"Faithful Witness" in the Crucible of the Roman Empire

In the Roman Empire of Justin's second century, the sociocultural climate maintained suspicion and persecution of Christians that continued from the Neronian persecution between 60 and 70 CE.[5] As Christianity began to be broadly recognized as essentially different from Judaism, Romans generally saw Christians as perplexing and uncomfortably subversive outsiders to be scrutinized, contained, or even neutralized. Christians were seen as politically divisive, uncivil, and unwilling to work proactively for the unity and flourishing of Roman culture and society. Romans saw Christians as superstitious and irreligious, denying the gods of others and of the culture more generally and severing the then taken-for-granted link between religion and empire.[6] As such, slanderous claims about Christians persisted. They were "accused of all kinds of wickedness," and "their assemblies for worship, instruction, and for the celebration of the Eucharist" were seen as "secret gatherings for incest, child murder, and cannibalism."[7]

Justin's *First Apology* and *Second Apology* were written between 151 and 155, and they constitute his rhetorical defenses against unfair charges, accusations, and assumptions not only about specific Christians but also about Christianity in general. The *First Apology*, formally addressed to the Emperor Antonius Pius and other political notables, features a general defense against erroneous beliefs about Christians and the charges leveled against them. It was designed "to disarm unbelief and to show that Christianity was not contemptible" but was instead "essentially rational."[8] Despite the specific and formal address at the beginning of the work, scholars generally agree that the apology was actually intended for a broader audience of "ordinary non-Christian people."[9] The much shorter *Second Apology*, on the other hand, appears to be a fragment of a larger work. Some scholars therefore hold that the *Second Apology* is part of or an appendix or postscript to the *First*,[10] while other scholars treat it as a separate work and date it shortly after the first.[11]

While Justin uses both *Apologies* to rebut specific claims, he also works powerfully to reframe the whole so-called debate about Christianity in ways that suggest not only that the claims about the nefarious features and influences of Christianity are simply not true, but also that Christianity can and should be seen as a uniquely positive force in people's lives and in Roman culture more generally. His concept of the Logos is the key vehicle by which he does this.

The Logos in Justin's *Apologies*

The concept of the Logos, as Justin applies it in both *Apologies*, is his theoretical move to harmonize Christian orthodoxy with the accumulated wisdom from the Jewish and Greek traditions. *Logos* was a significant and multifaceted term in second-century Platonism, and one that was generally familiar to Romans both within and outside the Christian community. In Greek, it generically translates as "reason," but—beginning with Heraclitus in the sixth century BCE—the term also began to take on a more specialized meaning, referring to the eternal and immutable truth that is accessed in varying degrees through philosophic inquiry and careful, self-reflective, synthetic, and philosophically deep engagement with art, literature, and poetry. According to archeologist and classicist Eva Brann, Heraclitus saw the Logos as a unified "cosmic Wise Thing," combining knowledge and wisdom of all things into a coherent and grand whole.[12] Plato's understanding of "Logos"—conceived in expressly idealistic (antimaterialistic) terms and captured in his theory of the "forms"—follows from Heraclitus and the pre-Platonic philosophers that followed Heraclitus's line of thinking.[13]

In the *Apologies*, Justin adapts this overarching sense of the Logos to frame his general rhetorical defenses of Christians and Christianity. More specifically, Justin adapts it to advocate how Christianity's monotheism is both distinct from and a fulfillment of Judaism,[14] how it explains Platonic thinking, and what some of its specific practices are. In Justin's view, the Logos in its full form is located in the person of Jesus Christ, and other people and other intellectual and/or religious traditions have traces of it. "Christ is the Firstborn of God," Justin writes in the *First Apology*, and as such, "He is the logos of whom every race of men and women were partakers."[15]

Justin elaborates on this connection in the *Second Apology*, claiming that since Jesus represents the Logos in its full form, those "in Christ" have the most compelling and most comprehensive access to the full measure of knowledge and wisdom that the Logos represents. This knowledge and wisdom is "greater than all human teaching," as "the whole rational principle became Christ." Those who are not Christians have some measure of access to the Logos—they can offer insight that is "elaborated according to their share of logos by invention and contemplation."[16] But because they do not "know all that concerns logos, who is Christ," their insights are incomplete and in some cases contradictory.[17]

Even so, those who are "outside" of Christ can participate in significant—even if not in total and/or salvific—measure. Justin mentions the historical Socrates as an abiding example of someone who achieved this. Justin declares, Jesus Christ "was partially known even by Socrates."[18] In so doing, Socrates exhibited enough of the divine character of the Logos in his quest for truth that he was accused of the "same crimes" as the Christians of Justin's day.[19]

As such, Justin's formulation of the Logos does much more than pronounce on epistemological and theological matters. It works additionally as a well-spring of rhetorical invention in probing common ground not only within the Christian community but also in the efforts of that community to engage those outside the community and in the broader culture.

"Faithful Witness" as Communal Identity and Rhetorical Sensitivity

Justin's struggle in living well in his own day is also our struggle in ours. Vincent E. Bacote spotlights this struggle when he pointedly asks, "Can there be Christian faithfulness in the public realm?" "If politics refers to our lives as citizens," he elaborates, "then what does it mean to be Christian and a citizen of a county, state, country, or world?"[20] Evangelicals living in the United States have long struggled to answer these questions and this struggle is seen in the markedly divergent approaches they have taken. On the one hand, there is the enduring triumphalism—or "Constantinian Christianity"[21]—that conflates theological purposes with political ones and sees public faithfulness primarily in terms of political influence. On the other hand, there have been the recent and growing calls for retreat, such as in Rod Dreher's book *The Benedict Option*,[22] that respond to the perceived hostility of "post-Christian" America. The latter approach focuses foremost on reclaiming subcultural identity and vitality at the expenses of broader cultural engagement and being fully present in the political realm.

There are two factors at work in exacerbating this contemporary struggle that Justin can help us work through. First, there is a lack of compelling communal identity on the part of evangelical Christians as a whole—an abiding and enduring sense of what they collectively have been called to do in engaging with those outside of their general faith tradition and with political and popular cultures more generally. Without a broad consensus, it has been far too easy for their voices—and religious voices more generally—to be profoundly coopted, to be "conformed to this world" (Rom 12:2 ESV).[23]

Philosophers Steve Wilkens and Mark L. Sanford call attention to the ease with which American evangelical Christians have in their political and cultural engagement succumbed to the hidden worldview of postmodern tribalism. Christians have placed considerable emphasis on the power and control functions of social structures; on the incommensurability of values and truth claims across "tribal" lines; on the elevation of the needs and values of the "tribe" at the expense of other communities and groups; and on the narratives of injury and marginalization that fuel moral outrage and the moral self-justification of all acts serving only the tribe—even (and especially) when those acts come at the expense of those outside the tribe.[24] This postmodern tribalism can be seen in the contemporary American political climate in which evangelicals participate with "decadence," meaning not "debauchery" but "terminal self-absorption—the loss of the capacity for collective action, the belief in common purpose, even the acceptance of a common form of reasoning." This kind of decadence is "a cultural, moral, and spiritual disorder."[25] And while it would be unfair to subscribe to a simple or monolithic motivation for the many evangelical Christians who voted for Donald Trump and continue to support him, it is fair to say that a significant motivation for many evangelicals—particularly conservative ones—has been not that they see Trump as someone like them, but as someone who will protect them, their interests, and their "tribe" against the transgresses and trespasses of the spirit of secular liberalism that they see in political figures like Barack Obama and Hillary Clinton.

For Justin, a countercultural stance of public faithfulness is a communal effort that addresses a primary need to create a unique and compelling communal identity as Christians. It is this purpose that helps to explain the rhetorical power of Justin's notion of the Logos. Justin's premises are that Christians "possess an inspired capacity to interpret the Jewish scriptures," and that they "have become the rightful recipients of the scriptural promises," that God made in the Hebrew Scriptures.[26] These premises worked to enable Justin, in explaining his notion of the Logos, to accomplish the important rhetorical task of melding both Jewish and Greek wisdom and locating that wisdom in the Christian community. This would give the fledgling and persecuted Christian community both a compelling communal identity and a powerful source of agency.

To draw from Justin's example to support this important communal work, then, we might ask questions like the following: What is the comprehensive scriptural witness about the kind of people that God has called the church to be, in ways that both adapt to and stand outside the broader political and cultural norms in which they exist? What does it fundamentally mean to exemplify—as individuals, as local church communities, and as the church as a whole—the apostle Paul's admonition to "not be conformed to this world, but be transformed by the renewal of your mind" (Rom 12:2 ESV)? How can the values of courage and self-sacrifice—and missional imperatives like *diakonia* (i.e., service to others)—be drawn upon in ways that not only help Christians of different denominations and specific theological commitments see their unity without effacing their diversity, but also create the impetus for effective, meaningful, and countercultural praxis that models an authentic and lived "witness"? In my hometown of Suffolk, Virginia, for instance, a diverse group of over twenty local churches have embodied *diakonia* by banding together to create and sustain the Coalition Against Poverty in Suffolk (CAPS), which offers a number of antipoverty, shelter, and job-training programs.[27] In particular, CAPS hosts the "Night Stay Program" in the winter months, in which churches open space to shelter people experiencing homelessness. In addition to having sleeping accommodations, guests are served dinner and breakfast in community with volunteers from that church. Individual churches rotate hosting responsibilities and share CAPS-held resources like air mattresses, blankets, and portable shower units.

Justin's intellectual witness also shines important light on a second factor that exacerbates the struggle over public faithfulness for contemporary American evangelicals: the lack of rhetorical sensitivity in public and cultural engagement. Rhetorician Wayne C. Booth describes the need for a deep rhetorical sensitivity, the deepest and most important goal of the art of rhetoric—a fully-orbed, systematic, and deep practice in which "opponents in any controversy listen to each other not only to persuade more effectively but also to find the common ground behind the conflict."[28] It acknowledges, as philosopher Eugene Garver does, that the cultivation and co-creation of trust is fundamental to effective and ethical persuasion.[29]

The questions that Justin's rhetorical example raises for us, then, might include the following: What are the fundamental values that are reflected in the civic culture and civic traditions of the United States? How can cultural features and values like "pluralism," "democracy," and "multiculturalism" be approached as conceptual and axiological "commonplaces" not only to think deeply about how religious faith and religious faith traditions can properly reflect and inform these features and values, but also about how these can be sources of common ground to appeal to people and communities that have different political values and commitments? How can the core cultural and civic value of "religious freedom" serve as a wellspring of renewal for thinking about religious purpose and for seeking to expand limited cultural understandings of this value, all in ways that promote the kind of common ground that makes ethical and effective persuasion possible?

Conclusion

Christian faithfulness in the public realm—as individuals and collectively as communities and the church—is difficult, requiring both insight and moral courage. That is why it is a struggle and always has been, from Justin's day to ours. Yet in this difficult but ultimately fruitful task to be shouldered by those individuals and communities that embrace the Christian tradition and the person of Christ, Justin provides important and timely guidance. Justin modeled well the importance of conviction, of speaking truth to culture, and of standing up at great cost for what is true and right.

At the same time, Justin modeled the modest, charitable, and rhetorically sensitive dimensions of bearing witness to the true God. It was very important for Justin to be right. But it was just as important if not more important for Justin to be faithful and effective in earning a fair hearing from others, in connecting them with truth in ways that they would find compelling, and ultimately in connecting them with the living God in authentic and vibrant relationship. Justin did all of this with his conceptualization and pursuit of the Logos, and in his work and his life more generally. We would do well to learn from his example.

CHAPTER 2

Saint Irenaeus of Lyon: Encouraging Patience in Learning and Humility within Christian Community

Tom Holsinger-Friesen

Abstract: In *Against Heresies*, Saint Irenaeus of Lyon (early second century–202) opposed second-century Christian gnostics who argued that God has nothing to do with material substance. By contrast, Irenaeus insisted that Christ's incarnation reveals the way God also reveals himself through Scripture: He works within human time and human tradition. Ultimately, it is the proper arrangement of the biblical texts as a whole that reveals a beautiful portrait of God himself.

Introduction

Irenaeus, bishop of Lyon in the late second century, lived on the frontier of Christianity—both geographically and theologically. During these "wild west" days of the small but growing church in the western Roman Empire, threats to his spiritual flock were both external and internal.[1] For example, Christians had recently been taken to the Roman amphitheater to be burned alive, gored, and tortured in front of cheering crowds. However, the wild and menacing "beast" that Irenaeus targeted in his work, *Against Heresies*, was an internal foe—a splinter group of gnostics, called Valentinians, masquerading as authentic Christians. Gnostics taught that the New Testament "God" (the Old Testament Creator "God," in their view, was separate from the New Testament version) was saving his chosen people from the evils of this world's time and space. Salvation was defined as realizing one's hidden identity as a bearer of the divine seed and simply awaiting a heavenly reunion with God.

Because gnostics employed the same biblical texts as did the church, Irenaeus recognized that the battleground would be Scripture—specifically, how it should be properly interpreted. Irenaeus argued that biblical interpreters should see themselves as artists arranging precious stones (i.e., individual texts) to form a mosaic. This completed biblical mosaic should reveal God's true image as that of a "king," yet gnostic arrangements yield an image of God that looks more like a "dog" or a "fox."[2] For these separate jewel pieces to collectively reveal God's glory, they must be set into the proper context and framework. It is the doctrine of incarnation, Irenaeus insists, that identifies this context as the expanse of time and space which God created and in which God became most fully revealed.

Popular Christian leaders today who insist that the marker of those who take the Bible seriously is their commitment to a modern doctrine of inerrancy might be unintentionally overlooking the "inefficient" and quite mediated ways through which God tends to lead his people by his word. As individual creatures, we best discern God's voice in the Bible when we are humble, patient, and receptive to the guidance of our broader community of faith. In the final analysis, Irenaeus would encourage digital citizens today to resist the dominant narrative that elevates maximum efficiency and instrumental control in all areas of life (including biblical interpretation) over co-presence and accountability in a community connectedness and virtue. Toward these ends, this chapter examines two specific passages from Irenaeus's work *Against Heresies* that highlight his conviction that in God's "economy," Scripture is a crucial means of grace enabling us to become more fully human, conforming to God's image.

The Gnostic Threat to Christian Teaching and Practice

The appeal of the Valentinians, the Christian gnostic group in Irenaeus's crosshairs, was, perhaps, unsurprising. Just as we, today, often prejudge the "latest" technology to be the "greatest," significant numbers of Christians in Irenaeus's flock were stirred by the Valentinians' innovative and novel biblical interpretations (think "technologies"). To Irenaeus, however, these readings were unfaithful to the gospel that was attested by Christ's apostles and handed down by the church. Irenaeus offers a strong rebuttal to his opponents on two points: their negative view of creation (particularly the creaturely limits of time and space), and their belief that true divine revelation bypasses the mediation of human tradition. According to Irenaeus, the Valentinians used Scripture to justify immoral and other extreme forms of behavior. For example, a leader named Marcus, who claimed to be the vessel of God's perfect divine knowledge and power, seduced women by offering to share this spiritual possession with them so that they could "become one."[3]

The cornerstone of Valentinian theology seemed reasonable enough when 1 Corinthians 15:50 was interpreted in a straightforward and literal manner: "Flesh and blood cannot inherit the kingdom of God" means just that. This text seemed to offer biblical support for a divided metaphysical worldview. Spiritual things (and beings) and physical things (and beings) had nothing to do with each other. Even God himself was divided. The highest God, Father of Jesus, is pure Spirit whose "essence does not [partake] . . . in time."[4] Physical reality was created by the lower God of the Old Testament, the Demiurge. Since, as gnostics observed, all matter—including the human body—decays, it must be inherently inferior to spiritual substance. It could have no part in God's salvation plan. Thus, although Christ might have appeared human, he could not have possessed a truly physical body. Such a union would have brought contamination into the unchangeable deity.

To convince would-be Valentinian converts that Gnosticism was incompatible with Christianity, Irenaeus needed to call into question the fundamentally negative view of creation held by gnostics. Adherents of such a worldview "located the doctrine of evil and the notion of a fall *within* the doctrine of creation—not . . . after and alongside it."[5] Time and space defined the habitat of physical beings. However, because the Valentinians understood themselves as spiritual beings, time and space were temporary nuisances and were wholly inappropriate to their divine nature.

Against this view, Irenaeus employed Scripture to defend the goodness of creation, given God's decision to reveal himself most fully in the incarnation of Jesus.[6] In fact, to Irenaeus, each distinct time period in Jesus' life (e.g., infancy, childhood, adolescence, young and older adulthood) was critical.[7] He "passed through every stage of life, restoring to all communion with God."[8] Irenaeus believed that, through Jesus, God restores all of human time to God's very being. Given that the divine redemptive plan is enacted *within* rather than *outside of* created time, God's people must remain patient through times of growth. As they receive the gospel that is revealed in Scripture, God brings about their gradual transformation and does so through time.

Gnostics claimed to have received inspired interpretations of Scripture without mediation in two respects. First, they presumed to acquire true biblical understanding without the mediation of time: instantaneously and without any process. Second, they denied the mediating role of the human community. They received and validated revelation individually and, as elect "spiritual beings," were subject to no communal accountability. From Irenaeus's perspective, such boasts expressed not only impatience but also arrogance. If time were to be gratefully embraced as the context within which God speaks, so also tradition (the collective experience of God's people through time) could be viewed as an invaluable resource and gift. According to Irenaeus, the apostles who experienced Jesus were in a privileged position to rightly discern the meaning of the gospel.[9] For Irenaeus, it is the gospel as interpreted and handed down by the apostles that is the "foundation and pillar of our faith."[10] Faithful biblical interpretation, then, is not done in secret by individuals sequestered from human influence. It is communal, open to all, and universally received.[11]

Individual biblical readers regularly find themselves in a community already in motion, a community Christ commissioned, a community the apostles established, through which all subsequent hermeneutical efforts participate. Irenaeus claimed that false teachers who separate themselves from the church community and reject its accepted readings have "alienated themselves from the truth."[12] They "deservedly wallow in every error . . . because they wish rather to be sophists of words than disciples of the truth"; by "disregard[ing] the order and the connection of the Scriptures . . . [they] dismember and destroy the truth."[13] For the Christian, true spirituality is not defined in contrast to physicality because spirituality includes the physical. Sadly, those who consider created time and human tradition to be irrelevant for knowing God actually dismiss the very means through which God chooses to reveal himself and his ways.[14] God's method of communication, in Jesus and through Scripture, is fully incarnate, not disembodied.

Against Heresies

In Book 4, chapter 38, of his five-volume work *Against Heresies*, Irenaeus continues to repudiate gnostic depictions of God, humanity, and salvation by specifically contesting Valentinian interpretations of 1 Corinthians 2, 3, and 15. The Valentinians insisted that Paul is dividing humankind into three groups according to their fixed natures (spiritual, soulish, and physical). Yet, Irenaeus queried, what are the Valentinians to make of Paul's frequent exhortations that God's people choose what is good and reject what is evil?[15] For this bishop, our destinies are not predetermined. They depend upon our actions in time. Irenaeus, however, must explain how human free will and divine omnipotence are compatible. The objection might be raised, "Could not God have exhibited man as perfect from the beginning?"[16] Irenaeus argues that although God was fully capable of creating humankind perfect from the beginning, it "could not receive this [perfection] being as yet an infant."[17] God's salvation works only through Jesus and the Holy Spirit, and in time, so that enables us to eventually contain in ourselves the Spirit and so fulfill our destiny as creatures.

Irenaeus saturates his arguments with the temporal language of growth and development. God, he claims, demonstrates both "power and goodness" in "ungrudgingly" giving us the gift of existence. Through God's wisdom, created things

> *receive growth and a long period of existence*, [and] do reflect the glory of the uncreated One. . . . For from the very fact of these things having been created, [it follows] that they are not uncreated; but by their continuing in being *throughout a long course of ages*, they shall receive a faculty of the Uncreated, through the gratuitous bestowal of eternal existence upon them by God. . . . [Human beings are] *making progress day by day, and ascending* towards the perfect, that is, approximating to the uncreated One.[18]

Christian gnostics believed that they were "perfect" because of their inherent nature and their secret knowledge of God as gleaned from Scripture. However, Irenaeus links the concepts of the progression of time and perfection and adds contemplation and love to them.[19] While Scripture does supply knowledge of God, even right knowledge is insufficient. It is when Christians take time to contemplate Scripture and are willing to be taught by the Holy Spirit that they can expect godly transformation and perfection. Knowledge gained through time results in a growing capacity to love God.

In *Against Heresies* 1.10.1–3, Irenaeus addresses that other crucible within which faithful biblical interpretation takes place: tradition. Tradition, for Irenaeus, is not the dead part of religion that gets repeated. Rather, tradition is the reason that no single Christian ever comes to the gospel on her own: all Christians drink downstream from the disciples who gathered around Jesus. Jesus entrusted his gospel to them, who would then communicate the gospel to all those who had ears to hear. Though the church in Irenaeus's time was dispersed, Christian life could not exist without the teaching Jesus left with the apostles. Comparing the apostolic tradition to the sun, Irenaeus argues that all Christian teachers depend on the teachings of Jesus the apostles passed on.[20]

Irenaeus's counterintuitive point against the gnostics is this: we are to beware of biblical interpretations that depart from the apostolic tradition because our understandings of God's identity, character, and way of salvation are at stake. In the same way God attached his identity to Jesus' earthly body, so too Jesus attaches his teaching to the mouths and memory of the apostles. This means that life with God cannot be separated from life with God's people. Such a life is dynamic, relational, and time-intensive, not static. Patience in time and humility in the context of church tradition—these elements are essential to our growth as biblical interpreters and, indeed, as human beings made in God's image.

Reading Scripture as Resisting the Idols of Efficiency and Control

When it comes to communication in the twenty-first century, technology seems to give us what we prize: ever-greater efficiency and control. These priorities are exemplified in a Verizon television commercial touting the power of a Droid smartphone. The scene opens in a humdrum corporate boardroom meeting, and a young man picks up his blinking phone. He begins to type, and as his pace accelerates we hear the sounds of metal clinking together. His human hands, now moving at lightning speed, morph into robotic hands composed of wires and steel parts. Abruptly, he finishes his work and confidently sets his phone down on the table, the others in the room none the wiser. The voiceover closes with the phrase, ". . . turning you into an instrument of efficiency."[21]

As this commercial demonstrates, our use of digital technology often betrays a desire for unchecked efficiency and control, and in so doing, it reveals a gnostic resistance to our time-boundness and communal connectedness. Efficiency is the desire to get things done as quickly and easily as possible and is the reason technological critic and lay theologian Jacques Ellul claims that magic is the first technology.[22] Why do the hard work of courting another person to fall in love with you when a love potion will accomplish the same end in a fraction of the time? In the commercial, the young man achieves greater efficiency at his job through multitasking. He sits at a meeting while simultaneously communicating with another person who is not there. His lightning-speed work transcends the time-boundedness of those around him, almost as if the phone allows him to perform magic. Similarly, the desire for control often runs the risk of isolating individuals from the communities they inhabit. A controlling individual often uses digital tools to arrange her environment in a way that favors her desires against those around her. In the commercial, while the young man sits in the meeting, his messaging isolates him from the people sitting in the room and the matter at hand. His desire for control cuts him off from the community he physically inhabits. In these two ways, efficiency and control suggest a gnostic resistance to time-boundedness and community.

A similar, perhaps gnostic, desire for efficiency and control is evident when Christians allow their imaginations and attitudes to be shaped by the modern doctrine of biblical inerrancy. Deliberations within this largely twentieth-century movement culminated in 1978 with the "Chicago Statement on Biblical Inerrancy." According to this statement, Scripture, "being wholly and verbally God-given . . . is without error or fault in all its teaching, no less in what it states about God's acts in creation, about the events of world history, and about its own literary origins under God, than in its witness to God's saving grace in individual lives."[23] Simply put, "What Scripture says, God says."[24] The mediated nature of divine revelation, thus, is largely overlooked. Receiving God's message for me can be envisaged as a highly efficient, almost magical process: I simply read the words on the page. This approach tends to ignore two realities: that all readings of Scripture pass through time-bound human experience and that all readings need the apostolic teachings as a hermeneutical filter.

An example of this tendency occurs every Sunday at one of the biggest churches in the United States. Before the pastor begins every sermon, he instructs his congregation to stand and hold their Bibles in the air. He then has them repeat the following mantra: "This is my Bible. I am who it says I am. I have what it says I have. I can do what it says I can do."[25] This biblical perspective may unintentionally encourage Christians to embrace efficiency (rather than time-boundedness) and control (rather than communal dependence) in their acts of biblical interpretation. Not unlike the aim of the gnostics, the mantra reflects a desire to take possession of an indisputable and perfect knowledge.

If, as the cliché goes, knowledge is power, then this view of the Bible might help Christians feel less vulnerable to time-boundedness and less dependent on those Christians who came before us. While this approach to biblical interpretation might help Christians feel less vulnerable and dependent, they also encourage Christians to feel less human and more godlike.

Incarnational approaches do not ignore our need to rely upon the Bible for truthful content, but the focus is different. Instead of embracing efficiency, control, and perfect knowledge, an incarnational approach asks, "How can I encounter the person of Jesus in these words of Scripture?" In the incarnation, God invites us to meet him through means that, while seemingly inefficient, promote a vibrant growing relationship.

The medieval practice of *lectio divina* ("sacred reading") is precisely the kind of incarnational biblical practice that embraces inefficiency and community. *Lectio divina* is sometimes practiced with a small group of Christians. The group selects a short passage—maybe even just a single verse or phrase. Then the text is read aloud numerous times, meditatively, with ample opportunities in between for individuals to wait, speak, and listen. Created time, no longer viewed as a scarce commodity, is a precious gift within which Christians can enter into prayerful dialogue with God and others. Ultimately, the practice of *lectio divina* aims to contemplate or listen to what God might be saying to the reader. In that word—mediated through time, Scripture, and the reflections of others—the Christian grows in knowing the Lord. *Lectio divina* offers the opportunity to read Scripture quite aware of human vulnerabilities and limitations. Irenaeus insisted that our Creator never bypasses the creation when He brings about salvation. It is fitting, then, that through *lectio divina*, God's Spirit uses frail, human language to cultivate seeds of spiritual growth within us.

Conclusion

If God's supreme revelation, Jesus Christ, expresses his preferred strategy of incarnation, so also does his revelation through Scripture. God teaches us in ways that are suited to our identities as creatures who must grow within our divinely given limits of space and time. For us, time is not to be grasped, controlled, or feared; rather we are called to lovingly receive it and do so with gratitude. Inefficiencies and communities are, ironically, essential conditions for personal growth. If divine activity and human activity are not mutually exclusive, then we must be humble enough to take the time to learn from others. God has certainly spoken to past and present Christians through Scripture, just as he speaks to us. To embrace that reality is to read the Scriptures like the creatures God made us to be.

CHAPTER 3

Saint Athanasius of Alexandria: Communicating Creatively, Clearly, and with a Prophetic Voice to Hostile Audiences

Paul A. Creasman

Abstract: De Decretis, a short work by St. Athanasius of Alexandria (c. 296–373) written in response to the Council of Nicaea, the Nicene Creed, and the followers of Arianism, attempted to resolve the growing discord among competing theologies and theologians. Athanasius encouraged the church to adopt creative and clear communication while maintaining a prophetic voice. *De Decretis* is remarkably applicable today as the modern church faces similar strains of discord, particularly when trying to engage the public sphere.

Introduction

Shortly after his appointment as bishop of Alexandria, fourth-century theologian Athanasius unexpectedly found himself to be public enemy number one. Other bishops, angered at Athanasius's fervent rejection of Arianism—the teachings of fellow Alexandrian theologian Arius—had accused the new bishop of murder, treason, and practicing magic.[1] The charges were eventually shown to be false, but the controversy was enough to drive Athanasius into hiding. Eager to clear his name, Athanasius took his case straight to Emperor Constantine. In a secret operation worthy of a spy novel, the bishop disguised himself, ambushed the emperor in the streets of Constantinople, and begged Constantine for an audience. The emperor agreed to hear him, but only if the other bishops were in attendance. The subsequent meetings were, however, unfruitful, and Constantine sent Athanasius into exile.[2]

In the fourth century, two views of Christ's deity had gained acceptance. On one hand, some Christians affirmed Arianism, that Jesus was not fully God. On the other, Athanasius defended what came to be known as the orthodox view, that Jesus was, in fact, fully God. In the middle, stood Constantine. His political power gave him the authority to declare one of these two views the law of the land. Ecclesial authorities on both sides recognized this power and tried to leverage it.

Similarly, many Christian leaders today long for political representation of their views and the legalization of moral positions that reflect Christian beliefs on social issues, such as abortion or gay marriage. In such longing for power, Christian teachings are often misunderstood, misrepresented, or simply dismissed in today's marketplace of ideas. Worse still, religious communities are sometimes at odds with each other, much like Athanasius and Arius, which only serves to compound the public perception that Christianity is too irrelevant to be of any public good. Coherent, faithful discourse and dialogue have trouble gaining traction among top political and cultural leaders when faith traditions are so misunderstood and so deeply divided.[3]

Athanasius's short letter *De Decretis* (*A Defense of the Nicene Definition*)[4] offers hope for resolving such convoluted communication. In *De Decretis*, Athanasius provides subtle parameters for how one might talk about Christ, particularly when engaging hostile audiences. Athanasius worked and wrote in contentious and hostile times for the early church, and the bishop did not always win the day. Written in exile, Athanasius's *De Decretis* not only addresses weighty theological issues like Christ's nature, but it also provides implicit answers to key questions about the very language we use to discuss faith. His work suggests that Christians would do well to engage in public dialogue with creativity, clarity, and a prophetic voice, three attributes that the pro-life organization Voice for the Voiceless models.

Nicaea, Arianism, and Athanasius

Written in the mid-fourth century, *De Decretis* was initially authored as a response to a friend who raised questions about the Council of Nicaea and why the bishops at the council adopted the particular language of the creed. At the same time, the book is a highly inflammatory attack against Arianism. Arius argued that if Christ was God's Son, and the Son comes from the Father, there had to be a time when Christ did not exist. As God's first creation, Christ was a creature, making him noneternal and less than God.[5] Athanasius was passionately opposed to this thinking.

Prior to the Council of Nicaea, Arianism had gained a foothold among the churches in Egypt. The spread of this new teaching threatened to fracture the church.[6] Eager to have a united church and empire, Constantine called for the Council of Nicaea in 325 CE. At the council, support for Arianism dwindled. The council approved language of Christ's divinity and wove it into the Nicene Creed. Arius was exiled at the conclusion of the council. Despite all of this, the issue of Christ's divinity remained unsettled for decades. When the work of the council proved unwelcoming to Arius's supporters, Constantine relented on Arianism. Two years after Nicaea, Constantine urged one of Arius's adversaries, Alexander of Alexandria, to readmit the exiled Arius. While Alexander refused, a synod in northern Asia Minor (modern-day Turkey) reinstated Arius, which led the way for Arianism to return to the church.[7] In 328, Athanasius advanced to become bishop of Alexandria and assumed his lifelong fight to unite the church and defeat Arianism. It would not be easy. The accusations against Athanasius of murder and magic were just the beginning.

The political and theological flip-flopping in Constantine's family continued for the next three decades. By some accounts, Constantine was baptized by the Arian bishop Eusebius of Nicomedia in 337.[8] The tipping points for Athanasius came in 353 and 355 when Constantius II, the last of Constantine's sons, twice ordered all sitting bishops to accept Arianism.[9] Athanasius refused. Amid growing political-religious turmoil and under threat of capture by Constantius's forces, Athanasius fled to the Egyptian desert in 356.[10] With his church nearly given completely over to Arianism and his government seeking to imprison him, it may have appeared to Athanasius that he was fighting the whole world by himself. It is in this tumultuous moment that Athanasius penned this important work.[11]

Perhaps motivated by a friend's request, Athanasius again took up his case against Arianism in *De Decretis*. He reinvigorated dialogue about Arianism by addressing a key moment in the debate at Nicaea. Nicaea was a major turning point for the church as it represented the church moving from a purely ecclesiastical organization rooted in its tradition and experience to one suddenly at the forefront of political and social power.[12] Athanasius certainly did not like the wedding of theology and political power that Nicaea seemed to represent, so it seems conceivable that he wanted to go back to that point in time and examine the actual arguments themselves.[13] It is worth noting, then, that the work is firstly a theological treatise. Athanasius does not give explicit direction about "how to renew dialogue" per se. However, careful examination of Athanasius's arguments reveals implied instruction about the proper means of engaging with others.

In recounting events of the Nicaean Council, Athanasius rehearses the arguments and behaviors of Eusebius of Caesarea and his followers—"Eusebians"—ardent defenders of Arianism.[14] At the council, they challenged certain portions of the proposed Nicene Creed, especially those related to Christ's divinity. In *De Decretis* Athanasius examines two key elements of the Eusebians' arguments at the council: (1) their rejection of the nonbiblical phrase "of the substance" which was used in the creed to describe Christ's nature and relationship to God, and (2) the way they used the word "son" to diminish Christ's divinity.

De Decretis

The greatest sticking point for the Arian supporters concerning the Nicene Creed was the use of the Greek term *homoousios*, or "the same essence or substance." The bishops at the council employed this phrase to clearly describe the nature of Jesus, that is, Jesus Christ was God; they were equals. The creed itself describes Jesus as "of one substance with the Father." Arian followers wanted to employ a different but similar term *homoiousios*, implying that Jesus was "like" God, but not necessarily of the same substance. Grammatically, the terms differ by their vowel sounds, but they were miles apart theologically.[15] To be "of the same substance as God" meant Jesus was the same as God, but to be like God was to be merely similar. Additionally, Arians felt *homoousios* was inappropriate, as it implied God had substance or materiality.[16]

The key concern of Eusebius and the Arians over *homoousios* was that the term was not found in Scripture. They felt the council was overreaching the boundaries of proper theology by using nonbiblical terms in the creed. Athanasius dismisses this argument early in *De Decretis* saying, "I marveled at the effrontery which led them . . . still to be complaining . . . , 'Why did the bishops at Nicaea use terms not in Scripture?' "[17] referring here to "of the substance" and "consubstantial." Later, he takes on the issue in more depth, explaining that the bishops felt compelled to employ the term as an ironclad means of communicating what they believed about God and Jesus. They wanted to express Jesus' nature in a way that the Eusebians could not exploit or twist.[18] "The Fathers," Athanasius writes, "perceiving their [the Eusebians'] craft and the cunning of their impiety, were forced thereupon to express more distinctly the sense of the words 'from God.' Accordingly, they wrote 'from the substance of God.' "[19]

The second key concern of the Arians addressed in *De Decretis* is how the Eusebians interpreted the phrase "Son of God." At the root of Arian theology was a unique perspective on the nature of Christ and what it meant for Jesus to be God's "son."[20] Athanasius quotes the Eusebians' arguments about Christ's divinity saying, " 'God was not always Father of the Son; but when the Son came into being and was created, then was God called His Father. For the Word is a creature and work, and foreign and unlike to the Father in substance. . . . Wherefore the Son is not true God.' "[21]

To counter this position, Athanasius undertakes a word study, examining how Scripture defines the word "son," thus revealing what is really meant by the term "Son of God." He seems to scold the Eusebians for not doing this themselves before they spoke to the council: "Now it may serve to bring home to them what they are saying to ask them first this, what a son simply is, and of what is that name significant."[22]

Athanasius maintains that Scripture provides a figurative and literal sense of the word "son," and the Eusebians fail to properly understand the difference.[23] Ultimately, Athanasius proposes that Jesus is the literal Son of God (i.e., his offspring), but not in the human or biological sense.[24] A divine understanding of the concept "Son of God" means that Christ fully reflects God's nature, including some characteristics that go beyond our humanness: "Men are created of matter; God is immortal and incorporeal";[25] "God calls into being that which is not; but men create by working some existing materials";[26] "God's nature is not bound by the conditions of ours."[27] In other words, God has always been and eternally is a Father.[28] Christ has always existed, yet he is also God's Son, because he fully reflects God's nature. Although that may be confusing for some, Athanasius encourages his readers saying, "It is possible . . . to understand something above man's nature, instead of thinking the Son's generation to be on a level with ours."[29]

Communicating Faithfully with Hostile Audiences

In *De Decretis* we can discern three strategies that help faithful communicators better engage with hostile or disinterested audiences, both within and outside of church communities: creativity, clarity, and a prophetic voice. Voices for the Voiceless (Voices) is a nonprofit pro-life advocacy group based in Phoenix, Arizona, that employs the communication techniques found in the life and work of Athanasius.

First, Athanasius's discussion of *homoousios* reminds Christians that as witnesses to their faith, they can and should be creative in sharing their beliefs. Is it right to use creative, nonbiblical means to articulate Christian truths? Athanasius says, "Yes." That is essentially what the council did. It is also similar to what Tertullian did in the third century when he employed the term *trinitas* to explain the Father, Son, and Holy Spirit.[30] One can also find evidence of Jesus himself employing creative means in his teaching. Scripture itself is not limited to propositional truth-telling. Rather, it is full of stories, songs, poems, parables, and other artistic means to communicate the gospel. Thus, Athanasius clearly advocates rhetorical creativity so long as the resulting message stays true to Scripture.

Similarly, Voices employs highly creative means to engage audiences in discussion of abortion issues. Through photography, podcasting, live events, and more, they artistically present personal narratives of those touched by abortion. It is worth emphasizing that the focus of these efforts is on sharing narratives, not biblical proselytizing or policy debate. In conjunction with a local church in downtown Phoenix, Voices hosts concerts and art demonstrations that further share the stories of individuals who have had abortions or have been affected by the issue in big and small ways. Like Athanasius's encouragement to use nonbiblical language to communicate biblical truth, Voices uses creative renderings of personal experiences to communicate a larger biblical reality: life is sacred.

In *De Decretis*, Athanasius makes the implicit claim that effective communication requires a clear and common vocabulary. Without it, communication is unclear and confusing. The Eusebians' arguments faltered because they failed to use words properly or, at least, in a way that everyone agreed upon. In this case, they conceived of "son" as having a strictly human interpretation. Athanasius defines "Son"—in this sense, a divine concept—by drawing upon the common denominator of Scripture. To that end, he proudly invokes Scripture no less than twenty-one times in clarifying his position: "I have incidentally referred to passages in Holy Scripture which speak of our Lord as the Divine Word and Wisdom, and the meaning of these titles, when carefully considered, is a confirmation that He is truly and literally the Son."[31] Even when the Eusebians try to use Scripture, Athanasius reminds them that it must be interpreted properly.[32] Thus effective communication and dialogue with others is dependent upon using a shared vocabulary and language.

Athanasius's concern over the Eusebians' flawed reading of the phrase "son of God" is instructive. It teaches us that words matter. If we fail to clarify our ideas or define our terms, or fail to draw upon a shared vocabulary, we potentially deepen the divide between ourselves and those we wish to reach. There may be great temptation to be overly creative, to gloss over important truths for the sake of being welcomed or deemed relevant by an audience. Athanasius shows us that we should not compromise clarity, especially when important truths need to be communicated.[33] Likewise, pastor John Piper argues that there may be times when propositional statements need to be made so everyone can be on the same page.[34] When we fail to practice clarity, miscommunication may result and may deepen divisions.

Voices takes such clarity and commonality with their audiences seriously. Other groups' faith-based initiatives involving abortion advocacy are often focused on creating legislation that restricts or end abortions. For these groups, legislation becomes the first step. Like Christians in the fourth century, these groups seek security for their positions in and through the machinery of politics. Voices, however, clearly states that legislation is not their immediate focus. Rather, they use the phrase "It *ends* here" with images of a courtroom or other legal symbols; such communication clearly states they do not intend to engage in a legal or philosophical debate as the first order. They do not collect signatures for petitions or immediate legal action. Rather, their focus is on individuals and their personal stories. They ask for anecdotes from their audiences, and Voices members share their own stories. By approaching the issue from the ground of common experiences rather than from heights of political power, Voices transforms the word "abortion" into one that bears highly personal significance. By focusing on the personal narratives of both the audience member and the member of Voices, they help create a common starting point for their conversations among their diverse and contentious audiences.

Third, *De Decretis* demonstrates that Christian communicators must some-times employ what communication scholars call "the prophetic voice."[35] Much of Athanasius's language in *De Decretis* seems abrupt, even rude. In describing the Eusebians' evasions he writes, "Such tactics are nothing less than an obvi-ous token of their want of Divine Reason."[36] Later he continues, "These impious men . . . [have] so little mind amid their madness."[37] Such a communication strategy recalls Old Testament prophets, many of whom employed powerful, truthful, and sometimes shocking rhetoric.

Athanasius is revered as "The Father of Orthodoxy,"[38] "The Black Monk Who Saved the Faith,"[39] and as the one who "saved Nicaea"[40] and "saved the Church,"[41] but he also had a reputation as a ruthless, harsh, and rigid bishop, both in word and deed.[42] Scholars who studied Athanasius's life kindly refer to his lifelong battle with Arianism as "vigorous."[43] It is easy to see how Athanasius was perhaps guilty of causing the infighting in the fourth-century church as much as he was noted for trying to heal it. I would argue, however, that such evidence reflects a prophetic voice, specifically the prophet's burden and the necessity of employing "shock therapy" to awaken audiences.[44]

Like Athanasius, Voices demonstrates prophetic talk. The leadership of Voices has a clear burden for speaking truth about abortion. Before form-ing Voices, core leaders formed other pro-life advocacy groups in Phoenix. While Voices does not employ such directly shocking rhetoric as Athanasius, the group demonstrates other prophetic qualities. Their creative methods en-courage believers and nonbelievers to "move toward originality and complexity" in thinking about the abortion issue.[45] Abortion is not simply a legal question. By focusing on individual stories of their members and audiences, it helps highlight personal alienation from God, a prophetic characteristic.[46]

Conclusion

The day Athanasius ambushed Constantine in the street, he did so with the best intentions. While he certainly wanted to be cleared of charges against him, he also yearned for unity in the growing church. His method then was confron-tational, and his audience with Constantine led to the bishop's exile. *De Decretis*, written well after this famous confrontation, reflects some wisdom gained. In fighting against the world, Athanasius learned to be creative and clear when engaging hostile audiences, all the while cultivating a prophetic voice. Eventu-ally, Athanasius and the orthodox view won the day. In 381, eight years after the bishop's death, the First Council of Constantinople affirmed the Nicene Creed, effectively ending Arianism. If we could nurture similar communication tools ourselves, perhaps we might foster better communication within our churches and in the public sphere, gaining influence on critical political and social issues.

CHAPTER 4

GREGORY OF NYSSA: REIMAGINING A HISTORICAL NARRATIVE TO HELP CONFRONT INSTITUTIONAL OPPRESSION

Naaman K. Wood

Abstract: Gregory of Nyssa (c. 335–c. 394), one of the first abolitionist Christians, spoke something unthinkable in his "Homily 4 on Ecclesiastes." He calls the institutional oppression of slavery a sin. Gregory understood the existence of a single slave as a violation against humanity, creation, and God. As a corrective to a minimization or outright denial of the sin of institutional oppression, Gregory helps us consider how narrative reimagination might be used to confront social sins of all kinds.

Introduction

In 376 CE, the Roman Emperor Valens exiled Gregory of Nyssa from his home in Cappadocia, a region in Asia Minor (modern-day Turkey). A few years earlier, Gregory had enjoyed a quiet monastic life filled with prayer and study. He reluctantly accepted the post as bishop of Nyssa primarily due to conflicts between orthodox Christians and Arian Christians, the latter of whom argued that Jesus was not God. While he was a brilliant theologian, he proved a less than able administrator and was even less capable at navigating ecclesial politics. Within a few years, an Arian faction accused the bishop of mishandling church funds, and, as a result, the Arian Emperor Valens sent Gregory into exile. While in exile, Gregory complained to his sister, Macrina, about his misfortune. Macrina responded in an unexpected way: "Will you not put an end to your failure to recognize the good things which come from God?" she asked.[1] "Churches send you forth and call upon you as ally and reformer, and you do not see the grace in this? Do you not even realize the true cause of such great blessings, that our parents' prayers are lifting you on high, for you have little or no native capacity for this?"[2]

Far from a word of comfort or a word of strategy to regain his post as bishop, Macrina spoke a word that was likely unthinkable to her bishop brother.

Gregory saw himself as a pious cleric who was suffering unjustly. Macrina saw him as a weak Christian who could barely pray, but one who was still blessed beyond measure. What Macrina displays in this moment is what Gregory so aptly demonstrates in his sermon "Homily 4 on Ecclesiastes," a sermon in which he calls the institutional oppression of slaves a sin and, therefore, calls for its abolition.

Gregory was one of the earliest Christians to understand the institutional oppression of slavery as a sin, and he can serve as a corrective to many contemporary Christians' inability to call the history of United States one of institutional oppression. In the bishop's time, as well as in most of the modern period, Christians did not see institutional oppression—the power to decide who is or is not a human being—as a sin. In contrast, Gregory spoke what was unthinkable in his time: he collapsed humanity, creation, and God onto the experience of an individual, hypothetical slave. "As goes one slave," Gregory might say, "so goes humanity, creation, and God." Christianity can follow Gregory in speaking the unthinkable: they can engage in the communicative practice of narrating U.S. history as a history of institutional oppression.

Gregory of Nyssa's Context for "Homily 4"

The historical record on slavery in both the ancient and modern periods suggests that slave masters did not see slaves as human beings, and, unfortunately, many Christians did not understand this institutional oppression to be a sin. In the ancient world, authors who discussed slaves demeaned them with stereotypical descriptions, calling them "childlike," "incompetent," "useless," and "wicked."[3] One major exception is Gregory's sermon, preached in 379 CE during the Lenten season, a season of confession.

The dehumanizing perception of slaves coincided with a legal right to perform violence against slaves and with the failure to preserve their voices, especially in the ancient period.[4] Many scholars see a strong link between slavery and violence, in both ancient and modern slavery.[5] In the ancient world, slaves often bore visible scars, the *stigmata* (or marks) of slavery,[6] such that by a mere glance anyone could see that a slave was a "bad" slave through their scars, tattoos, fetters, or crucified body. Violence reduced slaves from persons to bodies, as is evidenced in the Greek term *soma* (or body), a synonym for the term *orduolos* (or slave).[7] Additionally, slave voices are virtually absent from the historical record. What we know about ancient slavery comes from wealthy, educated elites, many of whom owned and dehumanized slaves.

In the midst of dehumanizing acts, most Christians uncritically accepted the institution of slavery, even those Christians who wanted to free slaves. Slave-owning was a "structural element" in Christian society and was supported by

parishioner and church leader alike.[8] While some critiques of slavery arose
in the ancient period, those critiques were isolated, short-lived, and mostly
inconsequential. More importantly, perhaps, the relative silence on these injustices constituted a tacit approval of the system of oppression. While there were
Christians who longed for justice, it was often a limited justice that accepted
various forms of systemic oppression as normal. Tolerance for widespread dehumanization of slaves and former slaves continued until the modern period.[9]

In 379 CE, the bishop's "Homily 4" appeared in a Lenten series of sermons
on the book of Ecclesiastes, a series in which he makes implicit reference to the
practice of confession of sin during Lent and freedom for some slaves on Easter
Sunday. Toward the end of "Homily 3," Gregory notes that Solomon, the writer
of Ecclesiastes, turns to the act of "the confession of things not rightly done."[10]
When Gregory opens "Homily 4," he notes, "We still find the occasion for confession controlling the argument."[11] Therefore, when Ecclesiastes 2:7 says, "I
got me slaves and slave-girls,"[12] the bishop argues that Solomon is confessing
the sin of slavery. The link between confession and slavery coincided with the
Lenten season. Lent, or the forty days before Easter Sunday, is traditionally a
season of confession and repentance. As a gesture of freedom, Christians of
Gregory's period sometimes freed an occasional slave on Easter Sunday, usually
good slaves. The bishop's sermon does not suggest that slave-owning Christians
free a single good Christian slave on Easter. Rather, he called the institution of
slavery a sin and called for its abolition.

"As Goes One, So Go the Rest" in "Homily 4"

To begin, Gregory collapses the individual human slave onto the rest of
humanity. The bishop starts with a single, hypothetical slave. He asks, "How
many staters [ancient coins] did you get for selling *the being* shaped by God?
If *he* is in the likeness of God . . .who is *his* buyer, tell me? who [*sic*] is *his*
seller?"[13] In these questions, Gregory repeatedly uses the singular pronoun,
referring to the hypothetical slave. However, immediately following, he pivots
from the singular human to plural humanity. "God would not therefore reduce
the *human race* to slavery, since he himself, when *we* had been enslaved to sin,
spontaneously recalled *us* to freedom."[14] In the move from the singular to the
plural pronoun, Gregory affirms that all of humanity is at stake in the single
slave.[15] If one human slave is a contradiction to the freedom of all of humanity,
then all of humanity is dehumanized. His thinking might be summarized this
way: "As goes one slave, so goes the human race."

Similarly, Gregory collapses humanity onto the "slave," whom he calls
the ruler of the earth who can be neither bought nor sold. The bishop insists
that a slave is a human being and therefore "rules the whole earth" and is the

"owner of the earth."[16] By "ruler" and "owner," Gregory does not mean that the human replaces God. Rather, all humans receive royal authority from God.[17] God decrees that each and every human rules "the islands, the sea, and all that is in them."[18] Gregory then imagines the irrationality of anyone purchasing a "ruler" and "owner" of the earth. As he imagines the transaction when the owner of the earth is sold, the buyer purchases that human and all of the earth with it. Therefore, when Gregory looks at a slave in his congregation, he does not see a slave. He sees the opposite. He sees a king, a ruler and owner of the earth. He continues imagining the transaction: Whenever a slave "is for sale, therefore, nothing less than the owner of the earth is led into the saleroom."[19] To illustrate the foolishness of such a sale, he articulates the impossibility of purchasing that which is beyond price: "So how much do we think the whole earth is worth? And how much all the things on the earth?"[20] They are "priceless" and cannot be purchased.[21] Purchasing a slave proves equally impossible. If the earth is priceless and the owner of the earth is worth more than the earth, then, "What will the buyer pay, and what will the vendor accept, considering how much property is entailed in the deal?"[22] This absurd transaction mirrors his previous thinking, this time collapsing creation onto the slave: "As goes one slave, so goes the earth."

In addition to collapsing humanity and the earth onto the slave, Gregory's thinking collapses Jesus, the God-man, onto the slave. Like the slave, Jesus is the Ruler of whole earth, a Ruler of all rulers, the King of all kings; he has authority over everything on earth. Since both the slave and Jesus are alike in that they are rulers of the earth, then the implicit connection runs in the opposite direction. In the same way that the slave is a ruler, Jesus was also a slave. Certainly, Jesus was never a slave sold or purchased at an auction, but his death brings him into a shared experience with slaves (see Phil 2:6–8). In the act of crucifixion, humanity treated the body of Jesus like it was the body of a slave in the ancient world. In taking up the cross, Jesus implicitly accepted the comparison, in the scars his body bore, the *stigmata* of slavery. Since Jesus is also God, then God is at stake in the slave's body. "As goes one slave, so goes God."

In collapsing humanity, creation, and God onto the single hypothetical slave, Gregory rejects the widely accepted idea that slaves were not humans; that instead they were bodies that could be bought, sold, owned, and dehumanized through stereotypes, violence, or silence. No master, Christian or otherwise, has the legitimate power to use money to transform a human being into a slave body. Gregory's sermon, therefore, rejects the idea that any human being possesses the power to decide who is and who is not a human being. In the context of Lent, a context of confession of sin, Gregory's conclusion was as inescapable as it was unthinkable: because the existence of a single slave is a violation against the very beings of God, creation, and humanity, the institutional oppression of slavery is a sin, and all sins must be abolished.

Reimagining the Narrative of the United States as One of Institutional Oppression

Gregory's rejection of the institution of slavery can help serve as a corrective to the tendency among many Christians today to minimize or deny this form of institutional oppression and the ways the church may directly or indirectly continue to reinforce such oppression. While institutional oppression is a political problem, it is also a deeply communicative one.

Several recent Christian narrations of race relations in American history illustrate what it looks like to minimize or deny systemic dehumanization. For example, pastor and theologian Douglas Wilson argues that while racism is sin, American slavery was not as bad as has been typically reported. In fact, he argues that slavery was generally benign for slaves.[23] Wilson's narration of history, therefore, effectively denies institutional oppression as a sin. In a more moderate register, pastor and theologian John Piper confesses to having been a racist[24] and claims the gospel demolishes racial divisions.[25] Nevertheless, while Piper mentions systemic injustice, his solution for racial divisions is essentially a denial that systemic racial problems demand systemic racial solutions. Rather, he "sides with the notion of personal responsibility" as the only real solution for racial divisions.[26] Finally, theologian and ethicist John Jefferson Davis acknowledges that institutional oppression is a problem in American history.[27] Nevertheless, his history of institutional racism concentrates almost completely on the Jim Crow era.[28] As such, he minimizes the possibility that institutional oppression was a problem before the Jim Crow era and that it persists today.

Against such minimization, Christians today can learn from Nyssa how to fully acknowledge and reject institutional oppression, specifically through the communicative practice of reimagining the narrative of a particular history, in this case U.S. history. Like Nyssa, Christians today can speak the unthinkable by rejecting the political reality that U.S. history is a history in which one class of persons possess the right to decide who is and who is not a person. They can do this through collapsing the whole of U.S. American history onto the experience of a single oppressed person. "As goes one oppressed person," Gregory would say, "so goes U.S. history."

Indigenous pastor and theologian Mark Charles narrates the history of the United States as a history of oppression institutionalized in its founding documents, in the nation's gradual suffrage, and in its current law.[29] First, the Declaration of Independence states unequivocally, "We hold these truths to be self-evident, that all men are created equal, that they are endowed by their Creator with certain unalienable Rights."[30] Several lines below this statement, the document complains that King George has failed to solve the problem of "merciless Indian Savages."[31] One might be tempted to read this dehumanizing stereotype as a contradiction to the first. However, such dehumanization is confirmed and institutionalized in the Constitution of the United States. Formalizing the inhuman status of indigenous peoples and black slaves, the document excludes "Indians" from representation in the democracy and counts black slaves as "three-fifths of a Person."[32] In these cases, it was the framers who decided who did or did not constitute political personhood in the eyes of the fledgling republic.

While Americans eventually recognized the personhood of black men, women, and indigenous persons, that recognition only worked under the rubric of institutional oppression. According to Charles, the power to decide who does and does not constitutes a political person has historically rested with white, landowning men.[33] In the Fourteenth Amendment, he argues, it was white men who declared that black men were persons, such that they possessed the right to vote.[34] However, in that document, those same men decided that indigenous peoples and women did not constitute persons and excluded them. In the Nineteenth Amendment, men declared that women were persons, but they still refused to recognize the political personhood of indigenous peoples. While individual states started to recognize indigenous personhood in 1948, it was not until 1962 that the last state, New Mexico, did so. The Constitution still does not recognize indigenous bodies as political persons. In the same way that granting freedom to good slaves in the ancient world unintentionally maintained the institution of slavery, these changes to federal and state legislations maintain the power of one group of people to decide who is and who is not a person.

Since the institutionally oppressive power to decide who is human is hardwired into the founding documents and in the process of suffrage, it is no surprise that this power continues to shape contemporary law. In the 1973 *Roe v. Wade* case, the Supreme Court decided that unborn fetuses did not constitute a human person, thus giving up their bodies to elimination. Likewise, through the 2010 *Citizens United v. FEC* case, the Supreme Court decided that corporations are political persons. In both of these cases, a group of people possesses the power to decide who is and who is not a person. That unborn fetuses are not persons while corporations are persons is part of the deep contradiction of institutional oppression. Charles concludes that the American social order constitutes a continuing order of institutional oppression. His narration of American history is an accurate extension of the manner in which Gregory collapses humanity, creation, and God onto the single slave. In this case, Gregory's thinking might be extended, "As goes one black person, one indigenous person, one aborted fetus, so goes American history."

Conclusion

When the ancient world looked at a slave, it saw an object of violence, a submissive body, a body marked with scars, fetters, and tattoos. When Gregory of Nyssa looked at a slave, he saw the ruler of the earth. It is difficult to under-estimate how deeply his sermon cut against the order of things in the ancient world—how deeply unthinkable and unspeakable "Homily 4" truly was. Today, Christians face a similar problem and opportunity. Christians can, like those in Nyssa's time, choose to minimize or deny institutional oppression. If Christians could listen to those like Mark Charles, then they could join him and Gregory of Nyssa in speaking what is unthinkable: the social order that upholds insti-tutional oppression can be rewritten. Such rewriting, Gregory reminds us, is the work of Easter Sunday.

CHAPTER 5

Saint Augustine of Hippo: Embracing the Practical Wisdom of Incarnate Communication in a Digital World

Calvin L. Troup

Abstract: Saint Augustine of Hippo (354–430), through the *Confessions,* narrates his pursuit of Roman orator Cicero's ideal for practical wisdom that comes to fruition in the person and work of Jesus Christ as living Word incarnate. This chapter considers how Augustine's commitments to incarnate communication as practical wisdom serve as a starting point for communication theory and practice for the digital world in which we live today.

Introduction

Saint Augustine of Hippo described his transition from childhood to adolescence as a time of sexual unrest and turmoil. For the young man who would later become bishop of Hippo and one of the most important Christian intellectuals, things were falling apart. He writes, "The bubbling impulses of puberty befogged and obscured my heart so that it could not see the difference between love's serenity and lust's darkness. Confusion of the two things boiled within me."[1] When his father found out about Augustine's sexual awakening, he did little to rescue his son from his restlessness. Rather, Augustine remembers that his father "was overjoyed to suppose that he would now be having grandchildren."[2] The only person that seemed interested in intervening in the young man's life was his mother, Monica. She warned him with "vehement anxiety," but to Augustine, "these warnings seemed to me womanish advice."[3] However, it was only in retrospect that the bishop realized these womanish words "were [God's] warnings and I did not realize it."[4] At this moment in Augustine's life, he longed for rest from his sexual confusion, and God's word reached out to him, incarnated in the voice of his mother.

These twin themes of rest and incarnation appear elsewhere in Augustine's writings. In the familiar statement from his now classic work *Confessions,* he says, "Our heart is restless until it rests in you."[5] Less quoted, but equally important, is Augustine's confession of faith in which he states, "Lord, my faith calls upon you, that faith which you have given to me, which you have breathed into me by the incarnation of your Son and through the ministry of your preacher."[6] It would be almost fifteen years until Augustine could begin to pursue true rest.[7] However, from the beginning of the book, we already know that Augustine's rest would come through God's eternal Word incarnate. He encounters this Word in ordinary, temporal life as he listens to many people, from his own mother to the preaching of Saint Ambrose, bishop of Milan, who became one of the most influential ecclesiastical figures of the fourth century.

Today we can look to Augustine as a reliable guide in the midst of the restlessness and emptiness of media environments dominated by digital communication technologies. Augustine's prime coordinate is the incarnation—the person and work of Jesus Christ. In the *Confessions*, it is only through the incarnation that Augustine can make sense of his disordered teenage years, the existence of evil, and the reality of death. Through Christ, Augustine learns a practical wisdom of communication that resonates with the deepest roots of historical Christian orthodoxy and fires the imagination of Christian thinkers from the Middle Ages through the Reformation to the present. This chapter invites readers to engage Augustine's confessional commitment to find rest in and through Christ's incarnation; to consider that the incarnation makes possible the reality that Christians can engage so-called pagan learning; and to reckon with the role of communicative practices in our daily, digitally driven lives that reside at the core of Christian thought.

Confessions

Looking back on his sixteenth year, Augustine recalls his life as a "disordered state in which I lay in shattered pieces."[8] The confession comes shortly after he reflects on his complicity in gratuitous teenage crime, "the pear-stealing episode" in Book II of the *Confessions*.[9] He admits that he committed the sin for no purpose except that it was forbidden, remarking that he and his friends did not need the pears and actually had better pears of their own at home. But through the story, he begins to explore questions about evil and the source of evil. Augustine finds the press of evil inescapable, because it resides both within himself and without. The pear-stealing episode reenacts the first sin in the Garden of Eden, and the bishop identifies himself with Adam in this sin. As he considers the problem of evil, he recognizes that evil is not created. Instead, evil is the corruption of good. Furthermore, the source of evil is not God the Creator; rather it is found in the turning of the creature's will away from God toward self. Pride is the prime evil. Because we are creatures made by God for the purpose of loving God first and foremost, turning from God disorders our love; turning from God diverts us away from God toward self. To love self first is a deficient form of love. To lack the proper love for God is the definition of pride, and pride is an act that corrupts the self and results in sin, evil, and death.

In the *Confessions*, Augustine faces the problem of death squarely. The death of a close friend tore him apart.[10] A disordered love of a friend led him to despair and fragmentation. Overwhelmed by grief, bitterness, and the fear of dying,[11] Augustine says, "To myself I became a great riddle."[12] The bishop would go on to lose a second close friend, Nebridius, and his mother, Monica, after his conversion. By the time Nebridius and Monica die, Augustine could grieve their deaths without pretense and retain hope both for them and for him. These deaths mark the problem of life and death as a diagnostic tool for marking the ordering of our love for God and neighbor. Loving in the proper order means loving God first and foremost according to the first great commandment and loving our neighbor with a kind of love that both actually loves the neighbor and also flows into the love of God. With these two priorities in place, love of self is included in the second great commandment, "Thou shall love thy neighbor as thyself." We may love ourselves third, for the sake of community and communion, so that we can enjoy God and love him fully together.[13]

From the problems of good and evil and life and death, Augustine turns to an equally personal but also cosmic question of truth and meaning. Augustine works out these problems in depth in Books XI and XII of the *Confessions*, engaging the skeptical question of his own day: "What was God doing before he created the heavens and the earth?"[14] This single question invites some of the deepest and most fruitful meditations in the Western history of ideas on origins, time and eternity, and eschatology. Augustine concludes that human beings reside or dwell in the midst of overwhelming truth and meaning established and secured through the incarnation.[15] As Christian theologian and apologist C. S. Lewis put it, Christianity "thoroughly approves of the body," including the incarnation, the resurrection, and eternal life—not in an ethereal netherworld of spirits but in a New Heaven and a New Earth in the body.[16]

According to Augustine, basic Christian beliefs predicate true understanding—that Jesus Christ is God come to us in the flesh; that Scripture is completely holy, completely truthful; and that the Word of God incarnate authorizes, inhabits, and participates in human communication. In the aftermath of his conversion, Augustine speaks of the incarnation: "Yet this your Word would be but little to me, if he had given his precepts in speech alone and had not gone on before me by deeds," and "We could think that your Word is far from union with men, and we could despair of ourselves, unless he had been 'made flesh and dwelt amongst us.'"[17]

Incarnation and Pagan Learning

A prominent question for intellectual leaders in the late fourth-century church concerned the admissibility of pagan learning for Christian study. For example, Augustine resigns his prestigious post as imperial chair of rhetoric upon his conversion. But by the time he writes *On Christian Doctrine*, which can be read profitably as a companion to the *Confessions*, he establishes legitimate protocols for Christians to study the liberal arts and sciences, including pagan learning.

Augustine's significance in the Christian intellectual discussion about pagan learning can hardly be overstated. We know it best by his extended debate through his correspondence with Saint Jerome (March 347 CE–September 30, 420 CE), who is known for his translation of most of the Bible into Latin (the translation known as the Vulgate) and his commentaries on the Gospels. Jerome took the position that Christians should only study Scripture. Augustine shares Jerome's deep commitment to scriptural study but argues that Christians should study pagan learning and accept truths that correspond with scriptural truth as valuable tools to enhance the knowledge of God's word in relation to God's created world. One of Augustine's most important observations in this regard is that to understand many things in Scripture we need to understand things in the world that cannot be understood from Scripture alone.[18] This principle is often summarized as an Augustinian maxim: *All truth is God's truth*. In *On Christian Doctrine*, Augustine says, "Every good and true Christian should understand that wherever he may find truth, it is his Lord's."[19]

The driving impetus in Augustine's call for the usefulness of pagan learning remains that a good understanding of the plain meaning of Scripture depends on just this kind of knowledge. For the Christian, however, the protocol for engaging pagan learning then becomes the central issue. *On Christian Doctrine* establishes the premises; the *Confessions* illustrate them in practice. As the bishop reflects on his encounters with the Manicheans, the skeptics, and the Platonists, or those who endorsed the philosophy of Plato in all things, he opens readers to the valuable knowledge in each of these schools and what he learned from them. Employing careful analysis of what was missing, he demonstrates their internal deficiency and the senses in which each was out of step with Scripture and the knowledge of Christ. Augustine maintains a clear priority on the word of God in all of its dimensions, the worship of God, and knowledge of God. He always turns pagan knowledge toward these good purposes, capturing his practice in the phrase, "plundering the Egyptians."[20]

> I had come to you from among the Gentiles, and I set my mind on that gold which you willed your people to take out of Egypt, for it was yours wherever it was. To the Athenians you say through your apostle that in you "we live,

and move, and have our being," as indeed some of them have said. In truth these books were from the Gentiles. But I did not set my mind upon the idols of the Egyptians, which they served with your gold, they "who changed the truth of God into a lie; and worshipped and served the creature rather than the creator."[21]

We hear in Augustine an unswerving priority on the word of God, the worship of God, and the works of God. The force of this exclusive commitment to Christian presuppositions enables Augustine to engage pagan learning in accordance with Christian truth while avoiding everything else. When he says "All truth is God's truth," he is wary of the dangers and deficiencies of pagan learning and is keen to turn the proceeds of pagan thought to good purposes.

This is important for communication studies today because Augustine explains that expansive learning is central to developing a Christian mind. Sound Christian thought begins with God's word and resonates throughout with the eternal truth of Scripture. Christian thought is not merely "religious" thought. It can boldly explore every intellectual and practical question, including philosophical, theoretical, and practical questions of communication.

Incarnational Communicative Practices in a Digital Age

Augustine's prime questions emerge from his deep commitment to the incarnate Christ and his expansive intellectual engagement. Augustine says he could never have come to faith unless Christ had come in the flesh. When, like Augustine, we see the life and word of Christ working together faithfully, we can listen to him as a teacher who addresses us person-to-person, as one who understands our lives from the inside out, in full humanity. Jesus' incarnation coordinates our communication practices vertically toward love of God and horizontally toward love of neighbor through the integration of word and deed.[22] Through the incarnation, word and work are simultaneous.[23] Therefore, the reality of the incarnation suggests that for ordinary people, the in-person union of word and deed constitutes the best communication practices for human beings and communities.[24] This is why, in the *Confessions*, Augustine calls ministers and teachers to imitate Christ in word and deed so that their parishioners and students might also learn the integration of word and deed in practice.[25] In practice, this leads to some specific priorities that apply within a world of digital devices.

First, the incarnation calls us to give priority to speaking in person. Put simply: Talk. Do not text. Do not opt for a digital alternative when conversing in person is possible. Spoken, incarnate language is the paradigm for human mediation. Everything we do has a media component; indeed, mediation is a synonym for communication. But language is a created good within human existence, not a technology invented and manufactured by us. Mediation works through points of communion between people, a word which shares a common root with *communication*. Therefore, we need to privilege live speech and listening over every communication technology. In the beginning, Augustine reminds us, was the Word. Jesus mediates as the Word and through words. The incarnation presents the one true mediator in the flesh. No medium made by human beings can accomplish the richness, depth, or potency of the created, spoken word. When we cannot communicate in person, then digital technologies are serviceable tools in such cases. The tools that carry video and audio with minimal delay serve us best. Text-based technologies such as e-mail and texting serve well when they support active, in-person mediation.

Second, the incarnation gives priority to bodily presence. When we go out into the world and meet people, we resist the distance maintained through digital media. Presence is the prime condition for well-ordered human communication and continues to be so in a world with digital technologies. Good communication practices work from a paradigm of bodily presence, the first-order practice from which all other forms derive. Precisely because nothing replaces bodily presence, other forms of communication have a place in the order of human communication, but only a subordinate place. God himself communicates with people in many ways—from words written in stone, to handwriting on a wall, to dreams and visions. But God's ultimate mode of communication comes to us face-to-face, through the full presence of Jesus Christ incarnate.

From an Augustinian perspective, digital devices are valuable as a subordinate remedy when we cannot converse in person, but not as an equivalent alternative. For example, the speed and clarity of digital technologies today may obscure their appropriate function, particularly if we fall into the false assumption that connecting digitally is "as good as being there." We may appreciate technologies that help us converse digitally with people on the other side of the planet, and we can affirm that digital communication is better than nothing. Messages can cover long distances almost instantaneously via digital devices, but the distance remains, and digital devices often generate separation and displace personal conversation. Strangely, digital media often accentuates distance, even among those close by, including family and friends. The incarnation encourages us to take care not to treat digital techniques as equivalent to bodily presence. In every meaningful relationship of life, bodily presence is the context for true human communication.

Third, the incarnation gives priority to word and deed in action together. Augustine's thought concentrates first on living faithfully among the people present with us. He insists that the test of our character and faithfulness resides in present, lived moments, not in distances beyond our reach or in hypothetical situations. Faithfulness, or a commitment to truthfulness in practice, emerges in the fidelity between what we do and say, a challenge for every person. The challenge of word and deed in person makes the time delay and distance of digital media attractive. We can be lured by the ability to present a fabricated representation of ourselves rather than our present reality. Present reality is not directly available within digital technology, since digital media rely on electronic mechanisms that necessarily separate us from the lived reality, even if only by fractions of a second. Therefore, every word and image in a digital world is a representation, never a presentation. The incarnation invites us to live in the present for communication purposes and accept the challenge presented by faithfulness in word and deed.

Digital communication technologies can support these practices. However, because digital technologies cannot participate in our bodily, present lives, they can never truly unite word and deed. Digital devices only offer representations. Thus "connecting" digitally is necessarily secondary and of lesser significance in order and practice. When we maintain the proper order and relationship, the digital tools we have made can serve us well. The best electronic communication is based on present bodily presence, whether it looks back to live conversation or anticipates future personal communion. But representation remains low in the order of good communication. Representative media may be preferable to us, but when we elevate digital devices through false equivalence, we become disordered, restless, and empty.

Conclusion

The wisdom to which Augustine directs us maintains a high priority on living by word and deed in bodily person. If God chose to reveal himself in the flesh through word and deed from all eternity, Augustine might suggest that we should take care to limit how much we divide such communication today. Digital technologies separate body from mind and spirit much more completely and decisively than anything envisioned by mind-body dualists of the past.

Augustine calls into question digital Gnosticism at its very starting point. Instead, Augustine calls us to live in a way that integrates word and deed in a world preoccupied with appearances. In the many ages since Augustine lived, Christian believers and many other readers of Augustine's work continue to find him thought-provoking and helpful. As the "Doctor of Grace" and a church father of the Christian faith for both Catholics and Protestants, Augustine is an indispensable guide for any serious consideration of communication from a Christian perspective.

CHAPTER 6

Saint Benedict of Nursia: Learning to Live Well with Others in a World of Contradictions

Diane M. Badzinski

Abstract: In *The Rule of Saint Benedict*, sixth-century monk Saint Benedict of Nursia (c. 480–c. 543) provides practical advice for living well with others, recognizing that life together is marked with contradictions that invite opportunities for growth. The central contradiction, to which all others relate, is the interconnectedness between ourselves and others. This chapter presents Benedictine wisdom on living life's contradictions and suggests several practical ways his insights serve to reframe relational dialectics theory in communication studies.

Introduction

As a young man studying in Rome, Saint Benedict—the son of wealthy and pious parents, born in Nursia—was so repelled by the wickedness in the city and the sinful lives of his "well-educated companions"[1] that he fled the temptations of the city and retreated to the caves at Subiaco, about thirty miles outside of Rome.[2] Despite Benedict's desire for solitude, knowledge of his wise counsel spread, and the monks of Vicovaro, Italy, asked him to serve as their abbot. Reluctantly, Benedict took this post and trouble followed. Although many of the monks resisted Benedict's strict adherence to monastic disciplines, his fame rose and disciples gathered. Eventually, Benedict grouped his followers into twelve communities, appointing an abbot to lead each monastery. Until his death, Benedict provided counsel to the monks as to how to live fully in community with others; these monasteries were seen by many as "islands of peace in a sea of turmoil and unrest."[3] Benedict's spiritual wisdom is preserved in *The Rule of Saint Benedict* (hereafter referred to as *The Rule*).

Benedict's life was one of penitential solitude and contemplative community, living out his conviction that learning to live with oneself is foundational for living richly with others, and yet paradoxically, truly knowing oneself is impossible apart from community. Likewise, communication scholars have theorized and conducted research centering on the role of contradictions in maintaining thriving relationships. Contradictions—often referred to as paradoxes, dialectics, or dialectical tensions—are central to a class of theories, with arguably relational dialectics theory the most prominent. "At the heart of dialectical theory is that contradictions or tensions are inevitable and necessary"; meaning is constituted from the "interpenetration of opposing discourses."[4] This chapter suggests that Benedictine wisdom offers a model for understanding the contradictions that mark our existence as individuals in community, providing guidance for rethinking relational dialectics theory.

Monastic Life

The Rule consists of a prologue and seventy-three short chapters, articulating "minute directions about the right ordering of daily life in the monastery, chapters which might at first sight seem tedious, irrelevant, remote."[5] *The Rule* is practical in its stipulations on many of the ordinary actions of the everyday life in monastic communities, ranging from the sleeping arrangements of the monks, proper amount of food and drink, manner of reproving boys, and the reception of guests. Benedict is quick to point out that *The Rule* is "nothing harsh, nothing burdensome," but it is for the "good of all concerned" that prompts "us to a little strictness in order to amend faults and to safeguard love."[6] *The Rule*, considered "one of the most influential and enduring documents of Western Civilization,"[7] was disseminated through many ancient manuscripts, the oldest of which was most likely written by the Benedictines of Canterbury sometime during the beginning of the eighth century, although the specific date is unknown.[8]

Benedict was born into an uncertain world in the wake of the collapse of the Roman Empire. Barbarians were pillaging and dismantling the empire. The church too was suffering, fractured by theological disagreements and struggling through wars and political discord; the church longed for "peace and order and light on a scene which seemed instead to be rapidly descending into chaos."[9]

When Benedict came to Rome to study at the end of the fifth century, the cosmopolitan city was full of temptations, and "all that was evil and corrupt found a home within its walls."[10] Refusing to be seduced by its bewitching powers, Benedict promptly abandoned his studies, fleeing the city to begin his life as a monk by first retreating to the caves outside of Rome, and then later establishing monastic communities. At a time of tremendous unrest, the monks gathered and formed communities, providing security and stability in the midst of a corrupt and strife-torn Italy. These monastic communities created a sense of place very different from the world around them, creating a truly countercultural way of living.

A rhythm to prayer and work marked day-to-day life in these communities. Prayer life was private and corporate, with hours each day set aside for "*lectio divina,* prayerful private reading, and *meditatio,* the memorization, repetition, and reflection of biblical texts."[11] *The Rule,* in eleven chapters, outlines specific details for corporate worship, everything from the times for saying "alleluia" to the number of songs to be sung, to the order of the psalmody. Manual labor also punctuated daily life in these communities, often in constructing and furnishing the monasteries and in cultivating the soil to provide sustenance.[12]

For guidance on how to carry out the everyday duties in monastic communities, living the dynamic of solitude and community, the monks turned to Benedict. *The Rule* was written as a "result of true *via media,* the middle way that holds centrifugal forces together to make them dynamic, life-giving. [Benedict] holds together the emphasis on the solitary, on the withdrawal and disengagement . . . with the emphasis on . . . the communal or shared life. Here are the desert and the city juxtaposed."[13] Here lies the chief paradox in *The Rule:* The apparent opposites of solitude and community are to coexist, and if we replace "either-or with both-and, our lives will become larger and more filled with light."[14]

Paradoxes in Life

Three dominant paradoxes in *The Rule* are solitude-community, descending (humility) and ascending (exaltation), and speaking-listening; however, the overarching paradox from which all others stem is the interrelatedness of solitude and community. *The Rule* stresses the importance of solitude, making time in our day away from others for silence and contemplation.[15] Although *The Rule* insists on solitude, the book was written as a guide for living in community. Community is "based on life with other persons in the spirit of Christ: to support them, to empower them, and to learn from them."[16] Community of this kind demands formation over time.[17] So important is community that monks who neglect to gather at stipulated times and places are to be reproved. Referring to tardiness at the table, Benedict warns that if "this failure happens through the individual's negligence or fault" he must make amends and if not "let him not be permitted to share the common table."[18]

Throughout Benedict's monastic life, he hungered for times of solitude, often retreating to the caves outside of Rome, living his conviction that contemplative and penitent solitude prepares one for community. This symbiotic connection between self and others is deeply intertwined with Benedict's perspective on humility, that is, it is in the day-after-day posture of descent that we are propelled upward to a closer connection with God and others.

Benedict begins his discussion on humility referencing Matthew 23:12 (ESV): "Whoever exalts himself shall be humbled, and whoever humbles himself shall be exalted." Benedict recognizes that a proper understanding of humility is intimately tied to an understanding of self in relation to community. *The Rule* states that a man loves "not his own will nor takes pleasure in the satisfaction of his desires," but rather he submits "to his superior in all obedience" viewing self as "inferior to all and of less value" to demonstrate love for God and others.[19] Benedictine sister Joan Chittister writes, "Humility, the Rule implies, is the glue of our relationships. Humility is the foundation of community and family and friendship and love. Humility comes from understanding my place in the universe."[20] Here Chittister provides an example of the interrelatedness of the contradictions: to live well in community necessitates a posture of humility.

In addition, Benedict understands that speech should meet the needs of the community. To know the needs of others, listening is key. Herein marks another example of the impossibility of isolating practices—speaking and listening—apart from community. Benedict counsels, "Guard your lips from harmful or deceptive speech. Prefer moderation in speech and speak no foolish chatter, nothing just to provoke laughter; do not love immoderate or boisterous laughter."[21] He further writes that when one does speak, it is of utmost importance to "speak the truth with heart and tongue."[22] Theologian and former Catholic monk, Thomas Moore, in his foreword to *The Rule*, declares that if we follow Benedict's advice and "never spoke hollow words of affection to each other, never turned away when someone needed an expression of our love, and spoke from the heart, we would automatically be making a different world, and we would find ourselves in the thick of real community."[23]

Although *The Rule* provides direction for speech, Benedict's chief concern is to listen. Listening is so critical for thriving communities that the first word that appears in the prologue to *The Rule* is *listen*: "Listen carefully, my son, to the master's instructions, and attend to them with the ear of your heart. This is advice from a father who loves you; welcome it, and faithfully put it into practice."[24] Within the Benedictine tradition, listening and obedience are intimately related, as the word *obedience* "is derived from the Latin *oboedire*, which shares its roots with *audire*, to hear."[25] Growing closer to others demands full attention and acting upon what is heard.

For Benedict, all practices, and by extension contradictions, cannot be understood apart from community, and embracing one pole of the contradiction without the other is ill-advised. If a person centers on one to the exclusion of the other, then trouble follows. The poles of the contradictions are wholly dependent on each other, and therefore the breakdown of one results in the breakdown of the other.

Rethinking Relational Dialectics Theory

Applying Benedict's ideas on contradictions to relational dialectics theory is a muddy task. It can be argued, however, that relational dialectics theory advanced by Leslie A. Baxter and Barbara M. Montgomery continues to be the most palatable, familiar, and research-generating dialectical theory in interpersonal communication.[26] Relational dialectics theory centers on individuals in relationships working through seemingly contradictory tensions; it is in struggling with these competing discourses that relationships grow and flourish. The three dominant, interdependent, yet mutually negating tensions are (1) autonomy-connectedness, (2) openness-closedness, and (3) novelty-predictability. Autonomy-connectedness is expressed in a variety of ways, including time spent alone or together, and one's rights and obligations to self and others. Openness-closedness contrasts candid disclosure with discretion and privacy of information shared. Finally, novelty-predictability pits the need or desire for consistency and routine against spontaneity and change.

There are parallels and distinctions between Benedict's positions set forth in *The Rule* and relational dialectics theory. The most important similarity is that Benedict and dialectical theorists recognize the contradiction between self (autonomy) and the other (connectedness). Not surprisingly, then, research confirms that this contradiction is prevalent in relational discourses.[27] Both also hold that contractions and concepts such as openness, rights, and obligations are essential for living together well. Without a doubt, Benedict and relational dialectical theorists concur that the opposites of life provide opportunities for relational growth.

Acknowledging these similarities, there are at least three important differences, and these differences offer suggestions for expanding relational dialectics theory. First, *The Rule* focuses on *why* contradictions exist. *Why* an individual craves autonomy, for example, is paramount. Is time apart an escape? Is time apart a way to be more fully present when together? Benedictine tradition holds that a time of separateness is not selfish but is embraced for the benefit of others, highlighting the importance of one's intentions; that is, it is one's intentions or motives or attitude that drive a need for solitude or community. Proponents of dialectical theory are firm that our attention should be on the competing discourses, sidelining the need to consider factors such as desires, motives, and intentions. If Benedict is correct that psychological states matter, including desires, motives, and intentions, then relational dialectics research might become more robust if it attended to competing discourses as language that reveals or conceals motives within a dialectical tension.

Second, where relational dialectics theory posits that no one single contradiction is more central than another, *The Rule* implies a hierarchy among the contradictions. In Benedict's view, contradictions are inexplicitly tied to the connection between self and others, and thus, it behooves us to study contradictions as they intertwine with the overarching contradiction of solitude and community. This interconnectedness among contradictions then requires researchers to move away from examining relational dialectics as separate entities to exploring how contradictions interweave and inform each other. I suggest that dialectical theorists consider self and others as the chief contradiction from which all others interrelate. If Benedict is correct in his stance that self and community are interdependent, and that it is only from solitude that true community is possible, then it suggests that as relational dialectics researchers, we should identify how self (autonomy, solitude) benefits others (togetherness, community), and how other contradictions interrelate to provide a richer understanding of community.

Third, *The Rule* and relational dialectics theory contrast in perspective related to how one is to view contradictions. Although dialectical theorists posit that contradictions are "normal phenomena seen as neither inherently positive nor negative—they just exist," leading to the possibility of both positive and negative relational ramifications.[28] In practice, however, contradictions are often seen as struggles or stressors that are to be negotiated within relationships, painting a portrait of relating to each other as a "messy, tension-filled business."[29] Communication, within this view, is conceptualized as "inherently tension-filled" and "meaning is unfinalized."[30] Although Benedict recognizes the unremitting struggles, he proposes that contradictions are best viewed as opposites that are to be appreciated. Rather than viewing opposites as tensions creating relational divide, *The Rule* suggests the need to hold both together; one cannot exist fully without the other. One's relational goal is not to escape from the tensions between the poles of contradictions but to learn to welcome and be fully present in both. This point is argued by Palmer: "Our first need is not to release the tension but to *live the contradictions*, fully and painfully aware of the poles between which our lives are stretched. As we do so, we will be plunged into paradox, at whose heart we will find transcendence and new life."[31] The implication for relational dialectics research is advocating for more work identifying the positive ways dialectics operate in flourishing relationally.

To make use of these three suggestions for rethinking relational dialectics theory—expanding to include desires of the heart, positioning self and community as the preeminent contradiction from which all others interrelate, and recasting contradictions in a more favorable light—I use them to analyze a research study grounded in relational dialectics theory: Semlak and Pearson's "Sandwich Generation" study.

Communication researchers Julie L. Semlak and Judy C. Pearson investigated the dialectical contradictions faced by women who simultaneously provide care for individuals both older and younger than themselves.[32] These women are said to be "sandwiched" between an older generation and a younger one. These caregivers completed a survey to measure their perceptions related to three relational dialectics and their satisfaction with their relationships with their older care recipients. The results revealed that as caregivers' perceptions of autonomy decrease, so does their satisfaction with their care-recipients. This finding showcases the stature of the autonomy-connectedness contradiction, supporting Benedict's position of its centrality. The question that arises is why these two variables relate. It is a very different picture if dissatisfaction is the result of resentment due to an infringement on autonomy, on the one hand, or is the result of an inability to provide sufficient care due to a lack of autonomy, on the other. If desires (motives, intentions) are embedded in competing discourses, isolating them would provide fuller insight as to why autonomy is negatively related to relational satisfaction.

Semlak and Pearson's study also reported that as openness between the caregivers and their care recipients increases, so do caregivers' perceptions of relationship satisfaction. It is not unreasonable to speculate that openness about a need for autonomy would impact relational satisfaction, yet by treating contradictions as separate entities, their interrelatedness is left unexplored. Relational dialectics theory accounts for multiple competing discourses, but the interplay among them is often ignored. Semlak and Pearson agree: we need to tease out "the complex relationships relational dialectic contradictions have on each other to better understand dialectic totality."[33]

Finally, there is a tendency to view relational dialectics/contradictions as negative—struggles, oppositions, tensions—and to see relating to others as strained. A negative view of contradictions operates as a perceptual blinder, slanting research toward focusing on negative interactions and impacts. Although recognizing positive outcomes with the caregiver-recipient relationships, Semlak and Pearson report that overwhelmingly studies show detrimental impacts. Such studies, however, were conducted primarily to isolate caregivers' challenges, coping strategies, and mental health issues. By attending to the struggles, the negative impacts of the caregiver-recipient relationship are highlighted. The same bias is prevalent in much of the research grounded in relational dialectics theory. Although contradictions—"formed when competing forces both draw two relational partners together and push them apart"—center on that which both unifies and divides, a negative bias prevails as research tends to identify that which fractures and to examine contradictions in "problematic" contexts (e.g., caregiving, stepfamilies, relationship termination).[34] More research effort should be directed to understanding how contradictions might very well draw others together and how they might function to promote healthy relationships.

Conclusion

As I write this chapter, Rod Dreher's much-discussed book, *The Benedict Option: A Strategy for Christians in a Post-Christian Nation,* becomes yet another example of a Christian reflecting once again on the wisdom of Saint Benedict and *The Rule's* potential for dealing with problems in our own moment.[35] Benedictine tradition offers insights for thinking more deeply about the opposites in life, inviting new ways to reframe relational dialectics theory. Benedict's unwavering stance that we are to see self in relation to community—the foundation from which all other practices stem—and that neglecting either self or community withers the other, demonstrates that it is possible to flourish relationally as we courageously live life's contradictions.

CHAPTER 7

SAINT ANSELM OF CANTERBURY: CULTIVATING SOLEMNITY AND HUMILITY BY OBSERVING HOW WORDS FUNCTION

Mark A. E. Williams

Abstract: Saint Anselm of Canterbury (1033–1109) views words as links in a great chain that will lead toward God himself. But these links will function to show that God is, in the end, a solemn and unspeakable mystery. Confronting this truth leads to the dual conviction of the importance of Christian intellect and of Christian humility. Were both of these lessons taken into account, Christians might find a new sense of calling, and Christian political activists might find a new way of speaking.

Introduction

In the Middle Ages, it was common for any man called to be an archbishop to make a public statement about his unworthiness for the high office. After this polite protest, he would assume his duties. When Anselm was appointed archbishop of Canterbury in March of 1093, his declarations of humility went a bit further. He ran and had to be physically seized and dragged (*"dragged,* not *led,"* his biographer emphasizes) into a nearby church to begin his consecration to the new office; Anselm wept throughout the entire service.[1] For months, he sought every possible means to derail the appointment. But almost a year after he was dragged into office, he acquiesced.[2] Anselm's disciple and biographer, Eadmer, takes a special pleasure in highlighting the Scripture reading that happened to fall on that day. Eadmer wryly notes that the Gospel text Anselm had to stand up and proclaim to his new congregation told of the master of the wedding banquet who issued the call to his friends: "Come; for all things are now ready. But they all began to make excuses."[3]

Eadmer's appreciation of that irony shows a sensitivity to the way words can become suddenly and unexpectedly robust. Many of us have had experiences where a phrase from a movie or a line from a poem we were forced to memorize in fifth grade comes back to us with new and unexpected relevance because of some crossroads we face. Such moments are, on rare occasions, life-changing. Usually they are less dramatic, serving only as imperfect hints that suggest small matters of chance may be nothing of the sort: that every word comes within the scope of God's providence and points back to him as its author. The experience of words reaching unexpectedly beyond themselves reflects exactly Anselm's views. He believed that words, when carefully crafted and properly understood, might show something about God that cannot be found anywhere else. His insights provide strong guidance on how the Christian individual and the Christian community can exercise a humility learned from careful observation of how words work—a humility that seems lacking in today's public discourse.

This chapter will first examine Anselm's view of how words function as presented in his two most famous writings, the *Monologion* and *Proslogion*. Turning to the setting of those writings, we will discover a crucial link between Christian life and linguistics, reestablishing a sense of divine solemnity at the end of what words can do. Finally, this parallel suggests a framework for Christian political speech rooted in the eternal but addressing the issues of daily life with a humility that is the only appropriate response to God.

The *Monologion* and *Proslogion*

In the *Monologion*, and the slightly later *Proslogion*, Anselm explains how he understands words and things—especially ultimate things—to be related. Anselm writes that there are three ways to think of how words function.[4] The first occurs when we use a word in common utterance. I say aloud to you, "I planted an apple tree," and because we speak the same language, these words (which are really just physical sounds I make in the air with my voice) function to communicate something from my mind to yours.[5]

A second relationship Anselm highlights occurs when I use such common words, but I basically communicate with myself. I may, for example, explain a situation to myself in my own mind so that I gain clarity. In such cases, words communicate meaning, but this time they are self-reflective and function to sharpen my own understanding of something.[6]

The third way Anselm thinks of words is as involving both images and understanding of things. I can imagine or picture an apple tree without the words "apple tree." If I know this type of apple tree well and have a deep and accurate "feel" for it, then I have an *understanding* of the tree. The *images* of things are part of the human imagination. Understanding a thing is the task of human reason.[7] When we have both images and understanding then we have in our minds the "principal word of the thing," according to Anselm.[8]

For Anselm, the ultimate goal of all language is to speak about and to encounter God.[9] We can easily see how this is accomplished in the first two functions of language: there is a sound we can make, "God," that can be used in common language to communicate. Likewise, we can think about God without ever saying the word "God" aloud. But when we come to the third function of words—having the "principal word of the thing" in our minds—we fail, and Anselm recognizes this limitation.[10] And yet words are the foundation of the human intellect.[11] For Anselm, this means each Christian must come as close as possible to understanding God, not as he or she imagines him, but as he knows himself. And this process begins by understanding the spiritual side of how words work.

Our contemporary world sees spiritual reality as vague, insubstantial, misty. The material world, in contrast, is specific, substantial, solid. You cannot stub your toe on spiritual things: they lack *substance*. Anselm's culture, however, had taught him to see the world in almost exactly the opposite way. While the physical world was real and (very literally) rock solid, that same solidity was thin, sparse, and shadowy when compared to spiritual realities. Set beside spiritual things, the material world was no more than a mist; the spiritual world was the solid reality that could pass right through it, almost without disturbing it.[12]

Note that Anselm is not saying, in some metaphoric way, that spiritual things are more important than physical things. However, for Anselm, material things were less real than spiritual things. For Anselm, a word spoken out loud is part of the material world—a mere disturbance in the air. That word becomes substantive, real, and meaningful only to the degree that it communicates something of the more real world beyond material time and space. Words become powerful and real only by becoming congruent with what is most real: the Spirit of God.[13]

So where does that leave the phrase "apple tree"? The oral phrase "apple tree" (a *physical disturbance* in the air) just refers to some other *physical thing* growing from the dirt in my yard. Or does it? For Anselm, God is the creator of all things, and all things exist in the mind of God before they are given to the human race.[14] The deepest reality of an apple tree is not found in the thing I planted in the yard any more than it is found in the sound I make in the air. The *actual being* of the tree in my yard is found not in time and space but in the thoughts of God, as God engages in the second form of communication: God speaks these thoughts to God's own self.[15] By planting and tending the tree in my yard, God permits me to participate in his creative acts of divine self-reflection.

Ambition, Humility, and Reason

Anselm composed his works while he served as abbot of the Benedictine monastery of Bec, in Normandy. Monasteries served as the center of education, and this meant a monastic life was sometimes a life of material opportunity. For dukes, clergy, and kings who needed an astute, literate, disciplined, and dependable person to serve in the court or cathedral, the obvious thing to do was ask the local abbot to recommend some studious, top-notch monk. Anselm considered this ambition a primary enemy of piety within the monastic community.[16] He wrote to teach his fellow monks how to pursue a genuine humility that did not push the self into the limelight but also did not demean the gifts God had shared with them, most especially their intellect.

In this context, the *Monologion* and the *Proslogion* serve as Christian devotions: meditations on the God revealed to the church in the living Word that is Christ Jesus. Anselm's preferred title for the *Proslogion* was *Faith Seeking Understanding,* and its first chapter leaves no question as to its purpose.[17] Anselm opens with an admonition: "Enter into the inner chamber of your soul; shut out everything but God and what can be of help in your quest for Him."[18] Anselm is writing devotionals, but these works are not "inspirational" in any modern sense of that word. His primary goal is a holy mind to accompany a holy heart. He is training his monks to think like Christians, and he offers neither comfort nor compliment nor even very much encouragement. Instead, he shows them a rigorous and demanding method that requires more focus, concentration, and uncompromising intellectual honesty than most university students today will ever meet. The goal is to love God entirely with every part of yourself, and that includes your mind.

Two elements meet in Anselm's writings. First, he demands a humility that refuses to seek recognition of self, while still pursuing excellence in every task. Second, he requires his monks to embrace the gift of human reason and apply it with uncompromising honesty and excellence. The rigorous and disciplined application of reason would also reinforce humility, since reason will discover and highlight its own limits (and so give one cause to be humble). But humility, rightly understood, would lead to increased devotion and intellectual discipline, since it enflames the desire to love God with all of ourselves, including our minds.

If we consider how words work, according to Anselm, and if we follow the links they form, this will assist us in moving toward an understanding of God's creative self-reflection. But even if one perfectly captured every thought of God's mind, one would still have missed God's self because, of course, God is not identical to God's own thoughts; God is the one thinking all those thoughts. And thinkers are not their thoughts any more than an author is a book.

Language and understanding may reach (imperfectly) God's words, but not God's self. Anselm notes that God's very being "is ineffable, because no words at all are capable of expressing it."[19] But Anselm's meditations work to come as close to that mystery as possible. For example, Anselm famously notes that God is "something than which nothing greater can be thought."[20] This is not a statement about God's being, but about our minds. And yet, by crafting the phrase in just these terms, he gives us language that, once we come to understand its implications, hems in some sense of God's very being, without ever addressing the unspeakable being of God directly. This is, among other things, what Anselm is teaching his monks about human communication. The goal is genuine humility, wedded to an unceasing pursuit of intellectual excellence, as an expression of love.

Obviously, these devotions do not demean, but instead celebrate, God's gift of human intellect, since they require the fullest possible application of that gift. But at the same time, these devotions teach the humility and awe necessary for approaching God, since they fail in their attempt to speak the only Word that really matters. That Word is, for now and forever, beyond all words.

Study as Worship and Humility at the End of Words

An infinite journey toward the unspeakable majesty of God has very practical ramifications. First and foremost, Anselm wants to avoid the obvious error of believing that, since God dwells in light inaccessible and cannot be comprehended (1 Tim 6:16), the human intellect is not really part of the journey of faith. Anselm powerfully shows this is not so, and he specifically notes that if a human loves God completely, that means seeking to understand God as deeply as possible. In taking this stand, Anselm highlights a robust tradition of Christian intellectualism: study as worship.

The failure to describe God's creation with as much precision and honesty as possible (in the sciences) and the failure to describe the experience of the human soul with equal nuance and honesty (in the arts) is a failure to love God with every part of ourselves and our neighbors as ourselves. Anselm believes that those called to study (whether chemistry or grammar) should study as if God were their professor. Some portray a rigorous intellect as something far removed from "real life" and dangerous to real faith. Anselm will have none of that nonsense. Reason that is contrary to faith is weak and barely any reason at all. But equally, faith that is contrary to reason is weak and barely any faith at all. In God, faith and reason are wed, and what God has joined together, none should seek to sever.

A second practical application is closely related to this first. Combining humility and intellectual rigor is not a need that passed away in Anselm's day, especially as Christians speak about politics. On August 30, 2016, Michele Bachmann, an evangelical and former Republican member of the House of Representatives, said in an interview that "God raised up" Donald Trump to serve as the Republican nominee in the 2016 U.S. presidential race because he was "the only individual who could win in a general election."[21] Earlier that same month, Pat Robertson stated on the Christian Broadcasting Network that "the Lord has handed Mr. Trump a gift" in the form of a weak quarter of U.S. economic growth—news which Mr. Trump should use to his advantage. Robertson encouraged Mr. Trump to avoid the devil's "rabbit trails" which would distract him and take him "off message."[22] Any number of other examples might be cited, and of course conservative evangelicals are hardly the only group with political shortcomings; others fail as thoroughly, but differently. The besetting sins of the evangelical right tend toward pride. The more liberal side of American political life tends toward conflating categories of thought.[23]

The statements above, however, suggest a serious problem in contemporary Christian speech: an overfamiliarity with God that significantly (and justly) undermines the Christian voice within culture. Without an awareness of God as unspeakable, it becomes far too easy to speak as though one were God. Christians without a humility born from the genuine sense of God's crushing solemnity and infinite mystery can casually state their own limited perspectives as though they spoke for God.

Anselm, of course, can address that problem. An awareness of the solemnity and mystery of God leads to the presence of humility and circumspection in speech. Rather than framing claims in terms of what I think *God wants,* believers could learn to speak more cautiously, claiming, "Here is how my reflections on my faith help me think about this situation. . . ." Such a frame around our political speech would do several things. It would acknowledge a distance between what I believe about the daily circumstances of my culture and what the eternal God knows about this moment. If my position turns out to be wrong or weak, this would not suggest weakness in universal Christian teaching, because I have separated my words from the Word. But when Christians state their political convictions without such humility, identifying their beliefs with God, they invite just such an association. Christian faith itself becomes a scandal and a target of criticism. The infinite unspeakable mystery of God is lost in the clatter of partisan meanness.

Ms. Bachmann, who in the past stated unequivocally that she was told by the Holy Spirit how to conduct her affairs in the House of Representatives, was certainly attacked after her statements suggesting God wanted Donald Trump to be the Republican nominee.[24] But Christianity in general was savaged far more, and to some measure that was because Ms. Bachmann left virtually no distance between her human perspective and God's eternal kingdom.[25] If I equate God's wisdom with my convictions about art, then I invite those who disagree with my artistic views to dismiss God. The same is true in politics, of course. But it need not be this way.

All physicists know how little we understand about the physical world, so they speak tentatively about their experiments and understandings. Christian physicists can add wonder at God's creative majesty to their study. For them, each new discovery increases both their understanding of creation and their awe of the Creator. And each new discovery highlights new mysteries about the natural world. This is exactly what Anselm would expect. Perhaps Christian politicians could learn from Anselm and the Christian physicist to start by acknowledging the limits of what they know and that God is larger than their understanding, larger than any political party, larger than all creation.

Statements that claim the backing of the will of God for any political convictions add a veneer of authoritative verbiage, but it is only a veneer. Genuine authority is found when a person in a dialogue finds common ground, stating fully and fairly what even an opponent would agree with. From there, the communicators reason their way toward conclusions. Each provides the reasons for their position; each objects to the other's reasoning as incomplete or mistaken. But the reasons given at every moment must be reasons the other accepts or at least understands.

If non-Christian scientists are wise enough to frame their strongest evidence in careful, studied, tentative claims ("Our best data seem to suggest . . ."), then perhaps Christian politicians could learn, in humility before the mystery of the Godhead they serve, to speak with more circumspection as well. Had Ms. Bachmann—or Mr. Robertson, or any other Christian—done so, their words would not have invited an attack on Christian Truth. Christian politicians who explained common ground reasons for actions and then suggested that such reasons were supported by their faith might invite a wise and reasoned discussion of how faith and power (especially political power) might interact.

Conclusion

Study is worship. Deep, honest, disciplined intellect prepares one to give a thorough, clear, and honest account of the hope in Christian life. Doing this with humility while listening to the objections of others is an act of love, Anselm notes, which is the core of Christian life. Solemnity and humility enable Christians to recognize their own limited understanding of God's ways and acknowledge the dignity and image of God in others, even when they take a different path and give different reasons for their convictions. Anselm hears clearly the call to love God with all his mind and understand him with as much depth as love, thought, and language can muster. In the *Monologion* and *Proslogion,* Anselm excitedly presents a call to the whole church to study and speak carefully. In the early twenty-first century, Christianity has much to learn from Anselm's call.

CHAPTER 8

John of Salisbury: Relying on a Tradition of Dialogue and Ethics as a Model of Education for a Post-Christian World

Brian Gilchrist

Abstract: In *Metalogicon*, John of Salisbury (c. 1120–c. 1180) acknowledged the intimate relationship between rhetoric and Christian education. He expressed how the *trivium* (grammar, dialectics, and rhetoric) offered the best means of teaching communication. John experienced a communication model of education that emphasized a choice of context, which contrasts with the digital age's information model of education that features a context of choice. Salisbury's *Metalogicon* offers today's Christian educators rhetorical teaching strategies to benefit their students.

Introduction

Catholic bishop and philosopher John of Salisbury began his education with crystal-gazing lessons.[1] His teacher claimed that anyone who looked into a crystal ball could gain vast amounts of knowledge. Although John was born into a lower-class family in twelfth-century England, he recognized that he could not achieve his goals by placing his faith in schemes or people who offered shortcuts. John ended his lessons with the crystal-gazer and later spent twelve years studying the liberal arts in Paris, France.[2]

In one of his most important works, the *Metalogicon* [*On Behalf of Logic*], John reflects on the liberal arts tradition and reminds us that a Christian education can make a positive impact on students. His reflections are especially relevant today as students prepare to live and work in a post-Christian age, or an age characterized by the loss of the Christian worldview's primacy in cultural and political affairs in favor of alternative worldviews such as secularism or nationalism. John describes liberal arts education as dialogic and ethical in character. John's account of education suggests that Christian education in an increasingly post-Christian age faces two temptations. Christian educators might be tempted to offer an information model of education and to craft an educational experience aimed at dominating the post-Christian world. Against those temptations, John suggests that Christian education can draw on its dialogic and ethical traditions to prepare students to engage in a virtue-informed, open-ended dialogue with all people in the post-Christian world, especially those who disagree with our beliefs.

Metalogicon

In *Metalogicon*, John of Salisbury notes the liberal arts were taught from the general framework of Catholicism and were fundamentally dialogic and ethical. The dialogic character of education was primarily displayed in the educational practice of disputations. During these performances, students would improvise arguments using logical reasoning and a diverse array of sources, like the Bible, writings from the church fathers, history, philosophy, and literature.[3] Using a military metaphor, John describes disputations as an arena in which the teacher functioned as the commanding officer or drill instructor, and the students trained as soldiers.[4] Relying on their memories, disputations demanded that students learned how to "propose and answer questions" and how to "prove and evade."[5] If students were knowledgeable, they could agree about what was said in each source. However, the real point of contention was found in arguing about what was meant in each source. Disputations were won through persuasive speeches that attacked the weaknesses in opponents' arguments.

While John begins his account of disputations with a military metaphor, his fuller descriptions suggest that good disputations were, in fact, open-ended and community-building exercises between two persons.[6] There was no room in this community for contentiousness or anger, and students were not to take the disputation as an opportunity to show off their skill or to "twist" the other's words or refuse to accept the other's "intended meaning."[7] More importantly, disputations forged an implicit binding, contractual relationship between interlocutors.[8]

In addition to disputations, a proper education should include an emphasis on ethics. John commends ethics as the highest and most important branch of philosophy.[9] As John explains, ethics considers the difficulties of questions of obedience and obligation as to "whether it is better to obey one's parents or the laws when they disagree."[10] Unlike today, however, John placed emphasis on the role that virtue and vice play in ethical decision-making and the formation of human beings into ethical people.[11] Education was to instill virtue into students at a young age, so that virtue did not "desert those who are becoming feeble with age."[12] Reading, learning, meditation, and application included some educational practices that encouraged the development of virtue among students.[13] Virtue was pointless if it "remained merely verbal," and students should therefore exemplify the virtues in a lived life.[14] Ethical virtue was not simply the province of education, but it was also integral to how the medieval world imagined the intersection of politics and religion.

Politics and Religion in Medieval Life

Although separating church and state may be a common feature to governments in our contemporary era, such a distinction between these two pillars of society was not practiced during John's life. Politics and religion were unified because Christianity operated as "the principal bearer of moral norms, virtues, and behaviors in Europe."[15] The Catholic Church served as the institution that combined religious and political life.

The Mass has played an important role in Catholicism from the time of the Last Supper until our post-Christian age because it offers a common dwelling space for all ranks of society to worship God.[16] Medieval Christians, whether peasant or emperor, practiced their faith as a community at Mass by celebrating the Eucharist.[17] Although medieval Christians affirmed the Eucharist as a significant sacrament, as contemporary Christians do today, their practices differed in some respects. Medieval Christians did not physically eat the bread on a weekly basis, as many contemporary Christians do, but consumed it visually. They participated in communion when their eyes gazed upon the meal and the priest prayed over the Eucharist to enact the miracle of transubstantiation.[18] What theologian and church historian Ann W. Astrell calls "Eating Beauty" might very well describe the best this practice had to offer.[19]

The Catholic Church drew from its theology to shape political imaginations across Christendom. Medieval society was comprised of the three estates—the nobility (or warriors), peasantry (or producers), and clergy (or priests and others in religious orders)—and those estates could meet the needs of the entire society to the extent that they fulfilled their duties to the other.[20] Furthermore, the Catholic Church served as an institution that could unify the diverse members of the three estates. If all members of society cooperated, then the whole society would flourish. In short, medieval politics recognized that the success of the entire society required the prosperity of all its members.

Despite this theory of political harmony, the estates were often locked in great struggles with each other. The clergy and nobility were the minority in Christian Europe, and these upper classes used the three-estates arrangement to put "workers [the peasantry]—the economic class, the producers—in a state of submission to the other two classes."[21] Those in power used literary production and other modes of communication to attempt to dominate and subdue the other.[22]

In this contested political space, medieval education operated to ensure harmony among the estates. To this end, the clergy and religious orders established and maintained a Christian educational system throughout the Middle Ages. The liberal arts and other courses of study were taught from the general framework of Catholicism. Christian educators pursued new knowledge and followed lines of inquiry they perceived was for the glory of God. Inside of this political arrangement, instructors embraced academic freedom and medieval classrooms served as spaces for robust debate that spurred intellectual and spiritual development.[23] Christian education helped students not only search for knowledge and pursue vocations but also apply those lessons to benefit society as they imagined it.

Applying Medieval Education to the Digital Age

John's account of medieval education promoted what can be described as a *communication model of education*, which differs from the information model of education so prevalent in contemporary education.[24] Communication occurs when human beings contextualize information to produce meaning, which they share in communion with other people.[25] In this approach, context represents the circumstances from which information emerged, specifically the time (when) and location (where). Rooted in context and communion, communication scholar Corey Anton distinguishes the communication model of education, which offers a choice of context, from the information model, which offers a context of choice.[26] A communication model offers a choice of context in that people make information meaningful when they acknowledge diverse opinions and engage in multiple forms of interpretation. In an information model, people are limited to a context in which only two choices are possible: they must label information as either correct or incorrect.

For example, the question "What did Jesus say in the Sermon on the Mount?" is rooted in an information model, in a context of choice. This question presupposes an answer that can be categorized in binary fashion as either correct or incorrect. Conversely, a communication model would pose a different question: "What did Jesus *mean* in the Sermon on the Mount?" This question does not limit answers to binary categories. The question invites an open-ended conversation among different perspectives and diverse opinions that might lead to multiple conclusions. One's distinct denomination of Christianity, personal experience, cultural background, and family traditions influence how one might answer that question. Questions tied to a communication model are much more difficult to answer than questions rooted in an information model because communication models involve interpretations—not merely definitions. Today, most educational institutions tend to prefer assessment based on information, on a context of two choices: right or wrong.[27] The standardized test remains the dominant form of student assessment, and such assessments only judge students according to how well they recall information.

Contemporary Christian educators today would do well to draw on John of Salisbury's model of education. First, John's account of the disputations emphasized the foundational dialogic character of education. While the disputations were a kind of intellectual combat, they served to create community invested in open-ended conversations. Such a vision for Christian education is difficult in our current age that increasingly feels like a secular or post-Christian age.[28] In a post-Christian age, many Christians often feel that their commitments are increasingly irrelevant or ignored, and, as a result, some Christian educators might construct insular, safe spaces for Christian voices. Inside these bubbles, teachers might also be tempted to give students "the correct answers" to the pressures and questions of our age and, with those right answers, dominate the conversation with those who do not share their commitments.

John reminds us that a Christian education, when based on the liberal arts, brings students into open-ended dialogue with other voices in the hopes of sustaining community. It is not a practice aimed at ending conversations. Rather than turn away from voices we perceive as threatening, a dialogic, Christian, liberal arts education would perform the exact opposite. Such an education might help white evangelical students engage black voices on matters of race; female voices on matter of gender; gay voices on matters of sex; Muslim voices on matters of peace; immigrant voices on matters of justice; Native American and indigenous voices on matters of land and identity; and so on. Since students will encounter voices that disagree with them and could be hostile to their beliefs, Christian educators must prepare them for oppositional perspectives. Put another way, open-ended dialogue aims to create a space where students can enter into community with anyone. Such open-endedness aims to resist the temptation that faced education in the Middle Ages, to communicate in an attempt to dominate others. Open-endedness aims to keep the conversation going in hopes that we Christians might be thought of as a people to whom the world should listen, even though what we say might sound scandalous.

Likewise, *Metalogicon* suggests that all Christian education should exist, at its core, as an ethical enterprise. Where Christians today may face the temptation to dominate a world where their voices might become increasingly irrelevant, ethical Christian education demands a cultivation of an instructive order of virtues and practices: patience, empathy, wisdom, humility, mercy, courage, faith, hope, and love. The virtue of patience gives students the wherewithal not to rush to conclusions with others who may be hostile and, instead, remain silent if need be. Such silence, as the author of the book of Proverbs suggests, might create the conditions in which Christians appear wise instead of foolish (Prov 17:28 NRSV). Listening might very well lead to and nurture the virtue of empathy. An empathetic Christian need not be defensive or angry. Such a person can lament with those who suffer and weep with those who weep.

Once moved to empathy, the Christian can search out the wisdom to engage in self-critique and the humility to confess any sins to a watching secular world. Self-critique and public confession can take many forms, but wisdom and humility of this kind are not masked forms of self-flagellation or self-destruction. Rather, these practices help Christians become more aware of how they attend to being a Christian in the world. Self-critique and confession also aim to create spaces where reconciliation is possible, reconciliation with both our God and our enemy.

Next, Christian education might address mercy. Mercy is not an abdication of justice but bears fruit when Christians find their opponents weakened on the verge of utter defeat. In that moment, mercy means looking these people in the eye, and, as Martin Luther King Jr. reminds us, refusing to issue the final blow, refusing to defeat them.[29] Having moved through all of these virtues and practices, then, and perhaps only then, might the Christian summon the virtue of courage. Courage might include a wide range of actions, but it would certainly include the willingness to say "No" to the secular, post-Christian world. This means that there will come a time and place where a Christian will need to engage in a critique of others, especially if the moment is fitting (Prov 25:11–15 NRSV). In a post-Christian age, this account of virtues and practices is recommended only after a Christian has engaged the world with these virtues in an extended, open-ended conversation aimed at creating community. Only then might those who disagree with Christians begin to hear their Christian critiques.

Similarly, however, a Christian education should cultivate the theological virtues of faith, hope, and love, and these virtues can help Christians imagine and co-create new political and social spaces with their "enemies." When Christians engage a post-Christian world, they do not do so thinking that they can bend the world to their will. Rather, they do so as an act of faith. When Christians engage a potential enemy with open-ended dialogue, that engagement bears witness to an alternative reality, a reality Jesus' resurrected body brought into existence. It is important to remember, however, that resurrection only comes to us through death. Like Jesus' body on Holy Saturday, Christianity has effectively died as the world's *modus operandi* or method. In such a world, listening, lament, confession, and mercy are acts of faith. They are acts of faith because they offer a post-Christian age evidence of a world yet unseen, a world where secularity does not have the final word any more than death does.

Ultimately, Christians should also engage in open-ended dialogue as an act of hope. In John's apocalyptic vision in the book of Revelation, he sees God's good future. He sees a world in which God makes all things right. He sees a world where all nations and kings will walk and rule according to the light of

God's glory (see Rev 21:24). An open-ended dialogue can serve as an act of hope, because we believe that only God can do the work of bringing all the contested and violent spaces we inhabit to rights. In a post-Christian era, an era where it looks like Christianity has lost, open-ended conversation with our enemies reminds us that we are not in control of God's good future. If we do not lose hope, our failures give us opportunities to learn and grow. Nor should we lose hope in God's good future, a future where God will "be all in all" (1 Cor 15:28), where he will reign over everything everywhere.

Conclusion

Like Christians in the the Middle Ages, Christians in a post-Christian world might be tempted to co-create a political space that inadvertently encourages communicative acts of domination and subjugation. However, Jesus' love for the world offers Christian education an alternative to domination and subjugation. When Christ encountered a political sphere of violence and domination, the encounter led to his death. The apostle Paul reminds us that in and through the cross, God obliterated social and political categories like "stranger" and "alien" (Eph 2:16, 19 NRSV). In a post-Christian world, open-ended dialogue with those who strike us as "stranger" and "alien" might feel like death for us. But Jesus' death suggests that it is only through such vulnerability that Christian education can properly love a post-Christian world.

As John of Salisbury recognized, a Christian education is no small task because it cannot offer shortcuts or mere information. It demands developing wisdom through a commitment to lifelong learning. John's work leads us from an information model to a communication model of education, which embraces a tradition of dialogue and ethics to meet the demands of a post-Christian age. Open-ended dialogue can be an act of love, because it helps us imagine a very different political landscape where Christians greet the stranger and alien not with a clenched fist, but with "a holy kiss" (see Rom 16:16; 1 Cor 16:20; 2 Cor 13:12; 1 Thess 5:26; 1 Pet 5:14).

CHAPTER 9

SAINT ANGELA OF FOLIGNO: EVANGELIZING THROUGH *KATAPHATIC*, OR REALISTIC, RHETORIC

Barbara S. Spies

Abstract: Saint Angela of Foligno (1248–1309), a medieval Franciscan mystic, left a considerable body of work in her *Book of Blessed Angela*. Angela tells of her conversion to a deeper faith and offers guidance to the church, moving beyond barriers imposed upon women which prevent public communication. She gains a following of disciples, and her style of prayer becomes her mode of speaking, creating a *kataphatic*, or realistic, rhetoric.

Introduction

In 1285, Angela of Foligno sat down at the doors of the Basilica of St. Francis of Assisi and screamed.[1] Angela's cry was one of conversion, an intense awakening of her faith, an experience of God's love.[2] Shortly thereafter, she participated in the sacrament of penance and changed her way of life, turning from her infatuation with wealth and social standing. In a very short period of time, everyone in Angela's family passed away: her husband, her children, and her mother. Her conversion and these events eventually led her into a life of religious leadership. "On that road to Assisi," Angela recalls, Jesus spoke these words to her: "I will do great things in you in the sight of the nations. Through you, I shall be known and my name will be praised by many nations."[3] *The Book of Blessed Angela* solidified Angela's role as a religious leader, particularly through her unique approach to mysticism. This approach can be termed *kataphatic*, or "realistic" and "positive."

Those who use a kataphatic theology "have recourse to metaphors, figures and images and understand them as referring to God in a realistic way."[4] *The Modern Catholic Encyclopedia* defines kataphatic theology as "a theology that makes positive statements about God in contrast to a negative theology (*apophatic*) which tells us what God is not."[5] The kataphatic mode "creatively constructs language in an attempt to name, describe, or theorize the divine," while the apophatic "recognizes and exploits the failure of language to speak of the divine."[6] Although "Angela seems to move easily between the two,"[7] this chapter emphasizes Angela's kataphatic mysticism in *The Book of Blessed Angela*, where she offers clear resistance to restrictions on women common in her time.

In this chapter, I examine how Angela sets a communication standard for any faithful individual, especially women, who must resist the status quo in order to participate actively in a faith tradition. First, I will examine *The Book of Blessed Angela*, where she outlines her kataphatic approach to faith. Second, I will describe the context of medieval Foligno, Italy, to illuminate why Angela's rhetoric has this approach. Third, I will focus on Angela's resistance and kataphatic instruction, which provide the contemporary Christian with responses to challenges of both being silenced and evangelizing well.

The Book of Blessed Angela

The text includes two parts: the *Memorial* and the *Instructions*. The manuscript was not written by Angela but rather dictated by her to a scribe.[8] The *Memorial* is an account of the steps of her conversion, offering wisdom to those hoping to have a similar experience. This section of her book goes back and forth between her comments and those of her scribe, Brother A., recounting aspects of the experience and her description of her conversion. Brother A. typically takes the position of an interlocutor, standing in for a curious but friendly reader. There are times when Brother A. asks for clarity, and other times he expresses doubts about her experience. Nevertheless, the text positions Angela as one who can listen to doubts and wrestle through them, affirming her experience as a trustworthy mystic who experienced a special union with God.[9]

Most sections of the *Memorial* give a heading followed by a kataphatic account of Angela's mystical experience, albeit not without moments of uncertainty. But it is through those moments of uncertainty that God provides even deeper assurance. At one point of struggle, Angela prayed to Jesus for a "tangible sign," something she could apprehend with her senses of sight and touch, a sign "that I could see, namely that he place into my hand either a candle or a precious stone, or whatever other sign he wanted."[10] She notes that Jesus does offer her something palpable but not in the way she desired. What Angela then describes is a kataphatic or realistic explanation, wherein she uses language to portray experience outside the realm of the senses. "This sign will be continuously in the depths of your soul," Jesus says in response to Angela; "from it you will always feel something of God's presence and be burning with love for him. And you will recognize in your deep self that no one but I can do such a thing."[11] Angela had asked for a containable sign of Jesus' presence, something that could be easily described. Instead, Christ gives an inexpressible superabundance of his presence; nevertheless, she is able to give a kataphatic description of something inexpressible: the feeling of a continual love that burns brighter than the candle for which she had originally asked.

The second part of *The Book of Blessed Angela* is the *Instructions*, where she offers specific descriptions of how the faithful might attain the kind of conversion that she experienced and how they might communicate their faith effectively to others. She starts with the general advice that her readers, both women and men, should follow the model of Francis of Assisi. Angela does not suggest to women the contemplative role of a cloistered nun. In fact, she opposes living a life typically reserved for women at this time. She suggests that women can and should take up the role of a public, action-driven, evangelizing itinerant who boldly follows in Francis's footsteps.[12] By way of preparation for such a public life, she offers spiritual direction in prayer through kataphatic description. "No one can be saved without divine light," she warns.[13] "Divine light causes us to begin and to make progress, and it leads us to the summit of perfection. Therefore if you want to begin and to receive this divine light, pray. If you have begun to make progress and want this light to be intensified within you, pray. And if you have reached the summit of perfection, and want to be superillumined [*sic*] so as to remain in that state, pray."[14] Her kataphatic language here is confident, concrete, and assured. Prayer is not some ambiguous, indescribable experience for Angela. Rather, her kataphatic language creates the sense that it is both spiritual and approachable to all who desire it, even to a woman in this restricted time for her sex, taking up Francis's mantle of public communicator for God.

In taking up a public role, Angela also invites others to put on the cloak of humility, minority, or weakness. Angela instructs, "When you are little, you do not consider yourself self-sufficient because of your knowledge or natural abilities, but rather you are always inclined to acknowledge your defects and your miserable condition; you question yourself and contend against yourself so as to convince yourself of your defects and strive to correct them."[15]

Angela's description of her experience of the cross emphasizes this notion of minority as she describes the scene: "This perception of the meaning of the cross set me so afire that, standing near the cross, I stripped myself of all my clothing and offered my whole self to him."[16] Angela's kataphatic language demonstrates and invites others to a posture of humility.

Medieval Foligno, Italy

Angela of Foligno practiced her faith in a church that did not often look to women for wisdom. Throughout history, the Catholic Church has valorized the voices of men in worship and instruction. Yet Angela was a woman who made her pastoral voice heard. In repressive circumstances, women like Angela often find a different rhetoric. In a context with little or no imagined feminine agency, Angela found a way to speak that broke new ground while remaining deeply faithful to the Catholic tradition. Part of what followers found attractive about Angela's rhetoric was "the scorching and completely feminine way in which Angela narrates her dramatic love affair with the 'passionate suffering God-man. . . .' The intensity of her account, flowing on every page like molten lava, has no match in Christian mystical literature."[17]

The explosiveness of Angela's kataphatic and feminine rhetoric was out of place in her context, and her conversion serves as a convincing example of that. Throughout most of Western spiritual history, "To be female is to be modest, yielding, and private . . .; to write or speak in public is not modest, not private and therefore not feminine."[18] Consider the details of Angela's conversion on the steps of the basilica: "She caught sight of the depiction in stained glass of Christ holding Saint Francis closely to himself, a window that still can be seen today. It left her stunned. After 'gently' and 'gradually' the rapture left her, Angela began to roll on the pavement at the entrance to the basilica shrieking: 'Love still unknown, why? Why? Why?'"[19] When Angela screamed at the threshold of the basilica, her vocal display embarrassed and scandalized those around her. Women were not supposed to act in this way. Angela ignored such restrictive social expectations for controlling her voice.[20]

Angela also exercised considerable influence on generations of readers. Some followers of Angela of Foligno include her contemporary, Ubertino of Casale, a Spiritual Franciscan; seventeenth-century Protestant theologian Johann Arndt; French feminist Simone de Beauvoir; and Trappist monk Thomas Merton.[21] As a result of her wide influence, she is known in the Catholic tradition as a "Teacher of Theologians."[22] Furthermore, Franciscans who followed Angela played a large role in the spread of Christianity in the Americas. The friars who had been in Mexico from the early 1500s established missions there and then moved up the coast of California in the 1700s. When those friars traveled north, "five copies of Angela's book were part of the library that a group of Spanish Franciscans carried on their way to evangelize the new World."[23] Angela's works continue to receive wide distribution today, although such circulation only occurred initially because of the approval by male friars.

Resistance and Kataphatic Instruction

Angela of Foligno offers two implications for Christian communication today: First, Angela bears witness to the reality that women's resistance is an effective means of expression and leadership. From the first moment of spreading the good news, when women told the disciples of the resurrection, the feminine voice has been questioned and minimized.[24] Often turning to the words of 1 Corinthians 14:34–35, people have argued that women must maintain silence. Many mainline Protestant churches finally ordained women in the 1970s, but women's role in the Catholic tradition continues to be limited.[25] However, like the first proclaimers of the gospel, resistant women like Angela have always shown a determination to speak.

Catholic women like the Nuns on the Bus have been using powerful rhetoric, like that of Angela of Foligno. In June 2012, a group of nuns started a campaign "to protest the radical cuts to social services included in Republican Congressman Paul Ryan's budget, approved by the GOP-led House and supported by his soon-to-be running mate, Mitt Romney. The tour is something of a calculated guilt trip—every stop is coordinated to confront Catholic lawmakers or Republican leaders who voted for the legislation."[26] The work of these Catholic women, indeed of Christians resisting oppression anywhere, can be well served by the approach of Angela of Foligno.

The Nuns on the Bus demonstrate the kind of resistance against the silencing of women that Angela of Foligno modeled. These sisters, along with the entire Leadership Conference of Women Religious, had been under scrutiny by the church hierarchy. Sister Simone Campbell, in a leadership role for the group of sisters who rallied against poverty and injustice, noted boldly, "At the very moment we were standing shoulder to shoulder with the bishops in their fight to protect the poor and advance the social justice mission of the Church."[27] She also argued that health care reform met the needs of the poor and that "The unborn were protected *and* those without care would get it."[28] The resistant rhetoric of these women demonstrates their refusal to be silenced while promoting the values of the gospel.

Campbell, as the voice of the Nuns on the Bus, resists without going against the church. David Gibson notes, "Campbell neatly folded her remarks in with statements from the Catholic hierarchy, which has had more than its share of disagreements with President Obama and the Democratic Party over issues like gay marriage and abortion." As Campbell remarked, "We agree with our bishops, and that's why we went on the road: to stand with struggling families and to lift up our Catholic sisters who serve them."[29] It is clear that being a voice for the underserved is a role that shapes their rhetoric. As one observer noted, "The Nuns on the Bus bear sacramental significance because the nuns' prophetic praxis—the bus tours themselves and the solidarity that they built—exposed and interrupted the prevailing irrational and immoral discourse about balancing the federal budget on the backs of poor people."[30] These women, with Sister Simone as their spokesperson, extend the kind of rhetoric that Angela of Foligno models.

Angela's second implication for Christian rhetoric is that kataphatic communication evangelizes effectively, graced with confidence and humility. All are called to spread the gospel, as explained in the Great Commission of Matthew 28:16–20. The question of how to accomplish that role is a perpetual communication problem. Religious studies scholar Denys Turner describes the kataphatic as "the Christian mind deploying all the resources of language in the effort to express something about God, and in that straining to speak, theology uses as many voices as it can."[31] Angela's work suggests that strong kataphatic imagery combined with humility proves an effective means of evangelization.

Sister Simone Campbell demonstrates what this kataphatic rhetoric might look like today. In response to the news that the Congregation for the Doctrine of the Faith, a body within the Catholic Church responsible for defending against heresy, would discontinue their investigation of the Leadership Conference of Women Religious, she described their kataphatic, embodied rhetoric as a demonstration of the gospel. She explained, "We now know that people do understand the value of what we do when we stand in solidarity on a daily basis with people at the margins who must contend with many forms of injustice—economic, racial, and so many more. We stand together and work to overcome injustice because that is the Gospel's call."[32] The picture of standing with those on the margins provides the listener a positive, realistic portrait of the gospel-in-action.

Another evangelist who uses a kataphatic approach is Barbara Brown Taylor, an Episcopal priest. In addition to her preaching, she is an author of several books on faith. At one point, in *Learning to Walk in the Dark*, she uses the kataphatic image of the chicken house at night to help the reader find comfort in the dark. She notes that in the day, chickens do not respond positively to a visit: "They crash into each other. They lose their feathers. They threaten to die of fright right there in front of you."[33] She contrasts that view with night a nighttime visit, when "it is like they have had two martinis. They chuckle to each other when you come through the door."[34] This imagery of the comfortable chicken house at night leads the reader into a discussion of darkness in Scripture: "Once you start noticing how many important things happen at night in the Bible, the list grows fast. Jacob wrestles an angel by a river all night long. . . . Joseph dreams. . . . The exodus from Egypt happens at night. . . . Manna falls from the sky in the wilderness at night."[35] Taylor comforts her audience with the presence of God through the darkness in our lives. Her kataphatic approach provides the kind of simple view to bring the audience into her teachings about the word of God.

Conclusion

Angela's initial conversion experience caused others to react in embarrassment and concern for her. Screaming on the steps of the Basilica of St. Francis resulted in quite a stir. But, more importantly, it acted as a foretaste of her *Book of Blessed Angela*. She resisted the conventions of the day: that a woman should keep silent about her responses to faith. She described her conversion in vivid detail so that others might have a sense of the realistic experience of religious transformation. Angela's kataphatic rhetoric, like those used by Nuns on the Bus and Barbara Brown Taylor, are displays of resistance to the constraints on women speakers. The communicative practices of these women, both medieval and contemporary, continue to be a role model not only for Christian women but for all Christians today.

PART TWO:

Renaissance, Reformation, and Early Modern Christian Thinkers and Theologians

CHAPTER 10

Nicholas of Cusa: Sharing Ordinary Things to Bridge "Knowledge Gaps"

Russell P. Johnson

Abstract: Cardinal Nicholas of Cusa (1401–1464) was passionate about teaching theology and philosophy to largely uneducated laypeople. Following his model, contemporary communicators can bridge the apparent knowledge gap between experts and their audiences by (1) explaining ideas to them through analogies with everyday objects, (2) convincing them that they already have the tools needed to understand themselves and God, and (3) encouraging them to meditate on their own work and play and thereby find divine truth in their active lives.

Introduction

The fifteenth-century writer Nicholas of Cusa was a cardinal in the Roman Catholic Church, a position second only to the pope in influence. Pope Nicholas V made him a special representative to Germany and tasked him with reforming German monasteries. For years, Nicholas of Cusa served as the prince-bishop of a city in present-day Austria. During this time, he traveled extensively and wrote treatises on theology, philosophy, mathematics, and physics.[1] Yet even with all of this political, intellectual, and ecclesial responsibility, he made the time to preach hundreds of sermons to peasants and often preached in the vernacular German rather than the more customary Latin. This dedication to preaching was very unusual for a bishop in his time, let alone for a bishop with as many responsibilities as Nicholas, but it reflects his lifelong commitment to sharing theological truths with ordinary laypeople.

A perennial problem faced by communicators is the gap in knowledge between educators and their audiences. Activists struggle to explain the consequences of a piece of legislation to a general public that does not know the history of the issue. Teachers try to explain difficult ideas to students who do not understand the concepts involved. Pastors and evangelists work to make deep theological truths accessible to laypeople who do not have any theological training and have not studied the Bible in depth.

Nicholas of Cusa was keenly aware of this challenge. His two short books, *The Layman on Mind* and *On the Vision of God*, demonstrate how he communicated in a way that overcomes knowledge gaps between educated elites and their uneducated audiences. The bishop writes against a wider backdrop of the fifteenth century, where uninformed audiences posed difficult problems for Nicholas. Many of these problems, as noted above, persist in the present day. Nicholas's writings offer three lessons for communication across knowledge gaps: using analogies with everyday objects, treating one's audiences as experts, and suggesting activities rather than expounding theories.

The Layman on Mind and *On the Vision of God*

Nicholas of Cusa's 1450 book *Idiota de mente* (*The Layman on Mind*) begins with a philosopher and an orator ducking into a spoonmaker's home to escape a crowd. They are eager to have a conversation about the nature of the human mind, and to their surprise they discover they have much to learn from the humble spoonmaker. The spoonmaker is called an *idiota*, meaning "layman," and he tells the scholars that he has had no formal education in philosophy or rhetoric. Rather, he learned about humanity and God by reflecting on his own work as a spoonmaker, and he uses analogies from craftsmanship to explain what he believes.[2]

The layman points out that each hand-carved spoon has its imperfections, yet from looking at various spoons we form an understanding of what an ideal spoon would be. We can see in each spoon the perfect goal toward which all imperfect spoons aspire. What is true of spoons is also true of human minds, the layman tells the two scholars. Humans are created in the image of God but show forth that image only partially. Thus, the mind of God is not wholly unlike human minds, but human minds never attain the perfection of the divine mind. Human understanding relates to divine understanding as the imperfect wooden spoons are related to the ideal spoon.

Hearing this, the philosopher exclaims that the great Platonic and Aristotelian philosophers of the past teach the same thing about human minds. He is astonished that the layman could reach the same conclusion simply by reflecting on the art of spoonmaking.[3] This exclamation gives us some insight into what Nicholas is doing rhetorically. He shows his readers that even an uneducated craftsperson can understand the truths of philosophy and encourages his readers—like the layman—to reflect on how the world around them reveals the truth about themselves and God.

There is a theological basis for Nicholas's confidence in laypeople's ability. If the fullness of God can be manifest in a simple carpenter, Jesus, then surely the woodworkers and shepherds of the world can comprehend the divine.[4]

Not only can theological truths be understood by the humble, they are already revealed directly to the humble. Nicholas's goal was not bringing ready-made insights from the academy to the laypeople; he was rather inspiring laypeople to recognize that they already had the tools to discover truth for themselves.

Nicholas's book *De visione Dei* (*On the Vision of God*) is an extended meditation on a painting of Christ's face. When Nicholas sent this manuscript to a monastery, he included an actual painting, which depicted the imprint of Christ's face staring directly at the viewer. The one Nicholas of Cusa sent to the monks and their visitors was, like the Mona Lisa, a painting whose eyes followed the viewer around the room. Nicholas used this painting as an analogy for the divine-human relationship, particularly as a way to enter a theological debate on the nature of God.

There was a divide in the fifteenth century between the transcendent, abstract God of scholastic theological treatises and the immanent God present in the everyday world of laypeople. Nicholas encouraged viewers of the painting to walk around the room while looking at the Christ's eyes. The eyes of the painting follow the viewer around, even though the painting does not change. Thus the gaze of the painting moves as the viewer moves, but the gaze also remains still and unchanging. Nicholas summarizes this phenomenon saying, "The icon's gaze is moved immovably."[5]

Elsewhere, Nicholas uses the example of a spinning top to make a parallel point. The faster a top spins, the more it seems motionless and at rest. A top spinning infinitely fast, Nicholas reasons, would both be in perpetual motion and perfectly at rest.[6] The top, like the painting of Christ, does not explain away the paradox but helps us understand how God could be both active in the everyday world and unchangingly transcendent. By considering the painting and the spinning top, we can begin to imagine how both of these aspects of God could be true at the same time. Through analogies with visible, tangible objects, Nicholas brings his readers to "that simplicity where contradictories coincide."[7]

Complex Ideas and Simple People

In fifteenth-century Europe, the universities were dominated by scholastic theology, which involved the study of massive, dense tomes. To understand scholastic theology, a student needed to be well-versed in a number of fields. Scholastic theologians emphasized systematic comprehensiveness and scholarly rigor at the expense of public accessibility.

Moreover, popular religion had little to do with abstract philosophy but instead was closely connected with the concrete, tangible world of villagers. People traveled for miles to venerate relics, which were usually the bones, clothing, or possessions of saints. The relics were hugely popular, but theological elites worried that people's attraction to them often got in the way of their knowledge of God. The veneration of relics in many places took on a magical quality that distracted believers from the truth of Christianity.

Like the scholastic theologians, Nicholas was well-read, had an excellent education, and had dedicated his life to understanding the God of the universe. But he recognized that laypeople yearned for a theology that was tangible, comprehensible, and related to their everyday lives, something they could see and touch. In his writings, he sought to bridge the gap between the lofty ideas of the theologians and the ordinary world of fifteenth-century peasants by reaffirming the connection between the transcendent aspect of God (the God beyond all created things) emphasized by the theologians, and the immanent aspect of God (the God at work in our everyday lives) central to the faith of the laypeople.

Nicholas wrote during the Renaissance, a time when the educated elites could amass impressive collections of books, and he was known around Germany and all of Europe for his collection of rare manuscripts. At the same time, roughly 95 percent of Germans were illiterate.[8] For the urban laborers and rural farmers, the profound intellectual developments of the age would have affected them only indirectly. The wide gulf between the educated and the uneducated was taken for granted, and it would not be until after the rise of the printing press and the surge in literacy following the Reformation that this would begin to change.

In addition, Nicholas was what we now refer to as a "Renaissance Man," a person with expertise in a diverse array of disciplines. He wrote treatises on topics ranging from mathematics to philosophy while working as a lawyer, a diplomat, and a clergyman. In spite of his rather comprehensive knowledge of the world, Nicholas did not divide the world into those who are "in the know" and those who are not. His writings challenged the common cultural assumption that some are "learned" while others are "ignorant." He recognized that each person—from the spoonmaker to the child, from the monk to the prince— has his or her own sort of knowledge that only needs activation through an act of reflection. Peasants and craftsmen do not need to be handed theological and philosophical truths from experts; they already have their own expertise and experience, which can become a gateway to understanding humanity and divinity. Just as the incarnation brings together the material world and the spiritual world, so Nicholas's theology of the extraordinary-in-the-ordinary brings together theological ideas and the tangible objects.

Undoing the "Knowledge Gap"

Though the twenty-first-century world is different from the fifteenth-century world, communicators still face the challenge of addressing audiences unfamiliar with the subject matter. In 1970, communication researchers showed that just as a wet sponge soaks up more liquid than a dry sponge, people educated about a topic can understand, remember, and process new information about that topic better than those unfamiliar with the topic.[9] Communicators hoping to reach nonexpert audiences cannot simply assume that the same communication style that experts can follow will also be beneficial for nonexperts. Nicholas of Cusa's sustained effort to overcome the perceived "knowledge gap" between educated people and laypeople offers three practical lessons for contemporary communicators.

First, Nicholas brings together the abstract and concrete by explaining philosophical and theological ideas through extended analogies with ordinary objects. He does not make his arguments by citing academic authorities, nor does he rely heavily on jargon or technical language. Rather, he communicates his points through extended meditations on spoons, paintings, and spinning tops.

In fact, Nicholas offers a wealth of analogies that draw together the extraordinary and the ordinary. "Whatever is said about God through affirmative theology," Nicholas writes, "is based upon a relation to created things."[10] In *The Layman on Mind*, Nicholas's analogies involve spoons, seeds, diamonds, wineglasses, compasses, candles, and lutes. Elsewhere in his work, he writes analogies about coins, measuring sticks, fire, paper, magnets, hunting, walls, clocks, and sundials. He wrote a whole dialogue about bowling as an analogy for the knowledge of God and another dialogue about eyeglasses as an analogy for the human mind.[11] These analogies take complicated insights and make them as familiar as household objects. Nicholas says, in effect, that a person does not have to understand the details of Aristotelian metaphysics to understand the nature of God. God can be found in wooden spoons, in children's toys, in bread and wine.

Even for communicators not explicitly talking about theology, objects make the ideas accessible and memorable, and analogies encourage readers to continue looking for connections and truths in their everyday world. The analogies also make the ideas seem practical, even tangible. Even though we do not venerate relics with the same fervency as fifteenth-century Europeans, we still live in a material world. Any ideals worth believing in need to be connected to this everyday world of cars, smartphones, lightbulbs, and warm meals, or else they will be too abstract to have any impact on how we live.

Second, by having the spoonmaker teach the lessons to the philosopher and orator in *The Layman on Mind*, Nicholas gives an example to his readers for how they can incorporate philosophical thinking into their workaday lives. Nicholas's layman did not need to stop making spoons in order to contemplate the mysteries of God but rather reflected on his own craft and the things around him to discover truths about the human mind and the divine mind. Nicholas believed that "all human arts are 'images' of the Infinite Divine Art,"[12] so people of any vocation could draw on their own livelihoods as resources for insight into theology. The spoonmaker did not need experts to tell him about human knowledge; he became an expert himself by contemplating faithfully on his own activities.

Nicholas's communication strategy in *Layman*—making his audience the authority—is one that challenges the assumption at the heart of the perceived "knowledge gap." By giving the example of the knowledgeable layman, Nicholas challenges the idea that only the educated can grasp complicated philosophical truths. This is an idea that needs to be challenged if one's audience is going to embark on a mission of contemplation and discovery. This sort of communication relies not so much on translating ideas into simple terms but on encouraging by example the process of discovering ideas for oneself.

Finally, when Nicholas of Cusa sent his book *On the Vision of God* to the monastery, he included a painting and instructed the recipients to walk around the room maintaining eye contact with the painting. This is very unusual for a book on philosophical theology. But for Nicholas, movement and activity are essential to understanding. In Nicholas's time, as in ours, there is an assumed dichotomy between the contemplative life and the active life, between thinking and doing. Nicholas, by contrast, urged his readers to think about what they do. For him, people learn not primarily by reading and absorbing but rather by meditating on their activities—carving spoons, viewing art, selling olive oil, bowling, hunting, growing crops, and measuring cloth. As communicators, sometimes our duty is to convey an already-known truth to another person, but often our duty is to encourage others to act and then learn from those actions. Nicholas of Cusa, the busy philosopher, communicates a message that can only truly be heard by active, moving, working people. His message, in the end, is simple—"God is revealed in everything, in everything that is known and done."[13]

In the twenty-first century, there is no longer a single "knowledge gap" between the learned and the ignorant. In the "Information Age," global knowledge is increasing at an exponential rate, and we now live in a world of many kinds of knowledge, a world where there are countless areas of expertise. Instead of one knowledge gap, we all find ourselves on different sides of hundreds of knowledge gaps. Art historians may know nothing about auto repair, physicists may know nothing about horticulture, and fashion experts may know nothing about astronomy. The "Renaissance Man" has become increasingly rare in the centuries since the Renaissance; nowadays we live in an intellectual climate of "specialization, subspecialization, and subsubspecialization."[14] One writer has suggested that the late eighteenth century "marks the end of an era in which a single human being was able to comprehend the totality of knowledge."[15] This feat may have been possible in Nicholas's century, but it is unimaginable in ours. To use Nicholas's terms, we have come to realize that we are all learned about some topics but ignorant about an ever-increasing number of other topics. These disparities in knowledge create problems for communicators who want to teach groups without training in the topic in question.

Conclusion

Just as the spoonmaker was able to teach the philosopher and the rhetorician in *The Layman on Mind*, so too individuals with varied areas of expertise can provide valuable perspectives and make points that experts may not have otherwise considered. Knowledge gaps need to be overcome precisely because collaboration between different minds is so powerful.

This is nowhere more the case than in the church, the diverse-yet-united "Body of Christ." In discussions about how to "love your neighbor," for example, different Christians draw on their individual areas of expertise. Christians schooled in the social sciences may provoke their congregation to activism and service that helps the underprivileged. Christians well versed in psychology may encourage their congregation to pursue practices of meditation and conflict resolution among themselves. Christians who have studied theology may instruct their congregation to a fuller understanding of God. Those laypersons sitting in the pew can teach the academics that their expertise is only useful as it intersects in everyday life. Each of these may face their own "knowledge gap" that they need to overcome in order to get their message across to an audience unfamiliar with the subject matter. Here Nicholas of Cusa's vision, in which people's everyday lives contain resources for apprehending complicated truths, provides guidance for Christian communicators hoping to overcome disparities of knowledge in the increasingly specialized twenty-first century.

CHAPTER 11

Martin Luther: Avoiding the Use of "Othering" to Construct Christian Self-Identity in a Pluralistic Society

Mark L. Ward Sr.

Abstract: Martin Luther's (1483–1546) infamous 1543 treatise *On the Jews and Their Lies* urged the destruction of Jewish synagogues and homes. Luther's intense criticism of the Jews was integral to his theology and his revolutionary emphasis on individual religious experience. Many Christian communities today, much as Luther did with the Jews, have responded to modern pluralistic society by "othering" perceived opponents as foils for constructing their own identities.

Introduction

The 450th anniversary of Martin Luther's birth occurred in 1933, the year that Adolf Hitler took power in Germany. The Nazi government organized grand celebrations of "German Luther Day" across the country, lauding the Reformer as a great German patriot whose 1543 treatise *On the Jews and Their Lies* urged civil authorities to burn Jewish synagogues, destroy Jewish homes, confiscate Jewish holy books, and force Jews into hard labor. Five years later, the Reformer's 455th birthday fell on the day after *Kristallnacht,* the infamous Nazi persecution in which rampaging stormtroopers destroyed Jewish synagogues, homes, and businesses throughout the land. On that occasion a prominent Lutheran bishop, Martin Sasse, noted with satisfaction that Luther's vision had come to pass. "On November 10, 1938, Luther's birthday," he gloated, "the synagogues in Germany are burning."[1]

The Nazis' appropriation of the Reformer makes a key point relevant to Luther's meaning for today. As the Holocaust illustrated, "rational" hatreds are also a latent possibility of enlightened Western modernity. The modern "self" cannot, like two sides of a coin, exist without constructing an opposite "other" as its foil—a phenomenon for which the Nazis and their "final solution of the Jewish question" are the modern examples. From his emphasis on individual belief emerges "a new understanding of what it means to be a person." This new subject could not stand alone. Luther's Christian self needed an opposite, an "other," to make sense of itself. Analysis of Luther's *Judenschriften* (writings about the Jews) reveals that "othering" is, like the reverse face of the same coin, interwoven with his theology and construction of the new Christian self. The point is not that Christian anti-Semitism originated with Luther but that it was bound up in emerging Western ideas about the autonomous self. Today, overt anti-Semitism may no longer be explicitly practiced in the church, but "othering" sadly remains a key strategy by which many Christian communities maintain their identity and vitality in a modern pluralistic society.

Luther's own othering, which reached its pinnacle in 1543 with *On the Jews and Their Lies,* was founded on the assertion that Jews can never be converted to Christianity. Thus the Reformer's work urged Christians to resist what he called four Jewish "lies," including their ethnic "arrogance," their "boasting" in circumcision, their "conceit" at receiving the Law of Moses, and their "pride" at being given possession of Israel, Jerusalem, and the Temple.[2] In fact, Luther had expressed anti-Semitic views from the start of his public ministry, four years before he sparked the Reformation by posting his Ninety-Five Theses on the Wittenberg church door. The horrific German Peasants' War of 1524–1525 put Luther in an apocalyptic mood so that his anti-Semitism intensified throughout the remainder of his life. In our present moment, othering remains integral to modern religious identity, especially among evangelical Christians. As evangelicals encountered an increasingly pluralistic world, they created "others" in politics and society as a way of preserving their own identity. In such a landscape, Christians must engage in interfaith dialogue to live at peace with others who may never convert to their faith.

On the Jews and Their Lies

At about 65,000 words, Luther's 1543 treatise *On the Jews and Their Lies* is the longest of his *Judenschriften,* the most ferocious in its scornful and even bawdy language, and the one most cited by the Nazis as a justification for their anti-Semitic program. The work is structured as a diatribe against four Jewish "lies" and then concludes with Luther's advice to the civil and religious authorities. Luther introduced his treatise by forgoing any attempt "to convert the Jews, for that is impossible."[3] According to him, such was foretold by the prophet Hosea in the Old Testament (Hos 1:9), and the rejection of the Jews fulfills Jesus' prophecy in Luke 21:20, 22.

Luther provided a description of four kinds of Jewish "lies" to resist. The first was the Jews' ethnic pride, even though "all the prophets censured them for it, for it betrays an arrogant, carnal presumption devoid of spirit and of faith."[4] After the prophets, John the Baptist and Jesus himself also castigated the Jews for their arrogance. The second "lie" was the Jewish "boast" that God gave circumcision to them alone and thereby set them apart from all other nations as his holy people. Since Abraham had his oldest son Ishmael circumcised before his second son Isaac, Luther argued, then "Ishmael is not only the equal of his brother Isaac, but he might even . . . be entitled to boast of his circumcision more than Isaac, since he was circumcised more than one year sooner."[5] For this reason, Luther added, Jewish prayers "provoke God's anger more and more" because they "defame God with a blasphemous, shameful, and impudent lie."[6]

The third Jewish lie stemmed from the Jews being "very conceited because God spoke with them and issued them the law of Moses on Mount Sinai."[7] Though styling themselves as the bride of God, "they were a defiled bride, yes, an incorrigible whore and an evil slut with whom God ever had to wrangle, scuffle, and fight."[8] Besides, Luther asked, why should the Jews boast that God spoke to them? God also spoke to the devils in hell and they are not accounted God's people.

Finally, Luther claimed, the Jews perpetrate a fourth lie as they "pride themselves tremendously on having received the land of Canaan, the City of Jerusalem, and the temple from God."[9] But this "boasting" is empty, he asserted, given the Jews' captivities and exiles, the destructions of the First and Second Temples: "they have been cast out, dispersed, and utterly rejected for almost fifteen hundred years."[10]

Concluding his treatise, Luther infamously urged civil authorities to enact seven "sharp mercies" against the Jews: (1) that people "set fire to their synagogues or schools"; (2) "that their houses be razed and destroyed"; (3) "that all their prayer books and Talmudic writings . . . be taken from them"; (4) "that their rabbis be forbidden to teach henceforth on pain of loss of life and limb"; (5) "that safe-conduct on the highways be abolished completely for Jews"; (6) "that usury be prohibited to them, and that all cash and treasure of silver and gold be taken from them and put aside for safekeeping"; and (7) that they be forced to "earn their bread in the sweat of their brow . . . [rather than] idle away their time behind the stove, feasting and farting, and on top of it all, boasting blasphemously of their lordship [as moneylenders] over the Christians by means of our sweat."[11] Luther then advised local pastors to support these actions and to denounce Jews living in their communities to the authorities, thus to "save our souls from the Jews, that is, from the devil and eternal death."[12]

"Othering" in Luther's Theology

On the Jews and Their Lies transformed the Jews into the ultimate "other" against whom Luther defined the Christian self. Luther's anti-Semitism was a product of systematic thought over his entire career. It was rooted in the "premise of a Christ-centered Old Testament [that] led Luther to distinguish between the old pious Israel . . . and a Talmudic Judaism, cursed by God for its rejection of Christ."[13]

Between 1513 and 1515, even before his Ninety-Five Theses began the Protestant Reformation, he delivered an inaugural series of lectures on the Psalms as the newly appointed chair of theology at the University of Wittenberg. Luther took ample occasion to excoriate the Jews. He began by expositing Psalm 1:6, arguing that the Jews are cursed under their own laws for their unrepentant rejection of Christ.[14] Two years later, when he reached Psalm 78:66, Luther was moved to crass rage against the Jews: "Their recta stick out, that is, the innermost feelings of their heart and their desires in opposition to Christ they display to the present . . . [as] their will to do harm and do evil appears, since they are not able to vomit the feces of evils against Him."[15] During his lectures on Romans, delivered between 1515 and 1516, Luther questioned whether Paul's eschatological promise in Romans 11:26 applied to rabbinic Judaism. In his lectures on Galatians delivered between 1516 and 1519, he rejected the traditional interpretation of Galatians 3:16 in which "seed" is held as a reference to the Jews, and instead argued that "the Offspring of Abraham means Christ, lest the Jews boast that they are the ones in whom the Gentiles are to be blessed."[16]

By 1520, in his *Treatise on Good Works,* Luther linked Jewish usury with gluttony, drunkenness, and "the excessive cost of clothes" that "suck the world dry."[17] For a few years in the early 1520s he softened his attack in hopes of winning Jewish converts. In this vein, he published *That Jesus Christ Was Born a Jew* in 1523. But then the German Peasants' War of 1524–1525 erupted into the greatest popular rebellion in Europe to that time. The uprising was opposed by Luther and mercilessly put down by the German princes through the wholesale slaughter of peasant populations. In 1525, Luther claimed that God had handed the Jews to the Gentiles "to be troubled by every sort of shame."[18] His hopes for Jewish converts were gone by 1526 when he wrote, "It does no good to preach to them or admonish them, to threaten them, sing to them, or speak to them."[19] In his 1538 treatise *Against the Sabbatarians,* Luther advanced a historical justification for his views.[20] Five years later, Luther penned *On the Jews and Their Lies.*

Luther lived until 1546. In his final sermon, three days before his death, Luther preached his last public words: "If the Jews want to convert to us and cease to blaspheme, and from whatever else they have done, we will be happy to forgive them. But if not, we should neither tolerate nor accept them among us."[21]

Christian Othering Today

Building on the work of Charles Horton Cooley and George Herbert Mead,[22] Social Identity Theory (SIT) holds that one's self-concept combines a "personal identity" based on individual traits with a "social identity" based on group traits.[23] Social identity is formed through five factors: the (1) distinctiveness and (2) prestige of one's in-group; an (3) awareness of and (4) competition with out-groups; and (5) in-group affinities such as physical proximity, interpersonal relations, personal attractiveness or similarity, shared backgrounds, and common threats or aspirations. The "other" is integral to all five factors, providing the reverse side to the coin of the self. For Luther, "the Jews" formed the out-group or "other" integral to his conception of the Christian self. However, the Christian formational practice of othering was not confined to the schisms of the Reformation.

Religious "othering" has arguably become even more integral to the identities of many Christian communities, posing a danger in our increasingly pluralistic world. Sociologist Peter Berger in 1967 proposed his influential "secularization hypothesis," which held that as religious believers encountered alternative ideas in modern pluralistic societies, their "sacred canopies" or religious worldviews would be increasingly difficult to maintain.[24] Thus, as the salience of religion dissipated, so eventually would religious strife. Yet thirty years later Berger admitted that, except in academia and Western Europe, his prediction was not borne out and global society has become "desecularized."[25] This trend has occurred, because pluralism causes social fragmentation that pushes many people to seek moral stability in religion.[26]

In a pluralistic environment, evangelical Christians have thrived in part because pluralism provides so many others against which they can define themselves. Liberal Protestantism has declined in the United States, because it "undercuts the assertion of explicit theological truth claims that would distinguish liberal churches from the wider 'secular but spiritual' culture."[27] By contrast, Americans evangelicals thrive by creating a "subcultural identity" that draws its strength from "battling" the surrounding culture and thus "constructing distinction, engagement, and conflict."[28] Put another way, the most vital religious community in the United States—the evangelical community with which one in four adults identifies[29]—derives its vitality from attacking "others" against whom it can then define its own identity.

Evangelical Christians often portray themselves as "a persecuted minority perpetually under siege at the hands of Communists, Hollywood, liberals, homosexuals, feminists, and Hillary Rodham Clinton."[30] During the 2016 presidential election, othering was prominent as leaders of the evangelical community exhorted the faithful to stem the "liberal" tide. Evangelist Franklin Graham warned that "same-sex marriage zealots," "elite sexual revolutionaries," and other "forces of evil that are allied against the free exercise of our faith" are waging "an all-out war on religious liberty."[31] Christian media personality Tony Perkins cautioned that Hillary Clinton's "liberal antifamily, anti-faith policies" would bring "a spiritual dark age descending upon us."[32] Evangelical author and radio host James Dobson blamed "the radical feminist movement, based on hostility toward men," for shredding the moral fabric of society.[33] Such are only a sampling of discourses that employed othering to establish Christian identity.

While evangelical othering has contributed to our present polarized civic discourse, communication scholars have claimed that interfaith dialogue can serve as one antidote. Many Christians are inherently anxious and uncertain when they encounter cultural "others" whose responses are unpredictable.[34] Thus, genuine communication is unlikely when, say, a team of student street evangelists drives away passersby with shouted sermons and "strange" questions such as "Are you saved?" while clinging to their own comfortable "church talk" out of anxiety and uncertainty at encountering "secular humanists." More hopefully, though, many evangelicals "will acknowledge . . . that their scripts are cultural artifacts and the scripts themselves are not Truth."[35] Furthermore, Christians can be receptive to the notion that their tribal language creates anxiety and uncertainty in others to whom such talk sounds strange. By setting aside one's own comfortably scripted religious lingo, they can minimize others' anxiety and uncertainty. Those of different faiths (or no faith) can thus dialogue and achieve reasonably accurate interpretations of each other's meanings.

Communication scholars James A. Keaten and Charles Soukup likewise hope to foster mutual understanding and dialogue between religious traditions. Their model distinguishes four types of religious believers. "Exclusivists" do not engage religious others and comprehend them based on differences, claiming their Truth excludes all other truths. "Reductionists" also do not engage religious others but comprehend them based on similarities, claiming all other truths are reducible to their Truth. "Relativists" engage religious others based on similarities, seeing all truths as leading to the same Truth. "Pluralists," however, engage religious others based on differences, acknowledging different truths and learning from each.[36]

Keaten and Soukup call on all religionists, including exclusivists, not to abandon their truth claims but, rather, to engage in "dialogic reciprocity" and the opportunity to learn from others. Such pluralistic dialogue "conceives of religious difference as an opportunity for insight and inspiration rather than a threat to one's own faith tradition"; it "focus[es] on faith rather than religion" and "requires a communicative climate in which religious differences and disagreement are interpreted as learning opportunities rather than sources of conflict that must be resolved."[37] Thus an evangelical Christian student preparing for a summer mission to the Middle East might ask a Muslim student how fasting at Ramadan and making the pilgrimage to Mecca influences her faith. The dialogue would then allow the Christian to glimpse the Muslim faith world and develop a respect for its sincerity and depth. In time, the evangelical student could learn to practice what Keaten and Soukup call a "humanizing exclusivism" in which the Christian duty to altruistically serve others includes "tolerance for the worldview, culture, and faith of those who are suffering." Though exclusivism may prevent full understanding of religious others, humaneness can still make possible interactions of "deep compassion, mutuality, and even reciprocity."[38]

Conclusion

The communicative act of "othering" is not new to Protestant Christianity. As this chapter has argued, it is epitomized in Luther's consistent anti-Semitic rhetoric. When taken together with contemporary Christian rhetoric, Protestant Christians are unfortunately being faithful to the tradition to which they fall heir. They often communicate in ways that are found at the fountainhead of Protestant faith. This communicative practice is not only deeply problematic and unethical, it is deeply antithetical to the Christian faith itself.

However, the sins of Christianity's fathers and mothers in the faith need not be repeated. Mindful interfaith dialogue is one communicative practice for Christians that can serve as an antidote to othering. When Christians invite and learn from religious differences, they reject the othering on which modern Christian identity is too often built. Rejecting othering as a Christian communicative practice is vital for modern Christians to be faithful followers of Jesus.

CHAPTER 12

Saint Ignatius of Loyola: Embodying Civility in Contentious Times

Blake J. Neff

Abstract: Saint Ignatius of Loyola (1491–1556) is primarily known for his *Spiritual Exercises* and for founding the Order of the Jesuits. But in a lesser-known letter, "Instructions for the Sojourn at Trent," Ignatius outlines a communication style of silence, humble self-correction on the advice of others, and helping others as a way to encourage civility during the contentious council debates. Those principles remain remarkably applicable for modern communicators today in a culture characterized by ideological division and incivility.

Introduction

The once-soldier and now convert to Christianity, the Spaniard, Ignatius of Loyola, set out on a journey to Jerusalem. In Manresa, a small town outside of Barcelona, Ignatius engaged in "long hours of prayer, fasting, self-flagellation, and other austerities that were extreme even for the sixteenth century."[1] Over the year of his stay, this regimen drove the new convert to profound spiritual and psychological crisis—his asceticism, or severe self-discipline to avoid all forms of indulgence, even drove him to thoughts of suicide. Soon thereafter, however, Ignatius retreated from the most severe measures of asceticism and a peace returned to him. He discovered that he could more easily help others as he engaged in quiet, inner reflection. From this experience at Manresa, Ignatius developed two of the core elements of spiritual practice that would define the Catholic religious order known today as the Jesuits. Ignatius's *Spiritual Exercises* turned from rigorous ascetic practices toward introspection and self-discovery. In addition, the Jesuits would aim to be of help to others in their spiritual growth.

Emerging from these central features of Jesuit life, Ignatius's letter titled "Instruction for the Sojourn at Trent" offers important insights for contemporary readers who are interested in regaining civility in public discourse. The substance of the letter suggests that civility is a result of a way of life that includes pastoral practices that aim to help others, the communal practices of sharing and correction that aim at self-help, and deliberative practices of silence that aim at understanding a speaker's argument and motivations. As a result, Ignatius's letter offers an alternative mode of teaching and learning in undergraduate education, particularly in courses such as Argumentation and Debate.

The Jesuits, Ignatius, and the Council of Trent

In 1537, after graduating from the prestigious University of Paris and being ordained in the Catholic Church, Ignatius and nine other recent graduate ordinands planned a pilgrimage to the Holy Land. By 1539, they realized the political tensions in the region would make their journey impossible. Committed to keeping their group together, the ten men gathered in Rome, drew up a proposal for a new order, and submitted their plan to the Vatican. On September 27, 1540, Pope Paul III issued a papal bull that recognized this new order as the Society of Jesus, or the Jesuit Order. The order almost immediately voted Ignatius as their leader, their Superior General. Although Jesuits, like men in other orders, took vows of poverty, chastity, and obedience, they also committed themselves to a "turn to the world" or a robust engagement with the world outside of the church.[2] In addition, the Society did not mandate a particular kind of dress and did not demand observance of Liturgical Hours. Rather, the order focused on missions, education, and the ministry of preaching, lecturing, confession, and the Eucharist. Jesuits sent men throughout the world where they started dozens of free schools throughout Europe, preached, catechized, and administered the sacraments.

The birth of the Jesuit Order took place during the tumultuous aftermath of the Protestant Reformation and at the beginning of the Catholic Counter-Reformation movement. Only a few years after the Jesuits came into existence, Pope Paul III called for a council to respond to the various doctrines and claims that emerged from the Protestant Reformation. The Council of Trent (1545–1563), met some thirty-five times over eighteen years. Pope Paul III provided three main subjects for the council to work out. They were to address the "purity and truth of the Christian religion," the "restoration of good morals," and the "peace, unity, and harmony of Christians."[3] The council did not accomplish all that Pope Paul III intended. It did, however, give momentum to the Counter-Reformation. In the years following the council, the Roman Catholic Church was revitalized and energized. It produced, among other things, theological scholarship, vigorous spiritual renewals, and new art forms.[4]

Although Ignatius of Loyola died seven years before the council ended, Pope Paul III had already called upon Ignatius to make a significant contribution to its deliberations by appointing a team of three Jesuits to serve as papal theologians at Trent. The team arrived in Trent on May 18, 1546, but one member died of a fever while traveling to the proceedings. Once at Trent, the Jesuit appointees set about creating abstracts of Protestant writings and establishing agenda items for the council stemming from propositions contained in those writings. In addition to their significant influence in arranging proposals, the pair had exclusive authority in reporting to the various commissions.

As the council addressed Protestantism, an air of contentiousness accompanied these debates and deliberations. Protestantism brought hidden differences between various Catholics out into the open, and these differences "threatened periodically to take over the deliberations of the council."[5] The most vociferous interchange occurred when a disagreement between two participants of the council escalated to physical violence. When one bishop apparently called another "an ignoramus or a scoundrel," the altercation escalated to a match of shouting and beard-pulling.[6]

It is likely that Ignatius anticipated the potential contentiousness of the debates and thus wrote a letter addressing such concerns to the men he sent to Trent. Penned in early 1546, Ignatius's "Instructions for the Sojourn at Trent" counseled his men to an unusually reserved and civil form of discourse.

The Letter: "Instructions for the Sojourn at Trent"

Ignatius advises his fellow Jesuits while at Trent to engage in a specific set of deliberative, communal, and pastoral practices. These practices were oriented to a single aim: the "salvation and spiritual progress of souls."[7] While Trent held out the potential for serious gains, Ignatius warned that failure could lead to a "great loss."[8] If Trent aimed to deal productively with the challenge of Protestantism, the moral integrity of the church, and differences between Protestant and Catholics as well as between Catholic defenders, then the stakes were, indeed, high. Thus, Ignatius counseled his Jesuit brothers to adhere to a "common plan" of practices.[9]

In the opening section, Ignatius first advises his fellow Jesuits to be slow to speak. Slowness opens up space for virtues of consideration and kindness and might also create the conditions by which these men could understand the "meanings, leanings, and wishes of those who speak."[10] To use rhetorical language, silence allows the listener to hold together both the *logos* (or argument made) and the *ethos* (or character) of the person speaking. Ignatius assumes that deliberation is not merely about understanding the content under discussion; productive deliberation also reveals people and their predilections, desires, anxieties, and all the other things that motivate their speech.

These practices for deliberation are minimal in comparison to the pastoral duties Ignatius expected the team to follow. In the largest portion of the letter, Ignatius indicates that he expects his men to continue in their normal Jesuit duties. They should preach, educate, minister the sacraments of confession and Eucharist, walk others through the Spiritual Exercises, visit hospitals, pray, and exhort others. While engaged in these practices, they were to hold together this pastoral work with the deliberations of the council in mind. For example, when they preached, Ignatius advises them to avoid "subjects on which Catholics and Protestants are at variance."[11] Instead, they should exhort their audience toward the virtues and awaken a "knowledge of themselves and a love of their Creator and Lord."[12] Given the deliberations at Trent, Ignatius advised public speech that fosters love. Similarly, the men should encourage others to pray for the council.[13] Ignatius here offers a counterintuitive way to frame the stakes of the council by implying that their pastoral calling—helping others—would provide the proper context for their duties at the council. If pastoral duties are their primary practice and helping others their primary aim, then all their other duties—like the deliberations at the Council of Trent—will find their proper orientation.

Finally, Ignatius closes the letter with communal practices. First, he advises the men to engage in regular sharing with each other about the contents of their day. "Spend an hour at night," advises Ignatius, "when each of you can share with the others what you have done that day and discuss your plans for the following day."[14] Second, he encourages his men to engage in communal correction of each other. "On one night," he says, "let one of you ask the others to correct him in what he may have done amiss, and he who is corrected should make no answer unless he is asked to explain the matter."[15] Such a practice would happen in rotation so that all the men would receive correction from the others. This communal practice was aimed toward the spiritual development of love in their lives, so that all the men could be "helped unto greater charity."[16]

A Call for Civility

Like the participants at the Council of Trent, modern North Americans live in contentious times. Vociferous voices dominate public discourse, and the loudest and angriest are most likely to dominate the news cycle. The incivility often reflects the polarized political rhetoric between Republican and Democrats in the United States. In that arena, the lack of civility has grown to the extent that in the midst of a nationally televised Presidential Address to Congress, a representative of the opposing party shouted "You lie" to the president, thus disrespecting not only the current office holder but the highest office in the land as well.[17]

But the problem is not just about national politics. Parents shout obscenities at volunteer coaches and referees. Shoppers square off over who was first in the checkout lane. In addition, there are widely publicized incidences of cyberbullying, vitriolic language on reality television shows, and the deep sense that we encounter more hostility in our interpersonal interactions at work, school, driving, shopping, and at home.[18] What makes the problem even greater is the fact that "everyone has a megaphone,"[19] creating "ubiquitous Tweets, blogs, and online reader comments."[20] Taking potshots from behind a cyber wall serves to increase the frequency and intensity of rude, insulting, and abusive comments.

Yale University law professor Stephen I. Carter defines civility as "the sum of the many sacrifices we are called to make for the sake of living together."[21] In contemporary society there is strong evidence that an increasing number of North Americans are unwilling to make those sacrifices. In one recent study, 95 percent of those surveyed expressed a belief that there is a civility crisis in North America.[22]

In response to this crisis of civility, some have called for the academy to take the lead by teaching students to practice higher levels of civil discourse. Proponents of the idea believe that higher education is not only precisely the place to begin the evolution to a kinder and gentler culture, but, in addition, "by teaching students about the importance of civility and thoughtfulness we may increase their chances for success in both their professional and personal lives."[23] The call is for higher education to graduate students "with an understanding of what it means to challenge ideas strenuously without attacking people as individuals or as a member of a group."[24]

If the academy is to accept the call to cultural transformation to civility, it will not be sufficient merely to insist that students disagree courteously while in classroom discussions, or live together amiably in university dorms. Nor is it likely that civility will be the result of undergraduates simply observing faculty as the latter treat students and one another with genuine respect. Instead, civility must become an intended outcome of undergraduate education that is monitored and assessed just as strenuously as any other outcome. In other words, "students need to be taught (and not simply exposed to or asked to use) civil discourse."[25]

One obvious place within the academy to begin is in a course in Argumentation and Debate. The instructor in such a course could adopt an outcome of teaching students civil discourse in addition to the more traditional goals of teaching classical theory, propositional development, and debate style. The Ignatian approach to civility offers particularly valuable suggestions as to the nature of a curriculum for such a course. In particular, three aspects of Ignatius's instruction appear applicable to the modern Argumentation and Debate classroom.

First, as previously noted, Ignatius's approach to civility includes the use of silence as a prerequisite to speaking. He instructed his men to slow speech and quiet listening. Ignatius believed that listening to the position of others would allow his representatives at the council to understand all points of view as well as the character of all debaters more completely.

By contrast, contemporary culture offers little opportunity for silence and the deep learning it affords. As a result, to simply instruct young debaters to listen to their opponent carefully will not likely yield the desired outcomes. Instead, early in an Argumentation and Debate course students may benefit from an exercise that calls for a protracted period of total silence including separation from social media. Spending six to eight hours of silence while engaging in otherwise normal activities may serve to awaken prospective debaters to the advantages of silence. A reflection paper or class discussion on the time of silence might further explore what the student learned about herself or about the nature of silence in general.

Second, Ignatius teaches that civility is not something we decide to perform. Rather, civil public deliberations are a result of certain practices that constitute a way of life. For Ignatius, in contentious times, his Jesuit brothers were to organize their lives around the practices of helping others. With their lives centered on helping others, these Jesuits should engage in communal forms of sharing, correction, and love. Ignatius's assumption was that if his men lived this life before they spoke, then their speaking would likely serve as an antidote to contentiousness.

The Argumentation and Debate course might teach the same principle by using cocurricular activities requiring students to experience particular problems prior to debate. For example, a unit debating the problem of homelessness might first require students to experience the everyday issues of living on the streets. Students who have confronted the real issues related to the problem would more likely emerge to acknowledge all of the various courses of action rather than dogmatically insisting on their particular solution as the only approach to solving the complex social issue. Similar approaches could place students in a rescue mission prior to debates on drug or alcohol abuse or as mentors to at-risk children prior to debating family issues in North America.

Finally, the Ignatian approach to civility includes a healthy dose of humility. To his representatives to Trent he wrote, "If the matters being discussed are of such a nature that you cannot or ought not to be silent, then give your opinion with the greatest possible humility and sincerity and always end with the words *salvo meliori iudicio*—with due respect for a better opinion."[26] Perhaps Ignatius's recommendation here is to remind his representatives that their opinions may not in fact be the best point of view. Perhaps it is offered as a challenge to the body to come up with a superior point of view. Either way, Ignatius's men were being reminded to debate with humility. The hour each night set aside for self-help through personal spiritual development also presupposed an attitude of willingness to be corrected and thus to improve.

Again, as in the case of silence, attitudes in contemporary culture stand in sharp contrast to the humble approaches suggested by Ignatius. Students will enter the Argumentation and Debate classroom from a world where debaters "who interrupt others, talk the loudest, make the quickest comebacks or insults, and compete to keep the attention on themselves" are considered the winners even if their position is weaker and where those who yield to a superior position are labeled "flip-floppers."[27] The successful instructor of civil discourse will need to discover ways to help students recognize that "all parties to an argument risk alteration of their positions as argument proceeds."[28] To that end, one possible assignment involves asking students to select a proposition with which they do not agree from a list of propositions on current social issues. The students could then write a position paper in support of that proposition. As students understand the strengths of positions that are different than their own, they may gain a more humble attitude toward their own positions in a variety of topics.

Conclusion

Historical records do not indicate whether the Jesuits in attendance at Trent followed Ignatius's instructions; however, we do have good evidence to suggest that even if they did, their civility did not necessarily solve the problem of contentiousness at Trent. Like the Jesuits at Trent, we should not expect that minority attempts toward civility will transform the entire contemporary culture. But if civility is to become the cultural norm, we must begin by behaving and teaching others to behave in a civil manner. Indeed, time is of the essence. For the betterment of North American culture in this most vociferous day, the Ignatian way of civility in public discourse must be taught promptly to the next generation of public debaters.

CHAPTER 13

ARCHBISHOP THOMAS CRANMER: UNIFYING AND RECONCILING THROUGH THE BOOK OF COMMON PRAYER

Thomas J. Carmody

Abstract: Archbishop Thomas Cranmer (1489–1556) understood that if there was any hope of lasting reconciliation between the various groups vying for power in English society he had to create a formational liturgy of worship that would help the people to grow in unity. To this end, Cranmer wrote and compiled one of the most significant works in the English language, the Book of Common Prayer. This chapter examines how Cranmer used theological and rhetorical concepts to achieve his goals.

Introduction

On March 21, 1556, sixty-six-year-old Thomas Cranmer, the degraded former archbishop of Canterbury, Cambridge professor, writer and compiler of the Book of Common Prayer, advisor to kings, and leader of the Reformation in England, was to present his last public speech. Previously, Queen Mary I and her government had tried Cranmer for treason and heresy. Following his conviction, Cranmer signed six recantations in which he denounced all his Protestant convictions.[1] In this, his final speech, the "traitor and heretic" was to stand in the University Church of St. Mary and announce these denunciations publicly. Immediately afterward, he was to be marched out of the church and burned at the stake. Cranmer took his place and he began his prepared remarks. When it came time for him to declare his final recantation, he paused. Instead of denouncing his writings, he proclaimed, instead, that all his written recantations were precipitated by his fear of death and contradictory to the truth that he knew in his heart. He also declared that the hand that had signed the documents would be the first to be punished in the flames.[2] He was forcibly removed from the platform and dragged to the stake. According to eyewitnesses, Cranmer was true to his word. As the flames leapt up, he thrust his offending right hand, the one that had signed the previous recantations, into the flames.[3]

Mary I viewed his reforms as radical and heretical, but Cranmer embraced the reality that any major reform of the religious life of the English could only be successful if it happened gradually and with the support of the monarchy. In the contentious infighting between Protestants and Catholics, Cranmer wanted to raise up a people who would embrace the hallmarks of the Reformation.[4] Concurrently, the archbishop realized that he had to provide the British people with a formational instrument of corporal and personal worship that would aid the reconciliation of a fragmented church and society. In such political and ecclesial turmoil, the Book of Common Prayer, more commonly referred to as the Prayer Book, proved to be Cranmer's most important and influential religious and rhetorical instrument.

Given the fractured social environment that is currently becoming normative in the United States and, sadly, in the North American Church, a study of a Christian theological and rhetorical work like the Book of Common Prayer is timely. This chapter will examine how Cranmer rhetorically constructed the Prayer Book to encourage the people to learn Scripture and lean on God's loving promises. In this way, he compiled an instrument that, through corporal worship and personal adherence to its precepts, is both relational and formational. Hence, it provides one possible antidote to the bifurcated times we are living in.

A Product of Its Time

The Book of Common Prayer was not created in a vacuum but arose in one of the most tumultuous times in English history, the Tudor period. This was a period in English history that most of us have learned about from watching a PBS or network series rather than from a mandatory college course. Much of it occurred during the reign of Henry VIII, whose stubbornness, lustful passions, pettiness, and capriciousness could change like the weather and come against friend and foe alike. He was a man who did not like to be denied something he wanted. When Henry VIII fell in love with one of his wife's ladies-in-waiting, Anne Boleyn, he decided that he wanted to have his current marriage to Queen Catherine of Aragon annulled.[5] He also hoped that Anne could provide him with a male heir, something Catherine had not been able to do.

Regrettably for King Henry, he could not divorce the queen without permission from the pope. Catherine had been the widow of Henry's older brother Arthur, so the couple had received a dispensation from the pope just to get married.[6] To make his case to the pope, King Henry summoned his advisor Cardinal Wolsey and deployed theological and legal scholars to the courts of Europe, so they might advance his position in support of the annulment. Thomas Cranmer was one of these scholars. When Pope Clement VII refused to annul Henry and Catherine's marriage, it triggered a series of events that changed the temporal and spiritual direction of England. Henry broke from the pope and the Roman Catholic Church and, through the Act of Supremacy, had himself declared Supreme Head of the new Church of England.[7] This new authority gave him the power to appoint or remove any clergy in England. It also gave the king control over all the doctrinal and liturgical modes of worship in the country. Hence, Henry VIII became both the temporal and spiritual king of England. Subsequently, the new archbishop of Canterbury, Thomas Cranmer, granted the annulment, and Henry was free to marry his new queen, Anne Boleyn.

Unfortunately, King Henry's love life did not settle into nuptial bliss and contentment. He had married four additional times when Edward VI succeeded him. Edward VI was only nine years old when he assumed the throne of England and became its first Protestant monarch. Edward VI, however, only lived until he was fifteen. During his short reign, Archbishop Thomas Cranmer and his colleagues were finally publicly able to advocate many of the tenets of Protestantism. Parliament passed the first Act of Uniformity in 1549, making the Book of Common Prayer the only legal form of worship in the nation. It looked like England would finally become a Protestant country, but it did not last. Edward's premature death led ultimately, after the nine-day reign of his cousin Lady Jane Grey, to the reign of Mary I (known as Bloody Mary). Mary I was a devout Catholic who was committed to returning England to the Roman Catholic faith. Under her reign, religious services in Latin were restored and the Book of Common Prayer was banned. It was under Mary I that bishops Nicholas Ridley, Hugh Latimer, and Archbishop Thomas Cranmer were burned at the stake.[8]

Some might wonder how, given Mary's religious perspective, the Book of Common Prayer and Protestantism survived and ultimately thrived in England. Mary's reign, like her stepbrother Edward's, was short. She was queen for only five years before her Protestant stepsister Elizabeth I succeeded her. Upon taking the throne, Queen Elizabeth I restored the Church of England, and the Book of Common Prayer once again became the standard religious liturgy of the land.[9] Elizabeth enjoyed a long and productive reign, and by the time she died, the Church of England and the Book of Common Prayer had become the standard for Anglican worship and would remain so for almost four hundred years. Though he did not live to see his ultimate goal realized, Cranmer's work helped to establish Anglican worship throughout the world.

The Book of Common Prayer

The political Acts of Supremacy and Uniformity forced England to go through the motions of acceptance, but Cranmer knew that such acts were not sufficient to bring about healing and unity from England's religious, political, and social upheaval. In that tumultuous moment, faithful Christians in England wondered if God had abandoned them because of the actions of their former king, Henry VIII. Cranmer understood the angst that the people were experiencing, and he wanted to convince them that God had not abandoned them.

His means of persuasion were prayer and liturgy. Today, liturgy is perhaps misunderstood as dead rituals performed in dark and dusty churches, but it means simply the "work for the people," a public or community service. In liturgy, worshipers are encouraged to participate actively, recognizing that they are members of the Body of Christ. To participate in the liturgy of the Book of Common Prayer is to experience a "form of theological speech."[10] There is a Latin adage often quoted in Anglican circles that states, *lex orandi, lex credendi,* loosely translated as "the law of praying is the law of believing." In other words, there is a correspondence between the words we use in our prayers and what we believe about the God we worship.[11] If allowed to take hold in the believer, it can change a person from the inside out, usually not overnight, but slowly though continual practice; like living water unhurriedly bubbling up from an underground spring, it can transform us.

Two liturgical examples from the Book of Common Prayer help explain how Cranmer sought to bring together mutually disparaging and diverse individuals and slowly, through continual practice, form them through the liturgy into a worshipping community of faith. One example appears in his second edition of the Book of Common Prayer (1552). In this version, the Morning Prayer service begins with self-examination and a confession of sin. The priest stands before the congregation and says,

> ALMIGHTY and most merciful Father, we have erred, and strayed from thy ways like lost sheep. We have followed too much the devices and desires of our own hearts. We have offended against thy holy laws. We have left undone those things which we ought to have done, and we have done those things which we ought not to have done, and there is no health in us. But thou, O Lord, have mercy upon us, miserable offenders. Spare thou those, O God, which confess their faults. Restore thou those who are penitent; according to thy promises declared unto mankind in Christ Jesus our Lord. And grant, O most merciful Father, for his sake, that we may hereafter live a godly, righteous, and sober life, to the glory of thy holy Name. Amen.[12]

In this act of confession, the congregation, together with the priest, kneel and admit that each one present has sinned through "omission and commission."[13] By the sheer act of praying together, the confession offers to the faithful an implicit realization: we have a responsibility to God and to each other. Regardless of the anger, hurt, or hatred that we may feel toward others and for whatever reason, we together confess and repent of our sins before God in hopes that we can be restored to him and to each other. Confession therefore becomes a corporate act of faith, and a belief that God is faithful, just, loving, and forgiving to the truly penitent.

Given the theological and social conflicts that were rampant in England at this time, Cranmer knew that he had to reassure the people that they were now forgiven by God. He expressed this assurance by incorporating a list of Bible verses designed to comfort the people. In the Book of Common Prayer, these are called the "Comfortable Words."[14] During the Communion service the priest, after declaring absolution of the people's confessed and repented sins because of the sacrifice of Christ, proclaims,

> Hear what comfortable words our Savior Christ sayeth to all that turn to him.

> Come unto me all that travail, and be heavy laden, and I shall refresh you. So God loved the world, that he gave his only begotten Son, to the end that all that believe in him, should not perish, but have life everlasting.[15]

Here in this liturgy taken directly from the New Testament is the source of true comfort: Christ. This is a reminder to the people that they can be assured of the depth of the Creator's love, and it was Cranmer's hope that this knowledge would impel them to put their trust in God's forgiveness and therefore forgive their neighbor, the first step in reconciliation.

Liturgy as Community Building through Communication

Today, Christians find themselves once again in a deeply divided landscape. Much of our worship follows the whims of the moment—either in popular worship songs, brief sermon series, or one-off sermons on an occasional biblical passage. Into this kind of rootlessness, much of evangelicalism also finds itself in a fractured political and social landscape in which the incivility of public discourse breeds disunity in the church by creating an atmosphere where the faith of a congregant is judged by others based on their endorsement of a political party, a social issue, or a candidate. Into this fray, the Book of Common Prayer offers us more than just a book that can ground us more fully in a deeper historic Christian tradition. It can also be for us, as it has been for generations of believers, a theological and rhetorical storehouse for engaging the hearts of those caught up in contentious times. Through continual, regular liturgical practices, the Book of Common Prayer has the potential to form a fractured church into a unified worshipping community of faith.

The Book of Common Prayer can do this because it is a "communicative playbook" designed to aid congregations and individuals to worship God in spirit and in truth.[16] It celebrates, guides, and comforts people through the milestones of life, love, and death with its various sacred rituals.[17] With sacred rituals and a common liturgical vocabulary, it creates a rhetorical community of members bound together in one holy and catholic church.[18] The Book of Common Prayer provides a pathway, not a guarantee. If practiced consistently, it can transform and equip even the most jaded person to navigate our dysfunctional culture. As one congregant observed, "Practically speaking, it is hard to physically or verbally assault your sister or brother over alleged wrongs if you are both on your knees before God."

As mentioned previously in this chapter, one of the hallmarks of the liturgical worship of the Prayer Book is the corporate and personal confession that is prayerfully spoken in each Morning Prayer and Eucharist service. Here we jointly confess in the words of the liturgy our sins of omission and commission to God and to each other. However, as with all interpersonal conflicts, just verbalizing the phrase "I'm sorry" does not heal all wounds or set everything right. To have the type of forgiveness that can bring about reconciliation and healing there has to be more than just confession. This is why the confession found in the Book of Common Prayer does not stop with the public announcement of sins but adds the need for corporal and personal repentance in the words "Restore thou those who are penitent." In this phrase, the word "penitent" means "one who repents," a person desiring to amend his or her life. The key to forgiveness, then, is a contrite heart desiring to turn away from those sinful actions that caused separation initially between the individual and God and secondarily between each other. These operative theological concepts of confession and repentance are the preconditions of true forgiveness and allow the truly penitent to accept the assurance of God's forgiveness.

If there is no repentance, can there still be reconciliation and healing? Yes, but it will be different. Without true repentance on the part of individuals, relationships must be modified. For instance, we may realize that what once unified us no longer keeps us together, and therefore, we may have to choose to graciously walk apart—not vilifying those that disagree with us but, as Jesus showed us in his response to the rich man, allowing them to walk away. Some may wonder how reconciliation or healing can take place if we are not walking together, but it can happen when we allow our personal spiritual formation into disciples of Jesus as reflected in the Book of Common Prayer to be infused in our corporate worship. We come to realize that we do not need to win all arguments, nor do we feel the need to seek retribution against those we believe have wronged us, the church, or society. Rather, we agree to disagree. In this case, reconciliation becomes recognition that our differences may never allow us to fully embrace the position of the other and personal healing takes place when we realize that it is not solely dependent on us. Just think what today's church would be like if we embraced the concept of gracious disagreement. We could embrace corporate and personal spiritual formation through a liturgy infused with Scripture that encourages us to worship God and seek the good of others, even if we disagree or walk away. What a Christian witness this would be in the midst of all the yelling and name-calling that we currently find in our society and, sadly, in the church.

Conclusion

First published in 1549, *The Prayer Book* has been in print in various forms for almost five hundred years and is often ranked with the King James Version of the Bible and the works of William Shakespeare as one of the most significant literary works of the English language. However, it is more than just a work of literature. The Reverend Dr. Ashley Null explains, "As the author of an exceptionally eloquent literary legacy, Cranmer bequeathed to the English people [and by extension to us] a liturgy that expressed the deepest aspirations of the human spirit with rhetorical potency and rational clarity."[19] The Book of Common Prayer through its relational and formational liturgy provides us today with a tried and tested rhetorical tool to aide reconciliation in the church and society.[20] It cannot accomplish this goal overnight, but to those who fully embrace its scriptural and sacramental liturgical rhythms, it will provide a means of personal and formational transformation. This is the very foundation of reconciliation. Therefore, returning to the Latin phrase discussed previously, *lex orandi, lex credendi* (as we pray/worship, so we believe) we can add a new expression, *lex vivendi* (so we live). May this be our urgent prayer.

CHAPTER 14

Menno Simons: Engaging Interpersonal Confrontation and Avoidance for Organizational Integrity

Bill Strom

Abstract: Menno Simons (1496–1561) required wayward believers to leave the church so they would take seriously the error of their ways and eventually become restored to fellowship. Simons understood that an organization maintains internal vitality and external integrity when it articulates a clear identity, signs on members who support it, and discerns when members require recommitment to its vision—principles that are relevant today for the believers in diverse organizations.

Introduction

By 1556 former Catholic priest Menno Simons was growing weak and tired. For twenty-five years he had been traveling under darkness of night promoting his conviction that salvation came not through infant baptism but through adult confession and repentance, and that the bread and wine at the Lord's Supper were not mystically the body and blood of Christ but meaningful symbols thereof. These convictions moved Simons to join the Anabaptists—a group who rebaptized adults—even though his theology and practice put a bounty on his head. Simons's beliefs were driven by freshly formed views of the Bible as authoritative, and from Scripture he took the ideas of exclusion and shunning which were difficult yet necessary practices to develop disciples and maintain church integrity. Specifically, he cited Paul's admonition to "stay away from" people who muddle doctrine and cause division and recommended following Jesus' words to treat blatantly unrepentant believers like pagans or tax collectors.[1]

The issue came to a head in Emden, Germany, in 1556 with the case of Mrs. Swaen Rutgers, the devout wife of a man who had already been removed from the church by elder Leenaert Bouwens. After removing Mr. Rutgers, Bouwens instructed Swaen to cut off all communication with her husband—to shun him.

Mrs. Rutgers refused, and some congregants agreed. When Bouwens stood firm, groups took sides, and both sides petitioned senior elder Menno Simons to intervene. In an initial letter Simons urged moderation and peace, but when this failed to help the situation, he held meetings. Ultimately Simons agreed with conservative colleagues that exclusion and avoidance were biblical, and thereafter he wrote and preached on the value of confronting, removing, and shunning unrepentant believers for their own good and the church's spiritual vitality. In a contemporary culture, Christians tend to avoid such confrontations, in part because we live in a postmodern context where all of us are tempted toward an excess of tolerance, a tolerance that threatens Christian identity today, just like it did in Simons's day.

In situations where Christian identity is threatened, his principles stand out because they take seriously the mission, vision, and goals of the church, Christian organizations, and specifically the Christian college or university. While confronting, removing, and avoiding people may seem tough, these actions merit our attention for organizational and communicative significance. In broad view, Simons's ideas relate to any Christian group that seeks to foster integrity for members and organizations. To this end, we will consider Simons's arguments in "Instruction on Excommunication" that help advance his case, explore his historical and theological underpinnings, and consider them within the Christian college context.[2]

Menno Simons's Teaching

For Simons, exclusion and avoidance must take place with the proper motive, in the proper situation, and with the proper aim to be restorative rather than punitive. These principles were biblical and redemptive as opposed to what he saw happening in some other churches. At the time he formulated his convictions, Simons witnessed the excommunication, torture, and martyrdom of numerous "rebaptizers" at the hands of authorities within the Roman Catholic and Lutheran churches.

In response to the abuse he witnessed, Simons believed that any pastor or church that excluded a member must do so with right motives. He indicated that exclusion is "done in sighing, tears, and a spirit of compassion and of great love."[3] To one of his critics Simons wrote that he had not rushed in to remove people from his local church. Rather, "We have admonished and entreated [wayward people], and have put up with some of them a whole year or two, ever waiting and hoping the best of them, and have not hastily separated them."[4]

Simons observed from Romans 2:1 that it was inexcusable for leaders to be motivated by wrath, pride, ambition, or envy when choosing to cut off churchgoers. God would pass judgment on anyone who did. Simons implored pastors to operate from a good heart with best intentions toward their brother or sister, as in the case of Mr. and Mrs. Rutgers. In short, motive mattered.

Simons also identified three types of people who might require confronting, excluding, and avoiding. First were situations as described in Matthew 18 where a believer had sinned against a fellow believer but refused to repent when approached by the offended person or by additional witnesses or when confronted by the entire church.

The second situation involved Christians who stirred the pot with controversial teachings. Simons got his cue from Paul's letter to Titus where Paul advises him to avoid foolish controversies and arguments about the law. The apostle tells Titus to warn the "divisive person" once, then twice, but if he continues in his dissention, to "have nothing to do with him" (Titus 3:9–11).[5] Simons called such people "schismatics" or "sectaries," meaning people eager to create schism (rifts or ruptures) through sectarian (rigidly narrow) beliefs.[6]

The third situation concerned people who were mocking the name of Christ and blemishing the church's identity with a flagrantly immoral lifestyle. Simons referred to passages such as 1 Corinthians 6 where Paul lists the sexually immoral, idolaters, thieves, and the greedy (among others) who will not inherit the kingdom of God.[7] In Simons's view, making attempts at reconciliation mattered before moving toward exclusion.

Assuming that confronting, excluding, and avoiding were done from a good heart, Simons went on to argue that all three must be done with the right aim, namely, that wanderers wake up from the error of their ways, repent, and be restored to fellowship with local believers. He pointed out that the church was not excluding people, but God was, and that the church was the local means to move offenders toward reconciliation with God and back into the community of grace. The goal of the church should be restorative, not punitive, and done in humility.[8]

Simons believed these matters required extreme care and consideration because at stake were the spiritual well-being of the congregation and the church's reputation. In a summary statement, he begs leaders to use tender wisdom in such matters: "Finally, I entreat all elders, teachers, ministers, and deacons in the love of Christ, not to teach this whole difficult matter recklessly, sternly and unwisely, but in the full fear of God, and with Christian prudence and paternal care, in a true, apostolic manner, not too hastily or too slowly, not too rigidly or too leniently."[9]

The Cultural Context of Menno Simons's Teaching

Simons's theology is better understood through his views of organizational identity and interpersonal communication. To him, church identity was closely linked to the means of salvation and evidence of the Spirit within, and interpersonal interaction was key in tearing down or building up the saints.

Regarding identity, Simons felt that the Roman Catholic Church had lost its biblical moorings and had created a manmade spirituality. He had experienced these things in that church as a priest. He was ordained in 1542—just three years after Martin Luther's excommunication. He performed the Mass hundreds of times in his twelve years as a priest and baptized infants for their salvation, all the while increasingly skeptical of their meaning.

The reason for his doubt was that Martin Luther and Ulrich Zwingli were arguing convincingly that salvation came by God's grace through faith alone or by God's choosing, not by infant baptism, nor by works, nor by paying off church officials. But oddly, Luther and Zwingli supported child baptism for various reasons including tradition and the fact that Scripture did not forbid it. Menno Simons thought otherwise.

Two years into his parish ministry Simons began to read the Bible for the first time. Therein he found no command to baptize children, only a command for adult baptism following personal conversion. The condition of the Catholic Church now made sense to Simons: if a child grew up believing salvation came from infant baptism, then his or her spirituality was likely not driven by a heart relationship with God but by following rituals and prayers created by church leaders. In "Foundation of Christian Doctrine," he addresses the point that "bells, churches, altars, holy water, tapers, and palms" may be used under God's blessed name but not be empowered by God's will or word.[10]

In short, Simons believed people who had been raised this way had yet to encounter the redeeming work of Christ and lacked the Holy Spirit for regeneration. To make the point, Simons asked church leaders for evidence of their new life: fear of God, love of neighbors, mercy toward the needy, visits to orphans and widows, and sacrifice of bodily pleasures.[11] In his estimation, genuine faith and worship had been replaced by "an external set of rites . . . [that were] pleasing to the flesh, such as bells, organs, singing, celebration, ornamented churches, beautiful icons" along with recited psalms, prayers, and sacraments.[12] Rather, in his view, the true church was the bride of Christ, a spiritual body made up of people who were "regenerate . . . meek, merciful, mortified [self-denying], righteous, peaceable, lovely and obedient."[13] To him the church's moral demise began with wrong theology regarding salvation and following that, lives devoid of spiritual fruit. Simons believed that to build a church of integrity one must begin with renewed theology and intentionality toward personal holiness. Thus it made sense to avoid people who stirred the pot with questionable theology or flagrantly immoral lifestyles.

To this end Simons also argued that close human communication was a primary means by which believers built up or tore down their spiritual identities. He likened tearing down to leprosy transferring skin-on-skin and leaven permeating bread dough.[14] Regarding family interaction, he claimed that fathers, mothers, husbands, wives, and children were especially apt to influence one another's souls and behavior for good or ill due to close proximity.[15]

This is why Simons believed that spouses should shun the other if the partner turned against God, because one's marriage to Christ trumped earthly commitment to spouse. He wrote, "We truly recognize through the Spirit and Word of God that the heavenly marriage bond between Christ and our souls . . . must be kept unbroken in willing obedience to the only and eternal bridegroom."[16] He claimed to have witnessed some three hundred spouses lose their faith altogether because they had ignored the teaching to shun.[17]

In sum, Simons's teachings indicated his commitment to establishing and maintaining the church's identity as a people reborn as adults and set apart as holy. He argued that one could recognize such individuals by the fruit of the Spirit's indwelling. Setting a believer outside the church for a season to come to his or her spiritual senses was a loving relational strategy to protect the "righteous" and win back the sinner.

Simons, Christian Identity, and the Christian University

Today, practices of exclusion are increasingly rare. Christians live in a culture that is increasingly tolerant of diversity. Postmodernism and relativistic accounts of truth have also won the day, and the wider culture tends to regard those Christians who claim to know the Truth as suspect at best or unethical at worst. Moreover, with church attendance declining and Christian institutes of higher education enrollments waning, it has become practical for both groups to attract new members through traditional marketing ploys (e.g., appealing to consumer values such as personal choice and member satisfaction) rather than distinct doctrine and religious rituals. In this context, it has become questionable for churches, Christian organizations, and Christian colleges to claim doctrinal certainty or strict practice. Tolerance, relativism, and an economic precariousness, therefore, all pose external threats to Christian identity.

In addition, avoiding practices of exclusion can also lead to damages within the Christian community, as the case of Mennonite theologian John Howard Yoder illustrates.[18] A brilliant and influential theologian, Yoder taught at Anabaptist Mennonite Biblical Seminary in the 1970s and 1980s. During this time, he sexually abused over one hundred women. Seminary leaders took no action against him until a new president forced his resignation. Only in 1992, six years following Yoder's departure, did his denomination begin disciplinary action. Moreover, it took another twenty-three years before the seminary took responsibility for Yoder's actions. In March 2015, seminary president Sara Wenger Shenk addressed Yoder's victims, "What was done to you, whether sinful acts of commission or omission, was grievously wrong. It should never have been allowed to happen. We failed you. We failed the church. We failed the Gospel of Jesus Christ."[19]

In this dangerous mix of economic pressure, relativistic morality, and tolerance of sin, Simons's practice of exclusion bears relevance for the church and Christian organizations.

The application here will focus on a Christian institution of higher education, Trinity Western University (TWU). Among the 4,700 degree-granting institutions of higher education in the United States, 1,000 identify as religiously affiliated, and 141 of these are members of the Council for Christian Colleges & Universities (CCCU), an organization that exists "to advance the cause of Christ-centered higher education and to help our institutions transform lives by faithfully relating scholarship and service to biblical truth."[20] While only two member schools claim Mennonite heritage, Simons's exclusionary practice shapes many of these CCCU schools when they require staff, faculty, and students to sign statements of faith and codes of conduct. TWU is no different, and its policy reflects many of Simons's concerns.

TWU has four different kinds of rules that correspond to some aspect of Simons's thought regarding exclusion. TWU's covenant rules describe a version of Simons's community that is holy and set apart. The university's motivational rules help those in leadership embrace what Simons says all leaders should have during discipline: good hearts and best intentions. The process rules TWU uses resemble the situations in which Simons claims exclusion might need to take place. Finally, the goal of TWU's rules parallels Simons's hope that exclusion be restorative not punitive.

First, covenant rules guide the process by which individuals come together to agree on the identity of their organization, including its beliefs, values, mission, and goals, and then invite new members to join willingly to develop personal and corporate vitality. The university asserts its Christian identity aimed at developing students into leaders with "exemplary character" and high competence.[21] The language of TWU's "Community Covenant Agreement" suggests that free choice and responsibility define its communal life. Everyone at the institution is said to "accept an invitation" into the community wherein they "commit themselves" to biblical virtues and practices and "voluntarily abstain" from attitudes and practices the university deems obstacles to spiritual and personal growth.[22] Should a student or employee engage in behavior deemed a threat to community safety, indicate ongoing breaking of the community covenant, or fail to perform the duties required of them by employment, the university reserves the right and responsibility to remove people from the campus.[23]

Second, motivational rules refer to the heart condition behind leaders' actions to hold employees and students accountable to the university's covenant code. Like Simons's view, the motive is not punitive but merciful, not vindictive but forbearing and restorative. This guideline recognizes that members are morally complex and similarly at risk of falling short of the university's ideals and preferred practices. Leaders are "to demonstrate care and acceptance for the individual even if behavior may be unacceptable" while attempting to "balance the needs of an individual along with the needs of the greater community."[24] Moreover leaders are encouraged "to prayerfully and objectively assess what has occurred and indicate to the student what violation(s) has (have) been committed."[25] Finally, the university considers the rights of the individual and the welfare of the community when writing up accountability agreements. The guidelines indicate checks and balances for leaders' motivations in both the accountability process and the goal of restoring members to good standing.

Third, process rules govern the communication and decision-making steps to discern appropriate actions with those it deems difficult members. At TWU the Harassment Policy and the Student Accountability Procedure reflect Simons's use of Matthew 18. University members should first approach the offender privately, then bring in a witness, and finally engage governing groups as a last resort. The harassment complaint procedure states that the person who feels harassed is to let the alleged harasser know that the behavior is unwelcome. If this fails to clear up the matter, the complainant is encouraged to consult a supervisor or in the case of a student, a student life staff member. If a failure to resolve the issue persists, only at this point is a governing body involved. Furthermore, only under severe circumstances is a member requested to disengage the organization. At TWU, those cases only include students failing to attain a minimum grade point average over several semesters; staff or faculty neglecting terms of contract; and individuals putting themselves and the community at risk (e.g., wielding a knife, threatening an attack, etc.). All people so removed are welcomed to reengage the campus community following personal renewal and commitments to the identity of the college.

Finally, end rules regard the goals of accountability, much like Simons's desire that disciplinary action serve to restore the shunned Christian. In TWU's case, end goals are twofold: to restore a person's integrity before God and to sustain the university's Christian identity. Simons would argue a person cannot have one without the other. To ignore people's wrongdoings shows neglect for their souls and disservice to the body. Simons would say ignoring misconduct is anathema to God's restorative love for people and Christian community.[26]

Conclusion

Menno Simons's theology and practice of discipline, and setting people outside the church, grew from his conviction that doing so would wake them up to the sin or heresy that threatened their spiritual well-being and mend the church's witness to the world. His ideas provide students of communication important insights as to how personal identity links to corporate integrity. These insights prompt questions for us to ask: Have we come together to agree on a corporate identity that is worth working toward and living for? Have members been given a chance to accept it freely, step out freely, and realize that owning organizational identity really matters? When conflict happens, are guidelines in place to provide avenues for reconciliation? If reconciliation is unlikely, do leaders proceed with best intentions to reprove and restore difficult people? Do we have the humility to see this process as intended for our personal growth and the organization's integrity? What is the aim of discipline? While shaped by sixteenth-century winds of change, Menno Simons's ideas and actions bear surprising relevance for spiritual well-being and corporate integrity today.

CHAPTER 15

John Calvin: Practicing Divine Accommodation to Manifest God's Love

Kenneth R. Chase

Abstract: John Calvin's (1509–1564) commentary on St. John's Gospel illustrates how he uses accommodation to explain God's strategic choices in leading people to faith. Calvin permits us to mirror God's own communication by accommodating our Christian messages to the needs of others. However, Calvin's view of accommodation in John 11 seems to require a split between God's strategic purposes and God's revealed message. Fortunately, Calvin's broader theology allows us to understand accommodation not as God's strategic choice but as a manifestation of God's love.

Introduction

At age twenty-seven, John Calvin began his ministry in Geneva under the tutelage of Guillaume Farel, a Reformed pastor who quickly sensed Calvin's gift for teaching and preaching. However, as a trained humanities scholar, Calvin could not envision ministry apart from lengthy hours in private study. Farel challenged Calvin otherwise. Calvin recalls that when Farel understood "a friendly request would get nowhere, he came with no less than a curse."[1] Calvin was not exaggerating. In an obituary published a bit more than ten years after Calvin's death, Farel's actual "curse" is printed in what purports to be his exact words: "I predict that, while you tell yourself that your studies will be in the service of Almighty God, God will damn you as one who does not seek Christ, but only himself."[2] With the threat of God's punishment weighing on his mind, Calvin accepted Farel's warning.

As a pastor, Calvin focused his scholarly acumen on the ministerial needs of specific audiences. Calvin's communication mirrored, to the best of his ability, God's own communication to humanity. This is a notable contribution of Calvin to our age as well. Calvin's God is the communicating God who considers the plight of his people and customizes his revelation accordingly. God bridges the gap between his own divinity and our humanity through his own communicative initiative. God adapts, alters, and adjusts his wisdom, justice, and righteousness in ways that accomplish his purposes in the lives of a beleaguered, ill-equipped, and sinful humanity. The story of God's good news is the story of God's accommodation. Relying heavily on the concept of accommodation, Calvin gives us permission to consider our communication as mirroring God's own practice. However, we ought not be too quick to draw conclusions from Calvin's warrant. As we will see, Calvin's use of accommodation raises difficult, and possibly troubling, theological questions.

In this chapter, I will focus on a representative example from the central years of Calvin's Geneva ministry, his 1553 commentary on St. John's Gospel.[3] John's account of Jesus raising Lazarus from the dead allows us to see both the value and the puzzle of Calvin's approach to accommodation. From this vantage point we can learn more acutely how love and persuasion in Christian witness needs to resist the temptation of consumerism.

Commentary on John's Gospel

Calvin celebrates John's Gospel as a treatise on how the sinful and undeserving receive eternal life through Christ's perfect sacrifice and the power of his resurrection. For Calvin, the Lazarus narrative in 11:1–57 is a case in point. John begins the story with a messenger telling Jesus that his friend Lazarus is near death. Jesus delays his journey by two days to Bethany, Lazarus's home; when he arrives he meets Lazarus's two sisters, both of whom are devastated that Jesus arrived too late to save their brother's life. Jesus then accompanies the sisters to the tomb, weeps in the presence of those who have joined the grieving family, and prays before commanding Lazarus to come out of the tomb. Lazarus exits the tomb, Jesus has his burial wrappings removed, and all are astonished.

Calvin's notion of accommodation is key to his exposition of God's strategic intentions. He explicitly uses the term "accommodation" when explaining Jesus' prayer to the Father that preceded Lazarus's exit from the tomb. In Luke 11:41–42, Jesus lifts his eyes upward and thanks the Father for answering his prayer, presumably the prayer (implied but not recorded) requesting Lazarus's resurrection. What is at stake here, for Calvin, is why Jesus would ask God to do something that Jesus already has the power to do. Calvin answers this question by first focusing on what the text says about the prayer. In verses 41–42, Jesus gives credit to the Father for demonstrating that Jesus is, indeed, sent by God. Calvin explains that Jesus' full majesty could not be perceived by the Jewish onlookers, so Jesus' acknowledgment of God eases those viewers into a more heightened appreciation for Jesus. This is Jesus "accommodating Himself to man's capacity" (16, v. 42), taking into account human limitations. Jesus vocalizes his prayer so that onlookers glimpse God's glory.

Calvin uses the logic of accommodation, then, to identify God's strategic purposes in reaching out to humanity. For instance, when Jesus delays going to Lazarus, thus ensuring that Lazarus would die from his illness, Jesus did so "for the disciples to acknowledge the resurrection of Lazarus as a truly divine work" (6, v. 14). Similarly, when John describes Jews traveling the two miles from Jerusalem to Bethany to "console" Mary and Martha (v. 19), Calvin indicates that God "had another aim" for those gathering to mourn: "that Lazarus' resurrection might not be obscure or that the witness might not be only his own family" (7, v. 18).

One of the most striking instances of Calvin's description of divine strategy is his explanation of Jesus' emotional response upon arriving at the tomb. John describes Jesus as emotionally moved in response to the weeping of Mary and her attendant mourners (v. 33). When Mary and the others directed Jesus to Lazarus's tomb, Jesus wept (v. 35), and he continued to experience emotional turmoil as he moved closer to the tomb (v. 38). Calvin honors the text and the humanity of Jesus, by affirming Jesus' sincere sympathy and emotional pain when confronted with the mourning of beloved friends. However, this also presents Calvin with another theological thicket. How could Jesus, who is the sovereign God incarnate, succumb to human emotions?

When he took on flesh, Calvin explains, the Son willingly submitted to the experience of human emotion. Thus, Jesus "shows by His groaning in spirit, by a strong emotion of grief and by tears, that He is as much affected by our ills as if He had suffered them in Himself" (11, v. 33). Calvin does not mention accommodation here, but elsewhere he views Christ's incarnation—the Son putting on human flesh—as God accommodating himself to human limitations.[4] By relying on this incarnational logic, Calvin explains that "when the Son of God put on our flesh He also of His own accord put on human feelings, so that He differed in nothing from His brethren, sin only excepted" (12, v. 33). Jesus' emotional display at Lazarus's tomb was an accommodated appeal to our humanity: "He wants to show us that He has done it with earnestness and feeling" (11, v. 33). So Jesus, in his humanity, genuinely experienced an emotional response. In his deity, though, Jesus submitted himself to human emotion for the purpose of conveying his genuine commitment to be a Mediator "ready to help" us because he, too, has experienced emotional grief (12, v. 33).

Calvin's commentary on John 11 helps us to see both the strength and the puzzle of his view of divine communication. On the one hand, Jesus' communication with those around him conveys God's compassionate offer of salvation to humans too stubborn and sinful to respond from within their own capacities. On the other hand, accommodating to humanity means that God designs his revelation to achieve specific outcomes that may be at odds with what God

actually states within his divine revelation. Calvin portrays God as having strategic intentions often hidden beneath, or even contrary to, what Jesus says or
does. This tension in Calvin's view of accommodation—the strength of God's
loving appeal and the hiddenness of God's persuasive strategy—is what must
be navigated to identify Calvin's contribution to contemporary communication.

Calvin's Rhetorical Approach to Ministry in the Sixteenth Century

Calvin's collected works in theology, biblical exposition, and preaching
evidence his rhetorical cast of mind in both how he describes God's communication and how he understands his own ministry.[5] Calvin saw himself as participating within the divinely orchestrated plan for the redemption of wayward
and obstinate persons.[6] In Calvin's view, God sees us in this same way; Scripture
is designed to guide, shape, and transform. Calvin's *rhetorical approach to ministry* emphasizes accommodation as central to God's redemptive work in and
through a minister's work.

When Calvin was writing about God's accommodation in the midst of the
sixteenth century, he was caught up in social, religious, and intellectual transformations, including the shift from Renaissance to Modern thinking about
rhetoric.[7] Within Renaissance humanism, rhetoric was a means of forming
character so that public influence was inseparable from the virtuous quality
of the persuader's life. As the first-century Roman educator Quintilian famously insisted, a true orator is "a good man speaking well." Modernist rhetoric, though, separated strategy from a person's character and message; rhetoric
becomes *instrumental*: a means to an end or a toolbox of devices useful for
accomplishing a persuader's strategic intentions. Calvin seems caught in the
transition from Renaissance to Modern rhetoric. In other words, his rhetorical approach to divine revelation and to pastoral ministry reflects Renaissance
humanism. Nevertheless, the ways he typically describes God's accommodation
reflect rhetorical instrumentalism.

We see the instrumental approach in the way Calvin explains accommodation in John 11: the divine persuader has a strategic end in mind and accommodates the message to the audience's circumstances as a means to an end.[8]
To put it in Calvin's own terms, "For who even of slight intelligence does not
understand that, as nurses commonly do with infants, God is wont in a measure to 'lisp' in speaking to us? Thus such forms of speaking do not so much
express clearly what God is like as accommodate the knowledge of him to our
slight capacity. To do this he must descend far beneath his loftiness."[9] God is
not actually "like" his accommodated revelation because, as Calvin emphasizes,
God is accommodating himself to creatures who do not have the capacity to see

and know Him as he actually is in all his sovereign glory. Thus, God's "loftiness" is not found within the accommodated communication but resides behind it, beyond whatever meanings we glean from divine words revealed to us for our instruction. God's recorded revelation, therefore, may not clearly reflect his strategic intentions.

This is the point, then, at which we must candidly reflect on Calvin's contribution to communication. We certainly embrace Calvin's commitment to God as an effective communicator, and we see Calvin himself practicing what he preached throughout his ministry. Through his use of accommodation, though, Calvin separates God's rhetorical strategy from God's delivered word. In his reading of John 11, Calvin sees God lisping through the recorded words of Scripture to achieve an outcome not explicitly identified within Jesus' words and deeds. When God "descends from his loftiness," then, this is a rhetorical strategy—an instrumental means—for achieving the ends of compassion and salvation. This separation between strategy and message means that, in theory, Jesus' lowliness and emotional expressions are not fully reflective of God's glory but merely tools that could be altered or discarded once the end is achieved. God becomes an instrumental user of the word; his rhetorical strategy differs from his delivered message.[10] This difference can undermine the confidence listeners have in God's divine revelation.

To be fair, Calvin firmly rejects any suggestion that God cannot be trusted or that God's self-revelation misleads. This is especially true when that revelation is the incarnate Son: Jesus as the revelation of God is himself fully God. Yet, despite his protestations, Calvin uses the concept of accommodation to enact the instrumentalism we see illustrated in John 11. His distinction has passed into the theological imagination of Protestant theologians, pastors, and congregants of subsequent generations. It is a distinction we still struggle to overcome today.

Accommodation and the Challenge of Consumerism to Christian Witness

The disappointing truth about contemporary communication is that the gap between strategic intentions and delivered message has permeated nearly every aspect of Western society. Through incessant marketing fueling a consumerist approach to life's promises and potentials, we see all persuasion as designed to sell something, whether secular or sacred. We cannot blame Calvin for this. But Calvin's view of divine communication did us no service by reproducing and advancing a distinction between the surface message and the strategy behind it. He passed down to us a weak view of persuasion as instrumental that gained theological and secular allies. Today's Christian preaching and evangelism, then, too often blends seamlessly into our market economies as merely another strategic pursuit of consumers.

Let us consider the case of Sarai, a young adult whose conversion to Christ at the age of twenty-seven was accompanied by a clarity of purpose.[11] With eagerness she took a week off from her corporate sales job and volunteered for an evangelistic summer camp as a counselor for high school students. Her growing theological sensibilities, however, were assaulted through the experience. Each evening featured an all-camp meeting with introductory-level Bible teaching. The skilled staff members engagingly introduced Jesus by highlighting events from the Gospel accounts culminating in the crucifixion and resurrection. Surrounding the evening's twenty-minute talks, though, were unending activities, entertainments, and luxuries that kept the teens attentive from breakfast to late night. Using terms like "circus" and "Disneyland," Sarai described activities including jet skis, go-karts, and dance parties; she expressed amazement at the professional concert quality of live music and visual effects; she described the meal times as combining gourmet food and constant entertainment, including staffers gliding through the cafeteria using carabiners connected to suspended cables.

Some of the high schoolers made decisions for Christ, but, in Sarai's eyes, Jesus was presented as a minor figure in the sweep of the camp experience, "as if Jesus was hiding behind all of the activities and every now and then the staff would allow a brief appearance." Did those who accept Christ make a true commitment to discipleship, or did they make a consumerist choice about an attractive lifestyle?

The staff at this summer camp certainly understands their target audience. If they want secular high schoolers to attend a summer Christian camp, and if they want those teens to attend to Bible teaching with more than a fleeting moment of focused concentration, then the staff must compete against the entertainment options that would keep those kids from giving such a camp even a moment of notice. The camp understands the rhetorical imperative: accommodate the message to the audience. The question, though, concerns the nature of this accommodation: Are the strategic intentions at odds with the delivered message? Is this camp, at some level (perhaps ever so subtle) a bait and switch?

Sarai wonders if the gospel is being "sold" to the students through instrumental means. In a capitalist economy, accommodation is indistinguishable from marketing: advertisers identify target audiences and accommodate products to consumers' capacities and values. In the evangelistic summer camp, Jesus was inserted into the midst of an all-out attempt to gain and hold a teenager's attention. The strategic intention (have the students commit their lives to Jesus) is presented through appeals to a student's desire for extreme fun and all-consuming entertainment; thus, the gospel is strategically accommodated to the target audience to achieve a desired outcome.[12] Sarai's summer camp experience seems consistent with economically motivated persuasion. Unfortunately, her experience also is consistent with separation of strategic intention and presented message in Calvin's use of accommodation. Calvin's contribution to communication, then, is flawed to the extent that he describes God's revelation in ways that would be consistent with advertisers, salespersons, and political spin masters.

At this point, though, we need to take a second look at Calvin's rhetorical imagination. Although he relied on accommodation to account for the gap between how God reveals himself and who he is, Calvin also vigorously resists the notion that God's accommodation to us is inconsistent with his message. At times, Calvin explains God's accommodation as fully consistent with his nature; God's adapted communication to humanity is both message and medium of his existence. We look at the accommodating revelation as a reflection of God who reaches out to his people through "wonderful condescension . . . led by a general feeling of love for his whole flock."[13] The God we see through his accommodation, therefore, is not a god who has hidden strategic intentions, but the God whose love is revealed in and through his communication.[14] When God accommodates humanity, God is loving humanity.

In consumerist persuasion, persuaders build exchange relationships with audiences (and vice versa) in which self-interest is a prominent consideration. Participants in the persuasion ask, "What's in it for me?" God's persuasion, though, is a manifestation of his love in which he has no "self-interest" at stake and in which his strategic action is simply another name for the appeal of his beauty and love. As John 12:23 and Revelation 5:5–6 both claim, God's loftiness is identical with God's lowliness; the majesty of God's glory is abundantly evident through Jesus' crucifixion. Jesus as God's accommodation is inseparable from Jesus as the fully sufficient revelation of God's love to humanity. God's persuasion always is self-giving; when God accommodates humanity through his own "condescension," God is revealing who he is.

In contrast to the use of persuasion in a capitalist economy, then, Christians ought to persuade by practicing loving others without a mismatch between strategic intentions and expressed claims. Within God's economy, our persuasion ought not seek competitive advantage or attempt to enhance the gospel's appeal; rather, God's economy requires that we fully participate in God's self-giving love toward his creation. We persuade others because we have been rebirthed into a new economy in which persuasion is characteristic of our response to God and his ongoing appeal to all people. We approach others not with strategic intentions that must be disguised, lest our true message be rejected, but with strategic intentions of how to faithfully utter the glories of Christ's good news. Our rhetorical relationships with others, then, are relationships of self-giving mutuality in which we live the persuasion of God. If we retrieve from within Calvin's corpus his use of accommodation as a synonym for love, then we can resist the dualism of strategic intention and designed message.

Conclusion

Wrestling through Calvin's view of accommodation allows us to ask the right questions of cases like the summer camp and provide resources to help people reflect on their own evangelistic practices. For instance, is the camp staff operating with a split between their strategic intentions and their presented messages? Or is the camp staff seeing their strategic intentions as participating in God's own loving appeal for all participants—staff and students—to be shaped into Christ followers? Does the camp experience mirror God's self-giving love or the temporary satisfactions of economically rooted needs and desires?

Calvin has modeled for us a ministry of persuasion reflecting God's own persuasive pursuit of his children. Perhaps accommodation is a desirable way of describing this persuasion. But Calvin's use of this term does not provide contemporary communicators with much confidence that proclaiming the gospel will be markedly different from consumerist appeals. Within Calvin's collected works, though, we find resources enabling us to restore persuasion to its God-given purpose as the everyday performance of love.

CHAPTER 16

Margaret Fell: Championing the Feminine Voice for Advocacy and Change

Joy E. A. Qualls

Abstract: Margaret Fell (later Fox) (1614–1702), authored the tract *Women's Speaking Justified, Proved, and Allowed by the Scriptures,* sometime between 1664–1666 while serving a prison term for speaking publicly as a Quaker—and a woman. Fell invites her audience, specifically women, to embrace their identity to speak publicly using rhetorical strategies that are focused on the feminine voice. This chapter explores how Fell's theology creates specific space for the feminine voice as a unique rhetorical strategy for advocacy and change.

Introduction

In 1660, King Charles II signed the "Declaration from Breda" that granted religious liberty to those who did not undermine the peace of England; nevertheless, the "tide of persecution" against Quakers "swept on," notably in the imprisonment of Quaker leader George Fox. However, Margaret Fell, one of the most prolific writers of the seventeenth century, wrote "an indignant letter to the magistrates"[1] and traveled to London to confront the king regarding these persecutions. As her biographer tells the story, the royal palace walls "are rich with tapestries of many colours, and the sunlight glints on armour and on swords. Lords and gentlemen, in rich attire, swagger in the anterooms, and with the ladies of the Court retail the latest scandal."[2] It was through this crowd that Fell walked "into the presence of the King," so that she might bear witness to the "growing persecution of the priests and justices" against Quakers and to recount the conditions of her "friends lying in cold, unhealthy dungeons."[3] She sought to attain "mercy" and "justice" for Fox.[4] What was true of this moment was true for the rest of Fell's life. She was willing to take an aggressive role within her own faith community and the broader society because she believed that God had empowered women to speak.

This chapter examines Fell's pamphlet *Women's Speaking Justified*,[5] by evaluating how her life and Quaker theology provides a basis for her sermonic rhetorical strategy that empowers women in the church and invites them to find their own voice to proclaim the gospel. Fell engages in a call for subversive rhetorical action for women by encouraging them not only to read her work but also to do so aloud in their own voices. This use of the feminine voice in the sermonic is meant to appeal directly to women making the case for women's collective voices as necessary for religious change and, by implication, for social change. Fell argues for women's equality based on their creation by God and his light coming upon them to proclaim his message. Because God created women and uses women in Scripture, there should be no limitation placed upon women in the church or in speaking about God. While it is no longer illegal for women to speak publicly in many cultures, women's voices in the church as sermonic proclaimers and leaders remains a contested arena.

Women's Speaking Justified, Proved, and Allowed

In *Women's Speaking Justified*, Fell presents a comprehensively argued defense of female preaching,[6] and she invites her audience, specifically women, to embrace their identity and to speak by the "Spirit and the Power of the Lord Jesus."[7]

First, Fell argues that women can take up full participation in the church due to the fact that God created man and woman in his image, and as such both possess the potential to serve as his prophets through the indwelling of God's Spirit. God's inward light, a Quaker term for the presence of God in a person granting them spiritual authority, enables both women and men to take up sermonic speech. Fell builds her case upon a basic premise of spiritual equality in Quakerism. She argues that those who use the Pauline Epistles (especially the letters to the Corinthians and to Timothy) to silence women are doing so against the created order and the Spirit of God.[8] Fell articulates that it is human beings, and specifically men (as a result of the Spirit of Darkness), who put differences between the sexes, not God, and that the time has come for all true believers to be released from the silence imposed upon women. However, even more so, it is especially time for women to attest and exercise their own authority.

The cornerstone of Fell's argument is the many instances in which women speak God's word. The comprehensive list of women found in Scripture is also a hallmark of her argument: the woman of Samaria, Mary and Martha, as well as Priscilla, Debra, Huldah, Sarah, Anna, Miriam, Elizabeth, Mary, Ruth, Rachel, Leah, the queen of Sheba, Esther, Judith, the wise woman of Abel, the daughters of Philip, Mary Magdalene, Joanna, Mary the mother of James, the woman who anointed Christ with precious oils, and so forth.[9] In particular, Fell focuses specifically on the women at the resurrection site and the apostles' response to them. Because women were the first proclaimers of the good news that Jesus had risen, they had and continue to have a providential role to play in spreading the gospel through sermonic proclamation. When women are told to keep silent, Scripture is being misapplied and terrible consequences may follow.

Fell is also thoroughly Quaker in her antiauthoritarian appeals. The sermonic feminine voice Fell both advocates for and employs challenges established hierarchies of authority and calls them into question. Fell's relationship to spiritual authority is noteworthy. On one hand, she is highly suspicious of established spiritual authority and power structures, and she cautions her readers about testing the truth of what any teacher says as well as having a general suspicion of educated ministers.[10] On the other hand, she places herself in the role of an apostle who possesses spiritual authority, or ethos, and is charged with admonishing, encouraging, and traveling from place to place as a means of leading others to the truth of the gospel. From Fell's writing, it is easily seen that she places a heavy emphasis on personal experience and on validating that one's faith is real through letting God's light search one's soul.[11]

Finally, Fell's sermonic feminine voice is not combative but expresses deep affection and care for those she is advocating for and those she is trying to persuade. Her writing style is characteristically apostolic in the way it communicates this deep affection to others following along in the faith. The tone that Fell takes makes her seem extremely sincere and desirous that the best would indeed happen to others, especially other women. Her apostolic authority is tempered with an emphasis on the validation of faith through personal experience. (This validation happened in her own life when she heard George Fox speak and converted to Quakerism.) She also encourages other Friends to be sure that they walk in the light by examining their own souls as well as her testimony. She tells her readers to let God's grace and salvation teach them and guide them. Further, she continues to exhort them to see whether there is evidence in their lives that they are bearing the fruit that comes from being in the light. Fell asserts that personal experience and confirmation in the life of the individual is paramount. This leads her to encourage women to use their own spiritual authority by taking personal responsibility to validate their own faith.

Women's Voices, Experience, and Authority

Fell wrote as she did to break the silence imposed upon women in the church and to encourage others to join her in speaking out.[12] She aimed to create rhetorical space for women to find their unique voices, granting both their personal experience and spiritual authority.

Fell wrote extensively throughout her life; however, she composed *Women's Speaking Justified* during her imprisonment in Lancaster Prison. While at Lancaster, she served four and a half years (1664–1669) of a lifetime prison term for treason. Quakers prohibit oaths to anything or anyone other than God, but Parliament, in an act of suppression, attempted to force Quakers to swear an oath to the king. When Fell refused to swear that oath, she was imprisoned and forced to forfeit her property, Swarthmore Hall, which had become a meeting hall and virtual headquarters for Quakers. This is not the first time Fell was threatened with prison, nor would it be the only time she would serve a prison term throughout her life. While married to her first husband, Thomas, a lawyer and later a judge, she had successfully avoided prison for holding illegal religious meetings in her home, speaking publicly as a woman, and supposedly being involved in witchcraft. However, following his death, she was imprisoned on several occasions for her religious teachings as a Quaker.

Fell argued that a woman's testimony spoken audibly and publicly carried real power to change society. This is also closely aligned with Quaker theological practice. Quakers become members of the Society of Friends by asserting their kinship with God through attesting to conversion and revelation of the Spirit of God. What Fell does in her writing is make the case, based on the testimonies of women in the Bible, that advocates for women to formulate their autobiographical testimonies and to share their stories with one another; their collective voice creates a shift and empowers others to turn toward the Spirit of God for empowerment and social change.

Fell engages in subversive rhetoric through the amplification of women's voices.[13] As a result of her work, women began to share their own stories, what we might call "testimonies," in a religious context. They found their collective voice and as a result discovered they were not alone in believing that a woman's goodness is not based on her submission in relationships and social structures. The narratives that women shared were painful and challenging but were necessary for others to recognize themselves in the voice of their fellow women. What Fell did was break the silence and call others to do the same. Those who followed her continued her work in ministry while she was imprisoned and after her death. They also continued to test boundaries and the sound of their own voices. This not only defined the religious position of Quakerism, but it created fissures in the patriarchal systems outside of the Society of Friends— fissures that need to be further expanded in modern religious communities.

Fell drew upon the spiritual authority she found in Scripture to validate herself as a leader in the Quaker church and thereby also empower other women to engage in similar activity and leadership. Fell's rhetoric reflects her emulation of the apostles. She boasts a high level of biblical knowledge and often quotes passages straight from the Bible, or she echoes sentiments similar to those found in Scripture. She provides commentary on the passages of the Bible she uses in her writing, giving both explanation and instruction on the purpose and use of these verses. She also traveled to encourage the Friends, opened her home up for meetings, and supported and directed itinerant preachers.[14] However, Fell's most striking rhetorical strategy that is similar to that of an early church apostle is the way in which she writes to various churches with a voice of authority and in sermonic form. Indeed, many of her writings take on a scriptural tone that often makes it difficult to tell when she transitions from quoting the biblical canon to speaking with her own voice.

Complementarianism and Christian Imagination

Fell's rhetorical negotiation of theology and culture is of particular interest to the study of the intersection between faith and communication. Like the church at Fell's time, many in the contemporary church exhibit a failure of imagination when it comes to the full participation of women in the church, most notably Christians who hold the so-called complementarian accounts of gender. Complementarian readings of Scripture argue that God created men and women "as equal in dignity, value, essence and human nature, but also distinct in role whereby the male was given the responsibility of loving authority over the female, and the female was to offer willing, glad-hearted and submissive assistance to the man . . . functioning in a submissive role under the leadership and authority of the male."[15] This submission not only excludes women from leadership in the church and marital relationships but effectively from any position in which women can have direct and personal authority over men. For example, in his podcast, a listener asked pastor and professor John Piper, "Should women be police officers?" While Piper does not answer the question directly, he does say that, according the Bible, "it would be hard for me to see how a woman could be a drill sergeant" who exerted direct and personal authority "over men without violating their sense of manhood and her sense of womanhood."[16] Given the similarities between police officers and drill sergeants, Piper's answer is an effective "No."

From Fell's perspective, complementarianism is a not a problem of biblical understanding—although it is certainly that. Rather, complementarianism constitutes a failure of a Christian imagination, an imagination that is unable or unwilling to envision a world where the gospel can be fully embodied in the lives of women. Fell helps us imagine an alternative possibility in which the contemporary church can read Scripture with an imagination that is longing to create rhetorical space for women's bodies and voices.

First, Fell's work encourages us to reread the biblical passages used by complementarians in an effort not to limit women's full participation in the church but to bring it into reality. For example, the complementarian Presbyterian

Church in America argues from Genesis 2 and Timothy 2 that God created Adam first, and his priority in creation means leadership over women. However, this reading seems incapable of imagining that Genesis 2:18 might have any bearing on the passage. Once God realizes that none of the animals have alleviated man's aloneness, God says, "It is not good for the man to be alone; I will make him a helper [עֵזֶר] suitable for him" (NRSV). The Hebrew word עֵזֶר, translated as "helper," can be rendered literally as "corresponding to." Read against the problem of the man's loneliness, only one who bears a close similarity to him (as opposed to the animals) can solve his problem. Furthermore, the term "helper" occurs nineteen times outside of Genesis. In every appearance, God is the "helper" to the biblical writer who is usually in distress, need, or want. If a reader allows the overtones of the rest of Scripture's use of "helper" to reach back into Genesis 2, then a hierarchical relationship of the woman as helper to the man becomes difficult to sustain.

If Christians could imagine a world in which the woman is a "helper" to the man in the same way God is a helper to many biblical writers (who are also men), then perhaps they might create rhetorical space in which men could acknowledge the reality that they need women to have a voice in their lives, institutions, and decision-making processes. Genesis 2 suggests not that women should be subservient to men but rather that where women's voices and bodies are not present, man is alone. The only thing in creation God declared as "not good" was the woman-lessness of man. When Christians create communities in which men have no rhetorical space to acknowledge their need for women, they insist on living in the loneliness God already solved at the beginning, If Christians can instead imagine a world in which all of its spaces are open to the voice and bodies of women, then they would be imagining a world obedient to the God of Genesis 2.

Second, if Christians can embrace a world with all its spaces open to the lives and bodies of women, then Christians will need to embrace the reality that the world will be an uncomfortable world in which change will happen, particularly a change regarding the assumption that women's bodies are offensive. For example, when asked if he reads commentaries written by women, Piper replies in the affirmative. "Here is a truth. A woman saw it. She shared it in a book, and I now quote it, because I am not having a direct, authoritative confrontation" with her in person.[17] He implies that a book creates an appropriate distance from the female author so that "she is not looking at me and confronting me and authoritatively directing me as a woman."[18] This preference for an indirect encounter means that, for Piper, it is the actuality of a women's body that makes her unfit to exert authority over him. Piper argues, as critics have put it, that the "offensive presence of her body"[19] is present in the "pitch of [her] voice and the presence of her breasts."[20] As long as her literal body is absent, a man can learn from a woman. Piper may want to create space for a women's written voice, but he cannot imagine a world open to her body and her physical voice.

In order to resist the temptation to exclude women's bodies from public spaces, Fell might celebrate how the female body and voice can be a bearer of the word of the gospel, that is, every woman's body can be for us like the body of Mary, the mother of Jesus—the bearer of the Word of the gospel. When a church creates rhetorical space for both voices and bodies of women, it may very well share their agency with other women, making visible their voices and bodies, their hurts, humiliations, and encounters with God. Such an expansive sharing of agency can take place only if both women and men learn to resist the temptation to see a women's body as an offensive body.

Conclusion

As women living in what many want to believe is a postfeminist society where the voice of women is equally valued, lessons remain that Fell speaks to regarding the feminine voice. Women must speak for other women and join their voices collectively. When women share their encounters with the divine, their hurts and humiliations, there is a powerful rhetorical space that is created, and it makes arguments against women's agency seem weak and lacking in persuasive refutation. What Fell accomplishes in her rhetoric is not merely a historic artifact of a bygone era but also a challenge to proclaim a feminine body and voice among followers of Christ and, as a result, upend challenges to the larger society.

CHAPTER 17

Jeanne-Marie Bouvier de la Motte-Guyon: Nurturing Attentive Silence as a Counterpractice for a Digital Age

Stephanie Bennett

Abstract: Christian mystic Jeanne-Marie Bouvier de la Motte-Guyon's (1648–1717) devotional posture centered on what some call the inward way, or the "prayer of silence." Guyon, who was imprisoned by ruling authorities for so-called heresy, broke the bonds of her captivity through perseverance in the spiritual practice of attentive silence. Individuals in the digital age can enjoy similar freedom from the temptations, injustices, and distractions that may hold them captive.

Introduction

Following the publication of Jeanne-Marie Bouvier de la Motte-Guyon's book *A Very Short and Easy Method of Prayer* (1685), the king of France accused her of heresy and immorality and placed her in various prisons. Her incarceration began in Vincennes, but then "church authorities moved her to a nunnery in Vaugirard. There she was frequently beaten on the face, while living in a decrepit room."[1] She was then held in solitary confinement at the notorious Parisian Bastille. After seven years of incarceration and abuse, the church exonerated Guyon. Although she was declared innocent of charges and ultimately released, imprisonment took its toll on her. She could not leave the Bastille on her own. She had to be carried out of prison "on a litter."[2] In the face of these injustices, she was always endeavoring to live by the words of 1 Peter 5:6–7 (NLT): "Humble yourselves under the mighty power of God and at the right time he will lift you up in honor. Give all your worries and cares to God for he cares for you." It was this humility that kept Guyon safe, sane, and strong, and her humility took the form of quiet, silent prayer. Guyon's experience cannot be a model for every Christian; not all should take up silence in the face of abuse and exploitation. Nevertheless, at times oppression may be impossible to avoid, and, in those moments, her example of looking to Christ and allowing God to sustain her can serve as a model, especially as we seek to break free from various kinds of prisons present in the digital age.

Jeanne Guyon's devotional posture centered on what some call the inward way, the "prayer of silence," or an attentive silence. Attentive silence is a means of communicating with God in humility, inward simplicity, and contemplation. Her willingness to share the freedom she found in silent prayer brought the ill-fated consequences of a tarnished reputation and prolonged physical confinement. It was the discipline of focused, intentional, prayer-as-communion with God that protected her sanity, helped her maintain hope, and gave her the ability to live a grounded, joy-filled life. As Guyon was able to break the bonds of her captivity through attentive silence, Christians in this digital age can enjoy similar freedom from the temptations, injustices, and distractions that may hold us captive. When the domination of our personal mobile media is tempered by attentive silence, God is discovered in a place of solitude.

Attentive Silence

In *A Short and Very Easy Method of Prayer*, Guyon reminds the reader of Luke's Gospel and writes, "The first thing you must learn, dear friend, is that 'the kingdom of God is within you' [Lk 17:21 KJV]."[3] Throughout the book she returns to the same idea—that the Lord's presence is not found outwardly but within, in attentive silence. Although waiting in silence may seem unproductive, passive, or even irresponsible, the choice to remain silent and attentive can be a practice used in the face of injustice. Guyon associated attentive silence with three vital postures: humility, inward simplicity, and contemplation.

For Guyon, silence made possible humility rather than self-magnification, and humility ultimately brings about confidence in God rather than in oneself. For anyone who has attempted to "become more humble," trying harder does not produce this fruit. Humility is not so much gained as it is issued forth from walking closely with the all-knowing, all-powerful God of Creation. Guyon understood that walking in the presence of such a God required her silence, and it was through her silence that she experienced true humility. Humility was not a feeling of smallness or weakness but a way of being in the world, a state of union with God's divine life. The silence of the soul, writes Guyon, "becomes both a wonderful transmission and receiving of divine communication."[4] She rightfully understood that humility was simply a synonym for communion with God, and she recognized that without Christ one will always be self-seeking. Against self-seeking, silence is an important step toward walking in humility.

Keen awareness of one's position before God, that is, one's humility, lays the foundation for an inward simplicity, or a faith that trusts him in all things, even in injustice or trauma. Guyon describes such simplicity as a childlikeness in one's faith, the same sort of posture that Jesus spoke about when he told his disciples to come to him "as a child" (Matt 18:3 NIV). Her silence as a response to oppression and suffering was far from passive. She writes, "We are not promoting the idea that the soul should be lazy or inactive. We are encouraging the highest activity the soul can engage in: total dependence on the Spirit of God. This should always be your main concern. It is in Him alone 'that we live and move and have our being' [Acts 17:28 NIV])."[5] Simplicity was a posture that defied the unreasonable demands and pressures placed on her life. Throughout the book, Guyon continues to recommend the way to this place of inward simplicity. The soul nurtured in attentive silence must press past all distractions of the senses. Those senses should fall away into a state of quiet solitude. The only thing necessary to bring one into such a time of prayer is the desire to surrender to him completely. "As you come to the Lord to pray," she writes, "bring a heart that is seeking nothing from the Lord, but desires only to please Him and do His will."[6] It is in the disciplined practice of this prayer that the transformation of the soul takes place; it is here that attentive silence can be an active response to outward conflict, confusion, or unrest.

Third, the prayer of attentive silence is most closely aligned with what most today would call contemplation. That is, instead of carefully meditating on Scripture or emptying herself of every thought, her practice was to dwell in Christ and seek his active presence within. There, she could meet with God, wrestle with the anxieties and perplexities of her situation, and ultimately experience rest. Unlike supplication, praise, or meditation, the prayer of the heart surrenders to the will of God. Guyon explains, "We must give our full attention to those activities that take place deep within our inmost being. These are the activities of the Spirit. The Spirit is inward, not outward. You turn inward to your spirit and, in so doing, turn away from outward activities and outward distractions."[7] This act of surrender has little to do with denying concrete experiences of daily life. Rather, outward actions possess spiritual value if they are a result of contemplation, of "something that has taken place deep within you."[8] Guyon goes on to say that outward activities can bear goodness with them to the extent that they are connected to "their source," to Christ.[9] It is here through regular, gentle turning of one's attention inward to the Lord that the soul becomes fully nourished and prepared to engage the world.

Marriage, Prayer, and Prison

Even before the humiliation of multiple stints in prison, Guyon encountered an earlier prison of sorts. This prison came in the shape of a demanding, disapproving husband to whom she was given in marriage at the age of fifteen. Her husband, Jacques Guyon, was a wealthy French gentleman of Montargis who did not share her love of God and refused to allow her to pray openly. In fact, his strident opposition to Jeanne's life of faith was so entrenched that he stationed one of his housemaids to accompany her as she moved throughout their home, just to make sure that she would not pray. It was there—actively silent in the midst of her oppression—that she learned what it meant to overcome adversity.

The ongoing distemper and denigrating control her husband levied upon her was compounded by his mother, who kept her isolated and cut off from the world. At the behest of Jacques, his mother kept a very close watch on her, making sure all her social interactions were monitored and that she was in compliance with all his wishes.[10] Of that extended season she wrote, "I was as one lost, and alone; so little communion had I with the creature, farther than necessity required. I seemed to experience literally those words of Paul, 'I live yet, no more I, but Christ liveth in me.' His [Christ's] operations were so powerful, so sweet, and so secret all together, that I could not express them."[11] Christ lived in Guyon, in part, through her practice of attentive silence. Her nearness to Christ kept her sanity and dignity intact.

When she was twenty-eight her husband died. It was then that Guyon began speaking openly of things she learned about silence and prayer. Her words encouraged many, and her popularity grew until King Louis XIV read one of her papers and decided her ideas could add flames to the growing movement of Quietism, which he considered heretical. Initially, her imprisonment was the result of a theological dispute between two archbishops—François Fénelon and Jacques Bossuet—both of whom were tutors for the sons of King Louis XIV. Fénelon admired Guyon and was enthralled with her ardent devotion to God. Bossuet was skeptical and prodded the king to quiet her voice. Louis found Guyon's faith divisive and petitioned the pope to have her censured. Though she remained steadfastly Roman Catholic, Louis arrested and interrogated her. Through much aggravated questioning and false witness, the French king crafted a case against Guyon. This began her long stint in prison.

Guyon was incarcerated at Vincennes and ultimately for seven years at the Bastille in Paris. When confined to the Bastille, her captivity was likely less pernicious than many other dungeons in seventeenth-century Europe, because the Parisian prison was used mainly to detain upper-class members of society and primarily used as a holding tank for judicial detention. The government provided its prisoners with a solid meal each day and the means to read and write. Her time in captivity, though intense and unjust, did not include physical torture, nor was it spent in the blackest part of the prison. Her final two years, however, were spent in the misery of solitary confinement.

Whereas the control of her husband attacked her dignity, imprisonment compounded such attacks with physical hardships, threats against her body, and implied peril toward her family. Though she did experience physical abuse and endured a rat-infested, cold, and windowless room, it was the relentless interrogations that Guyon reports as the most devastating. She faced countless false accusations, drummed up stories of sexual impropriety, twisted interpretations of her teachings, and condemnation as a witch. The emotional and psychological torture she endured became even more painful than the attempted poisonings or forced attention to the hysterical screams of other prisoners who were daily being driven to insanity.[12] These, along with separation from her family and friends, proved the most devastating.[13] In the end, the prolonged state of isolation and confinement plunged her into an attitude of attentive silence, one which allowed her to listen for an alternative to the abuse, threats, rancorous insults, foul smells, and myriad discomforts of a formidable prison. She sought to hear the voice of God and to find her own.

Digital Technology Can Hold Us Captive

In the digital age, attentive silence seems like even more of an anomaly than ever. Today, nine out of ten Americans are active on the Internet, and increasing numbers are gaining primary access through their smartphones.[14] Because mobile communication is now increasingly pervasive, the mobility factor of computer-mediated communication has exponentially increased; in 2011, 73 percent of cell phone users in America used their phones to text regularly and that number has increased.[15] Around 93 perecent of Americans use cell phones or wireless devices to communicate daily.[16] This impacts not only the social landscape, but also changes the tenor and tone of government, global politics, commerce, and the church. The ubiquity of digital communication has made possible e-mail-hacked elections, inflammatory tweets that come from the highest levels of government, cyber warfare, cyberbullying, and fake news. Like the current state of national political communication, interpersonal communication online is often impersonal, rude, and demeaning.

Additionally, the increased volume of communication and heightened pace of digital culture comes at a psychological cost: increasingly associated addiction and related mental health issues. Some older adults admit to checking their social media more than fifty times a day.[17] According to one study, the average teenage user checks his or her phone and social media as much as one hundred times a day.[18] A growing number of health practitioners have concluded that problematic Internet use has become an addiction and want to treat it as a legitimate disorder.[19] Although there is dispute about using the word "addiction" to describe such use, the psychiatrists and researchers who study the phenomenon note the prevalence of neurobiological vulnerabilities among those afflicted.[20] Furthermore, mental health practitioners cite a growing body of research that addresses the problems associated with this addiction such as depression, hostility, impulse control problems.[21] For many, the ability to resist the ubiquity and pervasiveness of the digital world seems impossible. As a result, it can seem as though our devices rule us. Although not physically constrained as Guyon was, our digital technology can, indeed, hold us captive.

Like Guyon, we might marshal the practice of attentive silence to serve as a counter-practice to the prison of our digital landscape, particularly through digital silence or periodic digital fasts. In those moments of silence, Guyon's postures of humility, inward simplicity, and contemplation can aid us in resisting such imprisonment.

If humility is that state that brings about confidence in God rather than in oneself, digital silence from our devices might show us that we have more confidence in our digital tools than we might want to believe. Our digital tools are empowering, but laying them down creates for many the opposite effect: a deep sense of uncertainty and vulnerability known as the "Fear of Missing Out," or FOMO.[22] Missing out on a key social event or a business opportunity can be a very real loss to one's social or economic power. But such fear illustrates a potential lack of confidence in God. When Guyon accepted her inability to control her imprisonment, she found confidence in God. This humility, this confidence, kept her from bitterness and despair. Likewise, through the negative experiences of digital silence (or setting down our devices), we have the opportunity to accept that we cannot control every aspect of our social and economic lives. It is in digital silence that we can find proper confidence in God.

Whereas Guyon understands inward simplicity as a faith that trusts God in the midst of injustice or trauma, our digital fasts allow us the opportunity to trust that God will not abandon us to diminished productivity. Because our digital technology allows for constant connection, it presents the temptation of being "always on" in relation to our social lives, work, or school. As a result, most acts of digital silence come with a cost of decreased productivity. It is not unusual, for example, for an employee to succumb to the temptation to return work e-mails while on vacation. Digital silence means that we, by definition, must enter a space where we lack productivity and possibly create the perception that we are bad employees or bad friends. Nevertheless, a digital fast creates conditions for resisting the temptation to always "be on." In "being off," we can quiet ourselves in the simple faith that God will protect us from the idol of productivity. Intentional silence in digital connection can produce the kind of inward simplicity Guyon experienced in her own captivity.

Finally, digital silence can create space for our own experience of Guyon's posture of contemplation. For Guyon, contemplation was an active seeking of the presence of Christ. In God's presence, she engaged the anxieties and perplexities of her imprisonment. Likewise, digital devices produce anxiety-inducing pings, vibrations, and audio-flags that keep many captive. Digital silence can create the conditions for contemplative prayer. Hauling our thoughts back to prayerful contemplation is impossible when our attention is constantly drawn to what might be happening online or who might be trying to contact us via text. Contemplative prayer is something akin to a hand grenade thrown into the pit of our busy brains. Regular practice will blow apart the hold our digital devices have on us. After the explosion settles, it is then that we can experience Jesus' presence and bring our fears, anxieties, and perplexities to Christ and in Christ find the possibility of peace and rest. Guyon's approach teaches us that digital silence is an important prerequisite to peace and rest in a digital world.

Conclusion

Methodist founder John Wesley said of Guyon, "How few such instances do we find of exalted love to God, and our neighbor; of genuine humility; of invincible meekness and unbounded resignation."[23] His admiration of her life was only possible because of the ongoing witness of Christ's light in the midst of her dark situation. In the deep humbling of one's self, "the soul's powerlessness," she reminds us, "is no longer painful now, but pleasant. Why? Because the very powerlessness is full of the life and power of the Divine life."[24] The rhythm of attentive silence can have a similar cleansing effect in the digital world that wounds us. Listening closely in the solitude of attentive silence, may we, like Guyon, seek Christ in the midst of our own prisons.

CHAPTER 18

John Wesley: Bearing Witness through Divine Gift, Sacred Choice, and Embodied Action

Elizabeth W. McLaughlin

Abstract: John Wesley (1703–1791), the founder of Methodism, wrote the 1785 sermon titled "On Working Out Our Own Salvation." In this sermon, Wesley describes how God's grace is actively working in the believer, and how each Christian must work out this grace in daily life through embodied action as a unity of mind, heart, and body. Wesley offers a refreshing paradigm of communication—as a gift, a choice, and an action—that expresses God's love to a skeptical and distrustful world.

Introduction

On March 4, 1745, minister John Wesley arrived in Falmouth, England, to visit the home of a "gentlewoman who has been long indisposed."[1] Just moments after he arrived, "an innumerable multiple of people" surrounded the house and yelled, "Bring out the Canorum! Where is the Canorum? [a Cornish epithet for Methodists]."[2] Wesley remembers their sound and fury as a "storm" or a "raging of the sea."[3] When the mob broke down the door to the house, Wesley, the gentlewoman, and her daughter took refuge behind a thin partition. The mob pressed upon the partition and threatened to crush them. "Indeed at that time," Wesley recalls, "to all appearance, our lives were not worth an hour's purchase."[4]

At the height of the eighteenth-century revival sweeping across Great Britain, Anglicans found Wesley's open-air preaching unorthodox and dangerous. At the very moment when his life was in danger, Wesley did not run or hide. "It is best that I just stand where I am."[5] He embodied charity and bravery and recounts the scene in his journal:

> I stepped forward at once into the midst of them and said, "Here I am. Which of you has anything to say to me? To which of you have I done any wrong? To you? Or you? Or you?" I continued speaking till I came, bareheaded as I was

(for I purposely left my hat that they might all see my face), into the middle of the street and then raising my voice said, "Neighbors, countrymen! Do you desire to hear me speak?'" They cried vehemently, "Yes, yes. He shall speak. He shall. Nobody shall hinder him."[6]

While we live in a different moment from Wesley's, our time is still witness to the reality that religion can be perceived as a hindrance to the public good. From nightly scenes of terrorist bombings to the heated rhetoric about sexual identity and politics, it may be tempting for secular observers to think the world would be a better place without religion in it. What can people of religious faith do to counter such perceptions? Wesley struggled with similar questions.

In the early 1730s, preachers John Wesley and George Whitefield joined together to lead what would be known as the Great Revival in Britain. Despite their friendship and success, the two preachers entered a serious theological dispute over the Calvinist doctrine of predestination. Wesley feared that the doctrine would harm the witness of the church, mainly through discouraging Christians from helping the poor. Wesley's most developed response came in his 1785 sermon "On Working Out Our Own Salvation" (Phil 2:12–13). Wesley describes, first, how God's grace is actively *working in* the believer, and, second, how each Christian must *work out* this grace in daily life by a sacred choice and in embodied actions of charity. To a world that may be increasingly hostile to religion, Wesley's work encourages religious communicators to bear witness to a watching world through gift, choice, and action.

Two Evangelists, God's Grace, and the Great Debate

The relationship and theology of John Wesley and George Whitefield are key to understanding the Great Revival in eighteenth-century England. These two great preachers partnered together to bring Christianity to all levels of British society. The pejorative term "Methodist" was given to members of Charles Wesley's "Holy Club" at Oxford University. Charles Wesley, John's brother and hymn writer, founded the club in the early 1730s to encourage its male members in their Christian faith. "Methodist" described their faithful practice and spiritual rigor.

During this time, George Whitefield and John Wesley met and became friends. While they shared a zeal for their faith, these two men were quite different. Wesley was a decade older and an educated Anglican; Whitefield had been an actor and server in a pub. Wesley was concerned with preaching and discipleship; Whitefield was an evangelist with a booming personality and rhetorical skills who led thousands to Christ.[7] In the spring of 1739, Whitefield preached in Bristol, England, to the coal miners in an outdoor meeting and invited the Wesleys to join him. Thousands were converted as Whitefield, with John and Charles Wesley, reached England's common people and served the poor. Whitefield focused his rhetorical skills to reach people for Christ; John Wesley organized groups for discipleship, charity, and learning.[8]

While their relationship together proved fruitful, harmony did not last. In March 1739, John Wesley preached a sermon, "Free Grace," against the doctrines of Calvinism and predestination. Whitefield requested that Wesley stop preaching this particular sermon. For a short while, the preachers kept an uneasy yet peaceful truce. Wesley preached an Arminian view of salvation proclaiming that God's grace is open to all persons and that this grace required a human, freewill response. Wesley feared that predestination created a deterministic perspective that made holiness and charitable works irrelevant. On the other hand, Whitefield turned to a Calvinist predestination that taught that God selected a few for salvation and the rest for eternal judgment. He believed that Wesley was denying original sin and preaching universal redemption.

Wesley disagreed with Whitefield's account of predestination, in part because he thought that believing God had already decided who was saved and damned eliminated the need to help the poor. For Wesley, charity, as embodied action, is a necessary part of obeying the gospel. Wesley also argued that if the poor are already chosen or damned by God, then feeding the hungry and clothing the naked becomes irrelevant in helping them find salvation.

Eventually, the truce came to an end. Whitefield eventually treated the Wesleys as hostile to his cause. In March 28, 1741, John Wesley wrote in his journal, "He [Whitefield] told me that he and I preached two different gospels. Therefore, he not only would not join with or give me the right hand of fellowship, but was resolved publicly to preach against me and my brother, wheresoever he preached at all."[9] The difference effectively ended Whitefield and Wesley's friendship and eventually led to a split in the emerging Methodist movement into two different camps: Arminian Methodists and Calvinistic Methodists.

In Sermon 85, "On Working Out Our Own Salvation" (1785), Wesley offers his most robust response to his Calvinist critics.[10] Wesley argues that God's "preventing grace"—or prevenient grace that goes before repentance—is available to all. Through human free will, an individual chooses whether or not to respond to the divine invitation. Wesley's position affirms the Christian doctrine of original sin, while standing firmly against predestination. He offers believers a clear understanding of how God is the source of the "work" that they enact within their lives. Wesley also offers a framework for individual believers to embody the love of God: through God's divine gift working in the life of the Christian, the Christian makes the sacred choice to work out her salvation and subsequently embodies actions of charity.

Divine Gift, Sacred Choice, and Embodied Action

Sermon 85 focuses on the passage Philippians 2:12–13, in which the apostle Paul says, "Work out your own salvation in fear and trembling for it is God that worketh in you, both to will and to do of his good pleasure." Wesley said this passage was "the greatest instance both of humiliation and obedience."[11]

Wesley structures "Working Out" in three major sections. In the first section, he unpacks God's divine gift saying, "It is God that worketh in you both to will and to do of his good pleasure." Second, Wesley turns to the opening phrase that relates to sacred choice: "Work out your own salvation in fear and trembling." Finally, the preacher stresses the connection between the two in a call to embodied action. This creates the context for the Apostle Paul's words that follow and offers the example of Jesus' freely chosen action for the benefit of humankind. God's grace is first and foremost a divine gift.

To explain the power of God's gift of grace and human dependence, Wesley transposes the two clauses of the passage to make his first point. "God worketh in us" demonstrates that the salvific process begins with God's gift and not with sinful human beings. All grace originates with God and is bestowed only by divine mercy. The preacher seeks to "remove all imagination of merit from man, and [give] God the whole glory of his own work. Otherwise, we might have had some room for boasting, as if it [were] . . . some goodness in us, or some good thing done by us."[12] The soul of the sermon is the lived, embodied response of the believer "working out" what God has "worked into" the person. God's loving action is the energy and catalyst for the life of the believer who is working in partnership with the divine to impart love to the world, through the body.[13]

Wesley builds on this point in the second part of his sermon, which emphasizes the necessity of human free will or sacred choice. The original Greek, which English translates as "work out," means not only doing something but "doing it thoroughly." Each must choose to work out his or her own salvation, for "you yourselves must do this, or it will be left undone forever."[14] For Wesley, this salvation comes in three movements of awakening: "preventing" or prevenient grace in which the person begins to see God's reality; "convincing" grace that leads to repentance; and "sanctifying" grace that calls us to depart from sin and "restore[s] us to the image of God."[15] This salvation calls humans to work out in their lives what God has done for them.

This working out calls for the whole person to respond. For Wesley, this means that the embodiment of grace calls for "everything [to] be done with the most earnestness of spirit, and with all care and caution" but also with "the utmost diligence, speed, punctuality and exactness."[16] This working out is done in the daily practice of spiritual disciplines: fleeing evil, "being zealous of all good works," praying, partaking in communion, and studying.[17] These disciplines require both human free will and divine grace.

In the third and final section of this sermon, Wesley addresses the necessity of embodied love. He asks the question, "If God works in us, why do we have to work?" His answer is, "God works; therefore you *can* work. Secondly, God works; therefore, you *must* work."[18] The power to live and embody love flows from divine energy enabling humans to live their everyday lives in acts of service to God and the world. This empowerment is not by human merit or effort, which cannot earn salvation, but is dependent on grace. In turn, humans must choose their response to God's grace, and, as Wesley argues, if they do not work with God, then "he will cease working."[19]

Divine Gift, Sacred Choice, and Embodied Action for the Common Good

Today, there is no shortage of secular voices that describe religion as harmful to the common good. Young adult "outsiders" to traditional faith like Jesus but believe that his followers are more "famous for what we oppose, rather than who we are here for."[20] In 2010, former British Prime Minister Tony Blair and religion critic Christopher Hitchens engaged in a public policy debate asking if religion was a force for good in the world. Much of Hitchens's critical work was to foreground the connection between religion and oppression. Hitchens claimed religions do harm when they teach that a woman is "an inferior creation," claim that "AIDS was not as bad as condoms," and fuel religious wars in Northern Ireland for more than four hundred years.[21] After the debate, a poll showed that Hitchens persuaded 68 percent of the three-thousand-person audience to his position.[22] Voices like Hitchens might help explain the rise of the "nones," Millennials who are leaving religion. The Pew Research Center finds that nones are disenchanted with belief and distrust organized religion.[23]

In a context where religion seems damaging to the public good, Wesley's notion of gift, choice, and action can offer an alternative witness, as embodied faith can speak louder than words. The public life and work of Charles W. Colson, felon and founder of Prison Fellowship Ministries, is an example of Wesley's gift, choice, and action, all of which demonstrates the good that religion can accomplish.

A little over five years after his death, Colson's faithful work for more than thirty-five years on behalf of prisoners, crime victims, and families lives on in a vibrant international ministry reflecting God's love to the world. As a public "sinner" and criminal, Colson's embodied example still communicates the love of God to the least of these as told through his memoirs *Born Again* (1976) and *Life Sentence* (1979). He experienced the divine as unmerited mercy, recognized his many experiences as God's working into his life, and finally committed to working out what had been put into him as a mission to prisoners and families through empathy and love.

Most baby boomers, and anyone who has watched the 1976 movie *All the President's Men*, know the disgrace of the 37th U.S. President Richard Nixon in the Watergate scandal. As Nixon's "hatchet man," Colson would do anything for his president. This loyalty sent him to prison for obstruction of justice. Motivated by his budding Christian faith, Colson confessed to this crime. He served seven months in Alabama's Maxwell Prison. In *Born Again* (1976), he describes the rise and fall of his life and career, as well as his conversion to Christianity just before prison. Colson's description of his experiences reflect what Wesley had preached: he worked out what God had worked in him through Christian action.

First, Colson describes his growing realization of the gift of God's mercy and his own sin of pride. Just before entering prison, Colson renewed his relationship with Tom Phillips, an old business associate. Phillips saw the empty state of Colson's soul and shared that dedicating his own life to Christ was "the most marvelous experience of my whole life."[24] Colson realized that he had to face himself and what he had done as a first step toward Christ.[25] As Phillips read aloud the first chapter of C. S. Lewis's *Mere Christianity* describing the cancer of pride, Colson saw himself in a new light. "*I* had done this or that, *I* had achieved, *I* had succeeded, and *I* had given God none of the credit, and never once thanking Him for any of His gifts to me. . . . While Tom read, I saw myself as I never had before. And the picture was ugly."[26] When Colson left his friend that night, he sobbed uncontrollably in his car, felt relief, and prayed for God to take him. Shortly after, Colson read all of *Mere Christianity* while on vacation with his wife Patty. By the ocean in Maine, he committed his life to Christ and experienced God's grace: "I felt the old fears, tensions, and animosities draining away. I was coming alive to things I'd never seen before; as if God was filling the barren void I'd known for so many months, filling it to the brim with a whole new kind of awareness."[27]

With his growing awareness of divine grace, Colson recognized God's active work in his life to prepare him for a new calling, one that invited him to make a sacred choice. Slowly, as he studied the Bible and spiritual writers while in prison and saw the true plight of his fellow prisoners, Colson came to see them as fellow image-bearers. Over months, he realized, "*There is a purpose for me being here, perhaps a mission the Lord has called me to.*"[28] He realized that his firsthand experiences of helplessness, anxiety, boredom, and desolation helped him empathize with his fellow prisoners and see them as brothers. Colson faced the choice to work out what God had worked into his life in an intimate relationship of trust and dependence.

Finally, after this initial choice or "yes" to God's call while in prison, Colson had to make plans for his future career, a career of embodied action and love for prisoners like himself. In his second memoir, *Life Sentence*, Colson speaks about obedience as the necessary choice to Christ's call to serve prisoners full time as his life's mission, serving prisoners, victims, and their families.[29] "In the depths of my heart, I had become convinced that I had gone to prison for a larger purpose than just getting my own life turned around," said Colson. "I wondered why it had taken me so long to understand."[30] Colson realized that God had worked in his life and that he had to work out his redemption in embodied actions of love.

Colson started Prison Fellowship in 1976, and today Prison Fellowship and Prison Fellowship International share the love of Jesus Christ and the opportunity for redemption and restoration with families and friends of the incarcerated. These public ministries provide resources for the incarcerated, those preparing for reentry, the Angel Tree program for prisoners' children, and training for wardens and prison staff. In addition, Prison Fellowship staff and volunteers advocate for restorative justice and reform for nonviolent offenses all over the world. An estimated sixty-five million people have been served from the willingness of Charles Colson to serve the least of these.[31]

Conclusion

By 1742, the anger over the doctrinal differences between Wesley and Whitefield began to calm down. These two great men agreed to disagree and did not get in each other's way or compete for followers. The two rivals parted as colleagues once more: "In 1770, the year of his death, Whitefield wrote to Charles as 'my very dear old friend' and described himself to John as 'your honoured brother.'[32] Further, Whitefield 'bequeathed a mourning ring' to each John and Charles 'in token of my indissoluble union with them in heart and Christian affection, notwithstanding our difference in judgment about some particular points of doctrine.' "[33] When Whitefield died, Wesley preached the sermon at his friend's funeral.

From Wesley's time to Colson's and our present moment, people of faith can contribute to the common good through charitable works that embody divine love. A watching and skeptical world can see these works. This communication, forged in the crucible of relationships, spans interpersonal, group, and public arenas. Both John Wesley and Charles Colson experienced the gift of God's grace and dedicated their lives to sharing this love of others in tangible, public action. Differing opinions remain on the value of religion, but actions that serve the common good embody divine grace nonetheless.

CHAPTER 19

HANS NIELSEN HAUGE: OFFERING A PRESCRIPTION FOR SOCIAL CHANGE

William J. Brown and Asbjørn Simonnes

Abstract: Hans Nielsen Hauge (1771–1824) inspired an unprecedented societal revolution in Norway at the onset of the nineteenth century during an extraordinarily prolific period of his truncated public ministry. Drawing primarily from Hauge's first book, this chapter specifically focuses on three critical conditions for incubating a societal revolution: living out personal devotion, becoming media literate, and embracing the hard task of community transformation.

Introduction

Hans Nielsen Hauge (1771–1824), an itinerant preacher without a formal education, was an unlikely social and political revolutionary. Hauge's commitment to preach the gospel throughout Norway is illustrated by his encounter with a wealthy woman named Maren Boes who lived in Bergen. Boes's conversation with Hauge is described as follows:

> You must sit down, Hauge. I have something to talk to you about. You are suffering so much for our Lord's cause that my heart has gone out to you in great tenderness on account on all your persecutions and tribulations. I am quite well-to-do, I have much property, and I'll soon be going home [dying]. So I thought I would leave it all to you—if you would come to Bergen and settle down.[1]

After many years of arduous ministry journeys and harsh imprisonments, there was nothing Hauge would have liked better than to settle down in Bergen. Hauge responded to Boes, "I am indeed grateful to you for the kindness you wish to show me, but I could not accept your offer, if you gave me the whole city of Bergen." And "Why not?" asked Ms. Boes, stunned by Hauge's response. Hauge answered, "Just for the Lord's sake. It would indeed be a great pleasure for me to stay here with so many dear friends. But think of all those all over this land who are waiting to hear a Word of God!"[2]

This zeal of Hauge and his followers created a spiritual movement that transformed Norway from an agrarian society of small farming and fishing communities to an emerging democratic independent state with a new constitution, religious freedom, new industries, and political reforms. In Norway, Christians spearheaded this "Age of Revolution," an age in which Christians sought the public good.[3] In our present moment, given the current political and societal unrest, heightened racial tensions, growing nationalism, and overall suspicion toward one's neighbor, Christians would do well to pursue a similar revolution.

In this chapter we explain Hauge's contributions to profound changes in Norway at the turn of the eighteenth century and discuss their implications, particularly Hauge's advocacy of personal devotion, media literacy, and community transformation. First, we discuss the key text, Hauge's first book, *Betraktning over Verdens Daarlighed* (*Consideration of the World's Folly*), which ignited a nationwide revival of personal devotion to Christ. Second, we explain the context of Hauge's ministry across late eighteenth-century Norway, focusing on the dramatic changes that he initiated through his promotion of reading, writing, publishing, and creating community businesses. Third, we consider the application of Hauge's ideas and work in the United States and other twenty-first-century Western cultures, especially on the need for media literacy in the midst of the proliferation of new communication technologies and communication networks.

The Primacy of Personal Devotion

Hauge's first book, *Betraktning over Verdens Daarlighed* (*Consideration of the World's Folly*), set forth both the tone and course for Hauge's short two decades of public ministry. In five chapters and seventy-six pages, Hauge exposes the failures of both the world and much of the state church's clergy in meeting the spiritual and practical needs of the Norwegian people.

Publishing *Betraktning over Verdens Daarlighed* (hereafter *BVD*) was difficult, as book publishing was not accessible to lay preachers like Hauge, who was not an ordained minister; neither was he a seminary professor, known scholar, or experienced author. He had to walk ninety-seven km (about sixty miles) from his home to Christiania (now Oslo) with his manuscript, convince the owner of a publishing house to print it, and finance the cost of printing and binding with $25 of his own money, a considerable sum at the time for a farmer.[4]

In *BVD*, Hauge demonstrated his pronounced ability to communicate in many "ingenious and striking aphoristic simplicities" with short narratives that common Norwegian farmers and fisherman could easily understand.[5] Drawing from Jesus' parables, he argued convincingly that church traditions without personal faith and devotion are impotent in overcoming the temptations of worldly pleasures and ungodly desires.

Hauge also shared his own spiritual journey from having knowledge of the religious doctrines of the state church, which he observed did not produce a vibrant faith, to personal revelation of his need to wholly surrender to Christ and devote his life to Christian service. The crucial event that triggered this transformation took place while Hauge was ploughing a field on April 5, 1796, two days after his twenty-fifth birthday. His own account of this experience has become a classic in the genre of religious historical autobiographies, imbued with descriptions of ecstasy and mystical vocabulary.[6] He goes on to reveal the social responsibility he embraced to communicate the gospel to others, devoting much of his first book to explaining the implications of his life-changing spiritual encounter.

Hauge accomplished many important tasks in *BVD*. First, he introduced himself to the public and legitimized his speech by "appropriating a genre of writing normally used only by the officials of the religious hegemony," thus creating a readership for spiritual content that was more accessible to common Norwegian people.[7] The subversive nature of Hauge's writing is revealed in his ability to turn the language of the hegemonic culture against itself by reworking it to serve his own purposes.[8] Although Hauge acknowledges that he is not an educated member of the elite clergy, he notes in the preface of *BVD* that all Christians are commanded to daily converse about the words of Christ, not merely in church but "as you are on the road, when you sit in your house, when you lie down, and when you rise."[9] He explains in the book's preface that teaching and preaching the message of Christ is his "greatest pleasure" and that he could not in good conscience dig a hole and bury his talent (his call to preach) "in the earth," alluding to Jesus' parable of the talents recorded in the Gospels of Matthew and Luke (see Mt 25:14–30; Lk 19:12–27).

Throughout *BVD*, Hauge's primary message is personal devotion to Christ. He also had harsh words for the clergy, alluding to them indirectly in scriptural terms as "wolves in sheep's clothing" and "false prophets." Hauge was so concerned about his thinly veiled criticisms of the state church that he struggled greatly with whether or not he should publish *BVD*, especially with the words of his brother Mikkel rattling in his mind: "This means prison for you."[10] Hauge concluded that he would be willing to pay a high price for being obedient to publish what he believed God had put on his heart to communicate.

Media Literacy and Community Transformation in Late Eighteenth-Century Norway

There was a stark contrast between the world that Hauge was born into in 1771 and the world in which he died in 1824. During Hauge's childhood years, only a minority of Norwegians could read and write.[11] Religious and political life in Norway was influenced predominantly by the state church, which practiced an institutional form of Lutheranism that relied heavily on knowledge of church doctrine and tradition with scant attention to personal devotion to Christ and to the inspiration and leading of the Holy Spirit in everyday living.

During his itinerant ministry, Hauge's preaching ignited a religious revival that swept across Norway, particularly among the peasant class.[12] Hauge and his followers, also called Haugeans, brought change not only to the Church of Norway, but also to the realms of education, business, politics, and social welfare. They launched new industries throughout Norway.[13] Many Haugeans became prosperous and influential leaders in Norway through their diligence, economic enterprise, and frugality, including three members of the constitutional assembly in Eidsvoll, the body politic that drew up a new constitution following Norway's independence from Denmark.[14] One of Norway's most respected writers, Anne Garborg, concluded, "it was Hauge that created the 19th century in Norway."[15]

Despite the pietistic elements of Hauge's books and sermons, he also discussed the practical problems of communities and strongly encouraged Christians to help solve these problems. By way of a solution, he firmly believed that Christians, by learning how to read, write, and publish, could revolutionize Norway, recognizing that literacy, or perhaps more rightly, media literacy, was the foundation of community transformation. Therefore, Hauge and his followers empowered the populace to write and publish their own ideas and experiences. Important changes in Norway initiated by Hauge broke the state's publishing monopoly, including that of the state church, which it had used to control religious and political thought.

Hauge's preaching and publishing influenced the advancement of media literacy and community transformation in Norway in three ways. First, he and his followers established groups of the Societies of Friends in Norway, who were often called readers or students because they studied the Bible and were highly experienced in reading and creating written works. The Societies of Friends were registered throughout Norway and consisted of several thousand members. These groups predominantly met in their homes and advanced literacy by reading and discussing Scripture together.[16]

Second, Hauge opened new literate space for the common people to write and publish their own works. Hauge "broke the unwritten rule of never publishing texts for a large readership without the necessary educational skills."[17] Before Hauge's publishing enterprises, the educational elites and ruling class controlled the means of media production in Norway. By creating his own published works in a style that peasants could understand, he inspired his followers not only to read but also to write and publish their own letters, pamphlets, and books. Hauge not only established his own publishing houses, he also financed those of other Christians, thus eliminating the publishing monopoly of the ruling elites.

Third, Hauge advocated for public education reforms to improve the media literacy of students, especially the writing skills of the peasant class. Haugeans advocated for compulsory teaching in writing for all Norwegians, granted in 1827 when the Education Act was passed. Writing skills were often handed down from the parents, many of whom were peasants, fishermen, and others from the lower and less educated classes of society. Yet these groups remarkably increased their writing skills within a few decades.[18]

These three changes increased media literacy in Norway, particularly in the country's extensive rural areas. In the late 1700s, only a small percentage of the Norwegian population could read and write.[19] By 1814, between 60 and 70 percent of Norwegian peasants were literate, a dramatic increase attributed to the publishing efforts of Hauge.[20] Haugeans were directly responsible for helping to turn Norway into a reading and writing culture that facilitated development of a "textual community."[21] As such, the textual community of Haugeans dominated over individual interpretation of religious texts as well as state authority.

Media Literacy and Community Transformation for Twenty-First-Century Christians

Like Hauge's moment, our opportunities to effect spiritual transformation are anchored in holding together the two elements Haugeans did: living out the gospel in both word and deed and serving the good of society. In aiming to live the gospel for the good of others, Hauge teaches us that the need for media literacy should not be overlooked. One of the barely recognized crises in American society is the woeful lack of media literacy.[22] New communication technology has diffused so rapidly that few Americans think about who controls the persuasive messages and technologies of today and how they have radically changed how we think and communicate. Public education has failed to systematically include media literacy in its curriculum. The church also has not taught Christians how to be media literate and to think strategically about how to harness the power of twenty-first-century communication technology.

Following Hauge, twenty-first-century Christians need to address three important elements of media literacy that can fuel community transformation for the public good. First, no society today will be adequately positioned for long-term spiritual transformation without a populace that is media literate. Our present moment is a moment in which false news stories are normative journalistic practice and young people look to comedy programs and other entertainment and social media as their primary sources for learning relevant social, cultural, and political information. Similarly, artificial intelligence, data mining, legal and illegal surveillance, and the creation of algorithms to manipulate attitudes, values, beliefs, and personal and social behavior are subjects most

Americans know nothing about as they mindlessly use and consume new media technologies with relatively little critical reflection on how such technologies are changing their lives.

Only a highly media literate public can adequately protect against the onslaught of false ideologies and beliefs perpetrated daily by popular media, multinational media companies, and political leaders. Christians can serve others by becoming leaders in media literacy education. Just as Hauge taught that all Christians should understand how to produce and consume written works, communication scholars with Christian sentiments argue that Christians must leave behind their media focus on culture wars and, instead, champion a media literacy approach that focuses on enhancing spirituality, creating appreciation for aesthetic value, and serving as a socializing function within local communities.[23] Communication scholars Stephanie Iaquinto and John Keeler echo what Haugeans might say to Christians today about our mediated culture: "If media are indeed our national religion in twenty-first-century America, as some scholars suggest, then who better to ask some of the most insightful questions about their values, images and stories than those for whom another religion is their standard?"[24]

Second, only the power of personal devotion will give Christians a powerful voice in today's popular culture. Church dogma, self-promotional ministries, irrelevant or poor church messaging, and ineffective use of entertainment media have created a Christian church with little power to affect our society and little expertise in meeting the most crucial social needs. The church in Western societies like the United States must break free from the overemphasis of knowing rather than being, a vestige of modernism that has crippled Christians' ability to communicate through the personal narratives common in postmodern societies.

Hauge also taught people how to write and publish their own stories. Christians today must do the same, becoming competent users of the powerful new twenty-first-century media technologies. Haugeans would encourage today's emerging enterprises like the Network of Biblical Storytellers International (www.nbsint.org), Christian Storyteller (www.christianstoryteller.com), and Christians sharing redemptive narratives on social media as starting points for engaging non-Christians with the love of Christ through personal story. Hauge would also advocate that Christians financially support Christian artists, media professionals, and entrepreneurs, believing that the next Bill Gates, Steve Jobs, and Mark Zuckerbergs of the world would be young men or women with a zeal to share the good news of the gospel worldwide.

Third, community transformation must be a primary goal and concern of every Christian. No one lives in a society today that is not in need of substantive transformation from the narcissistic, self-destructive, and depressing media landscape that promotes a culture of violence and death. The Haugean Movement in Norway revived the nation from a spiritual, economic, and political period of weakness to a period of spiritual, social, and political transformation in which all of Norwegian society benefitted.

Western societies like the United Sates need the same kinds of transformations. Open doors exist in every community to help the underprivileged by providing literacy programs, education, professional skills, and jobs through small business development. Community organizations such as the Life Enrichment Center in Norfolk (www.lecliteracy.org), a literacy-based ministry, and the Dream Center Foundation in Los Angeles (www.dreamcenter.org/dream-center-foundation), who have placed community-centered education as primary to their missions, are following in the Haugean tradition. Christians have enormous marketing power should they ever unite to support the businesses, entrepreneurs, and industries of Christians and refrain from supporting socially destructive enterprises. The Haugean-like textual communities of today could be networks of Christian professionals and church and community leaders collaborating to develop and fund literary programs, education, training, media and arts production, and entrepreneurship in economically struggling urban and rural areas throughout the United States.

Conclusion

Hauge's advocacy of personal devotion, media literacy, and community transformation in Norway has important implications for Christians seeking to contribute to spiritual transformation and social change in twenty-first-century societies. Hauge and his followers changed lives through the powerful influence of their own radical personal transformations. The ideas promoted and lived out by these transformed followers of Christ became the core values for the establishment of modern Norway. Haugeans were active in political, cultural, religious, business, and industrial life. They fought against the centralization of power, excessive public spending, corrupt privileges, monopolies, and rigid political and religious systems.[25] They were pioneers of building democratic institutions, the rule of law, due process, community entrepreneurship, social reforms, and a just society. Americans and other Westerners have much to learn from their example.

CHAPTER 20

William Carey: Adapting Messages to Audiences as a Redemptive Communication Strategy

Donald H. Alban Jr.

Abstract: William Carey (1761–1834) argued that Christ's commission to make disciples of all nations remains unfulfilled, and that a mission organization could address this deficiency by evangelizing diverse peoples in audience-adapted ways. Carey and several colleagues would eventually form a mission board, move to India, and launch a missional translation, education, and publishing initiative that enduringly impacted South Asia. Their accomplishments demonstrate the importance of audience-centered strategies in the crafting of redemptive messages.

Introduction

A hush filled the English meeting house in Northampton, a city about halfway between London and Birmingham, where the Particular Baptist ministers assembled for their fraternal gathering of 1786. As was his custom, the senior minister, Dr. John Ryland Sr., wanted to provoke beneficial conversation for the group and demanded that two of the junior ministers each propose a topic. After attempting to evade the challenge, William Carey, the twenty-seven-year-old lay pastor, rose to his feet. Carey proposed the ministers consider the question, "whether Christ's command to make disciples of all nations is to be carried out by Christians of all eras."[1] His query stunned those who were present. Unlike their General Baptist counterparts—who believed Christ died for all humans, that salvation is available to anyone, and that humans can be agents in the conversion process—the Particular Baptists viewed Christ's atonement as applicable only to God's elect and believed their conversion to be entirely a divine work rather than a human work. To propose otherwise, as Carey did, was to propose the unthinkable. "Young man, sit down," the elder Ryland riposted. "When God pleases to convert the heathen, He will do it without your aid or mine!"[2]

Carey raised the same question more formally, in 1792, in what became a landmark publication in the history of evangelical Protestant literature: Carey's eighty-seven-page treatise titled *An Enquiry into the Obligations of Christians, to Use Means for the Conversion of the Heathens. In Which the Religious State of the Different Nations of the World, the Success of Former Undertakings, and the Practicability of Further Undertakings, Are Considered* (hereafter *Enquiry*).[3] Although not widely circulated at the time, this work would prove to be monumentally significant in the history of Protestant missions.

The *Enquiry* introduced Carey's pro-missional thesis, backed his thesis with supportive data, refuted several counterarguments, and conjectured how the thesis, if accepted, might appear if it were put into practice. Throughout the work, Carey utilized Scripture, theology, church history, religious demographics, and practical advice to make his case. Carey is noteworthy as a communicator because he persisted against diverse obstacles and found strategic ways to implement his vision despite them. He spent years learning South Asian languages and producing a wide variety of literary works to ensure his targeted audiences had means for receiving the gospel. Carey also persisted against disparate obstacles. Taken together, Carey's audience-adaptive approach remains instructive to Christian communicators who face comparable challenges in the early twenty-first century.

The *Enquiry*

Carey built the *Enquiry's* pro-missional approach primarily on the basis of Scripture and his theology. He asserted that God's purpose in history is the establishment of his kingdom through humankind, an objective unfulfilled by previous generations. He ascribed this delay to the laziness of those entrusted by God with the responsibility of promoting the kingdom through evangelistic endeavor. He then targeted the antagonistic view by raising three objections to the position that Christ's directive applied only to the original apostles.

Carey's account of Christian missional communication began with New Testament accounts of early church leaders, not all of them recognized apostles—Peter, Philip, Paul, Timothy, Silas, and Barnabas—and with traditional accounts of these leaders taking the gospel to places as remote from Jerusalem, the church's birthplace, as Britain, Armenia, Ethiopia, and India.[4] He cited the examples of patristic Christian figures, such as Justin Martyr and Irenaeus, as well as medieval and modern figures like John Eliot, David Brainerd, and John Wesley, who had continued the missional tradition through their notable evangelistic outreaches.

Carey then cited global religious demographics to establish the need for missionary outreach. His third chapter began with a twenty-two-page compilation of statistics on the population, geographical size, and religious state of each nation of the world. The data partitioned the world's populations into four religious categories: Christian, Jewish, Muslim, and pagan. He concluded with observations that served, in his discourse, to show a need for the Christian gospel even in lands where a Christian presence had already been established.

In the fourth chapter, Carey refuted anticipated objections to his call for expanded Christian missional activity. He rejected the excessiveness of physical distance as a basis for inaction.[5] Carey also challenged the objection that a nation's incivility and barbarity are legitimate bases for refraining from evangelistically engaging distant peoples. Finally, he refuted the alleged difficulty of learning the foreigners' languages, which some might cite as a justification for inaction.

Carey concluded his work by painting a more detailed vision of the type of enterprise his treatise advocated. A supporting agency should equip a missionary with living necessities before departing for a distant land, and upon arrival a missionary must endeavor to learn native languages, build friendships with indigenous peoples, and relate to them lovingly and graciously. He also offered suggestions to enrich the missionary's ability to effectively communicate the gospel. Then, after briefly summarizing the previous chapters' content, he called for fervent and united prayer for the conversion of the spiritually lost.[6]

As Ernest Payne, a past president of the Baptist Missionary Society that Carey founded, observed, the *Enquiry* "had few literary graces," and its author was one who "shunned the limelight" and who "belonged to one of the less prosperous Dissenting bodies." Nor was Carey "a picturesque personality in the sense in which such a description is usually applied. Yet when he died forty years later, a revolution in the position and outlook of the Christian church had taken place, and by common consent he had himself had an outstanding part in it."[7]

Literacy, Literature, and Redemption

Carey was both a product and a producer of the communicative practices and media forms that were prevalent in his times. Carey grew up in a world progressively shaped by the printed page, one in which tracts, pamphlets, periodicals, and books enabled increasingly literate young people to encounter new ideas and to discover worlds that would have been inaccessible to them before the advent of the printing press.[8] Among the many writings that helped to shape Carey were the spiritual allegories such as John Bunyan's *Pilgrim's Progress*, the sermons of Anglican clergyman Jeremy Taylor, and the devotionals of Quaker mystic William Law. If works like these spawned Carey's pro-missional theology, his missionary vision derived as well from the missionary narratives of John

Eliot and David Brainerd, who had labored to take the gospel to native North Americans decades earlier, and by the adventurous accounts of Captain James Cook, the British pioneer and his descriptions of people groups half a world away.

Carey attempted to use the power of the printed page in his effort to engage then largely illiterate South Asians in a redemptive way. Along with educator Joshua Marshman and printer William Ward, who joined Carey in Bengal, India, less than a decade after his 1793 arrival, this trio was based in the Danish settlement of Serampore. They implemented the *Enquiry*'s vision by devising a missional communication strategy with two major objectives: expanding literacy in the region and producing native-language literary works for the emergent literate class's consumption. Carey functioned for decades as the mission's primary linguist, the visionary who quested to master the region's diverse languages, to translate religious and secular literature into these languages, and to author impressive original works of his own in the region's native languages. Marshman, drawing from his own expertise, launched and administered a network of native-language schools that grew to include ninety-two schools and ten thousand students by 1818 and became a large revenue source for the mission.[9] Ward worked to set up what soon became one of Asia's largest printing operations in its day, complete with typecasting and paper production capabilities.[10]

In a region with more than a dozen native tongues, gaining an aptitude in these languages for publication purposes was no small challenge. Nonetheless, the Serampore Mission Press, between 1800 and 1834, published biblical translations into no fewer than forty-seven languages and dialects.[11] Carey personally translated the entire Bible into Assamese, Bengali, Hindee, Marathi, Oriya, Punjabi, and Sanskrit and portions of it into twenty-one additional languages or dialects.[12] Carey and his colleagues also compiled grammars in Bengali, Sanskrit, Telugu, Punjabi, Kurnata, Marathi, and Bhotani.[13] The mission's grammars were complemented by its production of dictionaries for many of the same languages, with Carey himself compiling dictionaries for four languages.[14] His Bengali dictionary, considered to be his most outstanding, spanned two thousand pages, included eighty thousand words, and required thirty years of work before its completion in 1825.[15] Marshman, Ward, and other mission colleagues composed notable works of their own that were printed at Serampore.[16]

As some of these titles indicate, the "Serampore Trio" understood the strategic importance of using the press to produce popular and educational literature, not just to produce Bibles, tracts, and explicitly evangelistic materials. Their immediate goal, although ultimately evangelistic, was to bridge communication gaps between Europeans and Indians, and literacy expansion was their means for effectuating this. Accordingly, in an attempt to help Europeans better understand South Asians, they also published English-language translations of major cultural texts. Expanding native literacy and producing literature in native languages was an equally important aspect of the trio's missional strategy, and they aimed to inculcate "on every missionary the necessity of cultivating the literature of the country in which he resided, as far as it could be effected without relaxing his efforts to communicate the Gospel to the people."[17] Thus, in addition to its production of evangelistic material in native dialects, the mission published numerous secular works in native languages. The trio believed literacy and literature production to be essential as the means for dispelling what they believed to be native ignorance: "Under an enlightened and wise government, this mighty engine of civilization [the printing press] will in a few years compensate for the injustice of ages. . . . The press will bring the language of the people into general use, and dispel the clouds of ignorance, as the sun scatters the mists which the night assembles."[18]

Carey and his colleagues faced numerous obstacles as they implemented the *Enquiry*'s vision via literacy and publishing initiatives during their decades of operation. Undeterred, the Serampore missionaries persisted. The published word was their primary means for promoting their aim. As Marshman's son and Serampore historian John Clark Marshman observed a quarter-century after Carey's death, they considered the establishment of a press "one of the distinguishing characteristics of the missionary enterprise, that 'wherever a missionary goes, he prints.'"[19] By the time its press had ceased operations in 1855, two decades after Carey's death, it had become "the most prolific printing concern in India, producing works in more than 40 different languages and dialects."[20]

Communicating Redemptively Today

Carey's *Enquiry* and its implementation in South Asia during the early nineteenth century yield instructive insight to modern mass communicators who aspire to engage audiences via their medium in a redemptive yet effective way. A person functions as a redemptive communicator when his or her verbal and/or nonverbal behavior, as an expression of authentic love for God, intentionally manifests God's love to others in a way that promotes what God values in the world. Among these God-valued things, and particularly applicable to Carey, are the Christ-followers' attempts to communicate his gospel of forgiveness and redemption to those who do not know him (see Pss 67:1–2; 96:2–3; Isa 49:6; 52:7; Mt 5:14–16; 28:18–20; Mk 13:9–10; 16:15; Acts 1:8; Rom 10:14–15). Functioning effectively as a redemptive communicator in a pluralistic world requires a person to anticipate the unique rhetorical situation into which he or she will speak the message and to craft audience-centered messages accordingly. This requires the practice of three basic but vital strategic planning principles.

First, the communicator must know his or her redemptive and rhetorical goals. If rhetoric is "the strategic use of communication, oral and written, to achieve specifiable goals,"[21] the redemptive communicator's rhetorical goal is to send a message to others, in a God-honoring way, that promotes a God-valued end. For Carey, the goal was to challenge his fellow ministers "to use means for the conversion of the heathen," as the *Enquiry*'s full title indicates. This step requires the redemptive communicator, while visualizing or planning the anticipated venture, to define the venture's goal as precisely as possible and to do so by addressing several strategically interrelated planning questions in an audience-focused way. Whether through the creation of a desktop, mobile, or web application, a social, informational, or commercial website, a webinar, webcast, video conference, or broadcast, or a print publication, the question to ask is which God-valued outcome or outcomes will I attempt to promote through the venture? What do I want my audience to believe, to value, or to do in response to the message through which I will publicize the venture? If the venture materializes, how will I know whether I have achieved this goal? What, in a nutshell, is my redemptive mission? How can I most compellingly express this vision to an audience of potentially sympathetic others, as Carey did through the *Enquiry* and in subsequent mission publications, in a way that generates support from them?

Second, the communicator must know his or her audience, message, and medium. What do the audience members believe or value, and why do they believe or value these things? What are their preexisting associations and commitments, and how are these likely to impact their response to my message? Which language or message forms do they utilize? Can my message be channeled to target audiences in these language or message forms? If not, which alternative languages or message forms must I learn to utilize in my effort to realize my rhetorical goal? Moreover, which steps, if any, must I take in order to become a skillful user of these languages and message forms? Conversely, which steps, if any, must I take to enable my audience to use new languages and message forms that the message's impartation requires? In either case, which resources does this communication-enabling process require, and what costs do they involve? Are these resources and funding for these costs available or attainable? In the light of variables like these, how can I most effectively attempt to communicate in a redemptive way with this audience? Which messages should I construct or have I constructed, and in which form or forms should I express them in my attempt to have maximum impact?

As noted earlier, before knowing he would go to India, Carey manifested, in the *Enquiry*, his understanding that messages are most effective if mediated to listeners, readers, or viewers in audience-adapted message forms. Implementing this timeless principle in the digital age requires modern communication visionaries to understand, no less than Carey did in his day, that the would-be redemptive communicator is responsible for anticipating and attempting to bridge communication gaps that may prevent successful transmissions of the redemptive message to its target audiences. For Carey, the obstacles ranged at various times from the linguistic, cultural, and political to the technological and literacy related. For today's aspiring redemptive communicator, these situation-specific obstacle types warrant consideration as one evaluates the means through which he or she can most effectively promote the redemptive venture.

Third, the communicator must know which material resources and human resources his or her creation and transmission of redemptive messages to the target audience will require. Carey, a linguist, needed colleagues like Marshman, an educational entrepreneur, and Ward, a printer, in order to create means for channeling redemptive messages for target audiences. In order to be successful, an enterprise like theirs, as Carey generally anticipated in the *Enquiry*, would require them to acquire facilities, support personnel, printing presses, a type foundry, and resources for circulating their publications to target audiences. These necessities required initial capital and revenue-generating resources. As its early records indicate, the mission covered expenditures like these during Carey's lifetime with donations, with revenues from the mission press, and with monies generated by its native schools and its linguistic and translation works. Likewise, modern redemptive communicators must anticipate the resources and the revenue sources that their anticipated venture requires. Whether funding comes from gifts, grants, loans, sales, fees, personal resources, or elsewhere, the envisioned venture's capital and revenue needs will require funding in order for it to become a reality. It behooves the communication visionary, when creating his or her strategic plan, to devise a plan for generating such essential resources.

Conclusion

William Carey's *Enquiry* is noteworthy not only as a seminal document in the history of Protestant missions but also as a visionary statement that manifests a strategic way of thinking that is instructive to modern Christians who aspire to initiate redemptive communication ventures. Carey understood the importance of crafting persuasive messages to satisfy the rhetorical needs or demands of specific audiences. In the *Enquiry*, he did so by pitching the pro-missional cause to clergymen by citing biblical, theological, historical, and demographical supports and by refuting objections to his thesis. In South Asia, he did so by engendering native literacy and by advancing his redemptive goal through the production of native-language publications.

Whether one's redemptive goal is to promote conversion or to advance another God-valued outcome—through messages that are spoken, written, printed, broadcasted, digitized, or mediated otherwise to individuals, groups, or people in general—one's venture can only benefit from a preliminary guiding focus on discerning audience needs in specific contexts. As Carey's example suggests, skillful redemptive media strategists today should aim to adapt even the most timeless of messages to specific audiences, understanding through research and observation their rhetorically significant features and devising media strategies for reaching them.

CHAPTER 21

Søren Kierkegaard: Using Indirect Communication Strategies to Challenge the Complacent

Benson P. Fraser

Abstract: According to Søren Kierkegaard (1813–1855), a different kind of communication strategy is needed to awaken and empower those who call themselves Christian or those who possess some knowledge of the Christian faith but are resistant to embracing Christianity. This chapter examines one of Kierkegaard's most important pseudonymous works, *Concluding Unscientific Postscript* (1846/1992), to ascertain his understanding of two indirect communication strategies—overhearing and "making strange"—for awakening those individuals who are not living as Christians.

Introduction

Johannes Climacus, a pseudonymous character of renowned theologian and philosopher Søren Kierkegaard, tells the story of Kierkegaard as a young man contemplating what he was going to do with his life. According to Climacus, one Sunday afternoon Kierkegaard found himself smoking a cigar at a café. He began wondering what to do with his life. He recalled thinking that he was "getting on in years" and was "becoming an old man without being anything and without actually undertaking anything."[1] Wherever he looked, he saw the work of highly acclaimed people, those who were well-known or famous. Shortly after, a thought crossed his mind: "You must do something, but since with your limited capabilities it will be impossible to make anything easier than it has become, you must, with the same humanitarian enthusiasm as others have, take it upon yourself to make things more difficult."[2]

Climacus explains that when everything is made "easier in every way, there remains only one possible danger, mainly, the danger that the easiness would became so great that it would become all too easy."[3] If we are only interested in ease and comfort, we may not be really living as we should. Therefore, Kierkegaard wanted to alert the Danish church to live the truth it professed, even if it was difficult. Kierkegaard's chief concern was how to rouse those Christians whose ease and comfort had lulled them asleep to the cultural challenges before them.

Waking Danish sleepers was no easy task, especially since many in Denmark thought they were Christian simply because they were familiar with the doctrines and rituals of the church. Kierkegaard thus developed a communication strategy to help those who felt they knew the Christian message yet were resistant to living a Christian life. By examining one of Kierkegaard's most important pseudonymous works, *Concluding Unscientific Postscript*, this chapter articulates two literary devices of Kierkegaard's *indirect strategy* of communication—(1) overhearing and (2) "making strange," making something familiar look unfamiliar so that it can be freshly reexamined—in an effort to develop a strategy of apologetics that can awaken those who failed, both then and now, to appropriate the gospel.

Christendom in the Age of Reason

During the early nineteenth century, the church in Denmark was rich in liturgy, doctrine, and social life, but in Kierkegaard's mind, "the comfortable, civilized world of cultural Danish Christendom had done away with Christianity."[4] Kierkegaard understood the term "Christendom" to be a civil order of the official church of Denmark with its history and exercise of biblical pieties, yet its members were deficient of any authentic relationship to Christ. The church had become a theater of emptiness and vanity. He argued that "only religious inwardness, true spiritual solitude, can make possible a different order to life and reveal the inauthenticity of culture itself against the unshakable backdrop of a transcendent God."[5]

In addition, Kierkegaard lived in a time of great philosophical upheaval. The influence of modernity had taken hold of the academic and theological communities with the accompanying effect of marginalizing the significance of God's revelation.[6] He rejected the common assumption of modernist philosophers, particularly Danish followers of the German philosopher Georg Wilhelm Friedrich Hegel, who thought that "human rationality was sufficient for cultural progress and—more importantly—for individual human fulfillment."[7]

Contrary to these dominant views of objective reason, human beings were incapable of discerning the truth of Christianity by means of reason alone, not the least of which was because of the paradox of Jesus Christ himself. Paradox does not mean that reason does not contribute a part or have a positive role in Kierkegaard's thought. It does, however, mean that the basic human choice is not a matter of rational validation. For Kierkegaard, we cannot reason our way to God, because God is only known through spiritual inwardness, or a God-relationship. Because human reason is limited, there are limits to what fallen humans can know apart from God's divine revelation. Furthermore, Kierkegaard believed that Christ was the "absolute paradox." By this he did not mean "a formal, logical contradiction but rather some kind of tension-filled incongruity."[8] The incarnation was just one of these many tension-filled incongruities. People simply do not understand how Christ can be both God and man (eternal and temporal). This does not mean it is irrational; it is simply incomprehensible to human reason, and thus may truly be said to be above reason.[9]

Besides these philosophical changes, 1840s Denmark was also in the throes of major political changes as the reign of the monarchy was coming to an end. According to one historian, "Within a comparatively short period of time it became impossible to continue to exclude the great majority of ordinary people from public life."[10] In the late 1840s, for economic and political reasons, "Denmark was transformed into a constitutional monarchy with a representative government based on near-universal manhood suffrage, probably the broadest suffrage in the world at the time."[11] Despite some concerns, Kierkegaard came to "see the new democratic age as the inevitable way of the future."[12]

The church leaders were also under the influence of modernity, and they replaced a passionate encounter with Christ with pageantry, prose, and an easy understanding of Scripture. These leaders failed to understand a suitable Christian appropriation or assimilation. For Kierkegaard, "appropriation means *making the truth your own*; it is the personal assimilation of truth such that it transforms one's self."[13] He desired an existential and religious awakening; he longed for a greater inwardness, seriousness, and authenticity, all of which were lacking in the lives of many members of the church in Denmark.

It became clear to Kierkegaard that many belonging to the church in Denmark believed themselves to be Christian, while distorting Christian faith to fit their current social interests and cultural beliefs. For a great many in that church, Scripture had lost its prophetic force and could no longer challenge social structures or personal behavior. At the heart of Kierkegaard's challenge to the church is his insistence that Christianity is not an objective doctrine or a philosophy but a passionate relationship with Christ that influences how one lives one's life.

Therefore, Kierkegaard became a missionary to the Christians.[14] He did so with a special communicative strategy: indirect communication. As opposed to direct communication, indirect communication aims to nurture a Christian capacity, and it can be performed with the strategies of taking away and overhearing.

Direct and Indirect Communication in
Concluding Unscientific Postscript

For Kierkegaard, direct communication deals in the objective world of facts and figures, or, put differently, it is blunt talk that seeks to avoid ironic and elusive speech. Such communication has an immediate intent of providing content, as its meanings are explicit on the surface and clear. Kierkegaard suggests that Christians may have used the direct approach in an earlier time when the need for information was more prevalent because men and women had not heard the Christian message.[15] But in Kierkegaard's day the situation had changed.

Indirect communication can be understood as hidden or veiled communication, where "one does not begin *directly* with the matter one wants to communicate."[16] Indirect communication provokes honest thought. It stirs emotions and the imagination. It intends to convey more than what is said or seen. Although both direct and indirect communication were important to Kierkegaard's understanding of communication, in most cases he favored indirect communication as it most effectively addressed the needs of the church in his day, especially since the church had lost its Christian "capability."

The term "capability" is crucial to understanding indirect communication; for Kierkegaard, capability had to do with how a person lives—how one behaves and acts and not simply what one knows. Danish Christians were aware of the stories and doctrines of the church, but they were no longer moved by them. Rather than providing new information, indirect communication aimed to awaken a distinctly Christian capability to put into practice the knowledge they possessed. Capability is especially difficult to awaken if people live under the illusion that they already live in accordance with Christian beliefs, when, in fact, they do not.

Because Kierkegaard's Danish audience lived in such an illusion, that illusion needed to be "taken away" before they could attend to the truth of the gospel. Because his audience clung so tightly to their illusion, Kierkegaard suggests that they needed to be deceived into the truth.[17] By way of example, Climacus tells a story of a person whose mouth was so full of food, he could not chew or swallow, so he was starving to death. Since he was paralyzed by abundance of food, the best way to help this person, Climacus argues, would be to take away food from his mouth. In Kierkegaard's context, stories of faith were so redundant that they were no longer taken seriously. Christians were inoculated against truth. Therefore, indirect communication aimed to "take away" or "make strange"[18] the truths they thought they possessed, so that they might discover them anew.[19]

Overhearing can also function as a strategy of indirection. Kierkegaard experienced overhearing one afternoon as he quietly sat in a graveyard, hidden behind a hedge, and reflected privately. While he sat, he overheard a conversation between a grandfather and his ten-year-old grandson. With the hedge hiding him from their view, Kierkegaard discerned that the grandfather and grandson stood over the new grave of the grandfather's son, the grandson's father. The grandfather spoke with such deep sorrow, sincerity, and tenderness that Kierkegaard could not help but feel moved. The passionate and revealing conversation tempted Kierkegaard to leave, but he did not want to disturb the two visitors. So he sat silently, gripped by the intensity of the truth he heard.[20] Kierkegaard discerned that overhearing sidestepped his emotional resistance. Because no one was trying to persuade him, he could lower his defenses, listen, be moved deeply, and judge for himself the truth of what was said.

An example of indirect communication is found in 2 Samuel 12:1–7, a parable the prophet Nathan uses to confront King David regarding his adultery with Bathsheba and his murder of her husband, Uriah. Nathan realized that David did not lack information on this matter, nor was the king misinformed about his actions. Rather, the prophet had to "make strange" the truth he already knew. The prophet did not employ direct communication. Instead, he engaged in a holy deception. He told a story of two men, one rich with a large number of sheep and cattle and another poor with only one little lamb. The rich man, who could have easily chosen one of his many animals, took instead the poor man's only lamb to feed a friend who came to visit. Clearly seeing this gross injustice, David grew angry and condemned the rich man. Because David did not think this story was directed at his own acts of injustice, his defenses were down. He had room to be moved to anger and justice. In the midst of king's wrath, Nathan moved from indirect to direct communication. The prophet accused the king, "You are the man!" David had to make a choice. He could either face up to the wrong he committed or continue to attempt to hide his destructive behavior. He chose to confess his sin and plead his case before God.

Indirect Communication as a Tool for Apologetics

As one theologian rightly observes, "Much of the situation of his [Kierkegaard's] day is still reflected in the 'Western' world, in particular, U.S. Anglo-Christianity."[21] Furthermore, as Kierkegaard anticipated, many people today still believe that natural sciences are the sole arbiters of all legitimate questions about faith. This conviction is now clearly under contention within the academic community. For example, in *An Invitation to the Skeptical: Making Sense of God*, pastor Timothy Keller asserts, "Faith was making something of a comeback in rarefied philosophical circles where secular reason—rationality and science without any beliefs in the transcendent, supernatural reality—has increasingly been seen as missing things that society needs."[22] Accordingly,

Keller argues that although science can describe love and meaning as chemical responses in a person's brain, "if we assert, which virtually everyone does, that love, meaning, and morals do not merely feel real but actually are so—science cannot support that."[23] Furthermore, despite the fact that science and reason are sources of enormous and irreplaceable good for human society, they too have their limits. Keller argues that "Western secularity is not the absence of faith but a new set of beliefs about the universe."[24]

Christian apologists would do well to provide a Kierkegaardian Christian understanding of reason rather than simply uncritically accept modern and secular accounts. Theologian Andrew Davison makes such a gesture with his distinction between thin and thick reason. He states, "'Thin' reason is abstract and ahistorical; it is unimaginative," whereas thick reason "involves history and story, imagination and desire."[25] To imagine Christian reason as thick, historical, storied, imaginative, and desirable is to understand that Christian truths are perhaps best communicated indirectly. Contemporary audiences are technologically savvy and immersed in images that can awaken and enchant. Therefore, apologists might approach apologetics as visual and aural acts aimed at provoking a desire and longing for grace, rather than simply providing dry facts and doctrine.

However, Davison was not the first to imagine apologetics as potentially imaginative and indirect. A generation earlier, C. S. Lewis recognized the need for imaginative apologetics in a letter he wrote to evangelical journalist Carl F. H. Henry. In 1955, Henry invited Lewis to write an article for *Christianity Today*. By way of reply, Lewis wrote this to Henry:

> I wish your project heartily well but can't write you articles. My thought and talent (such as they are) now flow in different, though I think not less Christian, channels, and I do not think I am at all likely to write more directly theological pieces. The last work of that sort which I attempted had to be abandoned. If I am now good for anything it is for catching the reader unawares—thro' fiction and symbol. I have done what I could in the way of frontal attacks, but I now feel quite sure those days are over.[26]

In this statement Lewis signals his move to an indirect or imaginative apologetics. Lewis's phrase "to catch the reader unawares" sounds much like Kierkegaard's "attack from behind" and describes his own approach to "making strange." Furthermore, Lewis's reconsideration of the "frontal attack" comes very close to Kierkegaard's understanding of direct communication. Elsewhere, Lewis states that "God is everywhere but is everywhere incognito,"[27] much like Kierkegaard's notion that God is hidden. Finally, theologian Austin Farrer concluded in his homily at Lewis's funeral, "But his real power was not proof; it was depiction. There lived in his writings a Christian universe that could be both thought and felt, in which he was at home and in which he made his reader at home."[28] The intent for both men is to surprise or deceive the reader into reconsidering the truth they had dismissed or previously undervalued.

From the vantage point of an indirect or imaginative apologetic, the primary task of the church is not to create better arguments for the existence of God. Theologian Alison Milbank would argue that the "primary task of the church is surely to awaken people to their own creative capacity, and in so doing we shall quite naturally awaken also the religious sense."[29] It is not that reason does not play a part in our religious life, but coming to faith, especially in our current cultural milieu, may be better practiced as an imaginative provocation or indirect communication.

Conclusion

Years ago, I read a book by a prominent Christian author who was talking about how people come to faith. The author had a student. One day, the student admitted that the author had, indeed, "satisfactorily answered all his questions" regarding the Christian faith.[30] The author inquired, "Are you going to become a Christian?"[31] The student replied, "No."[32] Puzzled, the author asked "Why not?"[33] "Frankly," the student admitted, "it would mess up the way I'm living."[34] Clearly for this student, as for many people today, the question is not intellectually a lack of information. The Christian faith asks all of us to give up our entire lives, to take up our crosses, and follow Jesus. As this student attests, more information will not necessarily persuade anyone to lose one's life to save it. Rather, like the men on the road to Emmaus, Christians speak words that strike people's innermost being such that listeners ask themselves, "Were not our hearts burning within us?" (Lk 24:32 NRSV). Kierkegaard's indirect communication is a practice that enables such speaking.

CHAPTER 22

Alexander Campbell: Crusading for Pacifism and Abolition in a Time of War and Slavery

Kenneth E. Waters

Abstract: Alexander Campbell (1788–1866) used a small newspaper, the *Christian Baptist*, to spread his passionate plea for church unity. Campbell asserted that a logical outcome of focusing only on the New Testament as the guide for church unity meant condemning war and slavery. His writing and preaching about pacifism and abolition found much less acceptance than the rest of his message, one that eventually resulted in the founding of three American denominations that today count millions of adherents.

Introduction

In the fall of 1829, frontier preacher Alexander Campbell rode on horseback for eleven days through the Appalachian Mountains. He traveled from western Virginia to Richmond, the commonwealth's capital. His mission was to represent his neighbors in the revision of the Virginia Constitution. Two realities made his task more difficult. First, Campbell represented the "hillbillies" of western Virginia. Second, and most distressing to the former U.S. presidents, senators, and current Supreme Court justice assembled in Richmond, Campbell was a preacher arriving with the idealistic goal of trying to convince Virginians to abolish slavery. The preacher soon realized that the 1829 Virginia Constitutional Convention was not going to ban slavery. Despite his disappointment, he spoke often about the need at least to allow all (white) men to vote, not just landowners. His quest for a more democratic union was thwarted by the likes of former presidents James Madison and James Monroe as well as by Supreme Court Justice John Marshall who could not see clear to allow anyone other than white landowners to vote.

Still, none forgot Campbell's courage in challenging his better-known delegates. Former President James Madison regularly attended a church where Campbell preached while in Richmond. At the conclusion of the nearly four-month Constitutional Convention, Madison claimed Campbell was "the ablest and most original expounder of the Scriptures I have ever heard."[1] Campbell returned from the convention eager to resume his ministry as a preacher-entrepreneur, whose writing, speaking, and debating would result in the creation of three denominations—the Disciples of Christ, the Church of Christ, and the Independent Christian Church—that today count millions of members worldwide.

Anyone attending the Convention of 1829 who had read Campbell's initial newspaper, the *Christian Baptist*, knew well that this crusader for church unity, based solely on the New Testament teaching, was also a staunch supporter of abolition and pacifism. This chapter discusses his social justice stance, often overlooked by his biographers, and how his biblical justification for equality and peace based on church unity can inform the church today. The primary text informing this chapter is the inaugural essay Campbell wrote for the August 3, 1823, issue of the *Christian Baptist*, one of two newspapers he published and wrote in his lifetime. This essay and other writings formed the basis of one of his better-known sermons, "The Address on War," delivered in 1848, reprinted in his second newspaper, *Millennial Harbinger*, and later entered into the Congressional Record in 1937.

The *Christian Baptist*

The purpose of the *Christian Baptist* was to educate readers and to unify the splintered denominations with a return to the organizational structure and doctrine contained in the New Testament. In the first essay, "The Christian Religion," Campbell writes passionately about the corruption of denominational hierarchy, mission societies, clergy, and those who refuse to love as Christ loved. He advocates instead for congregational autonomy, weekly communion, prayer, baptism by immersion, and all church decisions being based solely on the New Testament Scripture or example. He saves a small but forceful number of words to advocate for pacifism and abolition.

Campbell concludes the article with an exposition on social justice in a sardonic critique of the contradictions of war. The preacher claims that it is strange that a military general claiming to be a Christian, "with his ten thousand soldiers, and his chaplain at his elbow, preaching, as he says, 'the gospel of good will among men,'"[2] would exhort the troops to go forth, "with the bible [*sic*] in one hand and the sword in the other,"[3] to make as many widows and orphans as possible. Once successful with the slaughter, the Christian general "will afford sufficient opportunity for others to manifest the purity of their religion by taking care of [the widows and orphans]."[4] The implication is that such actions, while claiming to be Christian, are anything but.

Second, Campbell condemns slavery. Too many Christians, he asserts, preach a gospel of civil and religious freedom, while simultaneously supporting

> a system of the most cruel oppression, separating the wife from the embraces of her husband, and the mother from her tender offspring; violating every principle, and rending every tie that endears life and reconciles man to his lot; and that, forsooth, because "might gives right," and a man is held guilty because his skin is a shade darker than the standard color of the times.[5]

Ministers who condone war and slavery encourage Christians to turn away from the truth of God's love for all humans. Quoting 2 Timothy 3:1–5, Campbell notes that in the latter days people "will be self-lovers, money-lovers, boasters, proud, blasphemers, disobedient to parents, ungrateful, unholy, without natural affection, covenant-breakers, slanderers, having a form of godliness, but denying the power of it. NOW FROM THESE TURN AWAY."[6]

Two years later, again in the *Christian Baptist*, Campbell unleashes another critique of war and slavery. In a fictitious and satirical letter to clergy, which he claims is the recently discovered "Third Epistle of Peter," Campbell claims that Peter admonished preachers not to rebuke believers who would go to war with each other. Instead, "Tell the one host that God is on their side, and the other host that he is on their side; so make them bold to kill."[7] He concludes by advising clergy to avoid the preaching of "'Peace on earth and good will to men,' but preach you glory to the victory, and victory to the brave."[8] He also satirically condones slavery:

> If any man go into a foreign land and seize upon his fellow man, and put irons on his feet and irons on his hands, and bring him across the great deep into bondage; nay, if he tear asunder the dearest ties of nature, the tenderest leagues of the human heart; if he tear the wife from the husband, and force the struggling infant from its mother's bleeding breast, rebuke him not![9]

The Epistle goes on to recommend to preachers that they do not tell the slave trader that he is doing the work of the antichrist: "For lo! he is rich and gives to the church and is esteemed pious, so shall you not offend him, lest peradventure he withdraw himself from your flock."[10] Later in a sister publication, *Millennial Harbinger*, Campbell describes slavery as "that largest and blackest blot upon our national escutcheon, that many-headed monster, that Pandora's box, that bitter root, that blighting and blasting curse."[11]

When Campbell returned from the Virginia Constitutional Convention, he stopped publishing the *Christian Baptist* and began the *Millennial Harbinger*. The tone of this publication was more measured, based on Campbell's belief that Christians—through achieving unity and living according to Christ—could help usher in Christ's return. In this publication, Campbell asserts that war and slavery lead to the "enduring wail of widows and orphans—the screams and the anguish of mothers and sisters deprived forever of the consolations and hopes that clustered round the return of those so dear to them."[12] This statement, in fact, is only a small part of his "Address on War," a culminating treatise on the sin of war he felt was not in keeping with God's will for humanity.

A Unity Based on the New Testament Alone

Alexander Campbell's social justice appeals were a logical extension of his crusade to unite factions of Christianity by restoring the organization and worship practices of the New Testament church. Enlightenment thinking influenced Campbell, particularly the belief that logic and God's revelation were compatible. Further, he asserted that people should read the Bible and determine for themselves what it said and how individuals and the church should encounter the world around them. If believers would follow this advice, they would see that church unity could only be achieved through baptism by immersion, congregational autonomy, lay ministry, the absence of missionary societies and Bible associations, and *a cappella* singing.

Campbell's standing among some frontier Presbyterian and Baptist churches grew after he soundly won a debate in 1820 with Presbyterian Reverend John Walker over the subject of baptism. Campbell spoke directly out of the New Testament, arguing biblically and rationally, that the only means of salvation was to be totally immersed as an adult. Over the next two years, several versions of the debate were published in book form, with around three thousand total sales across the United States.[13]

As the book's sales continued, Campbell began discussing with his followers whether the unification movement might spread more quickly if it were propelled by a newspaper. Throughout the young republic, opinionated journals that focused on religion took advantage of new printing technology to spread their ideas far beyond their local settings. Campbell and his supporters agreed that to have credibility their publication needed a foundation in an existing denomination. They eventually called the paper *Christian Baptist*, a nod to their affiliation at that time with local Baptist Church associations.[14] In the preface, Campbell wrote that the paper "shall espouse the cause of no religious sect, excepting the ancient sect 'called Christians first at Antioch.'"[15] Additionally, the paper's "sole object is eviction of truth and the exposing of error in doctrine and practice," relying only on the words of the Bible as its foundation.[16] Campbell wanted to "startle the entire religious community. This, indeed, was what he designed to do, for he conceived the people to be so completely under the dominion of the clergy at this time that nothing but bold and decisive measures could arouse them to proper inquiry."[17] While circulation never reached more than a few thousand, the influence of the paper spread internationally.[18]

Helping Campbell's crusade was the fact that during the Second Great Awakening, which began in 1790, Americans were devouring printed publications. While the Ivy League universities provided leadership training for clergy, less educated Americans were reading Bible tracts and other forms of printed text.[19] All forms of written communication took messages that were once geographically limited and allowed those messages to spread widely. Campbell leveraged printed materials to fuel his movement. Further, the early nineteenth century was ripe for the importation of Enlightenment teaching about individual rights coupled with the idea that anyone was free in America to become whoever he or she wanted to be. Church historian Nathan O. Hatch called this phenomenon "the democratization of American Christianity."[20] Hatch asserted that any young man with the gift of persuasion and a spirit of entrepreneurism, after finding fault with his local church or denomination, was free to start a new expression of Christianity and use his persuasive skills to build up a congregation.[21]

Although his teaching on pacifism and slavery occupied only a few pages of the *Christian Baptist*, Campbell held these controversial views primarily because of his understanding of eschatology.[22] He saw the work of God as encompassing three millennia: the patriarchal era ran from Adam to Moses; the Jewish era went from Moses to Christ; finally, the third era runs from the resurrection of Christ to the end of time. We live in the third and final dispensation, and thus we are under the covenant and commitment to Jesus Christ as revealed in the New Testament. To Campbell, God's commands to go to war in the Old Testament are confined to the second dispensation and are not found in the teachings of Christ or the authors of the New Testament. Further, war held the possibility that Christians would be trying to kill each other, thus undermining the unity of the church he preached with such passion.[23] The same sentiment was evident in his opposition to slavery as it was clearly a violation of the New Testament sense of justice.

Campbell lived to see some of his most cherished dreams crushed as the unity of the church and the movement toward the millennium lost ground to schisms within his own movement, and his appeals to pacifism and abolition fell on deaf ears in the United States at the beginning of the Civil War. Even his sons fought on different sides of the war. The Churches of Christ, the largest group of believers aligned with his Restoration Movement, have largely repudiated pacifism and "by the 1990s most church members were habitual pro-military conservative Republicans."[24]

Campbell's Relevance Today

While the movement did not create the church unity Campbell desired, his justification for pacifism and his opposition to slavery provide us with helpful teaching. First, a return to New Testament Scripture as the sole authority of truth can provide a common ground for rational discussion about disagreements between Christian individuals, churches, and denominations. Even when evangelicals wedded to biblical inerrancy disagree, their arguments often contain assertions drawn from church ritual and ecclesiastical history. Campbell would have us step back and only consider the words of the New Testament, with recognition that disagreeing parties might need to consult ancient Greek interpretations and even historical treatises to gain a complete context of what a given passage might mean today. Ethicist John Rawls provides a modern-day parallel to Campbell's method of dealing with biblical and social action disputes.[25] Campbell's vision for the church is egalitarian. Rawls's call for distributive justice uses a device called the "Veil of Ignorance" in which all parties go behind the veil, not knowing if the others are—in this example—a clergyman, a layperson with a college education, or a blue-collar worker with a high school diploma. Behind the veil, each person assumes the "Original Position," where his or her social status, education, and power are set aside as irrelevant. In the Original Position, people discuss what is right, how to distribute justice in a manner that seeks to do what is right, and how to protect the interests of all people.[26] To Campbell, a form of distributive justice or biblical consensus is achieved when all parties seek the New Testament as a guide for whatever issue they are deciding. Behind the veil, church tradition and extrabiblical ritual are not considered, only the words and examples found in the new covenant between God and his people, as exhibited in the early church.

Second, Campbell's teachings and his movement are outside the traditional boundaries of what Protestants would consider the "peace churches." His denominational progeny are considered mainline (Disciples of Christ) or evangelical (Churches of Christ, Independent Christian Church). While most of these groups embrace theories of just war today because it is practical, considering anew Campbell's justification for pacifism and his opposition to the oppression of any human being would be an enlightening exercise for pastors to consider from the pulpit or through small groups. Using only New Testament Scripture as the basis for this study would be enlightening and might revolutionize evangelical churches' engagement with the political and cultural landscape. In other words, Campbell's call for love based on New Testament teaching as the only rule to live by would radically alter the political landscape worldwide. Ministers and priests, for instance, might ask, "Should NATO forces have invaded Afghanistan to eradicate the Taliban and kill Osama bin Laden?" "Should the Western forces have invaded Iraq or intervened in Syria?" "What should be their stance toward other areas of conflict in the world?" Through Christian aid agencies such as World Vision, Compassion International, and others, Christians are great at helping victims of war and oppression after the human toll has been exacted. How different would the world be if along with rushing to aid the unfortunate, Christians politicians decried the use of force so no carnage occurred in the first place?

In encouraging Christians to stand against the racial injustices of slavery, Campbell would no doubt advocate that Christian unity cannot be achieved as long as Sunday mornings remain the most segregated hours of the week. And he would likely take seriously the calls for economic, social, and political justice made by historic advocacy groups like the National Association for the Advancement of Colored People (NAACP) and more recent groups such as Black Lives Matter. One can see Campbell using church facilities to create safe spaces for outreach to address the ills of a still-racist society and to encourage a dialogue based on love and unity between and among various ethnic and political groups. A casual visitor to most evangelical congregations today would likely find an emphasis on personal salvation and responsibility, but little teaching from the pulpit on what individual Christians should do to make the world a better place, one devoid of violence and subtle slavery, not to mention the worldwide phenomenon of sexual slavery that is only now receiving the headlines this tragedy deserves.[27] While Campbell would agree with evangelicals that salvation is personal and occurs between God and each of us human beings, he would also argue that the church's actions need unity, a more communitarian approach to ethics and behavior.[28]

Conclusion

Today we might still learn from Alexander Campbell's appeal to the New Testament as the authoritative source for Christian belief and action; we also find a gifted speaker and writer who incorporated sarcasm, wit, and an audience-focused rhetoric that inspired thousands of believers to seek a personal relationship with Christ unencumbered by centuries-old doctrines and rituals created by excesses within the Christian movement. A century before marketing firms began advising Christian celebrities on how to extend their brand, Campbell spread his message (and brand) by leveraging the available means of mediated communication. He also modeled to us in today's politically and religiously fractured culture the example of practicing what one preaches. His rational approach to Christianity and insistence that every person could read and follow the New Testament teachings without the intervention of church leadership and (hu)man-made doctrine is a strong example of how the church could still achieve a unified voice when addressing matters of cultural or political concern. He also contributed to the political landscape as a citizen while avoiding the temptation to mix religious fervor with the political process that seems to inevitably crush the credibility of those Christians who today cross the divide between church and state.

CHAPTER 23

John Henry Newman: Persuading through a Holistic Rhetoric of Belief

Janie Marie Harden Fritz

Abstract: In *An Essay in Aid of a Grammar of Assent,* John Henry Newman (1801–1890) presents an approach to persuasion that describes how we come to believe the claims of a religious tradition in a way that is rational but not based on formal reasoning. Newman's work is as applicable today as it was a century and a half ago as Christians face challenges to their faith from proponents of the "new atheism" and others skeptical of the claims of religion.

Introduction

John Henry Newman was deeply concerned about his good friend, William Froude, a scientist who had abandoned his religious beliefs because of his commitment to scientific rationality. Newman, a convert to Catholicism who had thought long and hard about the relationship between faith and reason, set out to offer the best case he could for why religious belief was reasonable, rather than being an inappropriate or even "immoral" use of the human reasoning capacity.[1] He was concerned not only with his scientific friend's inability to reconcile faith and reason, but also with all believers, particularly Christians who were untrained in philosophical and scientific reasoning and accepted the religious perspective taught to them as part of their upbringing without apparent reflection and careful judgment as to its truth or falsity. What if those believers had been brought up in another faith tradition or none at all? Could there be any justification for assenting to the truths of Christian tradition that were not arrived at through logical, formal thought processes so valued by scientists and philosophers?

In *An Essay in Aid of a Grammar of Assent,* Newman argues that humans are not primarily rational creatures. Rather, we are seeing, feeling, contemplative, and active beings. As a result, persuasive communication does well to appeal to our "illative sense," or that cumulative adding up of probabilities that produces confidence for humans. Writing this work in the late 1800s, Newman wrote in a moment where rationalists and agnostics of the Victorian era posed serious challenges to religious belief. Against this challenge, Newman saw that individual experience and personal history shaped people's first principles in a deep and profound way. Our own historical moment is one of multiple competing religious claims, including those touting the supremacy of the "new atheism."[2] Newman helps Christian communicators today with such challenges through an exploration of various means of persuasion, a life lived as persuasively powerful, and a critical stance toward rationalistic appeals.

An Essay in Aid of a Grammar of Assent

An Essay in Aid of a Grammar of Assent could be considered a project formulating a *rhetoric of belief*, since it focuses on the persuasive grounds for coming to faith and expressing that faith reasonably to others.[3] This work contains Newman's epistemology of belief—that is, it addresses how we can be justified in coming to believe what we believe.[4] He asks, how can we believe something that we cannot absolutely prove?[5]

Newman understood that, although the ability to reason is an innate human capacity, human beings are not only, or even primarily, reasoning beings—we are "seeing, feeling, contemplating, acting" creatures.[6] Carefully constructed verbal arguments laid out according to principles of logical inference about the wisdom of a course of action often are simply not persuasive; they have no hold on our hearts.[7] And some of our most dearly held beliefs cannot be proven through formal logical inference. They are formed by a different, but related, process that proceeds from an accumulation of good reasons but not in a carefully laid out, structured format like that of analytic philosophy. Our faith is a reasonable act, even when it does not emerge from scientific demonstration.[8]

Because logical inference works well at the level of abstract thinking but not so well at the level of the specific instance, to come to belief regarding concrete matters—about the truth claims of religion or the character of a friend, for example—we need an ability more sensitive and flexible than a verbal argument. Newman calls this ability the "illative sense," which permits people to grasp the truth of a proposition even when some of the logical steps for an inferential proof of the proposition are missing.[9] Through the illative sense, we are enabled to believe what the proposition states to be true even though we cannot prove it in a systematic, logical way.

In our daily lives, Newman argues, we take action regularly on the basis of decisions emerging from conclusions that are not supported by formal inference and proof. Our confidence in moving ahead with a particular course of action—whether boarding a plane that we trust will get us to where we believe we are going, selecting a major, or going on a diet that we believe will increase our energy—rests on many bits of evidence, stories, incidents, and experiences that add up to give us a strong sense that the proposition or belief or statement to which they point must be true, although it cannot be logically proven in the airtight fashion preferred by analytic philosophers.[10]

Newman offers, as an example, the proposition that England is an island. How does he know this proposition to be true? He lists several reasons, none of them airtight, but which together converge to provide a sense that it must be so. For example, the maps show it as an island; he had been taught it as a child; no one ever said it was otherwise; everyone takes it for granted; everyday interactions confirm or imply it—all these elements, or combined probabilities, add up to the absolute certainty "that Great Britain is an island."[11]

Newman refers to these combined probabilities as cumulative or antecedent probabilities. We come to give our assent absolutely and immediately, although the process of arriving at this point of assent ordinarily takes place over time and after exposure to multiple contexts in which information or experience relevant to the claim emerges—often implicitly, so that when we do give assent, we experience it as immediate and absolute. Newman believed that this way of being persuaded conforms to our nature as human beings. Indeed, Newman argues that we are obligated by our very nature to grant assent to propositions or claims that have sufficient antecedent probabilities, even if lacking formal proof; we can consider these claims to be "as good as proved."[12]

Newman believed that reflecting on what one has come to believe or has given assent to through reason and thought can strengthen our assent.[13] We may return to our beliefs to investigate them more fully to equip ourselves to offer an account to another person who may differ from us on some point.[14] Newman, in fact, considered that it is our obligation to investigate the reasonableness of claims to which we give our assent.[15]

A Moment of Challenge to Religious Belief

An Essay in Aid of a Grammar of Assent, along with several of his university sermons, represents Newman's understanding of holistic persuasion, an understanding of coming to claim a position or belief as one's own through a process that involves the entire person, including reason, emotion, and experience across multiple contexts of life.

Newman had ample reason to call upon the rhetorical resources he learned as a student at Oxford University, where he was tutored by the renowned rhetorician Richard Whately. As a Christian communicator, John Henry Newman responded to the circumstances of his time to assist the larger community of faith. His training as a rhetorician made him keenly aware of the nature of the intellectual environment he was called to address as he sought to defend the legitimacy of the foundations for faith of ordinary believers who were unable to offer formal evidence or reasons laid out in airtight logical form for their beliefs. Furthermore, as a convert to Catholicism, Newman felt compelled to offer an account of his conversion to Catholicism that would be convincing to those who questioned his change of religious allegiance. In *Apologia Pro Vita Sua*, for instance, he traced his own growing certitude that the history of the church, beginning from the earliest Christian writings, offered a convincing rationale for confidence in the continuity of the Christian narrative as expressed and preserved in the Roman Catholic tradition.

An Essay in Aid of a Grammar of Assent is a response to questions of a historical moment marked by challenges to religious belief by rationalists and agnostics of the Victorian era.[16] Newman recognized the need for a response to the prevailing view that heralded the scientific method as the only legitimate way of establishing knowledge. Trust in the scientific method rested on philosophical foundations of rationalism, positivism, and reductionism, which assumed that all phenomena, including human experience, could be explained by reference to the material world. Philosophers of the day questioned whether religious beliefs could be justified at all,[17] since the claims and tenets of religion could not be reduced to logical inferences involving propositions that could be tested scientifically.[18] Although Newman respected the scientific method and recognized the important role of reasoning in human affairs, he also recognized that science itself rested on assumptions that could not be proved, and he believed that emotion and experience, as well as the reasoning process, shape what we come to believe as true—the whole person is involved.[19]

Newman identified the role of individual experience and personal history in coming to believe, underlining the importance of what each of us brings to the table of decision-making. Where we start in the process of considering the truth of a claim or proposition makes a difference in whether and how we come to assent to that claim or proposition. Although he extended the work of thinkers like the philosopher David Hume and rhetoricians Richard Whately and George Campbell, Newman was ahead of his time in acknowledging the great variety in people's first principles—that is, the places they start from in making arguments or holding positions—and that belief is, to some degree, a very personal matter.[20] Newman also recognized the human being as an active information processor. Newman believed that the whole person was involved in both coming to belief and in offering persuasive messages—our background and experiences form the active context within which we come to interpret, understand, and communicate truth.[21] In fact, Newman considered the way we come to belief to be a moral matter, a matter of character. Newman believed that a person's character shaped whether or not that person would be able to give assent under appropriate conditions, and that persons of good and bad character were persuaded differently.[22]

Holistic Persuasion for Communicators Today

One arena of discourse today for which Newman's work is relevant is "militant atheism" or "the new atheism." Represented by thinkers such as Richard Dawkins, Christopher Hitchens, and Steven Pinker, this rapidly growing strand of atheism takes religious believers to task for placing faith in what cannot be seen or proved scientifically.[23] Although atheism is not a new phenomenon, the approach of this particular movement is more aggressive and more public than in past decades, with heightened visibility in the popular press and with an increased focus on "argument and debate in making the atheist case."[24] For this reason, the new atheism calls for a response from thoughtful Christians seeking to provide reasonable grounds for belief.

The arguments advanced by new atheists rest on foundations similar to those of skeptical intellectuals of Newman's day and can be addressed in similar fashion. Their position also requires a starting point: they, too, must assume something to move forward with their position, as Newman highlights.[25] Religious believers have different starting points but follow paths not so different from other thinkers to their conclusions. All belief requires reliance on that which cannot be proved absolutely, but there is a rationality that underwrites religious belief with epistemological ground as firm and stable as that upon which we walk in the ordinary course of daily life. Our disposition toward the world as it presents itself to us shapes our inclination to place confidence in the claims of religion, and it is always possible to find a way toward or away from religious conviction. Perhaps the margin of possible doubt around our experience provides a necessary opening for a faith that extends itself to the unseen with enduring conviction.

Indeed, much of what we believe about the world consists of propositions or assertions that we assent to in an immediate, unconscious, inexplicable, unconditional way—such as the existence of a city we have never seen before or our belief that the earth is spherical in shape. The conclusions we reach about people, events, and the many elements that make up our world seem inevitable, although our reasoning does not—cannot—take us all the way there.[26] The illative sense, therefore, could be considered a leap of logic rather than a leap of faith, a bridge constructed of a set of probabilities that all point in one direction, taking us over to the conclusion implied by those probabilities; they combine powerfully to give us a sense of being absolutely sure of something presented for our consideration by ourselves or others. Newman offers, as an example, as mentioned earlier, the proposition that England is an island. How does he know this proposition to be true? He lists several reasons, none of them airtight, but which, together, converge to provide a sense that it must be so.

Newman refers to these amassed probabilities as cumulative or antecedent probabilities. We give our assent absolutely and immediately to claims that are presented to us this way, usually over time and in multiple contexts. Newman believed that this way of being persuaded conforms to our nature as human beings. Indeed, he argues that we are obligated by our very nature to grant assent to propositions or claims that have sufficient antecedent probabilities and to consider these claims to be "as good as proved."[27] It is reasonable and right for us to exercise our faculties in this way, bestowing our belief unreservedly in such cases. This understanding of being persuaded applies across the board to human experience—to the new atheists and members of the faith community alike.

Given these considerations—namely, that we come to belief holistically, with many factors contributing to our decision to grant assent—what would Newman recommend to communicators today who hope to speak persuasively about their convictions to adherents of the new atheism? Or, to anyone else with whom we find ourselves in discussion or dispute about matters of belief?

First, Newman would advise us to be wary of formulas for persuasion that proclaim only one way of generating persuasive messages. We would be wise to consider the various approaches open to us to be persuasive. What one audience finds compelling and worthy of belief may not be work for another audience, given different backgrounds, experiences, and standpoints. A compelling story may speak to someone better than a logical argument. Understanding our audience—understanding the belief systems of those who believe differently than we do—may provide insights guiding our persuasive appeals. At the very least, being able to grasp the foundations of others' belief systems will add insight into what features of those systems secure allegiance from their adherents.

Second, Newman might suggest that our ethos or credibility as lived out in our daily practices may be a very persuasive message in itself. Our lives are one potential reason for another person to believe the story we tell; our faithfulness is one element in a collection of "cumulative probabilities" for another person. We do not know the extent of our influence, but we can be faithful in our daily communicative practices of what we believe in both explicit and implicit ways. As we enact the faith on a daily basis, our responses to others, events, and the world around us will build a living testimony to the trustworthiness of our own convictions, which may provide what another person needs in order to strengthen an already-existing faith or give assent to the gospel. Although much of the discourse surrounding the new atheism focuses on the rationality of belief systems, our everyday experiences involve responses to events that transcend rationality, and many decisions are not made on the basis of logical calculation alone. The integrity of convictions lived out over the long haul may invite openness to other ways of knowing, or at least the admission that living within a religious worldview has a logic and integrity worth respecting.

Third, concerning coming to terms with our own beliefs, Newman would ask us not to accept uncritically the claims of secular science and analytic philosophy. These ways of viewing the world rest on untested assumptions just as all beliefs and experiences do.[28] We must work with discernment to test our beliefs—through examining evidence and arguments, but also by other means, including our sense of the reasonableness of claims presented, how other people we trust think of the claims, and our own personal responsiveness to what is presented to us. Scientific knowledge and reasoning are necessary, useful, and appropriate in their proper place, but they must not hold other forms of reasoning hostage. Our experience of human knowing, the way real people make decisions in their daily lives, suggests the pragmatic usefulness of other ways of establishing confidence in beliefs about the world and the phenomena in it, including claims of religious traditions.

Conclusion

John Henry Newman encourages us to respond to our contemporary historical moment—to be aware of emerging intellectual trends, of ways of thinking and talking about issues in the public sphere, and of the personal nature of knowledge, as well as the call to provide publicly supportable reasons for positions we take and beliefs we hold. The nature of the support for these reasons may depart in key respects from formal logic or scientific proof, but they are no less legitimate. As the trend toward secularization continues, leaving a loss of transcendent meaning in its wake,[29] narratives of faith may emerge again as viable ways to make sense of human life. For audiences who are drawn to faith but who are reluctant to believe without some assurance that faith is at least minimally reasonable, Newman's work equips persons of faith with a fitting response to those concerns.

CHAPTER 24

CATHERINE BOOTH: DISTURBING THE PRESENT TO PROMOTE GENDER EQUALITY

Kathy Bruner and Kenneth Baillie

Abstract: Catherine Booth (1829–1890) was a persuasive communicator and cofounder of the Salvation Army. She is also known for her pamphlet *Female Ministry; Or, Woman's Right to Preach the Gospel* that argued for equality based on the exposition of Pauline passages and examples of women successful in ministry. Booth demonstrates how Christians can engage faithfully in public discourse and work to secure the full participation of women in the church.

Introduction

In the winter of 1867, Catherine Booth was engaged in a three-month-long revival campaign. Her Sunday and weeknight sermons were so popular that she packed churches, assembly rooms, and schoolrooms all over England. That she was a successful female preacher in Victorian England was, of course, unusual. But more unusual still was that her success rivaled that of the great preacher Charles Spurgeon, perhaps the most famous preacher of his era. Only a few years before Booth's revival campaign, Spurgeon built the Metropolitan Tabernacle, a massive structure that housed six thousand congregants. In the middle of her campaign, a committee of wealthy Methodists approached Booth and offered "to build her a church similar to Mr. Spurgeon's Tabernacle" if she would agree to be preaching pastor.[1] Booth turned down the offer.

Booth's life and thought might be best summarized in her claim that "There is no improving the future, without disturbing the present."[2] Booth's disruptions took many forms. She cofounded the Salvation Army with her husband William, and her ministry as a popular female preacher reached throughout Britain.[3] Booth wrote widely on the nature of holiness, evangelism, prayer, and temperance. One of her most important disruptions resides in a pamphlet she wrote. *Female Ministry; Or, Woman's Right to Preach the Gospel* (hereafter *Female*

Ministry) argued for women's equality in Christian ministry and aimed to "meet the most common objections" against women's full participation in ministry.[4]

Booth's writing resisted the assumption that women's place was in the private social sphere and instead embraced the Victorian desire for logical evidence and reason. She leveraged her success in the mediated world of the pamphlet in order to gain a wider audience for her speaking and fundraising ministry. Booth's successes suggest that Christians today need not reject our contemporary equivalent of the pamphlet: social media. Rather, we need to leverage it appropriately. Similarly, Booth's work with the Salvation Army underscores the need to protect women's equality in formal ecclesial policy and practice.

Female Ministry; Or, Woman's Right to Preach the Gospel

Booth addressed an objection to women's ministry in the nineteenth century, namely, that putting women in such a public role would be both "unnatural and unfeminine."[5] So strong were these Victorian assumptions that Booth had to refute the notion that a woman who steps into the pulpit "loses the delicacy and grace of the female character—in fact, ceases to be a woman."[6] Booth did not reject the stereotypes.[7] Instead, she marshaled these widely held assumptions to support her argument. These facets of a woman's nature, far from disqualifying her from public speaking, were rather "*natural*" or God-given "qualifications for public speaking."[8]

Despite the fittingness of women for public speaking, Booth acknowledged that women in the pulpit were a rarity; however, she argued this lack was a result of two cultural forces: custom and lack of access to education. "Use, or custom," she reminded her reader, "makes things appear to us natural, which, in reality, are very unnatural; while, on the other hand, novelty and rarity make very natural things appear strange and contrary to nature."[9] Custom also suggested that women were not qualified to speak in public due to lack of education, but Booth argued the real problem was the injustice of women's lack of access to education.[10] Even when men promoted the education of genteel women, they did so for the goal of "improving their performance as wives and mothers."[11] Like the practice of excluding women from public speaking, the custom of not educating women made their lack of qualification seem natural, when, in fact, it was nothing of the kind.

Second, Booth called the common claim that female ministry is forbidden in the word of God "the most serious objection which we have to consider."[12] She claimed Bible passages concerning women had been misinterpreted and began her argument in 1 Corinthians 11. In the passage, the apostle Paul reminds the Corinthians that when they are speaking in the assembly, or "proph-esying" for "edification, exhortation and comfort" of others, they do so with the appropriate head covering.[13] Men should not wear a head covering but women should. Here Paul was speaking literally of the human head. How-ever, most of Booth's contemporary readers took the passage to mean that women should not speak in church at all because they conflated the passage with Ephesians 5 where Paul speaks metaphorically about the husband as the "head" of the wife.

Booth claimed that in the New Testament church women spoke or proph-esied during the assembly, right alongside men; therefore, Paul's words ad-dressed *how* women should speak rather than prohibiting them from speaking. That women should speak in the assembly had been settled on the day of Pen-tecost (Acts 2:17). In making sense of the strange speaking of both women and men, Peter quotes Joel 2:28: both daughters and sons would prophesy on the day of the Lord. Therefore, Paul's words to the Corinthians should be read in light of Peter's. Moreover, Paul's admonition about head coverings only makes sense if both men and women are indeed speaking in the assembly of other Christians. Booth also addressed 1 Corinthians 14, a passage where Paul says women should remain silent in the church, "for it is not permitted unto them to speak."[14] Booth explained that Paul's use of the term "speak" (λαλειν) refers to a very specific kind of speaking. Paul was silencing the "pertinacious, inquisitive, domineering" manner in which some women were speaking, not prohibiting them from speaking altogether.[15]

Finally, Booth catalogued the reality that the ministry of women has been vital to God's purposes, and offered reflections on specific women in the Bible throughout Christian history. In the Old Testament, she lifted up Deborah's au-thority as prophetess and leader of ten thousand military men. She referenced Miriam, Moses, and Aaron as the trio who led the Israelites out of Egypt.[16] Moving to the New Testament, Booth listed fourteen women who ministered. Booth observed that Paul called Phoebe a *diaconon* (deacon), "nothing less than one of those gifted by the Holy Spirit for *publishing the glad tidings*, or *preaching the gospel*."[17] She lamented that translators substituted the word "servant" just because Phoebe was a woman.[18]

Booth praised historical and contemporary women whose "holy lives and zealous labours were owned of God in the conversion of thousands of souls."[19] She constructed a positive argument built on twenty-two women. She praised Madame Guyon, a medieval mystic who prompted the Quietist movement. The list also included Mary Bosanquet Fletcher, the first woman John Wesley autho-rized to preach. Taken together, Booth aimed to marshal biblical and historical evidence not only that women should be full participants in ministry, but also that God has and will continue to further the gospel through their labors and their preaching.

Female Ministry in the Nineteenth-Century Context

Implicit in Booth's writing was the nineteenth century's doctrine of separate spheres. The public sphere was the man's world of competition, profit, and rationality. The private sphere for women consisted of purity, submissiveness, and domesticity.[20] In *Female Ministry* Booth challenged the doctrine of separate spheres for women doing Christian ministry. She argued the holy nature of their work would shield women from "coarse and unrefined influences and associations."[21] Booth asked if the restrictions on women in her day were impeding the growth of the gospel, since more than half of the potential ministry workers were being excluded.

Second, in the nineteenth century, "carefully managed circumstantial evidence" was the key to successful public argument.[22] *Female Ministry* embraces this form of managing evidence, and her pamphlet read much like a lawyer's brief. In her use of reasoning and evidence, Booth was influenced by lawyer-turned-revivalist Charles Finney for whom preaching was like presenting a case in court. Like Finney, Booth applied piercing logic that confounded her audience. So persuasive was Booth that when Henry Davidson, father to the future archbishop of Canterbury, heard her speak, he remarked, "If ever I am charged with a crime, don't bother to engage any of the great lawyers to defend me; get that woman."[23]

Next, the printed pamphlet was an inexpensive topical booklet covering news, politics, social issues, and religion.[24] Pamphlets first emerged in the 1500s when their reputation was largely negative, but by the Victorian era they had become "the primary means of creating and influencing public opinion."[25] Entering contentious public spaces, preachers extended the reach of their sermons by reprinting them as pamphlets. Most pamphlet writers and readers were male, but women authors sometimes wrote under a pseudonym and participated in fierce public debates.[26] Booth embraced the pamphlet and published under her own name.

In addition, *Female Ministry* impacted Booth personally, catapulted her to international fame, and brought her to the forefront of the Salvation Army's ministry. She was an exceedingly shy woman who avoided public roles in her early years. After *Female Ministry* she felt convicted by her own writing and reflection. Booth testified that the Holy Spirit urged her to speak publicly,[27] so, as one of her biographers noted, "she applied her pamphlet to herself."[28] After the publication of the pamphlet, Booth received more speaking invitations than she could accept.[29] While it is unclear how many of her male clergy opponents were persuaded,[30] the publication struck a chord with the public. The original print sold out quickly and generated requests for reprints. As the Salvation Army became "the world's fastest growing Christian sect in an age of missions,"[31] Catherine Booth became the "prime apologist for the organization."[32]

Booth's convictions also had direct effects for women in the Salvation Army. She ensured that a formal policy of gender equality established "the right of females to act as evangelists or class leaders; to hold any office; to speak and vote at all official meetings of which they might be members."[33] This opened the way for "thousands of working-class women" to leave domestic and factory drudgery to join the ranks of ordained clergy.[34] Women preached, ran local ministries, edited periodicals, and opened the Army's work abroad.[35] By 1904 the Salvation Army was at work in forty-nine countries with 14,291 clergy, half of them being women.[36] Upon her death in 1890, the *Manchester Guardian* asserted that Booth had "done more in her own person to establish the right of women to preach the gospel than anyone who has ever lived."[37] In all, the pamphlet proved successful in popular terms and for women within the Salvation Army.

Social Media and Women's Place in Ministry

Booth's writing and success can help us engage at least two contemporary problems many churches and Christians face in the twenty-first century: social media and women's equality in ministry. For many, social media creates a space that is hostile to the reasoning and reflection Booth displays in her pamphlet. Facebook is full of off-the-cuff rants, hyperbolic language, and intemperate attacks, all too short to be nuanced. Twitter's 280 characters offer even less opportunity to write or read with any complexity or balance. Furthermore, "Dozens of studies by psychologists, neurobiologists, educators, and Web designers," observes journalist Nicholas Carr, "point to the same conclusion: when we go online, we enter an environment that promotes cursory reading, hurried and distracted thinking, and superficial learning."[38] Social media might be a space that malforms us, our reasoning, and our views of the world.[39]

However, Booth's use of the pamphlet offers an alternative view. The Victorian pamphlet bears some similarity to social media today. Pamphlets were sometimes accused of being untrustworthy and unruly, like Twitter and Facebook. Both the pamphlet and social media are contentious spaces where opposing voices compete for public attention. Pamphlets were as central to public debate as social media. Booth entered that fray of public debate, and her success created possibilities. Following the publication, her message reached across the world. She became the face of the Salvation Army and helped shape the group's policy on women. Social media have a similar potential. If Christians are eager to share biblical wisdom, they would be wise to leverage social media to gain attention and direct audiences to reasoned, deeper content.

In fact, author Rachel Held Evans demonstrates that engagement with social media need not produce the kinds of dire predictions Carr suggests. Evans tweets regularly on her own topics and re-tweets thoughtful material from a wide range of cultural influencers. While Facebook and Twitter are not ideal forums for intellectual rigor, they can entice audiences to read her blogs or books that allow for theological depth or to hear her when she speaks publicly. After the publication of her book *A Year of Biblical Womanhood*, Evans conducted interviews with major media outlets, emerged as a sought-after speaker on the topic of gender equality, and became a cultural influencer in her own right.[40] Like Booth a century before, Evans takes her ideological opponents to task and uses reasoned, biblical thinking to point out logical fallacies.

Further, Booth teaches that full equality for women in ministry must be formalized in written policies.[41] The enduring legacy of *Female Ministry* is that its concepts were written into Salvation Army polity.[42] Its female ministers are still 53 percent of the organization's international clergy today.[43] By percentage, the Salvation Army has more females in leadership than any other church, denomination, or Christian organization.[44] Unfortunately, when organizations fail to formalize policy statements affirming women's ministry opportunities, they tend to drift back into cultural patterns that limit women.[45] One example is Moody Bible Institute where women alumni in the early twentieth century were touted in the institute's publications for their wide-ranging ministries. Over time the institution slipped backward on the issue until a 1979 statement formally excluded women from the pastoral training major.[46] If we follow Booth's thinking, the gospel is at stake in exclusion of women. God has clearly used women in Scripture and in church history to accomplish divine purposes. When churches exclude women, they simply eliminate those persons God might very well call to proclaim the gospel.

One church that has formalized policies that allow for full participation by women is Willow Creek in Barrington, Illinois. In its early days of growth, women were significant in leadership, but the male church elders were unsure whether to make women elders. Willow Creek leaders commissioned a study "based not on 'feelings' but on the teaching of Scripture."[47] For eighteen months they consulted experts, conducted individual and corporate study of Scripture, and read extensively on the topic. In the end, Willow Creek adopted non-gender-based giftedness as one of its core values. Like the Salvation Army, Willow Creek wrote its commitments to women and men in ministry in a policy statement.[48]

Conclusion

Booth used the pamphlet for persuasion during the Victorian era, sharing the message that women have a right to equality in ministry. Booth's success with the pamphlet suggests that Christians can leverage social media to get attention and then point audiences to deeper content. Booth's pamphlet remains relevant because women's full participation in ministry is still "a subject of vast importance to the interests of Christ's kingdom and the glory of God."[49] In 1888, suffering from the breast cancer that would take her life, Booth delivered her last public address at City Temple, London. She urged those present to preach the gospel to the whole world. Her stirring reminder "There is no improving the future, without disturbing the present"[50] still rings true.

CHAPTER 25

SAINT THÉRÈSE OF LISIEUX: DEMONSTRATING HOSPITALITY TO DIFFICULT PEOPLE IN PRACTICAL WAYS

Mary Albert Darling

Abstract: Saint Thérèse of Lisieux (1873–1897) was asked to write about her life in her last six months on earth. Her collection of autobiographical materials in *The Story of a Soul* resulted in Thérèse becoming the youngest Doctor of the Catholic Church. Her work contains captivating stories of spiritual and communication practices that resulted in Thérèse showing hospitality to others in practical, "little ways." These same habits can be employed today as a means by which to generously welcome the stranger in our midst.

Introduction

At age fifteen, Thérèse of Lisieux entered a convent in nineteenth-century France. Her heart's desire was to daily demonstrate love for God and others in the context of a cloistered life. Thérèse quickly discovered that this desire was a daily, often intense, struggle to act in loving ways toward certain nuns she found especially difficult to be around. In her autobiography, *The Story of a Soul*, Thérèse writes about one nun who had "the faculty of displeasing me in everything, in her ways, her words, her character, everything seems *very disagreeable* to me."[1] When tempted to respond negatively to the nun in conversation, Thérèse became "content with giving her my most friendly smile."[2] At other times, Thérèse could not contain her negative responses. In those situations, she would flee the situation, running "away like a deserter."[3] When her struggles with this particular nun were not as intense, Thérèse decided to do for this nun what she would do for the person she loved the most. She committed to pray for this Sister and serve her however possible. Despite Thérèse's internal struggles, the Sister seemed to experience Thérèse's interactions as loving and affectionate.[4]

What Thérèse faced in her cloistered life is what the world continues to face in the twenty-first century: a difficulty to communicate in specific, civil, and

welcoming ways to those who are "displeasing" or different. A close reading of
Thérèse's *The Story of a Soul* suggests that her vocation of love involves three key
practices: solitude with God, acting *as if*, and communicating with intentionality. In nineteenth-century France, Thérèse's entered cloistered life at a very early
age, and once in the monastery, she participated in a way of life that centered
on the key values of prayer and contemplation, life in community, and service
to others. It was in this context that she wrote *The Story of a Soul*. For us today,
Thérèse's life and writing offers an important way to welcome the stranger in
our land, particularly refugees and immigrants (see Lev 19:34; Heb 13:2).

The Little Way

Thérése's *The Story of a Soul* reveals specific practices that led her to live her
life in a vocation of love for God. Although not named as such in her writings,
her "little ways" emerged from three interrelated practices: being alone with
God, acting *as if*, and communicating with intentionality.

First, Thérèse spent periods of time alone with God in prayer, and these
times of solitude included reflection on Scripture and silent contemplation.[5]
Thérèse's calling to a vocation of love occurred during one of these moments of
solitude. In September 1896, she was meditating on a desire to carry out "the
most heroic deeds"[6] for Jesus, like Joan of Arc. Thérèse opened her Bible to the
letters of the apostle Paul, hoping to find an answer for her intense desires. She
came upon 1 Corinthians 12:27–28 and read Paul's words that not everyone
can be apostles or prophets or teachers; instead, we are all different members
of one body. This gave her no peace, so she continued reading and found great
consolation in what Paul describes as the "most excellent way" of love (1 Cor
12:31 NRSV). It was at that moment that she discovered her vocation:

> I understood that LOVE COMPRISED ALL VOCATIONS, THAT LOVE WAS
> EVERYTHING, THAT IT EMBRACED ALL TIMES AND PLACES . . . IN A
> WORD, THAT IT WAS ETERNAL! Then, in the excess of my delirious joy, I
> cried out: O Jesus, my Love . . . my vocation, at last I have found it. . . . MY
> VOCATION IS LOVE![7]

Instead of desiring the grand heroics of Joan of Arc, Thérèse's life embodied her
vocation of love in the smallest of actions, her so-called "little way."

Next, Thérèse recognized that these actions, although small, were often
not easy, and she had to press into the difficulty through acting *as if*. Thérèse
discovered how imperfect her love was for her Sisters. She writes, "I saw I didn't
love them as God loves them. Ah! I understand now that charity consists in
bearing with the faults of others, in not being surprised at their weakness, in
being edified by the smallest acts of virtue we see them practice."[8] For Thérèse,

bearing others' faults meant she was to act *as if* she loved her Sisters, even when she did not feel loving toward them. As Thérèse encountered other nuns throughout her day, she would remind herself that she was to be motivated by love, instead of how she felt about the person. That conscious desire to act as if she loved the other gave Thérèse the strength to respond in "the most excellent way" of love (1 Cor 12:31).

She knew it was not hypocritical to act in ways that did not feel natural; rather, it was precisely in this little way that she was to become more loving. One such example was Thérèse's irritation with a nun who made a clicking noise that greatly annoyed her. What she wanted to do was glare at the Sister making the noise, but instead she "remained calm . . . and tried to unite myself to God and to forget the little noise. Everything was useless . . . and I was obliged simply to make a prayer of suffering. . . . I tried to love the little noise which was so displeasing."[9] Thérèse "took that irritating little noise and turned it into a feeling of love."[10]

Thérèse did not only act *as if* when she came upon a difficult nun in the course of her daily routines, but she also intentionally sought out and communicated with those who irritated her. Thérèse's intent was not to change others but to obey the command to love through showing a welcoming spirit to those who displeased her. Thérèse writes specifically of one such intentional encounter. She offered her services to one of the nuns who needed help, but the nun's physical state made it such that she was not easy to please. Furthermore, this Sister did not want Thérèse to help her because she was not one of her regular helpers. Although the nun finally accepted Thérèse's offer, she regularly complained that Thérèse was not helping her "correctly." Nevertheless, Thérèse found great satisfaction in helping, saying that she "did not want to lose such a beautiful opportunity for exercising charity, remembering the words of Jesus: 'Whatever you do to the least of my brothers, you do to me.'"[11] Thérèse found this memory particularly helpful, likening it to a perfume that helped her to be intentional in future acts of charity.[12]

The Little Way in Nineteenth-Century France

Thérèse of Lisieux was born Marie-Françoise-Thérèse Martin on January 2, 1873, in Alençon, France. It was a peaceful time for Alençon, having recently been liberated after the 1870 Franco-German war. Thérèse was the youngest of nine children, five of whom survived into adulthood. Both parents, Saint Marie-Azélie Guérin (Zélie), a lacemaker, and Saint Louis Martin, a watchmaker, were devout Catholics. All five surviving daughters became nuns, which was not uncommon in that day and age, especially with such deeply religious parents. In August of 1877 Thérèse's mother died, and her sister Pauline became a second mother to her. When Thérèse was nine years told, Pauline entered the Carmelite monastery at Lisieux, as did her oldest sister Marie. Thérèse was devastated at losing both of them and wanted to join the Carmelites but was too young. The desire, however, did not leave her and she kept trying to enter at an earlier than acceptable age.

When she was fourteen, Thérèse went with her father and a group from Lisieux on a pilgrimage to Rome that had been granted an audience with the pope. She took full advantage of the situation and asked the pope for permission to enter life at the convent at the age of fifteen. In April of the next year she started her cloistered life at the Carmelite monastery, a life she would live there until she died of tuberculosis on September 30, 1897, at the age of twenty-four.

Life in the Carmelite Order in Thérèse's day encompassed the same values as it does today: prayer and contemplation, life in community, and service.[13] Daily times devoted to prayer and contemplation are seen as the impetus for living in loving community and service to others and, as such, are the foundational values of the Order. Prayer in the Carmelite Order emphasizes *lectio divina*, reading and reflection on Scripture that then leads into a time of being in deep silence and contemplation with God.[14] These times of solitude are intended to infuse those in the Order with the love of Christ that then flows into community and service.

The Carmelite Order also values life in community, or the breaking down of barriers between and among people. These communities are intended to show the world that it is possible to live in harmony with those who are different from one another. Additionally, the service, or "apostolate," a nun could be called to would vary considerably. Nuns could be called on to go out into the world or to serve within the community. Prayer could also be seen as an intentional service, in terms of showing the world what loving communities could look like as a result of prayer. Although these values were and are admirable, there were strict expectations and punishments if those expectations were not met; the living conditions were at times uncomfortable; and not all nuns were easy to live with, as Thérèse's writing testifies.

Although Thérèse saw worldwide change coming from her writings as a real possibility, they were never intended for worldwide publication. *The Story of a Soul* consists of three manuscripts labeled A, B, and C. The first manuscript was for family; the second was for her sister Marie; and the third was for gathering information to be sent out on Thérèse's death.[15] Two months before her death, Thérèse made what is now considered her famous prediction: "I feel that my mission is about to begin, my mission of making others love God as I love Him, my mission of teaching my little way to souls. If God answers my requests, my heaven will be spent on earth up until the end of the world. Yes, I want to spend my heaven in doing good on earth."[16] As a result of this premonition, Thérèse asked her sister Pauline to edit as she saw necessary.[17] What resulted was a book that has sold millions of copies worldview. Thérèse's "little way" of being welcoming to others through smiles, kind words, and acts of charity, especially when she did not feel like it, clearly resonates today as well as it did in nineteenth-century France.

The Little Way for Today

One of the more divisive and complicated issues in the United States and the world is that of immigration and refugees. Many have labeled immigrants and refugees as lazy people, a drain on society, terrorists, and more.[18] This negative discourse was ramped up during the 2016 U.S. presidential election, especially as candidate Trump justified the building a wall between Mexico and the United States.[19] Trump's labeling here is an example of "othering." Othering is a strategy where groups form their own identity through the practice of disregarding certain people and groups that they are not like "us." As philosopher Simone de Beauvoir observes, othering has a kind of inescapability to it and appears in a wide variety of places:

> In small-town eyes all persons not belonging to the village are "strangers" and suspect; to the native of a country all who inhabit other countries are "foreigners"; Jews are "different" for the anti-Semite, Negroes are "inferior" for American racists, aborigines are "natives" for colonists, proletarians are the "lower class" for the privileged.[20]

In short, othering gives people a reason to alienate those who are seen as different and is counter to how Thérèse of Lisieux sought to consistently practice her little way of welcoming others she deemed different and displeasing.

Tragically, the church has been known to practice "othering" toward immigrants and refugees. For example, Robert Jeffress, senior pastor of First Baptist Dallas, delivered a sermon at St. John's Episcopal Church in Washington, DC, the morning of the president's inauguration. With the president-elect in attendance, Jeffress offered a reading of the book of Nehemiah that supported Trump's promise to build a wall between the United State and Mexico.[21] Similarly, a Pew Research Center survey found that 76 percent of white evangelical Protestants approved of Donald Trump's January 2017 travel ban, a ban that many Americans saw as othering Muslims.[22] Evangelical leaders who supported the ban included Jerry Falwell Jr., the president of Liberty University, and evangelist Franklin Graham, who offered a defense for the ban, stating that it was not a biblical issue.[23]

Thérèse saw the true test of welcoming to be that of following Jesus' command to "love your neighbor as yourself" no matter how difficult or displeasing that neighbor might be.[24] In relation to refugees and immigrants, Thérèse's vocation of love suggests that loving our neighbor means showing hospitality to these strangers, especially as we confront our fear of these peoples who are not like us.

For the church to move more in the direction of supporting immigrants and refugees in loving, tangible, and sustainable ways, it need look no further than Thérèse's practices of being alone with God, acting *as if*, and communicating with intentionality, all of which are evident at Dearborn Free Methodist (FM) Church, especially as the church welcomes Muslim immigrants and refugees. Consistent with Thérèse's vocation of love, before engaging in concrete acts of hospitality, Dearborn FM churchgoers are invited to meditate on a biblical passage and pray. Such encounters aim to let God's love transform the church, so that others' experiences are experiences of Christ's love in them. The selection of biblical passage is very important. For example, Christians might engage in reflection on biblical passages that urge readers to welcome strangers and foreigners. For instance, in Leviticus 19:34, God tells Israel, "The stranger who resides with you shall be to you as one of your citizens" (NRSV). The parable of the Good Samaritan also encourages North American Christians to love those we may consider our enemy (Lk 10:25–37). Solitude with God regarding passages such as these might very well encourage Christians to release their fear of those God tells us to love. As Pastor Dustin Weber maintains, "Everything that we do comes out of a place of prayer first," which also includes contemplation as a significant part of the prayer life and teaching in the church.[25]

In terms of acting *as if*, the leadership of Dearborn FM asks its members to show warmth and positive regard in their acts of hospitality. One such example is an ESL (English as a Second Language) Day Camp for refugee children. The weeklong camp aims to "provide elementary age refugee children space to learn and practice English in a safe and fun environment."[26] However, acting *as if* also includes a disposition appropriate to acts of love and hospitality. The church asks volunteers to be "friendly outgoing people willing to make a difference in kids' lives."[27] While church members might fear Arab immigrants and refugees, acting *as if* one is friendly toward them means pressing into one of the key difficulties of Thérèse's vocation of love. Christians may find it difficult to love their Arab neighbors. However, our feelings do not change the demand God makes on us to love. Acting *as if* one is friendly is simply a little way of showing God's love to a stranger.

For Dearborn FM, intentional community building and service to immigrants and refugees includes a range of embodied acts: community dinners,[28] providing meals in the first weeks of being in the United States, putting together food boxes, helping with rent and other expenses, donating home goods, and offering classes to help in their acclimation to a different culture.[29] Concerning community dinners, for example, Dearborn FM assistant pastor Megan Weber argues that the dinner is not about food. Rather, such acts of hospitality offer space where Christians can intentionally "lay aside our agenda—or our need to convert the other—and just be, and listen, and let God develop trust and relationship."[30] As Weber explains, the intention of the act is to change the Christian. In eating with those not like the Christian, a Christian has an opportunity to become a "good listener" first, after which trust and relationality may follow. The dinner, therefore, is best understood as a gift to the Christian, whereby God can release her from her fear of those not like her.

Conclusion

In conclusion, Thérèse's "little way" of showing hospitality, through specific words and actions, is actually not so little. It is full of everyday acts of hospitality that can lead to worldwide change when it comes to welcoming the stranger in our land. Thérèse's vocation of love involved time alone with God, reflecting on Scripture, and praying within the context of life in community. Those times helped empower her to respond in welcoming ways to others within that community.

We, too, can follow Thérèse's example. Taking what she learned from daily solitude with God into interactions with others is how Thérèse lived out her little way of love. This is how we too can act not only as individuals, but also in our churches and other bodies of believers, especially when it comes to welcoming immigrants and refugees into our churches, neighborhoods, and homes.

CHAPTER 26

WALTER RAUSCHENBUSCH: PROVIDING A ROAD MAP FOR SOCIAL CRITIQUE

Christina Littlefield

Abstract: Walter Rauschenbusch (1861–1918) inspired American Christians with a prophetic vision of the Kingdom of God. Rauschenbusch carefully balanced his belief in the sacredness of each person with his insistence on the social nature of sin, critiquing how rapid industrialization and urbanization had broken down human relations. His thought culminated in his 1917 work *A Theology for the Social Gospel*. His work provides a road map for communicating social critique and improvement in the digital twenty-first century.

Introduction

The dawn of the twentieth century witnessed the peak of revolutionary fervor over the social issues and class divides created by rapid industrialization and urbanization. The public perception of men like Standard Oil owner John D. Rockefeller shifted from captain of industry to robber baron as public outcry swelled against monopolistic practices.[1] Many Christian social reformers attacked Rockefeller directly, calling the $100,000 donation Rockefeller gave to the American Board of Commissioners for Foreign Missions in 1904 "tainted" and urged the mission board to reject the donation.[2] Strangely, the most socialist-leaning social gospel leader, Walter Rauschenbusch, stayed silent.[3]

Rauschenbusch's critique of the money powers went further than that of his peers, as he argued that natural resources like oil should not line one person's pocket but be managed as public trusts for the common good.[4] However, Rauschenbusch did not raise any direct critique against Rockefeller. Indeed, the two men, both Northern Baptists, were on friendly terms, as Rockefeller financially supported Rauschenbusch's work and Rauschenbusch sent Rockefeller his books and clippings of his lectures.[5]

This paradox between Rauschenbusch's condemnation of the consolidation of wealth in the hands of the few and his friendship with someone engaged in such behavior is perplexing until one understands the tension between Rauschenbusch's two convictions that, first, every individual is sacred and, second, that society's collective social sins were far greater than individual failings.

Rauschenbusch believed American capitalism encouraged Rockefeller's sins and that it was better to critique the system than to attack individuals; it was better to expose the root of the problem than to point at the bad fruit.

Rauschenbusch's 1917 theological treatise *A Theology for the Social Gospel* critiques the failures of the social order and provides the ideal for which individual Christians and their churches should strive.[6] In this work, Rauschenbusch's prophetic imagination inspires people of faith to attack social ills and provides them with an "alternative consciousness" to move toward.[7] His prophetic communication style of emphasizing social sins over individual failings provides a road map for how Christians can speak prophetically to the social order without resorting to personal attacks or partisan politics. Instead, Christians should recognize their own culpability, expose problems, and seek kingdom solutions. As Rauschenbusch focused on how economic inequality undermined democratic equality, this chapter will focus on how Christians might address those issues today.

A Theology for the Social Gospel

In *A Theology for the Social Gospel,* Rauschenbusch contrasts the Kingdom of God with the Kingdom of Evil, presenting a social view of salvation as a remedy for a social view of sin. Rauschenbusch defines the Kingdom of Evil as social sin organized to protect its ongoing evildoings against any attempts to bring light to the darkness.[8] Rauschenbusch rejected the idea that sin was between God and man alone. Rather, sin always undercuts human relations. Putting profit and ambition above the welfare of fellow human beings is to sin against God *and* our brothers and sisters.[9]

Rauschenbusch contends that the doctrine of original sin rightfully captures that sin is passed on socially and that "one generation corrupts the next."[10] The dominant culture of a society and the social powers within it endorse and normalize social sins from consumerism to racism to militarism, making it hard for individuals to see their own culpability in perpetuating those sins. Further, corporations benefit financially from social sins, and those corporations corrupt legislators, courts, police, the military, property owners, and religious leaders to stay in power and maximize their profits.[11] The social nature of sin is the only explanation Rauschenbusch sees for the suffering of the world. As he observes, "Society is so integral that when one man sins, other men suffer, and when one social class sins, the other classes are involved in the suffering which follows on that sin."[12] All of the above culminates in the Kingdom of Evil, and only an equally socialized Kingdom of God can correct it.

For Rauschenbusch, Jesus died not just to save human beings from their individual vices but also from the social sins that corrupt kingdom ideals.

Rauschenbusch contends that all human beings have coalesced in the social sins that led to Jesus' death on the cross. He identifies six social sins that collaborated in the death of Christ: the religious bigotry of the religious leaders, who used their political power for their own ends; the corruption of justice, in which innocent people are declared guilty; the mob spirit, or the social spirit gone mad; the militarist mentality of the empire, as the soldiers beat Jesus; and class contempt, as crucifixion was a punishment only for the lowest classes. The guilt of those who ordered Jesus' death spread to "all who reaffirm the acts which killed him."[13]

The Kingdom of God, however, is capable of summoning social force against the Kingdom of Evil. Rauschenbusch defines the kingdom as humanity reorganized to follow the will of God. Because of Christ's emphasis on the divine worth of every individual, Rauschenbusch believed the kingdom "tends toward a social order which will best guarantee to all personalities their freest and highest development."[14] Living in the Kingdom of Evil brings us into opposition with God, but following Jesus' example of living for the Kingdom of God fundamentally alters the relation between God and humanity, bringing God and humans back into "spiritual solidarity."[15] Those who seek the Kingdom of God fight the Kingdom of Evil with all their might, but they do not do so in their own power.

Rauschenbusch believed it was the prophetic power of the Holy Spirit that gave the social gospel its fervor, providing a spiritual impulse to reform efforts that allowed Christ's followers to outwork their secular peers. The social gospel "sees before it the Kingdom of Evil to be overcome, and the Kingdom of God to be established, and it cries aloud for an inspired word of God to give faith and power and guidance."[16] He argues the most fruitful contributions to Christian theology have come from those Christians who possessed a "prophetic vision" and rooted their theology in an understanding of the past, a deep concern for present social problems, and the hope for a future more in line with God's kingdom.[17]

The kingdom, therefore, is always present and future, where God's end purpose must be the end purpose for his people. It is a gift from God that cannot be ushered in with human initiative but toward which God tasks us all to work. Jesus Christ initiated the Kingdom of God as God's prophet, filled with the Holy Spirit. Through the Holy Spirit, God calls Christians today into Christ's kingdom work and into that same prophetic vocation. However, we always work in hope, because God's Kingdom will only be fulfilled through God's power and in God's own time.[18]

Rauschenbusch's Time

Rauschenbusch was attempting to vindicate Christianity and show that Christ had the power to heal the social ills that rapid industrialization, urbanization, and immigration caused at the turn of the twentieth century. Rauschenbusch's lifespan covers the post-Civil War Gilded Age and the Progressive Era, when American society rapidly shifted from primarily agriculture to industry, drawing millions from the farms to the cities, leading to awful working conditions, overcrowded tenements, disease, poor sanitation, unhealthy food, lack of clean water and air, rising alcoholism, and looser morals. The industrial revolution improved the quality of life for many, but it also created sharp divides between the haves and have-nots.[19] The rise of big trusts, labor unions, and economic socialism made both Christian and secular reformers fear there would be a revolution if social ills were not corrected quickly.[20]

Rauschenbusch perceived that churches were losing the upper and lower working classes, and that Protestant evangelicals were losing their influence on the nation's moral values. The old, individualized gospel had lost sight of the social teachings of the Hebrew prophets and of Jesus Christ. A more holistic gospel was needed, and the social gospel was born as an attempt to apply Jesus' teachings to every aspect of life: individually, socially, politically, and economically.

Rauschenbusch's work stems from his years as a pastor to the Second German Baptist Church in Hell's Kitchen, New York. The church was made up of working-class immigrants.[21] Of all the poverty, loss, and death he experienced ministering to the congregation, he wrote that it was the children's funerals that convinced him of the need for a more holistic gospel, one that would serve the spiritual, physical, emotional, and intellectual needs of humans.[22] He found that gospel in the kingdom ideal, which he had contemplated since reading Friedrich Schleiermacher and Albrecht Ritschl.[23]

American social gospel leaders spent several decades crying out in the wilderness before their arguments reached ascendancy within Protestant evangelical Christianity at the dawn of the twentieth century.[24] There was, of course, conservative pushback, notably in the publications of the *Fundamentals*.[25] The social gospel movement led to the establishment of the Federal Council of Churches and the 1908 social creed.[26] The social gospel provided the theological foundation for the Progressive Movement and many later social justice efforts.

A Theology for the Social Gospel was published during World War I. What makes this work unique is the systematic nature in which Rauschenbusch pores over Christian doctrines on sin and the atonement, and how he deepens the theology he shared with fellow social gospel leaders. Rauschenbusch also answers his critics who charged that his emphasis on environmental influences discounted the ubiquitousness of human sin.[27] While Rauschenbusch acknowledged the fairness of that charge, he wanted to widen conceptions of sin from individual sins, such as drinking or dancing, to social sins, such as those occurring under unrestrained capitalism.[28] Though later versions of the social gospel stray from Christian orthodoxy, the early social gospel under Rauschenbusch is evangelical to its core, with the ultimate goal of Christianizing the world.

Regaining a Prophetic Vision Today

The social sins that concerned Rauschenbusch run amuck in today's world, particularly in the United States, which still suffers from religious, ethnic, and class divides; power differentials between the elite and the disenfranchised; systematic racism in the justice system; the militarization of the police; the privatization of prisons; and the mob spirit dividing Right and Left in politics. Rauschenbusch argues that those who quietly benefit or silently acquiesce to these sins are as much of a part of the Kingdom of Evil as those who are active participants.[29]

Regaining a prophetic vision of the Kingdom of God requires first and foremost that Christians recognize their own culpability in perpetuating the social sins of the Kingdom of Evil. Kingdom ideals get slashed by a thousand little cuts. Rauschenbusch was primarily concerned with how economic inequalities undermined democratic relations, and he explored how average, everyday Christians helped perpetuate those economic inequalities. To him, Christians should consider the ethics of the products they purchase and spend every dollar with an eye toward stewardship of resources owed to God. Instead, greed, consumerism, and desire for a bargain, ignorance of the labor conditions in which a product is made, and turning a blind eye to the plight of the working classes all help economic inequalities to fester and grow. In response, Rauschenbusch argues that Christians need to lose their indifference, awaken to the realities of their own social sins, and leverage kingdom values for solutions to these sins.

First, Rauschenbusch argued that those with power and money continue to stay on top because good people give up what power they have through indifference. If he were speaking today, he might point to how lobbyists are allowed to influence legislation because too few people make their voices heard. He might also call attention to how the media focus on the horse race in an election instead of the issues, because that is what media consumers click on. Or he might preach on how the top percent pours their money into politics because splashy political advertisements are more likely to sway uninformed voters than rational debate. In a fallen world, dominated as it is by the Kingdom of Evil, Rauschenbusch argues that we all slowly and quietly accept the world's ways, and we need to wake up to its ways. As Rauschenbusch writes, "The social gospel opens our eyes to the ways in which religious men do all these things. It plunges us in a new baptism of repentance."[30]

Second, once awakened to how they contribute to economic inequalities or any issue of social injustice, Christians should work to educate others. Rauschenbusch was involved in early exposure work, what Americans often call "muckraking" after the Progressive Era investigative journalism movement. His publications and national lecture tours were designed to help expose Christians to the social problems in capitalist society and see an alternative that would bring the world into more brotherly labor relations. But he was also actively involved in his community in Rochester, New York, supporting religious and secular efforts to improve conditions for the working poor and hosting Sunday evening lectures to educate the community.[31] When the Holy Spirit has convicted a person on an issue of economic inequality or any issue of social justice, Christians today can spur reform in a myriad of different ways, from modeling practices such as buying fair-trade certified products (such as coffee, tea, and chocolate, which protect developing world producers and ensures they get paid fairly), to actively petitioning for laws that ensure living wages and safe working conditions, engaging in advocacy work such as social media campaigns to pressure companies to improve their labor practices, or actively educating others through Sunday school classes, sermons, or lectures.

The church's mission was primarily to educate the social conscience, and the individual Christian's job was to apply those principles, but both were called to pursue the Kingdom of God through active ministry to the "least of these" of whom Jesus speaks in Matthew 25. The church should promote the biblical ideal, digging deep into the words of Jesus and the prophets, helping their members wrestle with what Scripture might say about a social ill today. For example, I led my church through a twelve-week series looking at what Jesus had to say on social inequality in terms of race relations, immigration, Islamophobia, class stratification, and gender divides. Most social-gospel advocates inspired reform by exposing problems and identifying solutions. As Rauschenbusch remarked, "This is the chief significance of the social gospel for the doctrine of sin. It revives the vision of the Kingdom of God. When men see the actual world over against the religious ideal, they become conscious of its constitutional defects and wrongs."[32]

Third, Christians should go to the root of social problems while forging kingdom-inspired solutions. Rauschenbusch never attacked individuals. He kept his political party under wraps. Rather, he spoke broadly about the economic inequalities he saw and hoped his messages would convict those perpetuating those inequalities. Christians should not be drawn into individual attacks or mistake the prophetic voice for a political voice, Republican or Democrat. The prophetic road is higher than the attacks on cable news shows or from politicians purporting to be Christians. This means directing the prophetic critique at larger social institutions, rather than at individuals caught up in the sins of those institutions. The church should be asking the poignant questions about what Scripture might teach in any given situation and forever broadcast that kingdom ideal.

Rauschenbusch was concerned with how the social sins of materialism, greed, and selfishness corrupt local and national politics, buy legislation, and undermine democracy. This is particularly relevant today, with the Supreme Court's 2010 decision in *Citizens United v. Federal Election Commission*, which allows corporations and unions to spend unlimited funds on political campaigns as long as they do not give directly to a candidate.[33] Rauschenbusch refused to attack Rockefeller or other millionaires of his day who could buy political contests, but he did attack how those with money and power were undermining democracy. It is better, Rauschenbusch believed, to go to the root of how political contests have become all flash and no substance, necessitating billions of dollars in funds to run ever-longer campaigns. Better yet to point out how this broken political system undermined the brotherly (and sisterly) relations mandated by the Kingdom of God, which calls for Christians today to amplify the voices of all, particularly those who do not have the political or economic power to speak.

Conclusion

Rauschenbusch believed that pointing to social sins would convict individuals far more than personal attacks, leading them to make changes that would reverberate into society. Rauschenbusch's prophetic voice always showed the gap between human reality and God's ideal and pushed society toward the ideal. He called us to repentance, he called us to the kingdom ideal, he called us to fight for the Kingdom of God. He called each saved individual to become a redeemer with Christ, living his or her Christianity in the workplace, home, market, and public service.

Rauschenbusch's prophetic vision has had wide reverberations in society. *Huffington Post* Global Spirituality and Religion Editor Paul Brandeis Rauschenbush, the great-grandson of Rauschenbusch, described the 100th anniversary edition of Rauschenbusch's *Christianity and the Social Crisis* as "the classic that woke up the church."[34] The current Rauschenbush, who edited the 2007 edition, included essays discussing his great-grandfather's contributions from contemporary scholars such as philosopher Richard Rorty, Red Letter Christian leaders Jim Wallis and Tony Campolo, theologian Stanley Hauerwas, and philosopher Cornel West. Despite the church's struggle to fully implement his ideas, Rauschenbusch's work influenced these scholars and the likes of brothers Reinhold and Richard Niebuhr, Martin Luther King Jr., Mahatma Gandhi, and even President Barack Obama. As Rauschenbusch frequently wrote, there is always further progress to be made in pursuit of the kingdom. "The Kingdom of God is always coming, but we can never say 'Lo here.'"[35]

CHAPTER 27

Abraham Kuyper: Rejecting Approaches That Blur Epistemic, Academic, and Theological Boundaries

Mark A. Gring and Frank Fuentes

Abstract: Abraham Kuyper (1837–1920) challenged those who accepted pantheistic, boundary-blurring epistemic, academic, and theological assumptions. Kuyper's "Blurring of the Boundaries" speech presents Christianity as the antithesis of humanity's challenge of God for his place as supreme ruler. Kuyper uses his understanding of redemptive history, the sovereignty of Christ, revolution, and antithesis to encourage Christians to confront cultural norms and reestablish godly boundaries in thought and in the academy.

Introduction

In 1863, after earning a doctorate in theology, Abraham Kuyper received his first church appointment in the city of Beesd, Netherlands. Kuyper was born and raised as a Dutch Reformed Calvinist. However, as he proceeded through his formal education, the rationalistic enlightenment of his era swayed him, and he ended his formal education as an agnostic. Nevertheless, he took a church appointment, and as an educated, liberal pastor, he desired to meet his congregants personally. There was an uneducated, unmarried, miller's daughter, who at first refused to meet with him and then refused to shake his hand when they did meet. Her name was Pietje Baltus, a "pious malcontent" and less-than-welcoming congregant who assumed that Kuyper was just another liberal pastor who disdained her Calvinistic commitments.[1] While Baltus's faith at first appeared simple, it was based on biblical foundations that were certain, true, and unmovable. Over the ensuing years, Kuyper realized that Baltus's stubbornness had moved his heart to grasp Christianity as a world-and-life commitment and to accept Christ as the sovereign Lord over all. Kuyper went on to challenge the assumptions of his time and to begin communicating through the church, education, journalism, and politics as means to reform people and culture. By his death in 1920, Abraham Kuyper had been a pastor, theologian, educator, university founder, editor of a weekly and a daily newspaper, a politician, and prime minister of the Netherlands, who had published multiple essays, pamphlets, and books.

This chapter examines two of Kuyper's speeches at the Free University of Amsterdam and focuses on the way that an acceptance of pantheism—Kuyper's forewarning of postmodernism—destroys a Christian world-and-life view. Kuyper's system of thinking, known as "neo-Calvinism," argues that Christ did not come to just save sinners but also to transform people, institutions, and culture. Abraham Kuyper challenges intellectual norms and communicates reform by exalting the sovereignty of Christ, showing the divide between Creator and creation, and arguing against any system of thought that blurs God's ordained boundaries. We conclude by applying Kuyper's ideas to the presumption of communication as the queen of the sciences and the assumption that humans create reality by their speech.

Beware Blurring the Boundaries

Kuyper was a prolific author. From the hundreds of essays and presentations he gave, we briefly mention two of Kuyper's education-focused speeches presented to the Free University of Amsterdam with a focus on the second one. The first is Kuyper's October 1880 inaugural address to the Free University of Amsterdam titled "Sphere Sovereignty," and the second is his 1892 address as the outgoing university rector, "The Blurring of the Boundaries."

In his 1880 inaugural address to the university, "Sphere Sovereignty," Kuyper urges a marginalized Christian academic community to support the new university.[2] He justifies why each academic area should organize as its own sovereign sphere and emphasizes a broader Christian involvement in all of life under Christ's absolute sovereignty. His most famous lines from this speech, possibly his most famous quote, solidifies this relationship:

> Man in his antithesis as fallen *sinner* or self-developing *natural creature* returns again as the "subject that thinks" or "the object that prompts thought" in every department, in every discipline and with every investigator. Oh, no single piece of our mental world is to be hermetically sealed off from the rest, and there is not a square inch in the whole domain of our human existence over which Christ, who is Sovereign over *all*, does not cry: "Mine"![3]

Kuyper's biblical world-and-life view had an impact beyond academia. "Christ as Sovereign" is reflected in the mission and goals for the Free University of Amsterdam, in Kuyper's establishment of the Anti-Revolutionary Party and becoming prime minister, and in his encouragement to Christians to start their own social institutions.

In his 1892 speech "The Blurring of the Boundaries," Kuyper evaluates "the entire course of the nineteenth-century European culture"[4] by identifying and condemning philosophical *pantheism* as the normative assumption that eliminates the God-ordained line of distinction between Creator and created. Kuyper's stated main points are "to demonstrate, first *that* the spirit of our age in fact inclines in this direction; next, what *dangers* this tendency brings in its wake; finally, what *resistance* must be offered here."[5] He explains the assumptions behind postmodernist ideas by introducing Friedrich Nietzsche to the Netherlands and critiquing his God-defying arguments along with the works of "Hegel, Darwin and Schleiermacher, yogis and Gnostics, the cult of progress, and what we would call the demotion of 'character' to 'personality.'"[6] Pantheism can be defined as either believing God is in everything or that everything is God. If either of these perspectives is accepted, it eliminates the recognition that God is distinct from his creation because both become fused into one. As such, humans-as-God presume autonomy (self-law) and thus do not believe they are morally responsible to the sovereign Creator whose moral law is revealed to all. Similarly, it makes the worship of God (Christianity) equally a part of all things and all thought rather than maintaining the distinct biblical tension of being in the world but not of the world. Kuyper ultimately argues that "pantheism blurs all distinctions, obscures all boundary lines, and shows a tendency to wash out all contrasts."[7]

In this speech Kuyper mentions three areas that pantheism affects: religious, practical, and philosophical. He argues that the philosophical is most dangerous because it "systematically fuses every thesis and antithesis into a *synthesis* and, being fascinated by the concept of identity, casts all that seem dissimilar as similar, indeed, finally as being of the same substance."[8] When things and persons are perceived as being the same substance, it masks the fact that God creates people and things to have both similarities (unity) and differences (plurality). Kuyper was especially concerned that this "blurring of the boundaries" would push society to a fake uniformity based on a monism. As one theologian explains, "Nothing was more repugnant to Kuyper in politics and in the church, for example, than a kind of *forced and artificial unity or oneness.*"[9]

Kuyper urges scholars at the Free University to draw clear boundaries between Christian thought based on God's revelation and the dominant ideas of their day. Early in this presentation Kuyper argues that God is the one who makes distinctions and draws lines. He states, "In Scripture God is called by the Hebrew word *Hammadbdîl*, because He it was who drew lines, first between Himself and the created world, and then throughout the entire domain of the created world."[10] These boundary lines include distinction of design, demarcation, separation, contrast, and differentiation between God and humanity, animals and humans, day and night, work and rest, male and female, and good and evil—among many other distinctions. It is precisely these lines that pantheism seeks to eliminate and which Kuyper challenges by emphasizing the difference in the classical forms of thesis and antithesis. The anti-God norms are the thesis and God's revelation is the antithesis. Kuyper saw that Christians often need to act in ways that are counter (antithesis) to their culture and must challenge the prevailing assumptions and norms (thesis).

Kuyper in the Flow of (Reformation) History

The Protestant Reformation developed full-orbed through the sixteenth-century writings of John Calvin and later writings of the English Puritans, Scottish covenanters, and Dutch Reformers. These theological commitments influenced the political behaviors of William and Mary of Orange, coregents over the kingdoms of England, Scotland, Ireland, and the Netherlands, who brought an end to Roman Catholic rule in England in 1688, the so-called Glorious Revolution. The Reformation embodied the motto *Ecclesia reformata, semper reformanda secundum verbum Dei* ("the church reformed and always reforming according to the word of God"). This principle propelled the Protestant Reformation and dominated Abraham Kuyper's approach to life.

By the early 1800s, however, Protestantism encountered the political realities of the American and French Revolutions. For Europeans, the French Revolution brought not only a promise of greater democratic participation that energized thinkers and reformers but also a threat of destruction. This revolution caused grave concern and fear among those who observed its openly anti-God hubris through bloodshed and the executions of royalty, intellectuals, rich, and poor. This revolution, in particular, rejected the existence of God and commitment to God's revelation as the basis for knowing, seeing, and acting. French revolutionaries dismissed Christianity as overly emotional and zealous as opposed to the logical, scientific, and enlightened approach they chose. Ultimately the revolution framed science and religion as oppositional—setting the foundation for contemporary assumptions today.

The American War for Independence, on the other hand, was understood by Dutch historian Guillaume Groen van Prinsterer (1801–1876) and Abraham Kuyper as a godly challenge to British tyranny through duly-appointed sub-magistrates (that is, men elected to office). Van Prinsterer argued that the French Revolution, in all its phases, was a rejection of godly revelation, so a Dutch Anti-Revolutionary political party, based on Christian principles, was needed as a response.[11] In 1898, Kuyper concluded that Americans applied godly principles in reasonably good, but certainly not perfect, ways to bring about a biblical change. As such, the American independence offered hope, because it showed that representative democratic involvement and just institutions could be built on biblical, rather than revolutionary, principles. It was into this cultural context, based on these assumptions, that Abraham Kuyper presented his ideas, built his educational, social, and political institutions, and eventually became prime minister of the Netherlands (1901–1905) under the aegis of the Anti-Revolutionary Party.

Kuyper lived at the intersection of several historical trends and wanted to affect future sociopolitical directions but also retained the Reformed Christian heritage that had been influential in the Netherlands since the Protestant Reformation. Like other big-system thinkers of his time, he saw the intersection of Victorian systems, Reformed Christian commitments, German Idealism, and the rise of Modernism all coming together and bringing about the end of older political, social, and intellectual regimes. Although difficult, these changes also promised new possibilities. In particular, he was attracted to the fervor of German Idealism as opposed to the cold, dead religiosity that characterized the period before him. All of these changing ideas and revolutions repeatedly warned Kuyper that poor starting assumptions result in crumbling, failed outcomes.

Kuyper learned much from the critiques by van Prinsterer, who had written and lectured extensively about how "the Revolution" opposes God and his principles.[12] Van Prinsterer's reference to "the Revolution" encompassed all revolutions that dismiss godly principles and insert humanistic principles in their place—a blurring of the roles of God and humanity. Both of these men came to the conviction not only to be against revolutionary assumptions but also to be for a system of Christian thought that offered vision, direction, purpose, and hope.[13] Kuyper concluded that the foundation of thought needs to begin with an acceptance of biblical revelation and that Christians are called to build cultural structures and institutions based on a sovereign Creator God. Ultimately humans are dependent on God's general and special revelation to know or understand anything.

A Kuyperian Perspective on Human Communication

Kuyperian neo-Calvinism calls Christians to redeem people, culture, and institutions. This commences by first embracing and submitting to a sovereign God who superintends all of creation and whose created order arranges sovereign spheres and sets absolute boundaries between Creator and created. For communication as an academic discipline, Kuyper would argue that the field has its own rules, subject to God's revelation, for governing what it is and how it is to be studied. Boundary demarcations differentiate communication from anthropology, English, psychology, sociology, or theology, and communication should not be studied by the same rules that govern other academic areas.

While there may be mutually beneficial overlapping ideas between academic areas, each area of study is its own limited sovereign sphere and determines, based on God's revelation, what it is and how it should be studied. Ultimately, all academic areas are subject to God's revealed truth and should be studied for God's honor and glory with a recognition that God is Creator of all things and humans are, at best, sub-creators or re-arrangers of God's creation. We apply Kuyper's presuppositions to key assumptions predominant in the field of communication studies. First, current communication scholars tend to assume that communication should be seen as the queen of the sciences, and, second, the field tends to assume our speech creates truth and reality.

The role of communication in other academic fields and the relationship of speech to truth and reality are intertwined. The field's general reasoning assumes our speech creates "reality" and "truth," and no truth or reality exists separate from human talk. Thus it follows that the study of speech should be the basis for all study—the queen of the sciences. However, if we accept Kuyper's arguments about sphere sovereignty and Christianity as the antithesis of culture, then the study of communication has its own limited sphere, and it is not sovereign over other academic areas of study. It then follows that Christian communication scholars should not attempt to make their discipline the "queen of the sciences" as some contemporary scholars have tried to do.

The phrase "queen of the sciences" was used in the past to reference the high regard the study of theology had in the academy from the Middle Ages through the time of the Enlightenment. The term "science," at this time, was not limited to the application of the scientific method to naturalistic processes but is the Latin word for knowledge. The study of theology, then, was the ultimate study of knowledge, because God's general revelation through nature and special revelation through the Bible were the two ultimate sources of knowledge. Contemporary scholars who presume communication is the queen of the sciences want to make individual humanity or human processes the bases for all knowing and all knowledge. In contemporary communication studies, this argument has been most evident in the rhetoric-as-epistemic debate.[14] In this thirty-year debate, most scholars argued that no objective capital "T" truth existed, and if it did exist, it was beyond human ability to know it. Instead, these scholars argued that the only way humans can know is through a set of mental constructs, or abstract ideas about the mental constructs, that are either created by particular individuals or by the social groups to which people belong. Even two significant scholars, Richard A. Cherwitz and James W. Hikins, who argued for the existence of truth and humans' minimal ability to grasp it, were still unwilling to accept that all truth is God's truth and comes from God's general and special revelation.[15]

The study of human communication has much to offer other academic areas including biblical interpretation, psychology, sociology, business, and education, but it cannot, and should not, solely apply its own rules as the basis for understanding the other areas of study. Communication aids other academic areas of study in understanding language, how we use language to generate perspectives about God's revelation, and how we use language to ethically and unethically persuade. However, Christian communication scholars should not blur God-ordained boundaries that separate areas of study. They should ask questions about what those boundaries are, or should be. Because we are fallen, sinful creatures and our knowledge is affected by our creaturely perspectives and twisted sinfulness, the question about what is a God-ordained boundary is certainly open for academic and biblical thought, research, and debate.

Most importantly, the study of communication should maintain a clear view of the Creator-creature distinction that exists between God and humanity, and we should allow no one to blur these distinctions. God is the archetype and humans are mere ectypes; God knows fully and completely (*archetypal*), but we only know partially and incompletely (*ectypal*); God's knowledge is infinite and true while our knowledge is finite and frequently incorrect. These are biblical lines of demarcation between the Creator and the created, and to blur these boundaries places us in danger of presenting heresy as truth and placing ourselves above God.

A 2009 publication reports on an experiment that exemplifies the value of not blurring boundaries and what Christians can contribute to the rhetoric-as-epistemic debate.[16] In this study, the subjects were placed in an area they did not know well, a German forest and a Saharan desert, and were not allowed to view any fixed external objects like a sun, moon, stars, a mountaintop or other significant directional markers. In this "blinded" situation they were instructed to walk in a straight line. Even though the individuals thought they walked in a straight course, their GPS trackers showed they, instead, walked in ever-smaller concentric circles. The absence of an external fixed marker made it impossible to walk in a fixed course, but the presence of an external marker, like the sun or moon, allowed them to walk in a linear and direct course.

The situation is similar for us intellectually. If we have an external, fixed moral truth, such as we have with God and his special revelation, then we are able to "walk" in a clear, intellectually consistent way rather than revert to ever-smaller, subjectivist, and solipsistic assumptions about knowing. This fixed marker is significant when we engage in discussions about knowing, knowledge, our understanding of reality, and our ways of acting toward each other. If we grasp the self-attesting truth of Scripture, even with our inability to know it absolutely, then we have a reliable, external, fixed point by which we can evaluate our thinking and critique our understanding of what exits, what is true or false, and what is right or wrong. The acceptance of God's truth as a fixed certainty changes everything.

Conclusion

The conclusion to be drawn from Kuyper's arguments and actions is to take the Bible and God's sovereignty seriously. He argues against any syncretistic compromise with the "schemas of this world" (Rom 12:2) but, instead, argues that Christians can only challenge the norms of this world by thinking more Christianly and finding ways to apply a biblical world-and-life view to all aspects of our lives. Although imperfect, we challenge norms, communicate reform, and avoid blurring boundaries when we take seriously Kuyper's declaration that "there is not a square inch in the whole domain of our human existence over which Christ, who is Sovereign over *all*, does not cry: 'Mine!'"[17]

PART THREE:

Modern and Contemporary Christian Thinkers and Theologians

CHAPTER 28

Charles M. Sheldon: Promoting Accuracy and Advocacy in an Age of Constantly Competing Voices

Michael Ray Smith

Abstract: Charles M. Sheldon (1857–1946), author of the famous *In His Steps* novel, used his time during a one-week experiment as editor of the *Topeka Daily Capital* in March 1900 to provide an alternative model for the mainstream newspapers. Sheldon's Journalism of Accuracy provides a model for writers who want to include Christian-based faith in the multitude of voices lobbying to be heard.

Introduction

"If a thousand different Christian men who wished to edit Christian dailies should make an honest attempt to do so, the result might be a thousand different papers in very many particulars. In other words, these Christian editors might arrive at different conclusions in the interpretation of what is Christian," wrote Congregationalist minister Charles M. Sheldon in his one-week experiment (March 13–17, 1900), when he edited the Kansas *Topeka Daily Capital*, a mainstream newspaper using the question, "What would Jesus do?"[1]

Sheldon went on to write, "The only thing I or any other Christian man can do in the interpretation of what is Christian in the conduct of this paper is to define the term Christian the best that can be done after asking for divine wisdom, and not judge others who might with equal desire and sincerity interpret the probable action of Jesus in a different manner."[2] While Sheldon suggested that other Christian publishers might interpret the Christian-based approach differently, his editorials and news judgment are presented in his experiment as the dominant model for writers who want to include a Christian faith-based newspaper as characterized by the twin virtues of accuracy and advocacy.

In our age of false and "fake news," editorial misconduct, and infotainment, Sheldon's strident insistence on accuracy would be welcome and was certainly ahead of its time. To highlight Sheldon's model, this chapter explores an example of his use of a news story to generate reader response to famine relief. In addition, it examines Sheldon's conviction that the spirits (alcohol) industry was the evil of the day. The context of Sheldon's work will be explored by noting the conventions of the day and the controversial work of fellow publishers. Finally, I conclude with attention to Christian-based universities dedicated to both accuracy and advocacy in their teaching of journalism but always with an eye on the dangers of telling the unvarnished truth.

A Journalism of Advocacy and Accuracy

From March 13 to 17, 1900, the owners of the *Topeka Daily Capital* commissioned Sheldon to conduct his experiment for one week, more for the circulation bonanza than as a genuine test of an alternative journalistic model. They invited Sheldon to edit their paper, exploiting his reputation as a popular writer of fiction and his internationally famous novel, *In His Steps*, in which he told stories of dramatically reformed lives after the characters become Christians.

In asking, "What would Jesus do?" Sheldon broke from many traditions of the day. He chose to reject the content of sports and theater coverage, along with advertising for women's undergarments, for his version of a faith-based (Christian) daily newspaper. Similarly, Sheldon's Jesus would not associate with anyone in the liquor trade, much less publish their advertisements. Instead, Sheldon believed that the Spirit of God could use his words to provoke personal and social reform.

Sheldon used his news space for advocacy, but he insisted on accuracy.[3] For example, on March 13, 1900, in his first issue, Sheldon included an article, "Starving India: Fifty million people affected by the famine." The news, dated by weeks, led Sheldon to recruit the Reverend H. J. Bruce to write about the famine and the suffering. An editor's note followed the article saying, "The *Capital* knows of no more important matter of news the world over this morning than the pitiable condition of famine-stricken India. We give the latest and fullest available information of the progress of the scourge in the following articles."[4] Sheldon solicited a 10-cent contribution from every reader for a relief fund. For him, accuracy meant more than just reporting the facts. He blended accuracy with advocacy to promote social reform.

Sheldon's other stunning contribution in advocacy can be seen in his editorials. He broke from many traditions of the day by publishing daily editorials meant to influence newspaper policy and often published an appeal to social justice beside a routine news article.[5] He argued that placing the opinion piece beside the news article increased the linkage between the problem and solution, and he used his front page to make the point. The mainstream news industry condemned Sheldon's work of calling for donations to save starving people in

East India as part of the news story. Sheldon noted that the press could serve as a daily sermon to guide Christians in their spiritual maturity. He was not uniformly persuasive, however, even though he thought God was on his side and his news decisions were based on what he thought Jesus would do. To some extent, Sheldon's newspaper succeeded. Circulation soared from 11,223 newspapers on weekdays, and 12,298 in Sundays, to an average of 362,684 copies daily with subscriptions from forty-eight states and twenty-seven foreign countries.[6]

At the end of the experiment, the newspaper soon reverted to its original editorial policy of detached news reporting. Sheldon's work is a footnote to the history of newspapers, but it provides an intriguing example of a strident voice that leapfrogged over the routine calls for public policy reform and argued for personal reform available only through a personal confession of faith in Christ.

Social Gospel, Advocacy, and Accuracy in the Early Twentieth Century

In 1900, the Social Gospel Movement dominated Protestant circles. One scholar called Sheldon the chief propagandist for the Social Gospel Movement,[7] in which Christians manifested their faith by doing good works. These Christians believed that good works followed salvation.[8] Sheldon's sense of advocating a message of redemption meant that he omitted news of the Boer War, articles on the controversy of a silver vs. gold standard, and news of a politically charged gubernatorial race in Kentucky.[9] The same theme applied to paid advertisements and patent medicines. Sheldon said the social gospel impulse would be to include vital issues "that affect humanity as a whole"[10] The newspaper's commitment to the social gospel meant abhorrence of war, encouragement to seek first the Kingdom of God, and total extinction of the curse of alcohol.[11] Like publishers William Randolph Hearst, Joseph Pulitzer, and Horace Greeley, Sheldon used his newspaper as a bully pulpit. Like other famous advocacy journalists, Sheldon's lobbying proved successful in raising money for social gospel causes.[12]

In addition to Sheldon's reliance on the social gospel as a standard to reject typical news of the day, he made a point of challenging the sensationalism of the era. Sheldon rejected as wrong the fast-and-loose days of the Yellow Press with its screaming headlines and human-interest pieces, many of which highlighted the graphic details of murder and other felonies.[13]

For the social gospel pastor, accuracy was more than an ideal, it was a value he put into vigorous practice. To make sure each article was fact-checked, Sheldon counted on seasoned editor Harold T. Chase, and Sheldon credited Chase for his vigilance in checking the facts as well as getting the newspaper finished by deadline.[14] By 1914, Sheldon told Kansas editors at a conference that what he wanted most in a newspaper was reliability and truthfulness. If a paper did not know the facts, then it should keep silent.[15]

Sheldon's model, although panned at the time, would be praised today for its strident fact-checking. However, critics from the mainstream press may not like Sheldon's motivation—a Christian-based press that relies on an editor to discern subjectively the content of the printed press based on dependence of God for help. Sheldon wrote, "With the hearty cooperation of every person connected with the paper and with the help of the wisdom that I have prayed might be given me from Him who is wiser than any of us, I shall do the best I can."[16]

Editors tend to avoid a subjective evaluation of truth, but political scientist Lynn Vavreck found that the Mind and Society Center at the University of Southern California provides an accurate account of the process people use to evaluate truth.[17] As Vavreck observes, "When people consider whether something is true or not, they engage in either analytic or intuitive evaluations. Analytic evaluations are cognitively taxing and may involve searching for information like knowledge drawn from books or experts. Intuitive evaluations require less effort and are largely based on gut feelings like familiarity or ease of understanding."[18] Sheldon used the intuitive approach and while admitting that others could come to a different conclusion, his "What-would-Jesus-do?" formula was all he said was needed to include some content and omit other content.

Sheldon wrote from his conviction that the press would rally reform-minded readers to do good works and change the world, just as Christians are called to transform the world, not just reform it, because of a divine mandate. Sheldon was candid in his approach, but in this age readers must be vigilant and wonder who is behind the news that may be more the work of marketers than journalists. Sheldon's approach is best seen in his daily editorials that he published to explain what he called the ideal newspaper. For instance, he published two separate newspapers on Saturday to avoid having his staff work on Sundays, an example of practicing a type of journalism based on what he thought Jesus would do if he were a newspaper editor.

Student Media at Faith-Based Institutions

Journalism in the United States once relied on governmental authorities to approve of the content. Publishers who challenged the ruling authority faced the fate of publisher Benjamin Harris of the renowned *Publick Occurrences Both Domestick and Foreign*, who failed to get permission to publish. Historians considered Harris to have produced the first newspaper in the United States even though it lasted only one issue. The government forced him to cease publication, commonly called "prior restraint," because it did not approve of the content. Over the decades, the common understanding of the mainstream, general circulation newspaper is that it will provide both sides of an issue as part of its social responsibility function. That principle suggests that few people can mass produce a publication, which puts the burden on getting information out to readers as part of the social maintenance needed for a society to flourish. At its best, this social responsibility function requires that journalism works to make sure minority voices are treated with as much dignity and respect as all the others who possess a higher profile in a community. The reality is that newspapers, as well as other mass media, encounter pressures that sometimes influence them to neglect truthful reporting. By omitting an edgy article that may unduly embarrass a public official, the news outlet may hope that the omission will benefit the paper in some way. In such cases, the news is worse than inaccurate—it does not exist.

Similar pressures exist not only for big papers, but also for student media, especially at private, faith-based institutions, and Sheldon's work can prove valuable for negotiating political realities on the ground. While faith-based universities tend to elevate discovery and truth-seeking publically, some are quite cautious about student journalists choosing topics that could unduly embarrass university administrators. Sheldon's ideal of accuracy and his tireless work to discern fact from falsehood would seem to be the policy of choice among the Christian higher education subcultures.

On the university campuses that are members of the Council for Christian Colleges & Universities (CCCU), students often face the tension that Harris, Sheldon, and Chase encountered. According to its website, the CCCU exists "to create a broad association of Christian colleges that would support promotion and leadership activities for member schools and provide a unifying voice for Christian higher education in the public square."[19]

The concern by administrators is that students may still be maturing in the faith and not have the discernment necessary to apply a subjective rubric such as "What would Jesus do?" While private, faith-based universities allow students to have a laboratory to make and learn from mistakes, many are unwilling to allow mistakes to become public. Recruitment offices, boards of trustees, and others in powerful offices tend to be overly concerned that accuracy is not enough to make content worth disseminating. For instance, at the faith-based Palm Beach Atlantic University in West Palm Beach, Florida, my colleagues discouraged me from urging journalism students to report about business students who developed a smartphone app that allowed users to obtain a discount on alcoholic beverages at area bars and restaurants. The story, while accurate, was considered one that could be harmful to the alcohol-abstinence mission of the university. The university has since taken a different position on news and considers it valuable as long as all the typical conventions of due diligence are followed.[20] Similarly, in fall 2017, an article on extended visitation hours in the gender-segregated dormitories at Palm Beach Atlantic University was taken off the online news site almost as soon as it was posted. The reason: the middle-managers made the decision without checking with the board.[21]

While Sheldon's approach is useful in identifying news that should not be published, he is not as helpful when it comes to news that should be published. No one complains about his devotion to the facts and his attention to accuracy, but it remains unclear on what authority information should be disseminated.

What is missing in many faith-based universities is a policy statement that outlines its publications policy. Among the best is Spring Arbor University's mission statement: "Entirely student run. *The Pulse* is Spring Arbor's news magazine dedicated to telling the community's stories and providing a platform for discussions. We publish a 24 page [*sic*] magazine every month with stories varying from conferences held at the school to sports accomplishments to sa-tirical pieces; some still are true."[22] The statement does not mention factuality or censorship, and it emphasizes that the enterprise is "entirely student run." Would Sheldon approve? What would Jesus do?

For administrators and student media advisers, the most suitable approach is to give them Sheldon's notion to seek wisdom from on high and act accord-ingly. That posture does not guarantee that the university will be trouble-free, but if the goal is accuracy, at least journalists, whether students or not, will have a target that is about as realistic as any in 1900 or today.

College Media Advisers published a handbook that explores the free press on a private college campus.[23] The handbook recognizes that the First Amend-ment does not have to be followed at a private school, creating a flexible situ-ation much like Sheldon's newsroom. However, the handbook suggests that universities should aim to help students mature into citizens who recognize that a democracy must allow the marketplace of ideas to flourish. Furthermore, nearly all states have a provision that says it is unlawful to deprive someone of his or her right to free speech.

With those ideas in mind, the following is a start on making a faith-based policy that will do what Sheldon wanted. To help the community flourish, two principles must be in play on a faith-based campus: (1) ask journalists to do their duty in a spirit of mercy and a commitment to the truth, and (2) train reporters to fact-check every word of the article and check quotations with their sources.

Policy statements must be longer than these two points, but journalists should learn to balance the benefit of the public's right to know against the raw necessity of shielding the source, often a person of public notoriety, from the voyeurism of people who are not mature enough to avert their eyes and ears to something that is humiliating and dehumanizing. In the ancient Jewish culture, residents who shared a common courtyard knew that integrity demanded that even the public acts of some should not be observed, because privacy is a way to exalt the divine within us all.

The other virtue is to get the information right. It is hard work. The Bible demands two witnesses; the courts demand two witnesses; the mainstream press demands two witnesses. To establish a fact means that the writer will go beyond due diligence and seek the truth while ensuring that the information is not part of a hidden agenda or is a mean-spirited attack.

Conclusion

The result of Sheldon's grand experiment was a daily newspaper that avoided the superficial news of sports, the basest news of a suicide, or the names of tax evaders. One can hardly imagine the invitation for such an experiment today among the mainstream news media gods, no matter how renowned the editor. Sheldon's single greatest contribution was to insist that every word of a news outlet, including the advertising, was fact-checked, which provoked modest reform in the newspaper industry.[24] As one scans the horizon of twenty-first-century news outlets, such insistence is lacking, even among many Christian news media outlets.

Sheldon provides a model of a reluctant journalist who wants to redeem the world by getting his facts straight first. That may be a model that faith-based schools can adhere to and one that provides hope for generations of news seekers. Sheldon punctuates the truth that all news, regardless of the source, seems to have some bias, but that all news, regardless of the source, demands accountability to the truth. He provides the challenge, and a hope, to a society that asks "What would Jesus do?" when it comes to reporting the news. This question provides a launch pad for serious discussions about recurring issues of truth and justice in the newsrooms of Western civilization.

CHAPTER 29

C. S. Lewis: Constructing Relational Messages to Steal Past Prejudices against Christians

Steven A. Beebe

Abstract: C. S. Lewis's (1898–1963) classic book *Mere Christianity* remains popular due to Lewis's relational theology that is reflected in his ability to forge a relationship with his intended audience and overcome what Lewis called "watchful dragons"—prejudices against Christian that may keep the audience from listening. Lewis possessed a commitment to the idea that the Triune God revealed in Jesus was a God who related to humans. His commitment and message are well positioned to resonate with many of today's spiritual-but-not-religious seekers.

Introduction

Royal Air Force officer John Lawlor describes hearing C. S. Lewis's first radio talk when in the officer's mess on August 6, 1941.[1] Someone had ordered a drink. Just as the barman was about to hand the drink over to the customer, Lawlor remembers, "Suddenly everyone just froze listening to this extraordinary voice. And what he had to say. And finally they end up and there was the barman with his arm still up there and the other man still waiting for his drink. And they all forgot it, so riveting was that."[2] How Lewis developed a relationship with his listeners and readers—ongoing interpersonal connections between people—is central to understanding why Lewis was a powerful communicator both in the 1940s and today.

This chapter suggests that it is not just *what* Lewis said, but *how* he said it that makes *Mere Christianity*, one of his best-known books, a classic—ranked by *Christianity Today* as the best book about Christianity of the twentieth century and one that continues to sell more than a million copies a year.[3] Specifically, he presents a clear message in a conversational style that forges a relationship between author and reader, emulating a visit with an old friend. In an age when an increasing number of people describe themselves as "spiritual but not religious," there is evidence that a strong relational message resonates with both listeners and readers.[4] Lewis's relational style based on his relational theology can be imitated; it can help contemporary Christians effectively share the Christian message, especially with the growing number of those untethered to a specific religious denomination.

I first present an overview of the content of Lewis's book. I then look at the backstory of the book's development; the book is a classic not only because of its content but also because of the context in which it came into being. With World War II now on England's home turf, Lewis sought to bolster Christian faith at a time when he saw Christianity on the decline. More important than a specific creed, Lewis thought it was vital to develop a relationship with God. Specifically, the chapter identifies selected rhetorical techniques Lewis used to make a relational connection with first his listeners and then his readers.

A Mere Relational Message about *Mere Christianity*

In the title of the book, the word *mere* (borrowed from seventeenth-century author and theologian Richard Baxter)[5] means *essential* or, based on the Middle English use of the word *pure*. Lewis's intent was to identify those aspects of Christianity in a pure form that would be acknowledged as essential by the large majority of Christians. As Lewis notes in the preface, "I hope no reader will suppose that 'mere' Christianity is here put forward as an alternative to the creeds of the existing communions. . . . It is more like a hall out of which doors open into several rooms."[6] His goal was to invite us to stroll into the hall and eventually to explore the "rooms" where, as he put it, "there are fires and chairs and meals."[7] Lewis did not intend for his distillation of Christian ideas to substitute for denominational rooms but to identify the architectural elements that define common space shared among all Christians. He further clarifies his intent when he says, "Ever since I became a Christian I have thought that the best, perhaps the only, service I could do for my unbelieving neighbors was to explain and defend the belief that has been common to nearly all Christians at all times."[8]

Lewis's successful series of twenty-five, ten-to-fifteen-minute radio broadcasts was organized into four series, the first of which began on August 6, 1941. His last broadcast in his fourth series concluded on April 6, 1944. *Mere Christianity*, the compilation of all twenty-five talks, was first published as three separate books. *Broadcast Talks* included his first two broadcast series "Right and Wrong as a Clue to the Meaning of the Universe" and "What Christians Believe."[9] *Christian Behavior*,[10] the same title he used for his third radio series, and *Beyond Personality*,[11] which was titled "Beyond Personality: Or First Steps in the Doctrine of the Trinity," were each published as separate volumes before being included in *Mere Christianity*.

The big idea in his first broadcast series was to help his listeners understand that there is a Moral Law. Not only does he want us to believe that a Moral Law exists, but he also wants us to know we regularly break it. Moral Law is not merely descriptive but prescriptive; its purpose is to point to what we should do in order to live our lives as they were designed to be lived. Moral Law is practical.

In "What Christians Believe," Lewis seeks to articulate the essential beliefs that all Christians share. He first discusses the various "rival conceptions of God" and debunks Dualism, the belief that there are only two primary powers on earth—good and bad—and that they are equal.[12] As Lewis frames the argument, to judge one good and the other bad is to use a standard outside of both powers; Lewis's view is that there is only one standard for goodness and that standard is God.

Book three, "Christian Behavior" provides a taxonomy of moral rules and virtues that serve as "directions for running the human machine."[13] Cardinal virtues include prudence, temperance, justice, and fortitude. Additional chapters discuss social morality, which includes intersections between psychoanalysis and morality, as well as sexual morality—which Lewis believes, contrary to popular understanding, not to be at the heart of Christian morality. "The Great Sin," the sin of pride, is discussed in chapter 8.[14] Consideration of forgiveness, charity, hope, and faith rounds out his discussion of appropriate Christian behavior.

The last radio series, "Beyond Personality: or First Steps in the Doctrine of the Trinity," presents an overview of the function and purpose of theology, which serves as a map to guide us—a map prepared by those who have traveled our same path before us, to guide us along the way. Lewis concludes both his radio series and the published book with the chapter "The New Men," in which he explains that God does not desire improvement in people but total transformation. He challenges readers to become their authentic selves by following the One who is "Beyond Personality."

The Story Behind the Classic

Dr. James W. Welch, the director of broadcasting for the BBC, had read Lewis's *The Problem of Pain*, published in 1940, and was impressed with Lewis's ability to write clearly about complex topics. Welch wrote to Lewis to see if he would be interested in speaking to the British people on the radio. Welch suggested a couple of ideas, including "A series of talks on something like 'The Christian Faith as I see It—by a Layman.'"[15] Lewis wrote back, "I would like to give a series of talks as you suggest. . . . I think what I mainly want to talk about is the Law of Nature, or objective right and wrong."[16] Lewis added, "The first step is to create, or recover, the sense of guilt."[17] Lewis's original goal, then, was not to write a primer on Christianity, but to "create, or recover, the sense of guilt."[18] With World War II raging, Lewis believed the urgent task was to identify what the underlying sense of "good" is in order to establish a proper relationship with God and all people.

Lewis was a natural at using the broadcast media. His rich voice, skilled choice of words, and a message of interest to his audience combined for memorable broadcasting. In part because his first broadcast followed the Norwegian News (broadcast in the Norwegian language), his first listening audience was only slightly more than 500,000 people. But those who listened must have shared their enthusiasm for his message with others; his second broadcast had a listenership of more than 1.2 million people.[19]

There is evidence Lewis used his editing skills when fine-tuning the broadcast transcript. The original manuscripts of his radio broadcasts show where he crossed out passages and paragraphs at the last minute when he learned that some of his talks had to be cut from fifteen minutes to ten. His reductive edits are especially significant in the series "What Christians Believe." Lewis scholar Justin Phillips suggests that in addition to Lewis's general discomfort with radio, he did not spend much time listening to the radio except for a few news bulletins.[20] Phillips adds, "The broadcasting medium seemed increasingly trivial to him. In his books and his correspondence, references to radio listening are usually negative."[21] Yet, despite Lewis's discomfort with the medium of radio, it was the BBC broadcast talks that further solidified Lewis as a principle apologist for the Christian faith. Lewis took pains to make sure he was not speaking as an expert theologian but as a layman simply trying to be a translator of theological ideas. The "Lewis as layman" approach holds a key to the popularity of both the broadcasts and book.

Lewis wanted to connect to his listeners, not as an authority figure "on high," but as someone side-by-side on the journey with them. Additionally, although Lewis believed that communicating about religion does not require a unique liturgical language, he was aware of the particular challenges of communicating about theological ideas. As Lewis phrased it in his essay "The Language of Religion," "This is one of the great disadvantages under which the Christian apologist labours. Apologetics is controversy. You cannot conduct a controversy in those poetical expressions which alone convey the concrete; you must use terms as definable and unequivocal as possible, and these are always abstract."[22] Lewis wanted to be able to relate abstract ideas to his listeners using an accessible style. As early as the opening passage of his first broadcast talk, he uses simple, concrete language to help us relate to Christ as a person rather than an abstract "force."[23] As Justin Phillips accurately noted, "He carries you along as a good companion walking down a road. It is like listening to a benevolent uncle trying to explain the laws of cricket to his nephew."[24]

Lewis's theology is a relational theology. The Christian faith, suggests Lewis, should not be based on believing a specific creed (which is why he did not advocate any one, particular church) but on having a relationship with God. Lewis's journey to faith is less about conversion to a specific religious doctrine than about believing in the enactment of "the true myth." Jesus was who he said he was—not a liar or lunatic or "on the level with the man who says he is a poached egg," but our Savior.[25] God, as embodied in the Trinity, is someone with whom we can have an approachable relationship. Lewis embodies that commitment in his means of communication—not just in what he communicates, but also by *how* he communicates.

A Relational Message for the "Spiritual not Religious"

Contemporary Christian communicators could learn from Lewis's relational message. People increasingly describe themselves today as "spiritual but not religious" with a growing number of people less likely to affiliate with any specific denomination.[26] Such a perspective may result in skepticism from using explicitly proselytizing Christian messages that emphasize a theology-ladened, denominationally specific doctrine.[27] A relational theology is designed to "steal past watchful dragons"—a self-confessed goal of Lewis's own theological communication.[28] Although Lewis used his "watchful dragons" metaphor in reference to his Narnia books, his relational style and approach of *Mere Christianity* also sought to overcome preconceived "stained-glass and Sunday school associations" that had, as he put it, "paralysed much of my own religion in childhood."[29]

A key tenet of effective communication is this: Information is not communication. Information alone rarely convinces or inspires. Communication occurs when there is a meaningful *response* from the message presented.[30] A meaningful response is more likely to occur in the context of a positive relationship. Lewis develops a personal connection with his audience using three approaches that contemporary communicators can also deploy.

First, in his essay "Christian Apologetics," Lewis offers pithy communication advice for relating to any audience: "We must learn the language of our audience."[31] *Mere Christianity* was not attempting to pronounce the final word about Christianity but to provide an open invitation, especially for those who already believed in Christianity, to explore their beliefs more deeply. After delivering one of his early *Broadcast Talks*, he wrote to a friend with this assessment of his audience: "(I assumed last night that I was talking to those who already believed.) If I'd been speaking to those who didn't, of course everything I'd said wd. be different."[32] In today's vernacular, he sought to connect with the spiritual but not religious listener.

Second, Lewis further develops a relationship with his audience by using an oral style that appeals to the reader as well as the listener. His message has resonance, whether one reads it in a book or listens to it on the radio. We explicitly learn about Lewis's techniques for being sensitive to both speaker and listener when he discusses making the transition from the radio transcripts to the book *Mere Christianity*. In the preface he explains, "The contents of this book were first given on the air, and then published. . . . In the printed versions I made a few additions to what I had said at the microphone, but otherwise left the text much as it had been. A 'talk' on the radio should, I think, be as like real talk as possible, and should not sound like an essay being read aloud."[33]

In Lewis's transcripts he used for the BBC talks, his edits suggest keen awareness of the differences between speaking and writing. For example, a handwritten edit to the radio transcript reveals that he began his third talk on August 20, 1941, by saying, "I must begin by apologizing for my voice. Since we last met I've managed to catch an absolute corker of a cold."[34] He then wryly adds, "Should you hear this talk suddenly interrupted by a loud crash you needn't jump to any rash conclusions. It'll probably only be me sneezing or coughing."[35] Such informal commentary did not make it into print. He reveals that in early drafts of the book, "I reproduced [contractions and colloquialisms], putting *don't* and *we've* for *do not* and *we have*. And wherever, in the talks, I had made the importance of a word clear by the emphasis of my voice, I printed it in italics."[36] This glimpse of his editorial process gives us a behind-the-scenes look at Lewis the editor. Yet he does not wring all of the oral, conversational quality out of the text. He retains considerable oral-communicating-for-the-ear strategies (such as repetition, contractions, and personal references) that are key to enhancing the author-reader relationship.

Lewis's very writing practice involved speaking or mouthing the words as he wrote. Walter Hooper, Lewis's secretary the last summer of Lewis's life, writes, "When Lewis dictated letters to me, he always had me read them aloud afterwards. He told me that in writing letters, as well as books, he always 'whispered the words aloud.' Pausing to dip the pen in an inkwell provided exactly the rhythm needed. 'It's as important to please the ear,' he said, 'as it is the eye.'"[37] It is this oral quality of his writing that is one of the factors that make Lewis a skilled communicator.

Finally, Lewis also applied the technique that contemporary scholars of communication call *verbal immediacy*—using words to create a feeling of psychological closeness. Using immediate personal pronouns (such as *we, us,* and *our*), including personal examples (using *I, me,* and *my*), talking about personal experiences, and asking questions and speaking *with* readers and listeners (seemingly breaking into the lecture by providing personal commentary) rather than *at* them are all strategies of verbal immediacy. Perhaps his many years of writing literally thousands of letters honed his verbal immediacy style.

Lewis's voice, his language style, and his talent for writing for the eye and ear helped Lewis achieve immediacy with both his listeners and readers. It is as if he is there with us, conversing and anticipating our response rather than focusing only on presenting information. Lewis has presence.

Conclusion

Having a relational message need not mean disguising Christian principles or beliefs but describing the Christian message in a way that connects with contemporary readers. Lewis models the value of having a relationship with what he called "the true myth."[38] Jesus was a person who came to develop a relationship with us, and we are invited to have a relationship with Jesus, God the Father, and the Holy Spirit.

Mere Christianity endures not only because of the ideas it expresses but also because of the way they are expressed. Not only does Lewis speak what is true, but he also communicates in ways that continue to make the truth clear and relatable to millions. Lewis's communication lessons have application to today's Christian communicators. He models how to steal past the watchful dragons that may prematurely dismiss the Christian message as irrelevant, abstract, or unnecessary.

CHAPTER 30

Thomas Merton: Rediscovering Communication as a Message of Love for Communion

Jennifer Jones

Abstract: In the essay "Symbolism: Communication or Communion?" Thomas Merton (1915–1968) raises an important question about whether the purpose of communication is to convey knowledge or to encounter the transcendent. Merton argues for rediscovery of the latter, where communion may emerge through a symbolic message of love. Merton's wisdom guides us to consider communication that is subjective and symbolic to foster love and communion in human relationships.

Introduction

As a young college student at Columbia College, Thomas Merton had hopes of becoming both a novelist and a Franciscan priest. Both aspirations failed. Four of his novels were rejected for conveying "versions of the author's unresolved struggles to find meaning in his own life."[1] Then, when seeking to enter the Franciscan Order, he was asked to withdraw his application after confessing he had fathered a child for whom he might still have had responsibility at that time.

Despite these significant setbacks, Merton later became a monk of the Cistercian Order of Strict Observance, known as Trappists, at Our Lady of Gethsemani in Kentucky. In silent contemplation, ideas poured out of him into numerous books, essays, poetry, letters, and journals—the latter of which total 1.3 million words. His autobiography *The Seven Storey Mountain*,[2] translated in over fifteen languages, is likened to a twentieth-century *Confessions*[3] of Saint Augustine.[4] Through his prolific and profound writing as a self-proclaimed Christian existentialist, Thomas Merton has become recognized as one of the most influential contemporary spiritual writers.[5]

This chapter explores Merton's essay "Symbolism: Communication or Communion?" to help us see his contribution to a richer and more textured understanding of communication. He cautions us about the danger of slipping into instrumental forms of communication and the resulting objectifying treatment of others. By way of remedy, he encourages us to embody love, whereby we might experience communion with others, and then communion with God might arise. In particular, his approach responds to the issue of commercialized love that overvalues the accumulation of things and devalues the dignity of people. Against the forces of marketing, love and communion can ward off problematic notions of love. He posits that communication, when it carries a message of love, can bring forth a shared sense of unity and peace through community, which was the center of Merton's contemplative life of prayer and writing.

Love in a Time of Technology

To begin, Merton differentiates between sign and symbol. The purpose of a sign is to convey facts, inform, and explain. Conversely, a living symbol is not merely a sign for something else but it can also "makes us aware of the inner meaning of life and of reality itself."[6] Consider the example of the popular novel and movie *Life of Pi*.[7] The author, Yann Martel, posits that the story could have been told by using facts to document what transpired rather than using vivid symbols. He poses the question: Which is the better story? The symbolic approach makes the better story, not just because it is more entertaining, but because it also conveys profound meaning about the human condition and the transcendence of God that cannot be apprehended as easily through mere fact. The great spiritual teachers throughout human history used symbolic storytelling because it reached, as Augustine noted,[8] the inner-ear and heart, which cannot be qualitatively explained. Merton observes signs overtaking symbols because a technological society is driven to scientifically analyze data to arrive at facts. Yet a paradox emerges because while doing so, we lose a deeper understanding of human existence.

Merton observes that in contemporary society, even though we now have "the capacity to communicate anything, anywhere, instantly, man finds himself with *nothing to say*."[9] This predominance of signs becomes problematic when at the same time, according to Merton, symbols rich with meaning become trivialized and useless. While signs define, symbols honor the mysterious and lead to the humility of not knowing (in the technical sense). Therefore, Merton argues, if symbols "are not living signs of creative integration and inner life, then they will become morbid, decaying, and pathogenic signs of [one's] inner disruption."[10] As such, love will suffer spiritual decay when it is engaged only as an object or instrument, consumed in a technological society.[11]

Merton observes, "In a world where practical use and quantitative scientific information are highly prized, the symbol becomes meaningless."[12] However, this seemingly practical advantage is paradoxical because "the technological man finds himself in another artificial synthesis in which he has no longer any knowledge of anything except himself, his machines, and his knowledge that he knows what he knows."[13] Conversely, symbolism, when it leads to deeper communication, can bring about community with others, dynamism of thought, and action for meaningful existence. Merton uses the metaphor of an anthill.[14] If the purpose of our world is mere survival, then the anthill is sufficient; if, on the other hand, we desire communion, we should strive for something beyond our familiar and well-trodden tunnels. Communion cannot occur between subject and object; it may only manifest in subject-subject encounters. Through such encounters, subjects can be awakened to communion with God. Communion lets go of the need to know and define; it requires a humility that "relieves the burden of seeking definitive answers."[15]

Merton's push to elevate communion does not necessitate a total rejection of science and modern technology. Rather, he believes that science may be more fully appreciated when people have an openness and receptivity to the spiritual and mysterious realm. He writes, "Without this interior fulfillment, the mind of man is not equipped to cope with objective truth, and the spirit that has no interior roots will find that its 'scientific' knowledge of objects turns out to be 'a lie' even when it is materially correct. It completely misleads him as to the meaning of his own existence."[16]

For Merton, love is the most important positive force for communion. Furthermore, Merton writes, "Love has its own wisdom, its own science, its own way of exploring the inner depths of life in the mystery of the loved person. Love knows, understands, and meets the demands of life insofar as it responds with warmth, abandon, and surrender."[17] In love, people experience much more than companionship; they grow more alive and are transformed. Therefore, love provides value and meaning to human life, which is revealed through another. Love demands that we release ourselves as prisoners of our own egoism and let go of judging others.[18] Merton illuminates a profound truth, which is, where there is love there is life—a life more alive, real, mature, and fulfilling.

Love in a Time of Marketing

Merton calls specific attention to the blight of a marketing society. He writes, "The advertising imagery which associates sexual fulfillment with all the most trivial forms of satisfaction—in order to separate the buyer from his dollar—creates a mental and moral climate that is unfavorable to genuine love."[19] The modern view of love has been perverted and denigrated by the media's sexual objectification of people depicted to be in love. Merton makes a correlation between this corrupt depiction of love and consumerism, which he believes prevents people from living authentically. He observes that the corruption of love occurs in two forms. The first form is a *fantasy* where love means "falling" uncontrollably under some cosmic force. The second form is an *impression* where love is artificially created within the mind. Both forms are false because they are manufactured within the individual—either through the belief that one has no control over the spell of love cast from somewhere in the universe, or that one is entirely in control by molding a kind of knowledge of love by what one imagines. In either case, these two kinds of love are false because fantasy and impression are formed in the mind.

Merton argues that marketing sells us these corrupt versions of love as packages to be consumed. These corruptions are the taken-for-granted background in a "marketing society."[20] As such, love becomes an object, or a package, that is used in social and economic exchanges. Love as a package also transforms humans into objects. The human *subject* is replaced with a human *object*. When we look at ourselves as products, we see others in the same fashion. When love becomes a package, we can use it and throw it away when a new model is purchased. Such marketing encourages everyone to be unsatisfied with love, so that the exchange may continue. Merton challenges this mutilated view of love: "Love is not a deal; it is a sacrifice. It is not marketing; it is a form of worship."[21]

Although this objective exchange is mechanistic, a primary reason people support love as a package is biological. People in advertising and marketing know that urges can be satisfied with acquisitions. However, the consumer is never quite fulfilled, and true happiness is not experienced. And so, Merton posits, "The trouble with this commercialized idea of love is that it diverts your attention more and more from the essentials to the accessories of love. You are no longer able to really love the other person, for you become obsessed with the effectiveness of your own package, your own product, your own market value."[22] Quantity supersedes quality with an edict of "I need" that is perpetuated and exacerbated by "the saturation bombing of our senses and imagination with suggestions of impossibly ideal fulfillments," and thus "we cannot help revising our estimate of the deal we have made."[23] A term like "trophy wife" inherently sounds like doing business, a phrase that harkens back to the salesman whom people know can give them a better deal. Merton says that this all may be summed up in one word—narcissism, which "has disastrous effects, for it leads people to manipulate each other for selfish ends."[24]

This attempt to measure up to some ideal advertising image is hollow, immature, regressive, and self-defeating—a tragedy, according to Merton, that is purely infantile. However, we are not bound to this psychology of "getting" a package; we are free to existentially choose otherwise: "To love you have to climb out of the cradle, where everything is 'getting,' and grow up to the maturity of giving, without concern for getting anything special in return."[25] Thus, we may glean from Merton that communication, reoriented for communion, is not a sign, information, object, or package. Love, as the basis of communion, is an interior connection that is conveyed without consideration of the exterior package.

Communicating Love for Communion: Subjective and Symbolic

To enrich our lives and the lives of others in communion, we may take up Merton's wisdom by drawing closer to one another and to God by communicating love, which then leads to communion. This approach to communication is subjective and symbolic.

First, communication needs to be subjective. For Merton, to embrace the subjective is to be in self-giving loving relations with others who are viewed as sacred subjects. Being self-giving does not mean a total loss of self or a complete turning of oneself over to another. Self-giving focuses attention away from the self, or decenters the self. Moreover, a positive paradox emerges: self-giving garners an enlarged and more fulfilled self. Merton states, "We do not find the meaning of life by ourselves alone—we find it with another. We do not discover the secret of our lives merely by study and calculation in our own isolated meditations. The meaning of our life is a secret that has to be revealed to us in love, *by the one we love.*"[26] Hence, both the self and other are enriched through loving relationships.

The more different the other's life experiences are, the more we can understand the world and ourselves. My university has adopted the Narrative 4 program whose mission is to "build a community of empathic global citizens who improve the world through the exchange of personal narratives."[27] Participants in the program first contemplate a defining moment or story in their lives and then, in pairs away from the larger group, share their stories with each other. Returning to the group, they share the stories, but in the first-person voice of the other person. This program has been a great success in fostering radical empathy, a necessary life skill that is often not part of a college curriculum. Directing our attention toward others involves a sense of humility and respect in welcoming and learning from new perspectives and ways of being. As such we may become "transformed by the power of love."[28] Personal development and identity may flourish in communion with others. Merton proclaims, "I cannot find myself in myself, but only in another. My true meaning and worth are shown to me not in my estimate of myself, but in the eyes of the one who loves me."[29] Merton describes this phenomenon as revelation, and this is how our students have described their Narrative 4 experiences.

Second, communication should be viewed as symbolic. Appreciating the other person as a subject accepts that this other cannot be known as an empirical fact; the other cannot be quantitatively defined. This approach builds upon the idea of subjectivity where not only is the *person* viewed as a sacred subject, but the *encounter* between people is also subjective. We may come into a conversation expecting it to go a certain way, but Merton recommends that we again avoid prejudgment and allow the conversation to emerge. Merton argues, "Revealed truth is made present concretely and existentially in symbols, and is grasped in and with the symbol by a living response of the subject. This response defies exact analysis and cannot be accurately described to one who does not experience it authentically in himself."[30] If we enter into communication with others with the approach of "If I say this, they'll do what I want,"[31] we become objectifying manipulators or passive-aggressive cowards. Only God can know where an encounter may lead; therefore, our communication must always be a message of love, the result of which must be left to faith.

Merton recognizes the pragmatic purpose and necessity of communication, which is necessary for everyday life; however, he is concerned that this instrumental form of communication supplants communication that is symbolic, which is vital for meaningful communion with others and God. We may find relief in embracing existential moments with others by allowing a conversation to unfold. However, this approach also necessitates letting go of a feeling of immediacy that is often present in our "need to know now" culture. Efficiency has infiltrated our world but will not "produce" meaningful communion. Therefore, we need to be mindful when efficient communication such as e-mailing and texting is appropriate.

For example, a student once e-mailed me stating she wanted to interview me to fulfill a class assignment and asked if I could type responses to the questions she listed, which would help her complete the assignment more expediently. I replied that I would be happy to meet her in person to answer the questions and asked if she could visit my office. Merton's guidance of a symbolic approach, a face-to-face encounter, opened up an amazing conversation that neither of us could have predicted. As a college student from China studying in the United States, she was overjoyed to hear about my trip to China while looking at the souvenirs in my office. We shared an existential moment of transcendence in this conversation that would have been missed had I simply replied to her e-mail questions and communicated mere facts. Later that year she thanked me for "saving her life" because on the day she e-mailed me, she was feeling seriously homesick and depressed. If we had not met in person, she said she was not sure what would have happened that night.

Conclusion

We continue to read Merton because his wisdom, which is "smarter, deeper, more profound, more serious, more intense,"[32] touches our human condition and opens up greater possibilities for authentic and fulfilled living. As objectification persists in our world, Merton's works maintain relevance as he proclaims, "The tension in the West, especially in America, between naïve surface optimism (belief in scientific progress as an end in itself) and the deep, savage destructive tendencies of a technology and an economy in which man becomes the instrument of blind inhuman forces make us realize that the *degradation of the sense of symbolism* in the modern world is one of its many alarming symptoms of spiritual decay."[33] The effects this damage has on people's spiritual well-being, on their connection with others and their relationship with God, can be very discouraging.

A tragic accident that took Merton's life at the age of fifty-three left many in great shock and sadness, yet it compelled his devotees to honor his legacy by poring over the millions of words he left behind. Merton "was essentially a man of tradition, striving to recover authentic Christian and monastic values in a time of change and upheaval, during which he often reads the sign of the times better and more clearly than others."[34] Merton engaged both the theoretical realm and practical reality to offer us spiritual maturity.[35] In a world rife with dehumanization, there is much work to be done to repair our world. However, the good news is that the world of communion, which is most salient to Merton, is within and among us. Communion may be revealed to humanity when subjective and symbolic communication entails a message of love.

CHAPTER 31

MARTIN LUTHER KING JR.: LOVING YOUR ENEMIES BY DEVELOPING "*AGAPE* IN THE SOUL"

John R. Katsion

Abstract: Martin Luther King Jr. (1929–1968) was a Baptist minister who helped to shape the Civil Rights Movement during the 1950s and 1960s in the United States. In the midst of this turbulent time, King preached the sermon "Loving Your Enemies" in which he lays out three principles to help the church members develop "*agape* in the soul" as they seek to love their enemies. This chapter applies these principles to one of the greatest enemies facing the church today: radical Islam and the Islamic State (ISIS).

Introduction

On the evening of January 30, 1956, an assailant threw a stick of dynamite onto the porch of the home of Martin Luther King Jr., the pastor and civil rights activist. Coretta Scott King, his wife, and a family friend were able to get to the backroom with the Kings' new baby Yolanda seconds before an explosion ripped through their home. On hearing of this attack, many people showed up with guns and other weapons to protect the King family and, for many of them, to exact revenge.[1] In the middle of this mob, King arrived home and, to calm the crowd, began to speak of a concept that was the foundation of his work in the Civil Rights Movement: Love for those who hate you. "We must love our white brothers, no matter what they do to us," said King. "We must make them know that we love them. . . . We must meet hate with love."[2]

This idea of loving one's enemies speaks to many of the challenges our culture faces today. Christians of all colors today across the globe face the horror of hate. Meanwhile, many North American Christians feel that the broader culture is beginning to hate them, especially because of their views on issues such as gay marriage, transgender rights, abortion, and contraception.[3]

How might Christians—and other marginalized and persecuted groups— respond in the face of hate, cultural opposition, and violent persecution?

Throughout church history, Christians tended to take two polar extremes: to hide and hunker down or to respond with angry diatribes. Neither approach actually transcends the cultural divide or speaks to wider church or societal concerns. King offers a better way. In the face of a terrorist attack upon his family, he told his enemies that he loved them and wished good for them. How was King able to do this, to love in the face of such hostility?

A close reading of his sermon "Loving Your Enemies" provides insights into two questions King addresses that are instructive for our current cultural climate: How should we love our enemies, and why should we love our enemies? This chapter examines principles of loving one's enemies laid out by King in his conception of "*agape* in your soul," and then applies them to the American church, and specifically, how it can learn to develop love toward one of its greatest enemies today: ISIS and the followers of radical Islam. In the end, King's "*agape* in the soul" offers a way for the church to ask deeper questions about the human condition that drives hate and to help the church cultivate a love for one's enemies in a culture racked by incivility, racial tensions, and ideological divisions.

Loving Your Enemies

On November 7, 1957, Martin Luther King delivered a sermon titled "Loving Your Enemies." Early in his sermon, King quotes Matthew 5:43–44: "Ye have heard that it hath been said, 'Thou shalt love thy neighbor, and hate thine enemy.' But I say unto you, Love your enemies" (KJV). King tackles loving one's enemies through the two interrelated issues of how and why people should love their enemies.

King says that to love one's enemy, the Christian must first analyze or examine his or her own life. He admits that, in some cases, people are going to make enemies for reasons beyond their control. His congregants might attract enemies because of their strong work ethic, their height, or the color of their hair or skin. Therefore, King warns his audience that "there might be something within you that arouses the tragic hate response in the other individual."[4]

As his key example, King turns to the tension between the United States of America and Russia. While King counts communism as unacceptable to Christians, America has often succumbed to the evils of capitalism. "Isn't it true," he asks, that America has "taken necessities from the masses to give luxuries to the [upper] classes?"[5] What is true for economics is true for civil rights. "Isn't it true that we have often," queries King, "trampled over individuals and races with the iron feet of oppression?"[6] Amplifying the need for self-analysis, he asks a final, perilous question, "Isn't it true that through our Western powers we have perpetuated colonialism and imperialism?"[7] What is true for America might be true for his audience, and to avoid similar mistakes, Christians need to examine themselves.

King then implores his audience to find good in and refuse the opportunity to defeat the enemy. King submits that there is a "split" or a dividedness between good and evil in every person. It is as if the self is engaged in a civil war, as if "there is a recalcitrant South of our soul revolting against the North of our soul."[8] King's audience might have been willing to admit, following King, "that within the best of us, there is some evil," but it might have been harder to admit that "within the worst of us, there is some good."[9] Not even the worst human has lost this goodness, the image of God. This goodness in the enemy may motivate love toward her or him.

In addressing the "why" question, King argues that his audience should love their enemies because hate begets hate and closes off the possibility of the redemptive power of love. King implores his church members to love their enemies because hateful actions give way to other heinous actions. "If I hit you and you hit me and I hit you back and you hit me back and go on, you see, that goes on ad infinitum,"[10] he remarks. It takes a strong person to "cut the chain of evil" that hate perpetuates.

Finally, King urges his audience to resist hate because "love has within it a redemptive power."[11] For King, love is the greatest power in the universe, and it is the only power that helps people relate the right way to their enemies and motivates them on their long march for freedom and civil rights. Love also redeems those who practice it by changing them at their very core. King gives historical examples of the power of redemptive love, culminating in the example of Jesus and his death on the cross: "It is an eternal reminder to a power-drunk generation that love is the only way . . . that love is the only creative, redemptive, transforming power in the universe."[12]

Living with Hatred and Fear

Martin Luther King Jr. preached this sermon to a primarily black audience. King and his church members daily experienced the hatred of a racist society. Whites forced blacks to use separate seats on buses and at restaurants, separate drinking fountains, and separate schools. In 1954, the Supreme Court ruled in *Brown v. Board of Education* that racial separation in education was unconstitutional, and the court ordered the desegregation of all school systems. However, many whites were resistant to the ruling. For instance, Governor Fabius of Arkansas called out the National Guard to stop the integration of black children into the Little Rock school district. Later, the whole Little Rock public school system was shut down for a year rather than allow black and white children to learn together.[13] The next year, a black woman named Rosa Parks refused to comply with segregated seating on a public bus. Her arrest led to the Montgomery Bus Boycott, which lasted for 381 days.[14]

Martin Luther King Jr. eventually led the boycott, and, as a result, the intensity of hatred directed toward African Americans intensified, including hatred toward King himself.[15] The year King preached "Loving Your Enemies," many black churches were bombed and attacks on African-Americans seemed to continue unabated.[16] In the 1950s and 1960s, whites killed as many as two hundred black persons involved in the Civil Rights Movement in "an effort to uphold and maintain the racial order in the South."[17] These murders could be categorized as "a tool of racial terrorism" in an attempt to "uphold white supremacy."[18]

These particular acts of murder took place against a larger context of lynching. Lynching was a premeditated killing that included torture, burning, and mutilation of the victim. Lynching was a way for those in power to control others through terror and intimidation. Whites committed the majority of lynchings against blacks, with 79 percent of all lynchings between 1882 and 1968 occurring in Southern states.[19] Two of the most notable were the lynchings of Emmett Till and Willie Edwards. Whites lynched Till for allegedly flirting with a white woman, and whites accused Edwards of having an affair with a white female.[20] In both of these cases, the whites who killed them were never convicted. The members of King's church intimately knew these threats upon their lives, and King's call to love their enemies was costly. King asked his congregation to love the people who might lynch and murder them. In the middle of these frightening and chaotic times, King called for love for one's enemies, for "*agape* in the soul."

The American Church and Developing "*Agape* in the Soul"

Who are those the American church needs to develop love toward, even as they practice hate toward us? One enemy of the North American church that seems to be growing in its open attacks on the church in the West is that of radical Islam, particularly those involved with the terror organization ISIS.

ISIS has claimed responsibility for many attacks against Christian communities and churches. In the Middle East, radical Islamic terrorists are systematically eliminating many Christian centers in that region. ISIS has abducted and murdered Christians in Iraq, Syria, and Libya.[21] In the West, ISIS has claimed responsibility for religiously motivated attacks in Germany and France. One example of the targeting of churches in the West was the murder of a Catholic priest during Mass by ISIS operatives in France in 2015.[22] In December 2016, the Department of Homeland Security stated that ISIS sympathizers "continue aspirational calls for attacks on holiday gatherings, including targeting churches."[23] ISIS, with the rise of radical Islam, is a growing enemy of the church and all that it teaches. With this enemy in mind, then, how can the church implement King's ideas and develop "*agape* in the soul" for these people?

King would have the church start by finding good in those who inhabit the world of ISIS and radical Islam. The question facing the American church is how to find good in the faces of those one considers pure evil: the faces of those who behead their prisoners, abduct children, and rape women left in the towns and villages they overrun. King was faced with the same question when challenged by his God to love people who tried to kill him and his family and lynch blacks in the South. He must have struggled to search for the good in the face of what he most certainly must have seen as pure evil.

For King, the place to start is in seeing each person on this planet as created in the *image of God*: "When you come to the point that you look in the face of every man and see deep down within him what religion calls 'the image of God,' you begin to love him in spite of [*sic*]. No matter what he does, you see God's image there."[24] Those hands that slit the throat of the Catholic priest in France were hands that once touched a mother's face or were maybe even used to play with a child.

Preemptive Love Coalition is a group that is willing to show the love of Christ to those who persecute them, and specifically to members of ISIS. They show the way forward in seeing the good in the face of the evil of ISIS. One of their workers describes ISIS in a way that tries to see the good in an enemy: "You may have seen . . . [ISIS] described as monsters, animals, and an apocalyptic death cult. Those words just obscure the fact that these are largely men and boys and in some cases women, who want to belong, a place to feel safe, and to have meaning. Who are looking for a way to put food on the table for their kids."[25] The perspective that Preemptive Love Coalition takes toward its enemies mirrors King's call to find the good in one's enemy, and it demonstrates that it is possible to find good in those who kill our Christian brothers and sisters.

The next step, according to King, would be to start with a feeling, but if we are going to love our enemies, it must be in action. Love as an action is a profound idea, one that has immediate, practical implications and lives out the call of Jesus for all of his followers to "do good to those who hate you" (Lk 6:27 ESV). Love in action is demonstrated once again with the work of Preemptive Love Coalition, when they show their love to followers of ISIS by giving them food and cold water to drink. One of their workers "gave water to a bound prisoner dressed in a yellow jumpsuit, who [*sic*] he recognised from an ISIS propaganda video posted online. This man, a tribal sheikh loyal to the Islamic State, had stood and watched as a friend of Sadiq's was brutally executed. 'You killed my friend,' Sadiq said, as he poured water into the man's mouth. 'But I've come here to feed you.' "[26]

The church needs to analyze how it can better serve followers of radical Islam, and one simple way would be to provide food and care for Muslims in their surrounding areas. Could churches include a group like Preemptive Love Coalition in their annual giving budget, or is there a university in their region with Muslim exchange students who could use food, clothing, or simply encouragement? Love in action should prompt the American church to find ways to show love in a practical way for Muslims and even for those who are seeking their destruction.

The final way for the church to love the followers of Islam, based on King's ideas, is to remember that love is redemptive. If we are going to develop "*agape* in our souls*," then Christians need to grasp this important point: love is the only way forward that redeems both the Christian and her enemy. As King observes, hate does not have any redemptive quality; it only destroys. We may feel the urge to walk down the path of hatred, bitterness, or unresolved anger; but as King states, continuing down this route will eventually distort our personalities: "Jesus says love, because hate destroys the hater as well as the hated."[27] In opposition to the destructive power of hate stands the redemptive power of love. The power of love is an idea that we all may know about, but King's sermon is a reminder that we as Christians are all called to this radical love and, in the end, it is the only thing that will change the world we inhabit.

King's conception of love comes from the example of Jesus Christ on the cross and his call for his followers to love their enemies, to love those who hate them, but it is also a conception of love that King developed in the realities of the crucible of suffering. King had borne the brunt of physical and verbal assaults; he dealt daily with the stress of living in a segregated society and suffering from an oppressive system. Even as he faced daily oppression, King was able to say that he sought to love his enemies because that was the only thing that was going to change the world.

Conclusion

On April 4, 1968, Martin Luther King Jr. was assassinated by his enemy. His assassination would seem to point to the victory of the system, the victory of the oppressor over the oppressed. But in his call for love, King showed his followers the best way to react to his death, and that was with love toward those who killed him. In so doing, King helped to stop the cycle of hate that could have erupted after his tragic death. In the end, the life of Martin Luther King Jr. demonstrated the principles that he espoused in this early sermon "Loving Your Enemies" and can be summed up in this one theme: To love our enemy, we all need to develop "*agape* in our souls."

The church needs to heed King's words, and, specifically, we need to start living them out toward those who follow the tenets of ISIS and radical Islam. To find good in those who would kill us, to show love in practical ways by feeding and clothing and helping those who hate us, to say "I love you," and then to see something redemptive in that love—all of these choices will help the church to develop "*agape* in the soul." It would be an *agape* so entrenched that no amount of hostility would be able to root it out of us, an *agape* that would allow us to say to our enemies, as King said to his, "I love you. I would rather die than hate you."[28]

CHAPTER 32

REINHOLD NIEBUHR: PLACING REASON AND REVELATION IN HISTORICAL DIALOGUE

Thomas M. Lessl

Abstract: Reinhold Niebuhr's (1892–1971) powers of religious persuasion among nonbelieving as well as believing North Americans are especially well illustrated in *Human Nature*, the first volume of *The Nature and Destiny of Man* (1941). Rather than appealing to the authority of revelation alone, Niebuhr puts the alternative understandings of human nature offered by classical rationalism and modern naturalism in dialogue with a biblical understanding. His unusual persuasive success illustrates what religious communication may gain from such an apologetic framework.

Introduction

Reinhold Niebuhr is perhaps the most publicly visible theologian ever seen in North American history—one of the few ever featured on the cover of *Time* magazine.[1] We get a sample of the persuasive power that brought him into the public eye from Langdon Gilkey, an unbelieving Harvard undergraduate student who attended one of his lectures in 1940. When the talk was over, the student found himself on a different path.[2] He writes that the talk was "from the beginning to end a challenge to the assumptions of my sophisticated modernity," but also a challenge that gave rise to "a vividly new interpretation of my world."[3] What was it that worked this sudden intellectual conversion, a conversion that led Gilkey to become an influential theologian in his own right?

A big part of any answer may be found in one biographer's description of Niebuhr's communication career as "constant dialogue."[4] In Niebuhr's case, dialogue meant a concerted effort, not just to express theological concepts derived from the Bible, but also to do so in answer, as Gilkey wrote, to the "challenge" posed by competing modern ideas. For Gilkey, this challenge came from Bertrand Russell, John Dewey, and George Santayana, three prominent figures in modern philosophy of that time, and it was because Niebuhr successfully answered these voices that Gilkey was suddenly able to appreciate an alternative biblical perspective.

That Niebuhr preferred to call himself an apologist or preacher rather than a theologian perhaps also tells us something about this dialogical approach.[5] Of course preachers and apologists are theologians, but the presentation of the gospel cannot always succeed by theology alone. Theologians, we might say, answer the question, "What does the Bible tell us?" The preacher-apologist also sets out to answer another question: "What does the nonbelieving world tell us differently?" For many listeners who have already embraced the opinions of the secular world, the first question can only be meaningful in light of the second. A communicator who puts the Bible in conversation with alternative modern ideas answers questions on both sides, and thus there is a close connection between Niebuhr's characteristically dialogical approach to communication and the usual concern of the apologist.

My general aim in this chapter is to explain why Niebuhr's dialogic practices might be helpful for audiences that are likely to be receptive to the gospel only if it is apologetically framed. The main example of Niebuhr's dialogic approach to communication is *Human Nature*, the first volume of his influential Gifford Lectures, *The Nature and Destiny of Man: A Christian Interpretation*. I will first recount how Niebuhr makes sense of and critiques modern notions of human nature in this work, tracing how problems in ancient Græco-Roman philosophy plague modern rationalism. In a second section, I will situate Niebuhr's apologetic efforts in his own life context and, finally, explore applications or lessons Niebuhr's dialogic approach can teach us today.

Human Nature

To engage in dialogue is to work upon some common ground shared by two sides, and since God is not part of this common ground for both the believer and the skeptic, Niebuhr found one that is—human nature. It is only in the second volume, *Human Destiny*, that he offers a specifically Christian view of this subject. He stands to make the Christian viewpoint more intelligible and compelling by deliberately setting it alongside competing views.

The problem with modern self-understandings for Niebuhr is that they mix together incompatible ideas that come from two historical cultures. Rather than being distinct, these modern views are in fact "adaptations, transformations and varying compounds of primarily two distinctive views of man: (a) The view of classical antiquity, that is of the Græco-Roman world, and (b) the Biblical view."[6] In looking at the classical components of modern thought historically—that is to say, in their original Græco-Roman setting—they can be separated out from the biblical ones they are blended with now. Once readers have a clearer understanding of how classical and biblical thought contrast, they can also begin to understand which parts of modern self-understanding come from which source.

Examining classical ideas in historical context, Niebuhr draws attention to two inadequacies that now plague modern self-understanding: the modern world's inability to account for the persistence of evil and its inability to sustain the human individuality it so prizes. Because these two problems arise from the limits of the classical worldview, Niebuhr shows that these modern hopes in fact have their basis in the other source that has shaped modernity: the Bible.

To name the core of our classical inheritance, Niebuhr uses the term "rationalism," by which he means the tendency of Græco-Roman thinkers to identify "rational man (who is essential man) with the divine," and, in fact, to regard reason as a "creative principle, identical with God."[7] Therefore, the essence of human nature shifts into a transcendent, impersonal, and universal domain of reason. The pure rationalism of the classical thinker relies upon a dualism that gives the spirit, but not the body, a divine reference point. A human essence that finds its true bearings within a disembodied realm disconnected from the material world, Niebuhr argues, will be powerless to address evil within that world.[8]

Modern thinkers are now disposed to reject the rationalism of Plato and Aristotle in favor of something more like scientific naturalism or materialism, and so they may not instantly recognize their own world in this classical one. But Niebuhr is careful to show that modernity's materialism and naturalism are only variations upon classical rationalism. The "naturalistic rationalism" of antiquity, much like the scientific worldview in modern times, proposed to sidestep dualism by insisting that all that exists is matter, but these classical naturalists, no less than Plato or Aristotle, exempted their own powers of thought from this web of material causality. These efforts only gave rise to another form of matter-spirit duality.[9] Like the classical materialists who sought to locate the rational spirit within nature, modern materialists have not escaped dualism. The immanent rationality of naturalism is no less disembodied than the heavenly rationality of Plato.

Unable to escape this dualism of mind and body, the classical world gave little place to the historical optimism so characteristic of our time. Such modern hopes, as Niebuhr shows, are only possible because, under the Bible's influence, the modern world continues to regard the individual embodied spirit as having purposeful significance. There were some inklings of this hope in Greek tragedy, as Niebuhr points out, when it depicts the "human passions as something more than mere impulses of the body."[10] But ultimately antiquity found itself unable to discern how humans could "be creative without being destructive," how the creative aspirations of the tragic hero could rise up without disturbing a more ultimate "rational principle of order."[11] By relegating evil to the material side of human nature, classical rationalism thus made it inevitable that virtue was otherworldly and evil was worldly.

Only creatures made to reflect the image of a God who is both "will and personality" could possess freedom and individuality, and only the ones who see themselves from the "standpoint of God" could hope to amend worldly evil.[12] However, the Bible understands evil as intrinsic neither to spirit nor nature—both of which are made by God. Evil was instead a willful breech in the relationship between a free human creature and a loving Creator. Thus, while biblical writers take evil seriously, they also hope for redemption from it. The classical mind regards human evil "complacently as the inevitable consequence of [man's] finiteness or the fruit of his involvement in the contingencies and necessities of nature," but the biblical mind cannot. If the "law" of human nature is "love, a harmonious relation of life to life," we are compelled to exercise our freedom "in obedience to the divine centre and source" of this life.[13]

The Modern North American Context

Born in Wright City, Missouri, in 1892, Niebuhr was a first-generation North American, the son of a German pastor who immigrated to the United States in 1881. He once described his father as a man who "combined a personal piety with a complete freedom in his theological studies," and this formative influence gave rise in the son's maturity to a figure who was likewise deeply conversant with the thought patterns of the world at large but always anchored in his own faith.[14] Throughout the whole spectrum of his work, Niebuhr brought the precepts of faith into open interaction with alternative beliefs.

One scholar used the term "dialectical" to describe this practice.[15] In its classical sense, this was the practice of setting one's ideas against competing or different ones in order to test and refine them. Dialectic has had important significance for public communication since classical times—so much importance, in fact, that Aristotle regarded it as a logical discipline necessary for responsible and effective persuasion—what the Greeks called rhetoric.[16] As a method of inquiry, dialectic supposes that the truth-value of ideas is assured by their ability to withstand refutation, and it contributes to effective communication by perfecting and clarifying these ideas in the process. Dialectic supports good communication not only because it helps ensure that the claims we advance stand on solid ground but also, and perhaps more importantly, because it ensures that a particular position is understood in relationship to the complexity of different ideas and experiences that might stand opposed to it.

Another formative idea reflected in Niebuhr's communication practices was the pragmatism of William James and John Dewey that he was introduced to during his formal education at Yale University.[17] The pragmatist holds that the measure of an idea's truth is how well it translates into practical experience and, conversely, that real world experience provides the most appropriate testing ground for developing sound ideas. Pragmatism reflected North American culture's energetic and active spirit as well as its characteristic resistance to the abstract philosophical reflections more typical of European schools of thought. Since North American theologians were accustomed to following this traditional European path, it is perhaps not surprising that Niebuhr never saw himself as a member of this profession but instead as an "academic vagabond."[18] But his pragmatism also accounts for his lifelong activism in public affairs and the fact that the Christian ideas discussed in his many books and essays almost always address social and political issues of the time. Theology, as Niebuhr would put it in one of his early essays, was meant to aid "the ethical reconstruction of modern society."[19]

Niebuhr's own brand of pragmatism, which he would later called "Christian realism,"[20] was already manifest in the first part of his career, the thirteen years he served as the pastor of a Detroit church. Niebuhr felt that he could serve his parishioners only through active involvement in the worldly struggles that surrounded them, the social and racial inequalities and economic injustices and hardships suffered by those now laboring in urban factories. Niebuhr was soon intimately involved with the secular "Left," and even with some of the political efforts of Marxists and socialists, and this pattern continued on a national scale after 1928 when he settled into the academic position at Union Theological Seminary, which he would occupy until his retirement in 1960. But his engagement with secular ideologies, rather than prompting him to dilute his Christian beliefs, in fact had the opposite effect. As Niebuhr began to articulate the theological insights that arose from his activism, he also became increasingly critical of the tendency within Christian liberalism, then popular among proponents of the social gospel, to absorb many of the precepts of the modern secular culture.

Apologetic Applications

Niebuhr's unique strength as a thinker and communicator lay in his "ability to make tangible the links between theological abstraction and social realities, without reducing religion to slogan or sentimentality."[21] Summations of this kind are likely to make us think of him, as many do, as a Christian activist, and certainly he was. However, in Niebuhr's case it was precisely the intensity of his worldly involvement that also made him so effective as an apologist, and there are several things that the church in our own time can learn from this.

One general lesson that we learn from Niebuhr is that social activism is, in some sense, an activity of apologetic dialogue and should therefore be recognized as an opportunity to communicate the gospel. Thoughtful believers who labor alongside other activists have an opportunity to put their own faith premises into interaction with secular ones. One might just as easily say that this is a necessity. The Christian activist needs to be concerned with those premises of the broader culture that do not agree with those of the gospel, and because these premises become especially visible in the operations of secular activism, the believer who works in this realm will also develop a more intimate understanding of these challenges.

The opportunity that this gives to apologetic communication can be illustrated in the example of environmental activism. Secular environmentalists have frequently claimed that God's commandment to Adam and Eve in the book of Genesis to "fill the earth and subdue it" (1:28 NIV) encourages environmental degradation by suggesting that nature is ours to do with as we please. Any Jew or Christian who has thought about this charge will recognize its obvious fallacy, that one of the consistent themes of the larger biblical body that this passage belongs to is that the creation is not ours but God's. If God gave us the freedom to fill and subdue the earth, this could only be on the assumption that we would do so by executing his creative will. But the believing activist who addresses this challenge also has an opportunity to show that the Bible can resolve inconsistencies within the arguments of secular environmentalists. For instance, while it may be true that harm may be done to the earth by those who believe that it is theirs to act upon, every policy that proposes to repair our planet assumes something similar. One cannot enact policies to protect the earth without also assuming human authority over nature. The believing activist who recognizes this contradiction is also in a better position to communicate one important advantage of the biblical perspective to his or her unbelieving associates.

Environmentalists believe that nature has intrinsic value and that we are not therefore at liberty to determine its fate, but in contradiction to this, they also believe that we must take that fate into our own hands. No merely naturalistic worldview can resolve this contradiction, but the biblical understanding of human nature can. The Bible teaches that nature belongs only to the God who made it and thus that ultimately it is not ours to do with as we please. Because the Bible also teaches that we are, as creatures made in God's image, capable of knowing God's will and purpose, therefore compelled to care for God's creation—as both servants and ambassadors.

Niebuhr teaches us a second and related lesson about apologetic communication through dialectical habits, the active way in which he brings into play every side of the disagreements that separate believers and unbelievers. Communication scholars in our own time are more likely to call this approach "dialogic," "two-way," or "interactive," but whatever terms they use, all will agree that this is at once an ethical and effective approach to communication.[22] It is ethical because it is honest, and it is effective because honesty opens people to all the complexities and difficulties that coincide with inquiry. Our convictions may make it certain that we will never agree with an opponent, but messages that fairly voice every side of an issue simultaneously demonstrate respect for our opponents even as they put a more elaborate understanding of these complexities in play.

The value of dialectic can be illustrated by the problems that arise when defenders of the Bible fail to employ dialogue in their efforts to address worldly challenges. The communication practices that coincide with what is often called "creationism" often exemplify this failure. By "creationism" I do not mean the doctrine of creation, the basic premise of the Bible that God created the natural universe. I mean interpretations of that teaching that presumptively rule out and therefore fail to hear science's evolutionary claims. Those in the scientific world charge creationists with dishonesty for refusing to examine evolutionary claims, but we may also want to consider whether creationism honestly examines what the Bible claims. If nature is God's work as the Bible teaches, then believers can confidently assume, as a matter of faith, that any thorough examination of the natural world will bear out God's revelations. Faith commands us to assume that when scientific explanations appear to contradict Scripture, this is only because they are incomplete explanations. We believe that nature is a creation, because the God who alone knows the full story of the universe has revealed it as such. Faith then gives us confidence that we can examine the claims of science without fear, and a fearless encounter between the Bible and science will naturally occur as dialogue. If faith means that we cannot rule out scientific claims merely because they appear to contradict the Bible, we will then do better by listening to those claims. The believers who make themselves receptive to science by engaging it in dialogue are not being unfaithful to God; rather, they are obediently carrying out what faith assumes about the creation—that the more we know about it the more we will know the glory of God.

Conclusion

As an apologist who was able to reach a very broad audience in the United States, Reinhold Niebuhr is somewhat comparable to the twentieth century's most famous apologist, C. S. Lewis. It was Lewis who insisted that Christians recognize that the circumstances in which we communicate the gospel have changed fundamentally in modernity. When he used the phrase "God in the dock" to represent this, he meant a shift in what is traditionally called the burden of proof.[23] Presumption now lies with modernity against the Bible, and this means that Christian communicators can only hope to succeed by more actively engaging the claims of the modern world.

I think that this is true in general, but it is more especially true in the academic universe that both Lewis and Niebuhr inhabited. I also believe that the general goals of communicating our faith can only be achieved if we follow the example of these great apologists in targeting learned culture more actively. We often forget that the modern university has evolved from original universities that were created to execute Christ's Great Commission (see Mt 28:18–20). Because of its Christian roots, the modern university continues to have a missionary influence upon our world, and so if believers can reclaim a voice within this academic culture, they can more effectively continue its traditional work.

CHAPTER 33

FRANK SHEED: INITIATING
DIALOGUE ABOUT BELIEF

Margaret M. Mullan

Abstract: In Frank Sheed's (1897–1982) dialogic approach to theology means meeting relevant questions, engaging the power of language to explain reasons for belief, and seeking meaning in relationship with God. Sheed's invitational questioning offers believers and nonbelievers a way of reflecting on meaning and encourages participating in today's "Speakers' Corners" like social media. Through public discussions as a sharing of beliefs, participants understand why one's own particular beliefs matter enough to be shared.

Introduction

"All right, you say Christ claimed to be God and proved his claims were true. So what?"[1] The question rang out from the audience before the platform in Speakers' Corner in Hyde Park, London. Catholic platform-speakers Frank Sheed and his wife Maisie Ward long remembered this question: "That 'So what?' rang in our ears. . . . It was no use to prove a doctrine to [men and women] if they did not understand what it meant."[2]

Sheed, as an Australian law student studying in England, was first attracted to understanding his faith through listening to these lively discussions about Christian beliefs in Hyde Park. A speaker would introduce a topic, people might stop to listen, an audience member would shout a question or challenge, and the speaker's response might lead to more questions or to listeners walking away. As a platform-speaker for forty-eight years and writer/publisher for over fifty years, Sheed spent a long time engaging in the "So what?" question.

The provocation "So what?" still invites believers to question if belief matters enough to be discussed.[3] Sheed did not wait for people to go to a brick-and-mortar church to learn about religious belief; he shared his reasons for his belief amid a park's busyness of everyday life. Always attentive to openings for possible religious dialogue, Sheed might go in search of today's public platforms, like social media, to talk about belief.

Amid environments of people avoiding public discussions about religion, Sheed's writing extends an invitation to use a dialogic approach for initiating religious discussions. A dialogic approach begins in acknowledging one's own particular perspective and remains invitational to ongoing learning.[4] This chapter focuses on the 1966 book *God and the Human Condition* (hereafter *Condition*) in which Sheed addresses pressing questions of his day and proposes that a relationship with God offers a reason and purpose for living.[5] Sheed offers communicative gestures for inviting public discussions about personal beliefs, and one could extend these invitations to dialogue in our contemporary public meeting places: social media sites.

God and the Human Condition

In *Condition*, Sheed invites seeking an encounter and understanding of God as a personal and a shared experience. For Sheed, many church attendees lived religious ritual without personally knowing the God of their creed or understanding why they practiced this faith.[6] Theology, he posited, should be rooted in learning about and loving God: "Each new thing learned about God is a new reason for loving [God]."[7]

First, Sheed begins *Condition* meeting the questions of his day, as a dialogue of *aggiornamento*—a bringing up-to-date—with his response to the Catholic Church's *aggiornamento* happening in the 1960s. Sheed engages questions such as: Is faith necessary? Can the mind know or understand God? How does someone experience God? Sheed offers possible responses to these questions by describing what a relationship with God might look like and why this relationship helps one handle life's problems. He suggests that an encounter with God is a real experience, a true reality. He hoped that all those reflecting upon the questions might be open to a possible experience of "what the same truths might mean for [her] too."[8]

Second, to those who would propose that religious beliefs stay in the unspoken, personal realm, Sheed responds that God—by nature as the Word—promotes communicating the meaning one finds in belief. God endows language as a powerful communicator of theological meaning. If words are imbued with meaning, then reflecting upon and sharing these words helps both speakers and listeners come to understand the meaning of God's messages.

Sheed describes how language both communicates well and falls short of fully communicating theological realities. While "our Lord's human concepts and their utterance in human words bore the infinite,"[9] "our language is naturally soaked in the finite."[10] Words that are "light-bearing," by analogy, may point to a reality beyond the meaning of a word or concept.[11] In Christian tradition, words may be infused with the presence of God, with the incarnation of Christ as the quintessential communication of divine presence.[12] Sheed, speaking in particular to Catholic Church members of his day, invites believers to privilege reflection on the word of God in Scripture and through God's Son who reveals God.[13]

Even if all language is limited in its communication of the meaning of realities, reflective communicators courageously and humbly select language to describe reasons for belief. Sheed states, "God we see as in a glass darkly (1 Cor 13:12)—and we *say* more darkly still."[14] Jesus calling his followers to "Go and teach all nations" (Mt 28:19) includes helping people "to see deeper into [words'] meaning and unpack the reality concentrated in them."[15] According to Sheed, the communicator, inspired by those who have gone before her, who have talked about Scripture, revelation, and God's love, feels she does not speak alone and is joining an ongoing conversation about the meaning of these powerful words.

Third, Sheed describes belief as a discovery of a meaningful relationship with a living God. Accordingly, "God is not a problem to be solved, not even a solution to be admired, but a reality to be possessed, contemplated, conversed with, loved, enjoyed."[16] Furthermore, one may come to know God through and beyond philosophy. "Philosophy is the work of men seeking to know more of God; Scripture is the work of God seeking to be known by men."[17] The words in Scripture communicate a God seeking to be known by all people. While one can come to know the divine through human experiences like sensing the infinite or experiencing joy, only Jesus reveals love as the defining characteristic of God.[18] Reflecting on Jesus Christ leads one to understand God through a relationship.

For Sheed, "What really matters . . . is the impact revelation makes upon us,"[19] which can lead to loving God. Because "love craves knowledge," therefore, "it would be strange to love God and not want to know more about that God. Love craves not only to know but to be known."[20] A believer continues to be impacted by revelation and to seek understanding of God. Sometimes a believer may not be able to explain how a relationship vitally impacts her, and yet she can still experience that a relationship is significant to her. Throughout *Condition*, Sheed encourages reflecting on the meaning of revelation, the words used to understand that meaning, and the persons intimately linked in meaningful relationships.

Meeting Questions

In the 1920s, when he first visited the platform for the Catholic Evidence Guild[21] in Speakers' Corner, Sheed did not fully understand his own religious beliefs and saw platform-speaking as a way to learn about his faith.[22] He wanted to understand truths about God and the world and believed this living truth could be shared with others.[23] Although Sheed did not thoroughly document his own personal questions about his faith, he continually proposed and addressed hypothetical questions arising in response to his street or book reflections. Throughout his speaking and writing, Sheed's discussions voiced and responded to real questions.

Although he had an outgoing personality, Sheed did not initially—or ever—feel completely comfortable going to Hyde Park for the discussions.[24] He felt that his words were sometimes unclear and that his audience sometimes misunderstood him. However, every Sunday from 1920 until 1970, he publicly reflected on why and how he believed in God and his religion. Public dialogue about one's own belief involves an ongoing encounter—however uncomfortable—with questions from others or from oneself. Communicators like Sheed offer encouragement for sharing one's beliefs however certain or uncertain one is about one's beliefs. Sheed shared not because he believed that he held all the right ideas; rather, he bore witness to a relationship that was vitally important to him.[25]

Throughout his years of speaking, Sheed broadened his discussions to address a wider audience and an alternative to written and spoken apologetics. Catholic Christians in London in the 1920s did not typically participate in street corner debates. The Catholic Evidence Guild presented a unique forum for Catholics to discuss their faith on public street corners. This particular guild initially took an apologetic approach of defending their religious beliefs.[26] At first, Sheed had also directed his books and public speaking to Catholic Christians who did not understand their own beliefs,[27] so his explanations were a defense of those Catholic beliefs. In these initial books, he used strong appeals to logic to convince his listeners of the reasonableness of his ideas. Yet during the years on the public platform, Sheed discovered that his audience did not seek reasonable logic for belief; they sought belief that something, or someone, mattered.

In response to the reactions of his audiences, Sheed switched from offering a defensive argument about his beliefs to an open discussion about belief. He realized, "I did not know when I began that one must never talk for victory—to show oneself right and the other [person] wrong."[28] Distinct from his fellow Catholic theologians, Sheed was shifting from delivering one-way lectures to laying ground for dialogue. He sought to meet the listener or reader as a fellow-seeker looking for meaning in experiences.[29]

This broadening of the audience within Sheed's work parallels, and at times precedes, the opening of the Catholic Church to its own dialogue with the people of the day.[30] Sheed believed the church must continue to grow in understanding, translating beliefs to guide believers in differing situations.[31] He encountered people who had no patience to listen to long explanations of reasons for beliefs. Thus, his writing style is very distinct from classical theologians engaging the same questions about faith. He uses words that make sense to an ordinary reader and a conversational tone that invites interruptions.

In Absence of Religious Discussion, Initiating Dialogue

Religious discussion outside familiar groups seems increasingly rare,[32] and today a decreasing number of young Americans attend or affiliate with an official church.[33] So, where are religious discussions taking place?

Studies report that typically offline religious practices align with online religious engagement.[34] If young people are not attending churches offline, they may not be engaging religion online, or religious online discussions, either. An absence of religious dialogue invites the presence of impassioned communicators: people, like Sheed, willing to initiate the conversation about belief. Sheed's life and messages invite religious believers into three communicative gestures as they seek to initiate such conversations: acknowledging their personal questions about faith, assuming their posture as learners about their faith, and embodying the posture of a learner through the act of speaking.

First, Sheed approaches religious conversations by acknowledging his own questions. He did not take the platform as the expert teacher or the one who knew more; he took the platform so as to continue engaging his own questions of faith. Before every public discussion, Sheed reflected upon his personal reasons for his own beliefs[35] and sought to understand his faith by confronting his own questions about this faith.

Sheed's questioning engages what German philosopher Hans-Georg Gadamer calls the art of dialogue as an art of questioning, considering, and working out common meaning.[36] Dialogue is an art of strengthening ideas through shared questions and expressed words and of questioning words to uncover the meaning in what is said. No one person determines the interpretation or fixes the outcome, but all who join in dialogue through questioning engage in proposing possible answers. In his personal reflections, Sheed noted that he always heard the imagined voices of the passersby shouting out valid questions in Hyde Park. As he practiced the art of dialogue, Sheed's questions came into focus and moved him to continue exploring his faith.

These questions drive Sheed's books. He contends that God has commanded seekers to ask questions: "Ask and you will receive" (Mt 7:7). Questions asked today by Millennials or by seekers of any age indicate openings for dialogue. Fellow-seekers who hold differing beliefs meet in the sharing of questions. As Sheed found in the Hyde Park platform a place for engaging questions, today religious believers might find social media a site for informal conversation, a sharing "out loud"—or online—of their own questions and/or possible answers. Communicators approach religious discussion by first acknowledging their own questions.

Second, Sheed assumed a posture of ongoing learner about the faith. His confidence to engage questions about faith sprang from his commitment to continue learning about all religious beliefs, and *Condition* encourages believers likewise to continue learning about their beliefs. He prefaces his discussion of belief claiming, "You and I are not great creative theologians, working on the frontiers of revelation. . . . [W]e are students of theology, doing our best to enter into and make our own [those] truths."[37] His position as a learner resists a privileging of himself as a teacher standing above the students. Engaging religious explorations alongside other students, believers who communicate about religious belief refuse to claim a high ground of certain understanding or interpretations.

By listening reflectively before, during, and after speaking, Sheed demonstrated his commitment to learning.[38] He sought the best words for describing "what the same truths might mean for [others] too."[39] While speaking, he did not seek to win arguments but to share—as clearly as he could—beliefs that he found vital for living. On leaving the platform, Sheed would again reflect upon his speaking and assess the effectiveness of his explanations.

Dialogic communication emerges through learning from others.[40] Taking a position as co-learners, religious believers are reflecting alongside fellow-learners. Aware that "the speaker and his message reach the hearer together,"[41] Sheed practiced respectful speaking and listening. He stressed showing courtesy, even reverence, toward each audience member, because the speaker was a fellow-seeker trying to describe her own life-giving truths.[42]

Third, Sheed lived his commitment to learning by actively, publicly, and willingly speaking about his faith. Sheed brought personal belief into spaces where religion was not discussed, because he felt more people needed to learn how to talk about why they believed what they believed. Maybe believers or nonbelievers do not feel comfortable speaking about faith because they do not know how to explain their own beliefs. Sheed learned to talk about his faith by stumbling through attempts to speak clearly and thoughtfully. One learns about one's own belief by verbalizing it.

One might read about God endlessly, but these words might bear no real meaning for a person.[43] One who has found that God's words do bear important meaning in one's own life is prepared to talk about God in public settings.[44] Beliefs considered to be vitally important are worth expression in public discussions. Sheed found that publicly expressing his beliefs led him to get behind his beliefs in a living, deeply personal way.

Expressing one's belief indicates one's confidence about and openness to reactions to one's messages. Sometimes in public discussions, questions are asked and the speaker has no immediate answer.[45] In online discussions about religion, Sheed's example can lead one to continue the conversation through tough questions or misunderstanding. Even as participants seem to log off from the discussion, or leave the group discussing the question, believing communicators hope for future discussion and believe that meaningful dialogue will happen.

Conclusion

Does belief matter enough to be shared publicly? In a world of people avoiding discussions about meaningful realities like religion, Sheed's commitment to finding or starting the conversation encourages believers to voice their reasons for, and even uncertainties in, believing. Sheed felt that the Christian faith offered meaningful answers to life's questions, answers compelling enough to be shared. His dialogic approach to religious discussion offers believers and nonbelievers a way of reflecting on meaning and encourages participating in today's Speakers' Corners. In the sharing of beliefs, we understand why a particular belief matters at all. Even if no one else ever joins the discussion, the believer who speaks from and about her own questions hopes to receive insight from the questioning.[46] Like Sheed, we believe communicating about belief can be meaningful for someone else—if only the communicator herself—and we hope that expressing answers to our life questions resonates with someone. In the absence of religious discussions, simply speaking about belief starts the conversation and opens the way for possible dialogue.

CHAPTER 34

Hans Urs von Balthasar: "Kneeling Rhetoric" in Dark Times

Craig T. Maier

Abstract: This chapter examines the significance of Hans Urs von Balthasar's (1905–1988) work, specifically *The Glory of the Lord*, for Christian communication theory and practice. Balthasar contends that Christianity has lost its ability to acknowledge and wonder at the awesome beauty of God. His work suggests a new understanding of Christian communication—*kneeling rhetoric*—that attends to and proclaims God's glory amid the spiritual darkness of our times.

Introduction

Following his ordination to the Catholic priesthood in 1936, Hans Urs von Balthasar planned to settle into a quiet ministry as an editor of a respectable Jesuit journal in Munich. The increasing oppressiveness of the Nazi regime, however, ended this dream. By 1940, he had fled to Basel in his native Switzerland, where, alongside his pastoral responsibilities, he supported himself by translating classics of French poetry and theology into German. Balthasar enjoyed this humble work, seeing it as an opportunity to highlight voices that he worried might be lost. He also saw it as a chance to preserve the Western Christian tradition amid the terrors of the Second World War and the seemingly unstoppable advance of technology and secularism. Gradually, though, he felt the pangs of a new vocation to speak a fresh word into this moment of terror and uncertainty. "The tree of tradition must put forth new branches," he wrote. "Why should the one who gives form to what has been handed down from the past never do anything more than express his own thought through other people's voices?"[1] With this insight, Balthasar embarked on a new path, responding to the encroaching darkness by calling not for vigorous action but for the quiet contemplation of God's beauty.

This chapter explores the first and largest part of a seven-volume work titled *The Glory of the Lord*. Over the course of these volumes, Balthasar seeks to reorient Christian theology from an overreliance on reason toward a rapturous wonder at the glorious beauty of God. In fact, he places this sense of wonder at the center of Christian theological reflection. Balthasar described his project as articulating a kneeling theology.[2] Balthasar's kneeling theology suggests a new way of speaking Christ into the world, grounded in the discernment and proclamation of God's eternal beauty. This chapter calls his approach to Christian communication "kneeling rhetoric." Amid the chaos, disorder, and violence that defines our world, kneeling rhetoric has important implications for Christian communication. Balthasar invites us to deepen the formation of Christian communicators, explore the spiritual effects of media, acknowledge the revelatory power of communication, and embrace Christian communication as a means of bringing meaning and hope to dark times. Today, the loudest, angriest voices often seem to dominate in political, cultural, and religious discourse. In contrast, Balthasar urges us to recognize that Christian rhetoric always begins in silent, discerning, patient listening.

The Glory of the Lord

At the beginning of *Seeing the Form*, the first volume of *The Glory of the Lord*, Balthasar makes a twofold claim. First, he argues that our ability to perceive the Beautiful is intimately connected with our ability to believe in God. Second, and consequently, we must believe in God if we are truly to acknowledge the Beautiful.[3] If we read too quickly, we might dismiss Balthasar simply as a Swiss mystic seeking to cut away rituals and dogmas that would inhibit our encounter with the divine. However, he makes it equally clear that we cannot see God's splendor without the "form" provided by the Christian intellectual tradition, just as a painting without lines and shapes becomes a meaningless mess of color.[4] Balthasar argues that "seeing" and "form," always work together. Contemporary society has encouraged the separation of the two, forcing Christians to make a false choice between their hearts and their heads and stripping Christian belief of its spiritual power.[5] If Christians are to speak to a world filled with terror, he writes, we must recover our ability to wonder. When we begin with wonder, Christians encounter a glorious beauty that renders us speechless. Balthasar wants that speechless wonder of divine beauty to be the inspiration and starting point for our intellectual and spiritual lives. Thus, he declares that before we can embark on a Christian theology (which explores the true) or a Christian ethics (which concerns the good), we must have a Christian aesthetics (which accounts for the beautiful).[6] For Balthasar, then, Christian reflection must always begin with aesthetics.

At the beginning of his Christian aesthetics, Balthasar describes the beauty of God's redeeming work using four metaphors: *charis*, self-communication, *kenosis*, and *eros*. The first, *charis*, "refers to the attractive 'charm' of the beautiful" and describes the brilliant luminosity of God's glory.[7] The Greek word *charis* is the root of the words *charism* and *charismatic*, but *charis* here represents the ultimate gift that comes from God's constant revelation throughout Creation. Balthasar describes God's revelation as self-communication. This self-communication is ultimately *kenotic* or self-emptying, in which God "pours out his limitless love for the creature . . . into the void which is empty of himself."[8] Balthasar argues that the proper human response to this outpouring of love is *eros*. Though we often associate *eros* with sexuality and romantic love, *eros* in a spiritual sense represents the existential longing that carries a sinful soul out of its creaturely bondage and "enthuses and inspires man to collaboration" with God in the redemption of the world.[9] These four terms capture the essence of Balthasar's message: God communicates with Creation through his self-emptying Gift of Christ, and the Christian's first and foremost spiritual and intellectual calling is to receive this wondrous gift like a lover longing for the beloved who is absent.

The second and third volumes of *The Glory of the Lord* highlight twelve Christians who provide models of this type of longing. Five are theologians: Saint Irenaeus, Saint Augustine, Pseudo-Dionysius the Areopagite, Saint Anselm, and Saint Bonaventure. The other seven come from other fields: the medieval poet Dante, the Spanish mystic Saint John of the Cross, the French mathematician and philosopher Blaise Pascal, the German Romantic philosopher Johann Georg Hamann, the Russian novelist Vsevolod Soloviev, the Jesuit poet Gerard Manley Hopkins, and the French poet Charles Péguy. The fact that the five theologians Balthasar examines lived before Saint Thomas Aquinas is no accident. Aquinas, Balthasar observes, represents a dividing line in Christian theology, the moment when reason begins to supplant beauty as the heart of Christian reflection.[10] He argues that if we are interested in a Christian aesthetics today, we must therefore begin with Christian artists—poets, novelists, painters, sculptors, musicians, dramatists—and mystics, because they alone have remained attuned to beauty and wonder. For Balthasar, the absence of aesthetic reflection in contemporary Christian thought mirrors the unabashed worship of reason.

In response, Balthasar makes a stunning claim: To recover our voice, Christians must understand everything that they think, say, and do as a conscious blend of artistry and thought. For Balthasar, this linkage between faithful art and intellect was strongest in the early church. Balthasar sees the early church as struggling to craft a "bridge" between the competing influences of art and philosophy,[11] a bridge that he believes is vital for Christian life. Without philosophy to provide intellectual and ethical rigor, myths, rituals, and other artistic expressions of the divine soon become formless fantasies unable to sustain serious belief. But without artistic expression, philosophical logic and dialectic transform religious beliefs into bloodless abstractions lacking resonance and power. In the midst of the gulf separating art and philosophy, Balthasar believes our true spiritual vocation is to become guardians of wonder. When we become these guardians of wonder, we discern, understand, and proclaim God's glory to a world in danger of forgetting God's presence.[12] Today, this calling is especially difficult. When much of the Western world can look up everything from the physics of the Big Bang to the latest celebrity scandal on our smartphones, wonder can be in short supply. Against the tide, guardians of wonder are everyday mystics, recognizing the infinite mystery of creation, longing after the everlasting gift of God's love, and inviting others to join them in praise of God's glory.

The Glory of the Lord's final two volumes focus on the histories of Israel and the early church, respectively. Here, Balthasar suggests that the guardianship of wonder starts with what this chapter calls "kneeling rhetoric." During "the long twilight" of the exile and postexilic period,[13] in which a fallen Israel contended with God's apparent absence, Balthasar contends that the Jewish people kept their faith alive through two practices, which he calls "events." The "speech event" describes Israel's constant interpretation and proclamation of the Scriptures that gave meaning to their lives.[14] The "blood event" expressed and enacted Israel's constant interpretation and proclamation in and through sacrificial liturgy.[15] Christianity continued these traditions. Where Israel's hope was bound up with the destiny of the Jewish people, the church's proclamation of the gospel and sacramental liturgy call all of humanity to acknowledge and participate in God's glory.[16] Balthasar's aesthetics acknowledges the power of speech and action in bringing the gospel to the world. His kneeling theology allows for a kneeling rhetoric that opens a space for the sacred in an aggressively secular age. Balthasar's moment, however, reminds us that this rhetoric must always retain its contemplative heart, lest it perpetuate the darkness it seeks to dispel.

A Moment of Artificial Light

The Glory of the Lord appeared in Germany between the years of 1961 and 1969, turbulent years during which the Second Vatican Council plunged the Catholic Church into an era of tremendous change, and a divided humanity lay under the threat of technological domination and nuclear annihilation. The stresses of the previous centuries had come to a head, and all branches of Christianity were struggling to adjust. The increasing demands of the Age of Enlightenment during the eighteenth and nineteenth centuries led many Christians to focus on what they saw as the inherent reasonableness of Christian doctrine. However, their attempt to speak to Christianity's secularist critics did nothing to stem the rising tides of relativism, skepticism, and apathy toward traditional Christian teaching.[17] In response, many Christians became increasingly militant, focusing on apologetics to defend what they understood to be their increasingly beleaguered worldview from external threats.[18] These assumptions lay behind the aggressive neo-Thomism that dominated Catholic seminaries in the early twentieth century, a pedagogical approach that frustrated Balthasar.[19]

Against those who believed that Christians could and should use reason to argue others into the faith, Balthasar sees the drive toward both "reasonableness" and defiant apologetics as a symptom of a deeper spiritual affliction in Western Christianity. Accordingly, Christians assume that they can define or defend particular teachings as if they were purely intellectual abstractions without stopping to wonder at the gift that lay beneath those beliefs. All too confident in their theological frameworks, they hammer home the tenets of their faith without ever allowing them to change their hearts, or the hearts of anyone else. This mind-set amounts to defending the walls of Christendom without stopping to consider whether those inside the fortress are spiritually starving to death.[20] Even as he appreciates the Second Vatican Council's attempts to renew the church, Balthasar argues that the council's attempt to make the church relevant did little to encourage Christians to recover the sense of holy wonder and divine awe that secularism and technological advancement had stripped away. Like ancient Israel, Balthasar suggests, Christians have found themselves in a long twilight of their own creation.

In describing contemporary Christianity as lost in twilight, Balthasar echoes Hannah Arendt's characterization of modernity as a moment of "dark times."[21] Arendt observes that the notion of dark times reflects a deep sense of confusion. When human life is beset by a constant murkiness, it becomes impossible to tell the difference between what is true and what is false. For Balthasar, contemporary society's influences—its media and technology, its rationalism, its preference for totalizing ideologies—often make it impossible for human souls to recognize the authentic Light of Christ. How should Christians respond to this moment of what Balthasar called "the *anima technica vacua*"[22]— literally, "the empty technological soul"? Perhaps we can look to Arendt. "Even in the darkest times we have the right to expect some illumination," she writes, adding that "such illumination may well come less from theories and concepts than from the uncertain, flickering, and often weak light that some men and women, in their lives and works, will kindle under almost all circumstances and shed over the time span that was given them on earth."[23] Balthasar urges a new sort of saintliness and a new sort of Christian discourse, both seeking Christ's light and speaking it unto the darkness. This is the calling of kneeling rhetoric.

Kneeling Rhetoric in Dark Times

Where kneeling theology strives after God's glory, kneeling rhetoric engages in speech and action that communicates this glory. While Balthasar himself never articulates a rhetorical theory in detail, his work suggests that kneeling rhetoric possesses three elements, each with its own implications for the theory and practice of Christian communication today.

First, and most fundamentally, Balthasar's work shows us that Christian communicators must have their hearts and minds formed spiritually and intellectually and cannot simply be trained in the latest communication technologies and techniques. For Balthasar, Christian communication necessarily begins in contemplation, and he reminds us that jumping to action without prayerful reflection—something that today's world often demands that we do—can do great harm. Such a point calls to mind Saint Augustine, who emphasizes that, before polishing their arguments and selecting their rhetorical strategies, Christian communicators must begin with prayer "to drink in what [they are] about to pour forth."[24] Here, we see the importance of providing Christian communicators with the depth of thought and faith necessary to respond to today's complex ethical, cultural, political, technological, and religious environment. Christian communication educators, especially at the college and university level, must help their students begin and continue this journey throughout their lives, while practitioners bear the responsibility of ensuring that their well never runs dry. A daily practice of prayer, worship, and discipleship remain vital, but Balthasar also urges us to interweave our diet of communication theories and strategies with readings from Christian mystical and spiritual writers. Christians such as Meister Eckhart and Saint Catherine of Siena, Charles Wesley and Anne Bradstreet, and Thomas Merton and Dorothy Day can all help us find wonder as we encounter the world.

Second, Balthasar's work allows us to see Christian communication as not only informational and persuasive but also potentially revelatory. We can tend to view communication simply as a tool for transmitting information, making people laugh or cry, or persuading others to do what we want them to do. Such a perspective can lead Christians to see rhetoric as a set of purely decorative techniques that help "get the Message out" or, less charitably, "dress up" ideas that are unpleasant or difficult to understand. In contrast, Balthasar's aesthetics suggests that the practice of communication itself has an influence on us. The images that we create, the metaphors that we use, the arguments that we make shape how we talk about, reflect upon, and ultimately encounter God. The vibrant mosaics of medieval cathedrals inspire a different type of awe than the simple walls of Quaker meeting halls. Describing God as a "mighty fortress" opens one way of thinking about God, while the metaphor of "loving parent" opens another. How Christians encounter the increase of nonbelievers in American society depends on whether they choose to frame this demographic trend as a disaster or an opportunity. Kneeling rhetoric calls Christian communicators to appreciate how their rhetorical and stylistic choices create the form that allows persons to see in particular ways. Style and substance remain inextricably intertwined.

Third, and perhaps most important, Balthasar's work challenges us to see Christian rhetoric as "artful practice"[25] that reveals God's beauty to people through discourse, image, and action. As discussed above, Balthasar's theological aesthetics draws heavily from Plato, who advocates a passionate rhetoric that fires the human soul with the beauty of Truth.[26] Contrary to neo-Thomist theologians, who tended to look toward reason as the foundation of their faith, Plato believes that people can never be argued into the truth but instead must be coaxed into its embrace, a process that Plato describes through metaphors of love and courtship.[27] Similarly, we might say that a Christian communicator in a Balthasarian sense should be what C. S. Lewis calls "a 'romantic theologian,'" someone "who considers the theological implications of those experiences which are called romantic."[28] Several have noted how C. S. Lewis's *The Chronicles of Narnia* use literary form to raise complex theological questions and invite Christians and non-Christians alike to think differently and more fruitfully about faith. Balthasar's aesthetics suggest a similar path, one that uses the artful play of language and imagery to awaken persons to God's glorious presence, to inspire their imaginations, and to call them to respond to God's love. In this way, kneeling rhetoric strives to speak to people who might long to know Christ but have forgotten how to recognize his presence in their lives.

Seeing kneeling rhetoric as an artful practice opens exciting new frontiers for Christian communication. While we might immediately think of Christian artists who pepper their work with Scripture references and use their art to preach with a heavy hand, kneeling rhetors elect to be more indirect, weaving faith in subtle but substantive ways into their work. The Irish rock band U2 is an important example. Through songs like "I Still Haven't Found What I'm Looking For" and "Walk On," they articulate a Christianity that transcends sectarian boundaries. We can see kneeling rhetoric in countless other places: in Shakespeare, whose plays ask profound existential questions that simultaneously reflect a deeply Christian sensibility; in the Catholic writer Flannery O'Connor, whose short stories deal with faith and ethics amid the stresses and struggles of ordinary life; or in the pop artist Andy Warhol, a devout Catholic throughout his life whose work struggles for meaning in an age of mass reproduction. In fact, Balthasar urges us to recognize the potential of all artistic expression to ask profound theological questions. Theological questions can appear even if its artistic content—love and murder, cross-country trips and family dramas, Marilyn Monroe and Campbell's Soup cans—is not explicitly theological. Kneeling rhetoric recognizes that the arts, when faithfully engaged, offer means for provoking thought, inspiring hope, pursuing peace and justice, and resisting oppression. Taken together, we can read Balthasar as offering a simple but powerful theology for an emerging church of communicators, "creatives," and "makers": pursuing beauty in the name of Christ can transform the world.

Conclusion

Balthasar's theological aesthetics leads us to see that, in dark times of war, social confusion, technological change, and economic uncertainty, Christian communication must always begin by looking toward the light. He challenges Christian communication scholars and practitioners alike to realize that our foremost task today lies in discerning, acknowledging, and bearing witness to the wondrous *charis* that imbues our efforts with confidence and joy. Each of the elements of kneeling rhetoric builds on the others: through formation that deepens our contemplative hearts, Christian communicators become aware of the spiritual significance of media and communication's revelatory power, transforming our work into an artful practice that maintains and manifests the authentic light of Christ in dark times. Balthasar's work poses urgent questions: Can we allow ourselves once again to be seduced by wonder at God's glory? Can we differentiate the Light of the World from the intoxicating glow of our smartphones and television sets? Can we communicate this wonder, this beauty, to others? Can we open a space for the sacred in a moment of spiritual twilight? As we ponder these questions, he writes, we may feel as if we are casting a message in a bottle into an uncertain sea. Still, Balthasar is not without hope. "To find land and to have somebody actually come across [this bottle], now that would be a miracle," he writes. "But sometimes even miracles happen."[29]

CHAPTER 35

Jacques Ellul: Communicating Wisely with Hospitable Resistance in a Technological World

Quentin J. Schultze

Abstract: Jacques Ellul (1912–1994) acknowledged that *The Presence of the Kingdom* (1948) was the departure for the rest of his work. In it, Ellul considers the problems of being a Christian "in the world" but not "of it" (Jn 17:14–16). The result is a classic book that helps Christians to communicate wisely through authenticity, hospitality, faithfulness, and community.

Introduction

As a teen studying law in 1932, Jacques Ellul had a remarkable experience while translating Faust. "I knew myself to be in the presence of something so astounding, so overwhelming that entered me to the very centre of my being."[1] Ellul says he "was converted—not by someone, nor can I say I converted myself. . . . From that moment on, I lived through the conflict and contradiction between what became the center of my life—this faith, this reference to the Bible . . . and what I knew of Marx and did not wish to abandon. For I did not see why I should have to give up the things that Marx said about society and explained about economy and injustice in the world. I saw no reason to reject them just because I was now a Christian."[2]

About fifteen years later, at the end of World War II, Ellul felt called to write *The Presence of the Kingdom* (hereafter *Presence*),[3] "a little book that would essentially provide a critical, Marxist-like Christian perspective on the presence of the Christian in today's world—not in the world in general, but in the world as it was."[4] It addressed the relationships among faith, technology, society, and media. Ellul considered the problems of being a Christian "in the world" but not "of it" (Jn 17:14–16); the dialectical tensions that govern human existence and order reality; the way society and the church elevate technological means over ends; and the tendency of public discourse to function as propaganda. He addressed these topics from multiple perspectives: as a professor of history, sociology, and law; as a lay theologian; and as an outspoken Reformed church leader in Bordeaux, France, where he also served in the French resistance to Nazism. The result is a classic book that helps Christians to communicate wisely through authenticity, hospitality, faithfulness, and community.

The Presence of the Kingdom in Historical Context

In *Presence* Ellul addressed, in the post-World War II period, the age-old biblical question of how to be "in" but not "of" the world (see Jn 17:14–16), and he puts communications media front and center. The same totalitarian concerns that drove the development of the scholarly discipline of mass communication under scholars such as Paul Lazersfeld, Harold Lasswell, and Wilbur Schramm led Ellul to discern the ways evil is spread and maintained institutionally in society.[5] Ellul proclaims, "We need a new form of communication between human beings, in order that the relations between them, distorted by their conditions of life, by class feeling, by prejudice, may, by a renewal of their intelligence, be recreated upon a personal and living plane."[6] To live faithfully God's command to be "in" the world but not "of it," Ellul argues that Christians need a fuller understanding of the dialectical tensions that govern human existence and order reality, the way society and the church elevate technological means over ends, and the tendency of public discourse to function as propaganda.

First, Ellul argues that human culture, or ways of life, exists in dialectical tension between good and evil. There is no perfect good or evil in culture and society; the Christian faith is a kind of idealism that cannot practically be institutionalized with perfection in the fallen world. Christians will discover "the opposition that exists between the Christian faith, the claims of revelation, and the life in the world and its demands, its faults, and its compromises."[7] Christians are caught "between two necessities." On the one hand, they themselves cannot make the world less sinful. On the other hand, it is impossible for Christians to accept the world as it is. They must act faithfully in the world without becoming wholly accommodated to the world.[8]

This distinction between the way things are and the way they should be in the world—including in the church—produces dialectical tension. Discovering, describing, and deconstructing the dialectic requires real-life, hard-nosed, clear-minded discernment. The Christian should, says Ellul, shuttle between the ways of the world and the claims of biblical revelation, looking for the points of tension that can illuminate the nature of specific human struggles and particular institutional brokenness. What exactly is wrong with the church, media, government, or economy? What are the media and everyday people saying about current issues? Upon what do they base their claims?

Ellul says the faithful communicator needs to reject any simple descriptions and solutions. The world is rarely so neat. A good-bad dialectic runs right down to the hearts of people. Moralistic slogans based on opposing ideologies wrongly assume that one ideology captures all of the relevant questions and has all of the real answers; everyone else should simply listen. Ellul calls such simplistic categories part of the "attitudes of the world."[9] In Ellul's historical context, Christians were arguing that "the Christian ideal" was represented in such categories as Communist, Liberal, Pacifist, and Personalist.[10] Instead of adopting such worldly categories, faithful communicators are called to live an "agonistic" way of life, wrestling continually with uncertainties and discontinuities while bringing salt and light to the world and becoming "sheep in the midst of wolves."[11] The faithful communicator realizes that judgment and grace exist simultaneously in society and in the lives of individual Christians.[12] By addressing such dialectics, a communicator is more open to the radical nature of human problems and to creative communicative possibilities.

Second, Ellul writes, "The first great fact that emerges from our civilization is that today everything has become 'means.' There is no longer an 'end'; we do not know whither we are going. . . . We set huge machines in motion in order to arrive nowhere."[13] Individuals still have their own personal ends—such as a higher salary or a job promotion. But church and society increasingly lack a vision of what they hope to be or should become. For instance, today the church chases after technological means—in worship, in outreach, in numerical growth—but often forgets how to be a faithful, prophetic community in the world. In recent years many church leaders simply assumed that employing screens in worship venues would make services more attractive to teenagers. In Ellul's prophetic vision, humans themselves become means in society. For instance, each person becomes "an obedient consumer, and with his eyes shut he swallows everything that economics puts in his mouth. Thus, fully persuaded that we are procuring the happiness of man, we are turning him into an instrument of these modern gods, which are our 'means.'"[14]

The rapid development of so many amazing communication technologies has outpaced humans' ability to understand how, when, where, and especially why to use them. Communication technologies mightily capture humans' imagination because they symbolize revitalized human relationships. Who would oppose improved relations in church or society? But new technologies never quite deliver on the utopian promises. They do not need to, because there are always newly emerging technologies that promise to overcome the limitations of the previous ones. But to what ends—purpose or *telos*—are the older and newer technologies aimed? "Until now," Ellul observes, technological methods or "means were created for the sake of the end: now the end no longer inspires, for it is only a word, it is not even a myth. It no longer creates anything, and the mechanism of the creation of means is very different. The latter reproduce themselves mutually."[15]

Third, Ellul argues that media tends to function as propaganda, and he grounds his critique in the inability of audiences to see through the mass-mediated portrayals of reality. He argues that most people no longer believe in their own life experiences, judgments, and thoughts.[16] Instead they willingly adopt the views they receive via media. In addition, the more that any particular view of reality—such as expressed in news reports, opinion pieces, or documentaries—is shared by contemporaries, the more likely a person will accept that opinion as truth. Ellul calls this the "basis of all propaganda."[17]

Ellul calls the flood of mediated content "the shadows."[18] He contends that these shadowy messages become a person's "life" and "thought," replacing firsthand experiences. As a result, a person "gets used to living in complete incoherence, because all his intellectual activity is taken up with furtive visions, themselves without a past and without a future, and without any substance even in the present."[19]

I imagine this today as the life of a multimedia, multitasking person overloaded with incoming and outgoing messages via e-mail, social media, and other digital media. This modern person's life is filled with instantaneous messages but often devoid of connections with history, tradition, or a sense of God's overarching redemption of humankind. Even more than in Ellul's day, an individual has to address so many interesting distractions that she or he may lose intellectual and spiritual traction.

According to Ellul, people simply accept simplified and condensed "explanatory myths" spread by the media themselves and adopted and reinforced by many citizens.[20] In the post–World War II era, Ellul points to ideological myths that animated large political, economic, and military movements, such as "the bourgeois myth of the Hand of Moscow; the Socialist myth of the Two Hundred Families; the Fascist myth of the Jews; the Communist myth of the antirevolutionary saboteur."[21] These types of myths, he says, help the individual "avoid the fatigue of thinking for himself, the disquiet of doubt and of being questioned, the uncertainty of understanding, and the torture of a bad conscience."[22] He holds that the modern individual can pretend to have a clear conscience by employing a widely believed myth to justify his or her own actions or inactions. The myth may be partly true, but it at best clouds people's perceptions of reality. Myths are like popular stereotypes that become dangerous when people act upon them. When Christians hold such myths, they find it is "impossible to live one's faith, to bear a genuine witness."[23]

Today the explanatory myths are spread most powerfully by media designed to appeal to a social or ideological group. In television, MSNBC and the Fox News Channel represent liberal and conservative perspectives, respectively. Hosts and guests create "talking points" that are mini explanatory myths. These and other broadcast and Internet outlets pay writers, researchers, and archivists to support on-air celebrities' ongoing use of explanatory myths about the latest news events, sometimes even creating news themselves by referring critically to each other's media coverage. Explanatory myths often reflect assumptions about race, gender, economics, social class, power, and religion. They are supported by labels like "progressive," "socialist," "rightwing," and "fundamentalist." Additional explanatory language includes "social justice," "liberty," and "homophobia." Such terms are highly evocative, but they obscure the underlying complexity of social reality. Who *really* are these people? What do they *really* believe?

Perhaps Ellul's most significant point is that public, mediated discourse is largely self-confirming, self-legitimizing propaganda; the media give audiences the mythical content they believe or want to believe, not what is true. Furthermore, the myths are promulgated by media personalities, political operatives, and special-interest groups who do not understand reality and who demonize their opponents. There is very little real communication based on mutual understanding of the reality behind explanatory myths. Today such "communication has become practically impossible," concludes Ellul. "In order to understand each other we need a minimum of ideas which are common and valid for everyone, of prejudices and values which are the same for all—and most often unconscious."[24] And in order to achieve any such consensus about reality, we need to pursue the right kinds of communication practices that will open dialogue, engender listening, and equip people to see beyond and beneath the myths of the day.

Moving Forward with Wise Resistance

For Ellul, the most critically important practices for renewing human communication are authenticity, hospitality, faithfulness, and community. Together they represent a wise and revolutionary departure from contemporary public discourse.

First, authenticity describes one aspect of Ellul's call for Christians to create an honest, integrated "way of life."[25] Ellul contends that Christians no longer know who they are because they have so deeply accommodated themselves to the language, explanatory myths, and everyday practices of the secular world. In order for Christians to authentically mean what they say and say what they mean, they must know what they believe, understand how their beliefs are distinct from those of the world, and determine how to communicate those beliefs. Ellul recalls how in the sixteenth century, Reformed Christians employed a distinct style of life in opposition to Renaissance living.[26] He contends that it is not adequate for Christians to have individual virtues; they need a shared, authentic way of life that will speak to others and to themselves about what it means to be radically faithful in a fallen world.[27]

Today the lack of authenticity in public discourse is especially apparent in public perceptions of institutions such as government, business, and church. For instance, the church must contend with the rise of the "nones"—the fastest-growing religious group, made up of people who claim no religious affiliation and are highly skeptical of religious institutions even if they personally claim to be spiritual. In the United States, the nones represent about 20 percent of the population.[28] For the church to be an authentic witness in the world, Christians must believe and live out what they profess. Their lives must authentically speak the gospel.

Second, Ellul additionally calls for communication based on hospitality, namely, opening up one's heart, mind, and space to those who are different—to the stranger in one's midst. A communicator must avoid simplistic stereotypes in order to speak to particular individuals and groups; she or he can do this only by becoming more intimately knowledgeable of people's actual feelings, beliefs, and attitudes. Stereotyping is the opposite of hospitality; it makes no room in our minds and hearts for who others really are. Explanatory myths, which are society-wide stereotypes, deceive us into thinking we know others.

In the ancient Hebrew and Christian traditions, such openness to learning from and about others is the basis for hospitality toward the stranger.[29] The key practice is listening, or attending to reality. Listening is not just hearing. It is understanding, along with the naturally human responses of sympathy and empathy. And, at its best, it produces sympathy and empathy toward those with whom we are called to communicate. When we invite others to tell us their stories—of life, faith, fear, and joy—we can become moved by their individual experiences. They are no longer stereotypical persons easily dismissed by explanatory myths. For instance, listening to stories of homeless people will invariably undermine people's assumptions about the causes, nature, and impact of homelessness.

Third, Ellul also calls Christians to be faithful rather than merely effective communicators. Faithfulness means, first, not depending solely on human intellect and ingenuity but necessarily on the work of the Holy Spirit, who can "break through" the separations among people. The world relies on technique, whereas the Spirit alone can give Christians the language they need to speak to their biblical neighbors.[30]

Faithful communicators also believe in "the event," the gospel. This historic event—unlike news reports and other "trifling incidents"—"includes within itself the meaning of all the development of the past, and significance for the future."[31] To use more contemporary language, God's intervention in history through Jesus Christ established the metanarrative that faithful communicators employ as the basis for all of their own storytelling. This metanarrative is the church's revolutionary alternative to mass-mediated explanatory myths.

Perhaps modern prayer has become one of the biggest stumbling blocks to faithful communication with God and neighbor. Instead of viewing prayer as humble dialogue—especially listening—with an almighty and omnipotent God, we tend today to see prayer as a way, or technique, for getting what we want. This concept of prayer as mere technique contributes to the inauthenticity of the church, especially when people decide to give petitionary prayer a try and are quickly disappointed with the outcome. Faithful prayer, like faithful communication in general, offers all petitions and celebrations to God in the knowledge that the Holy Spirit will hear and respond according to God's good will, not necessarily according to our limited understanding of what is best for us and others. Put another way, faithful communication does not occur in a closed system of cause and effect but in an open system in which God knows and does what is best in tune with his covenant to be our merciful Father.[32]

Finally, Ellul calls for communicators who are anchored in local communities of faith where they can "learn afresh what the fruit of the Spirit is." By rebuilding parish life and rediscovering Christian community, faithful communicators can revive "the concrete application of self-control, liberty, unity, and so on."[33] In other words, worship and fellowship form right communication practices.

At a time when individualism is afforded such a premium in society, Ellul's call for community seems romantic and naive. The movers and shakers in society, the proud and the mighty, are the more domineering persons who seek publicity and love the limelight. Gaining celebrity status in all areas of life—from church to business and government—is a sign of personal success and a measure of a laudable career. Ellul will have none of this. The communists and socialists created powerful personas in his era, and with dismal consequences. Hitler and Stalin ruled with iron fists, not community-nurtured fruit of the Spirit. They spread powerful explanatory myths about the social benefits of collectivistic nations and undermined the church as a source of valuable prophetic insights.

Conclusion

Ellul recognized that the most authentic, hospitable, and faithful human communication practices are nurtured in communities of truth and love. "We need a revolution," concludes Ellul, "a revolution that attacks the bases of a civilization," a civilization "whose efforts tend solely toward transforming people into swine—all people."[34] Addressing the issues of faith, technology, society, and media, Ellul shines a light on much in modern society that needs to be understood and dealt with better. His book *Presence* offers excellent insights, as well as correctives, that are relevant today and, given the proliferation in technology, will remain so for the future.

CHAPTER 36

JOHN HOWARD YODER: ADVOCATING PATIENT PROCLAMATION THROUGH THE USE OF MIDDLE AXIOMS

Gerald J. Mast

Abstract: John Howard Yoder (1927–1997) advocated patient proclamation—what I call "gospel communication"—as a biblical framework for offering Christian witness in changing cultural contexts that are free to reject it. Yoder's forms of gospel communication embrace the particularity of evangelical truth and refuse to coerce the audience through appeals to self-evident knowledge or an imperialistic wider wisdom.

Introduction

While attending one of Swiss theologian Karl Barth's seminars at the University of Basel in the early 1950s, Mennonite missionary David A. Shank recalls sitting next to John Howard Yoder, who was also studying with Barth at that time. According to Shank, on this occasion Barth was explaining how the memory of Jesus Christ's death and resurrection on the one hand and the anticipation of Christ's future return on the other hand constitute the defining components of Christian hope. In response to a student who asked about the calling of Christians in the present time between the resurrection and the return, Barth said, "In between we look back and remember and we look forward and hope. We remember . . . and hope." Shank says he heard Yoder muttering under his breath in response to Barth's claim about memory and hope: "We obey."[1]

This often-repeated story about John Howard Yoder's correction of Karl Barth displays well Yoder's central theological conviction that the shape of the Christian life arises directly from the social and political posture of the Master and Teacher whom Christians profess to follow: a posture defined most profoundly by service to neighbor and love for enemies. In this chapter, I explore how John Howard Yoder envisioned gospel-centered communication in the contexts of both the church and the secular public policy arena. First, I examine the Mennonite tradition that shaped his theological vision. Second, I summarize the development of his theology of political communication in terms of two key concepts: middle axioms and body politics. Finally, I apply this model of evangelical political communication to the specific case study of a public Christian witness against capital punishment.

Mennonite Background

John Howard Yoder grew up in Wooster, Ohio, at the edge of a large Amish-Mennonite community, a descendant of influential ministers and leaders in that church community. An unusually gifted intellectual in a culture that did not place great value on academic skills, Yoder attended Goshen College during a time when this Mennonite school had become a center for renewing Anabaptist historical and theological knowledge among the Mennonites and in the guild of church history.[2]

Following his graduation from Goshen in 1947, Yoder accepted an assignment in France with the Mennonite Central Committee to renew their peace convictions and help lead the agency's relief efforts in Algeria.[3] While in Europe, Yoder earned a graduate degree in theology from the University of Basel and formed a network with other North American scholars committed to the transformation of the Mennonite Church in North America, known as the "Concern" circle. They published a series of pamphlets under the title of "Concern" that challenged the Mennonite church to recover the practices of the Anabaptists and the early church.[4]

Between 1955 and 1962, Yoder participated in the landmark postwar theological conversations in Europe between the historic peace churches (Brethren, Mennonite, and Quaker) and Protestant communions (Reformed and Lutheran) on the topic of the "Lordship of Christ over Church and State." Yoder's presentations at these conferences anticipated many of the theological and ethical arguments that he would develop in books like *The Politics of Jesus* and *The Christian Witness to the State*. Yoder's 1973 publication of *The Politics of Jesus* was a landmark moment in Mennonite theology, giving new and credible visibility to Anabaptist perspectives about politics, ethics, and biblical interpretation in evangelical and ecumenical circles.

Yoder was clearly a brilliant scholar and writer. At the same time, he was also a deeply flawed man whose relationships with women often crossed over the line into harassment and abuse.[5] This fact needs to be acknowledged since for Yoder theology must be lived, not merely taught. In other words, Yoder's life and actions are an important expression of his personal theological convictions—including both his inspiring advocacy for peace and his troubling abuse of power.[6]

Yoder shaped his innovative and influential theological vision in response to the defining events of his life. The most important of those events was the disaster of modern war that he witnessed as a relief worker in Europe. Another defining development was the increasing assimilation of Mennonite communities to Protestant denominationalism with its emphasis on social responsibility and leadership.

Yoder's vision drew from historic Anabaptist understandings of peaceful nonresistance and Christian community, but he also incorporated insights from his teachers at Basel such as Barth and Oscar Cullman.[7] A central claim that Yoder developed in his theological vision is that the gospel of peace proclaimed in the life, death, and resurrection of Jesus is not merely an ethic for unusually spiritual people gathered in, say, monastic or sectarian communities, but rather an expression of the created order.[8] For Yoder, the teachings of Jesus are actually realistic ways to deal with human problems and challenges. This is because Jesus Christ, who was present at the creation of the cosmos, is deeply in touch with how things really work in the world, even if it does not seem that way. Because of the deep and large truth that Christian disciples bear witness to, they can be patient with the diverse and contrasting norms by which their neighbors—including political authorities—make ethical choices. At the same time, Christians should expect that when the church displays the way of Jesus Christ in its social relationships and ethical decisions, it becomes the central vehicle for God's work in human history. From this perspective, the church, not the nation, is where the most truthful political action is unfolding.

Middle Axioms and Body Politics

Yoder's model of gospel communication incorporates two mutually reinforcing but distinct practices: middle axioms and body politics. First, in his 1964 book *The Christian Witness to the State*, he develops an approach to political communication based on "middle axioms," defined by Yoder as "mediating between the norms of faith and the situation conditioned by unbelief."[9] Yoder is critical of approaches to Christian political witness that are based on the assumption of the national state as the primary subject of God's action in history. This is because Yoder understands the biblical witness to define the church, not the state, as the central subject of God's action in history. As such, the church does not seek primarily to improve society or to make the state more nearly like the kingdom of God, since that is not where the future of God's peaceable reign lies. Instead, through God's providence the state "does not bear the sword in vain" (Rom. 13:4) but channels violence against violence so that enough order is maintained for God's principal project to unfold in the life of the church.[10]

So while the church does not expect representatives of the state to reflect the premises of the gospel, the church is nevertheless able to bear witness to the state about the lordship of Christ over history. This includes Christ's judgment of the idolatrous violence the state utilizes to legitimate and protect its own absolute autonomy. Such witness may include tactical interventions into public discourse through the use of premises that are accepted by the national culture and that represent the national culture's best human commitments. For example, in American society, the church may make constitutional arguments about matters such as human rights and religious liberty that reflect the lordship of Christ but that are articulated as an interpretation of the U.S. Constitution. Such interventions are designed not to persuade the nation to be more Christian but to bear witness to Christ's ultimate authority over the state. In short, middle axioms, when construed properly, assist the church in making the its witness accessible in language that can be recognized by those who are not yet ready to hear the church's full witness, who are not yet ready for complete surrender to Jesus Christ.

The church's self-understanding and biblical worldview is expressed by contrast in the practice of "body politics," a practice that Yoder developed more fully in his later writings. This practice should be viewed as the other side of the coin of middle axioms. Middle axioms convey what the church's witness looks like when it addresses itself to a context defined by an alien cultural language that may include disobedience to Christ. Body politics by contrast display the form and content of the gospel in the idioms of the church, including such practices as binding and loosing, breaking bread together, baptism, gift discernment and empowerment, and consensus decision-making. These practices show the surrounding world a picture of God's will for the world: "the people of God is called to be today what the world is called to be ultimately."[11]

In Yoder's body politics theology, then, a "sacrament" like the Eucharist—breaking bread together—becomes a performance practice that exhibits the beginning of economic sharing.[12] Likewise, the process of binding and loosing described in Matthew 18 inaugurates the practice of restorative justice as a gospel response to transgression and offense.[13] Baptism is a display of the new life of reconciliation to which believers are called, a life in which old divisions and identities are exceeded in a new humanity defined by "interethnic inclusiveness" and created by "inducting all kinds of people into the same people."[14] Confirming the gifts of every member of the body expresses the human dignity that the fullness of Christ now defines each person who has become part of the community of faith.[15] The unforced consensus that arises in meetings following the "rule of Paul" found in 1 Corinthians 14 respects the diversity of voices entailed in a "truth-finding" conversation genuinely attentive to the Holy Spirit.[16]

Yoder's vision of the church's body politics offers an insightful tool for describing collective communication as practices and routines by which a social body both takes action and displays what it knows. Intriguingly, Yoder invokes the well-known terms of media theorist Marshall McLuhan to explain why the "shape of God's people" matters: "medium and message cannot be divorced."[17]

This invocation of media theory situates the form of the church's life together as the medium in which the gospel message is conveyed.[18] The practice of sharing bread and wine is as important as the theological meaning of communion. The way committee meetings are conducted is as important as the decisions that are made.

How to Make Political Witness That Is Good News

Yoder's twofold model of political communication works in application to an issue like capital punishment—although a Christian could develop a tactical and practical framework to other issues like abortion, war, poverty, health care, or minimum wage. In the case of capital punishment, Yoder provides the cues for both the body politics and middle axioms by which state-sponsored execution may be opposed in a gospel manner.[19]

Yoder begins by describing an example of Christian forgiveness publicly expressed in collective action. On July 18, 1957, Cleo Peters was released from prison and embarked on a violent rampage, during which he shot and killed Amish farmer Paul Coblentz. Before the trial, twenty-eight people, mostly Amish, were refused for jury duty because of their opposition to applying the death penalty. Peters was found guilty and sentenced to die in the electric chair.

In response, the Amish community took seriously Jesus' command to forgive their enemies as taught in Matthew 6:14–15. They embodied the commandment in a body politics. Amish families invited the parents of the killer into their homes. Many signed petitions to the governor asking for the commutation of Peters's sentence. Acting in response to these petitions, the governor commuted the sentence, only hours before Peters was scheduled to be executed. Following the commutation, many Amish—including the widow of his victim—sent him letters of forgiveness and invited him to repent. When a group of Amish ministers visited him in prison, they learned that Peters had become a Christian, partly due to the forgiveness the Amish extended to him. Their display of forgiveness received considerable attention from the surrounding public, thereby confirming Yoder's insistence that such collective Christian practices both obey the gospel and communicate it.[20] These practices are examples of what Yoder called body politics.

To undergird his account of the church's body politics, Yoder explores biblical principles on human life. Reflecting the story of Paul Coblentz and the conversion of his killer, Yoder suggests that human life is sanctified—created and set apart by God—and therefore belongs to God alone.[21] As God's image bearers, human beings even in their corrupted and sinful condition have capacities for repentance and restoration denied by capital punishment. Thus, taking human life under any condition is an attack on the basic evangelical testimony of God's patience: "not wanting any to perish, but all to come to repentance" (2 Pet 3:9 NRSV).

Yoder then develops a biblical perspective on the place of killing in the moral order and as a function of the state. He interprets Old Testament laws about killing to function primarily as a restraint against unbridled vengeance. Such restraints are based in God's original response to Cain's murder of Abel: God protected Cain from the vengeance of those who wished to execute him for killing Abel.[22] In the New Testament, this restraint against unbridled vengeance is amplified by Jesus' call in the Sermon on the Mount to refuse to take an eye for an eye but to instead love enemies and return good for evil. This demonstrates that God's highest intention for both divine and human response to evil is to oppose it not through vengeance but instead to "swallow it up, drown it in the bottomless sea of his crucified love."[23]

Yoder makes it clear that affirming the biblical testimony of respect for human life does not necessarily address the question of what we should expect of an "unbelieving society and of the state."[24] However, it is important to be "clear where we begin" as Christians: with the "certainty that death is not God's highest will for any man."[25] Christians who engage in public witness must be aware of their own deepest convictions about the way and will of the God of Jesus Christ as revealed in Scripture, even if their public argument with the state assumes secular grounds.

Next, Yoder shifts his perspective from the biblical grounds for the church's own "body politics" to the public argument addressed specifically to the state. In developing this middle axiom argument in the context of U.S. public policy, Yoder defends two key claims that are focused on popular and constitutional grounds. The first of these claims is that capital punishment does not serve as a deterrent to crime. Here Yoder is acknowledging and challenging a popular understanding of the role capital punishment plays in protecting society from lethal criminals. He cites psychological studies to argue that most people who commit murder do so under emotional circumstances in which they are unlikely or unable to weigh the consequences of their actions.[26] He compares crime statistics in states with and without capital punishment to show that the "murder rate is from two to three times greater in states which have and enforce the death penalty than in those which do not."[27]

The second argument Yoder advances on the ground of a middle axiom is the possibility of judicial error or prejudice. Because the death penalty, once carried out, cannot be reversed if new evidence appears or a mistake in forensic analysis is discovered, it contradicts the American constitutional system of checks and balances that assumes the possibility of appeals based on further knowledge or evidence.[28] Moreover, given how costly it is to effectively defend a person accused of murder, particularly if the death penalty applies, those with wealth have an unfair advantage over the poor in such cases. Yoder also argues that "the death penalty is used in the southern states as an instrument of racial discrimination."[29]

Conclusion

For Yoder, both body politics and middle axioms constitute proclamation of the gospel in a specific context: either the church with its biblical worldview or the nation with its constitutional and political premises. Thus, instead of seeking validity through appeals to a wider world, gospel communication patiently submits to the "conditions of meaning" available to its audience, accepting the possibility of rejection.[30] In fact, for Yoder, the good news "accepts as a price of its communicability that it must suffer at the hands of the audience."[31]

A proclaimed message is sometimes mistakenly regarded to be an aggressive imposition of an absolute or irresistible truth. Yoder helps us see instead the violence associated with persuasive messages that have been reworked and massaged for broad appeal, rather than for specific audiences and purposes. An example of such violence is the effort throughout church history to gloss over or even remove the specifics of Jesus' Jewish heritage from the story of salvation as told by the church—from the rejection of the Hebrew Bible by the Marcionites in the second century to the anti-Semitism of the German Christian movement during the Nazi Holocaust. Gospel communication is rooted in an unvarnished and particular truth as good news: in the life, death, and resurrection of the Jewish teacher Jesus Christ, the world has been reconciled. This evangelical knowledge is a truth that makes us free, not the least so because it gives us the opportunity to take it or leave it.[32]

CHAPTER 37

Carl F. H. Henry: Indicting Evangelical Inaction on Social Problems

Michael A. Longinow

Abstract: Carl F. H. Henry (1913–2003) confronted Christian fundamentalists in his day about a misguided emphasis on the external trappings of life, while other Christians and unbelievers were finding ways to fight racism, corporate injustice, and help feed the hungry. This chapter focuses on Henry's practical call for Christians to use education and political action to speak into the larger issues they had neglected, and how such suggestions still bear consideration in our day.

Introduction

Journalist and theologian Carl F. H. Henry claims that he once spoke to "a company of more than one hundred representative evangelical pastors."[1] He asked this esteemed group how many, in the last six months, had preached a sermon that condemned such social evils like "aggressive warfare, racial hatred and intolerance, the liquor traffic, exploitation of labor or management, or the like."[2] These were not personal sins Henry was asking about. He was asking about preaching that offered Christian solutions on societal vices. And when he asked these pastors to raise their hands if they had given such a sermon, not a single hand went up.[3] He recounts this moment in his 1947 book *The Uneasy Conscience of Modern Fundamentalism* (hereafter *Uneasy Conscience*). While some evangelicals have embraced Henry's social conscience, many still resist it; however, his call for practical faith rings as true today as it did in the 1940s.

In *Uneasy Conscience*, Henry suggested that Christian higher education and political action were key mechanisms evangelicals should use to place societal evils at the center of the Christian imagination. In their passion for saving lost souls, many fundamentalist Christians in the early 1900s turned their backs on such problems as racism, addictive lifestyles, broken homes, neglected children, and the effects of greed in the United States and around the world. Evangelicals were not unaware of social problems around them; their response, though, was to seek a return of the United States to what they believed were its religious roots, by means of soul-by-soul regeneration.[4] But their mind-set on how to do this marginalized them from mainline Protestants and Catholic Christians. Henry's world is very similar to ours, and the final section of this chapter tries to imagine what Henry might say to us about today's Christian higher education and politics.

Henry's *Uneasy Conscience* Laid Before Modern Fundamentalists

Henry used the first five of eight chapters in *Uneasy Conscience* to make the case for fundamentalism's problems, and chief among them was its conception of sin. Fundamentalists focused almost entirely on personal vices, preaching against drinking alcohol, attending movies, dancing, playing cards, gambling, and smoking. But this focus had unintended consequences. Fundamentalists and evangelicals with this mind-set inadvertently conceived social change as possible only through individual lifestyle choices. Henry considered this approach dangerously myopic, because it ignored the biblical reality that justice was also a function of social systems and institutions.[5]

The answer, Henry believed, was for evangelicals and fundamentalists to recover a biblical view of sin. He argued that God's redemptive message had social and political implications, not just personal ones. "The emperors," Henry reminds his reader, "must come to terms with Jesus" as God's divine challenge to earthly political and social authority.[6] Christianity does not simply challenge individuals; it challenges the greatest of human institutions. Henry called this wider perspective "a proper temporal focus."[7]

In the final three chapters, Henry turned to practical matters—to schools and political action among other things. While these pages show his care for elementary and secondary schools, his main focus was on Christian higher education. He spoke of the need for evangelicals to produce "a competent literature in every field of study, on every level from the grade school through the university,"[8] but not the kind that would be immediately shunned as simplistic or theologically monotone. The works put in students' hands would have to provide balance, showing "implications from the Christian as well as the non-Christian points of view."[9] Henry also called for a teaching of writing and communication that could, with skill, "contend for a fair hearing for the Christian mind, among other minds, in secular education."[10]

But Christian scholarship and writing would be of little use without classrooms in which to place them. Christian educators needed space and teaching tools to do their work. Separate institutions, no less rigorous than their state-funded counterparts, "must be reaffirmed,"[11] he insisted, with a new emphasis on training teachers with evangelical Christian values. There would need to be fresh attention to the forming or maintaining of these Christian schools, at all levels, "to concentrate the thinking of youth upon the Christian world-life view as the only adequate spiritual ground for a surviving culture."[12]

With such preparation, Christians might better engage the wider social ills of the world and peacefully work with those who disagreed with their views to bring the Kingdom of God more fully to fruition. While Henry opposed the "us vs. them" dichotomies that fundamentalists used when countering prominent liberal thinking, he did call "enemies" those who directly opposed traditional virtues and Christian beliefs in the public sphere. And he called believers to "pursue the enemy in politics, in economics, in science, in ethics" and to do so "girt in the Gospel armor."[13]

Yet even in this stance Henry was a peacemaker. One should work alongside those with whom one disagrees theologically, always ready to explain one's deeper purpose. "We join them in the battle," he urged, "seeking all the while more clearly to delineate the enemy, and more precisely to state the redemptive formula."[14] Ultimately, when Christians care for others, God has a way of making the gospel known even in the actions themselves. "Without minimizing the redemptive message," he wrote, "the church ministers by its message to those who stop short of commitment, as well as to regenerate believers."[15]

Henry's 1940s America

Henry's writing of *Uneasy Conscience* grew out of a unique personal experience with faith and learning and with the public marketplace of ideas. He was the first in his family to attend college.[16] Noted evangelical Frank Gaebelein, then headmaster of the Stony Brook School on Long Island, New York, suggested to a teenage Carl Henry that he look at Wheaton College, a liberal arts school outside Chicago, Illinois. His choice to attend there put Henry squarely on the path of evangelical education.[17] But this type of training was becoming a shrinking option. By the 1930s only one-fourth of state-run colleges and universities still had any sort of required (or optional) chapel services.[18] Schools like Wheaton that put a firm commitment to Christ at the center of their identity steadily diminished through the twentieth century. Today they number less than two hundred amid some four thousand accredited colleges and universities across the United States.[19] Henry's call for Christian schools, then, in *Uneasy Conscience* bore a sense of urgency drawn from his own experience.

Part of his experience, one that led to his mandate for strategic and informed political action, included news journalism. Henry had served as a hard-driving reporter for daily newspapers in upstate New York before attending college; he continued his reporting for Chicago publications part time while he was in college, and his skills, along with his theological grasp, later earned him an invitation to serve as the first chief editor for *Christianity Today*. But it was a tough job: his task was to draw a cohesive audience from across fractured Christian communities.[20]

The early United States had seen journalism, Christian faith, and education grow up together. The spread of media-crafted messages, along with a push for literacy and awareness of the marketplace of ideas, was vital to the expansion of Christian faith communities across the American colonies and through the frontier.[21] Yet while Christianity's growth in America was tied to media and communications, that force was an unwieldy one. By the time Henry took his first reporting job in the late 1920s, the religious press in the United States had mostly denominational roots, and publishing for Christians had splintered into warring theological approaches.

Some of the media discord in the early 1900s came in response to the ninety widely published essays comprising *The Fundamentals: A Testimony to the Truth*[22] and to those who aligned with the fundamentalist movement. Fundamentalists fought to return to the nation's religious roots, but Henry saw this as a failed project. Modernists within Christianity had, for generations before him, been turning to science for answers; but where fundamentalists called for separation from such believers, Henry saw a path to cooperation with them as one growing out of conversation. In *Uneasy Conscience*, he noted that modernist believers were those Christians "whose ideology was divorced from New Testament supernaturalism," and who had brought into their faith "the Renaissance humanism of modern philosophy"; as a result, these Christians were, in the late 1940s, a vocal force against fundamentalists.[23] He believed, however, these modernists were nonetheless disillusioned people,[24] ready to hear new suggestions. While suggestions that could bring common ground were few, one with the most potential was social change.

In 1947, the year *Uneasy Conscience* was published, two years after the end of World War II and a return home of more than a million American troops, the U.S. poverty rate had spiked upward.[25] Nearly 35 percent of Americans met the poverty classification.[26] Hunger was a national problem as prices after the war for food shot to unprecedented levels. Federal assistance for the elderly was in question as costs for Social Security seemed to make it unsustainable.[27] Unemployment had been epidemic in the United States since the collapse of the U.S. stock market in 1929 and, in the postwar years, seemed to be hitting youth particularly hard.[28]

Racism was also rampant in the mid-1940s. Segregation had been firmly entrenched in the United States despite some degree of integration of the armed forces and Major League Baseball.[29] Federal law had, by the mid-1940s, attempted at least a measure of labor protection for racial minorities, but it was meager and slow to spread nationally.[30] And change was slow, as well, within fundamentalist churches.[31] Mainline Protestant denominations, those that fundamentalists would consider liberal, were taking the lead on fighting racism and pursuing social justice issues among believers and in society.[32]

The Classroom and the Legislature

Early twenty-first-century evangelicalism finds itself in a similar social space to what Henry saw in the 1940s. In the wake of the numerous deaths of black men at the hands of police, grassroots movements like Black Lives Matter[33] argue that racial intolerance is alive and well. Some evangelical Christians seem indifferent to such claims or resist such movements' remedies to the problem.[34] Like many in the United States, they remain remarkably silent or speak only hesitantly in political forums or media settings. They seem to show little public concern about social injustice on the streets of U.S. cities, about the plight of refugees fleeing combat zones in Libya, Syria, and bordering nations, or about the effect of corporate greed on migrant laborers and their families in the United States who have, since before Henry's time, suffered painful exploitation.[35]

Part of Henry's lament in *Uneasy Conscience* was a loss of voice for Christian evangelicals in the public marketplace of ideas of his time. By pouring their energies into condemning what Henry considered nonessentials—practices like playing cards, social dancing, lighting up a cigarette, grabbing a beer—evangelicals lost their ability to build dialogue over much larger issues. Opponents of an evangelical approach to Christian faith, in the 1940s even as they do today, push back against what they hear as severe, condemnatory attacks on liberal lifestyles. Given that approach, such opponents have little appetite for listening to what Christians have to offer that transcends these externals.

For Henry, the classroom was one place where Christians had more to say, and more to do, than in perhaps any other venue in the mid-twentieth century. The other was political discourse, tied to public policy formation—lawmaking that could solve social problems and bring help to those in need. These two, the classroom and the legislature, were inseparable for Henry. He called for "a formula for a new world mind with spiritual ends, involving evangelical affirmations in political, economic, sociological, and educational realms, local and international."[36]

Thomas Jefferson had envisioned education in a democracy as a tool for building a virtuous society. John Dewey, in *Democracy and Education*, had argued in 1916 that education of the practical kind—hands-on learning—was crucial for building a sense of morality in young people.[37] But Dewey's moral compass for the classroom, drawing on a false assumption of innate virtue in all people, fell short, in Henry's thinking. And by the 1940s, Deweyan humanism had become a powerful force in the public schools and in ever-growing state and private nonsectarian universities. For children and young adults to have a sense of God's redemptive power through Christ, they would need the practical learning Dewey called for. Even better, students also needed the ability to articulate the redemptive power of their faith reasonably in ways that showed how biblical ethics were applicable to all of life, even for people who were not yet believers in Christ. Henry believed in the power of a rigorous curriculum and of thorough pedagogy, and speaks of these fondly in his own memoirs. So his admonition to twenty-first-century evangelical Christian educators would be to engage young people's minds as well as their imaginations in the classroom. He would endorse experiential learning, much as Dewey did, but with the groundwork of Scripture as a mandate for knowing and understanding experience.

Henry called for researchers and writers to step up and create "a competent literature in every field of study, on every level from the grade school to the university, which adequately presents each subject with its implications from the Christian as well as non-Christian points of view."[38] Henry believed Christian schools were crucial: Christian colleges, universities, and seminaries, he believed, were crucibles shaping potential thought leaders and social change agents in his day. He noted in *Uneasy Conscience* that "the spirit of the evangelical seminaries and colleges may largely determine the interpretation of social need."[39]

Certainly, these schools needed the highest quality teaching materials, produced by Christian scholars. But for Henry, the best researched scholarship by Christians, for the best teaching, could be applicable and even sought out in secular schools and universities. Henry was adamant about the need for evangelicals to go life-to-life, mind-to-mind, with those struggling with doubts—or who scoffed at evangelical beliefs. "The Christian life must be lived out, among the regenerate, in every activity," Henry wrote, "until even the unregenerate are moved by Christian standards, acknowledging their force."[40]

Furthermore, in the post-World War II era of hopeful political resolve, Henry said the voice of Christians in public policy settings needed to be evident, but so did their actions. "The world has awakened suddenly to the astonishing potentiality of an individual veto," he wrote, adding that "a single statesman with the convictions of [St.] Paul would echo the great evangelical affirmations throughout world politics."[41] Henry understood well the messiness of compromise in democratic governance. But he would nonetheless call evangelicals to involvement in the discourse that creates public policy undergirded by biblical principle: compassion for the vulnerable, care for the underserved, and protection through checks and balances against negligent and uncaring rule by elected leaders and unelected bureaucrats.

Conclusion

Evangelicals struggle no less today than they did in Carl F. H. Henry's day with legalism, an inability to dialogue constructively with ideological opponents, and a tendency to miss the real facts behind issues that divide them. Racism, poverty, greed, and economic injustice are still too little discussed by evangelicals if weighed against the time and energy put into discussion of evangelism and theological distinctions. Christian education and active involvement in political and social change are no less necessary now than in Henry's day, though their place in a liberalizing culture faces increasing scrutiny in an era when judicial interpretation of the First Amendment's Establishment Clause is being favored over the Free Exercise clause in that same amendment.[42] While there have been improvements since the 1940s, there is still much work to do in the twenty-first century for evangelicals, whose voices are too often marginalized by those whose observations of what Christians do, or leave undone, drowns out what they say. The road forward will be one of patient listening, reasoned dialogue, persistent action, and a commitment to go where the needs are, even when the road is shared with those of differing beliefs, or no belief at all.

CHAPTER 38

Chiara Lubich: Mediating Unity and Love

Dennis D. Cali

Abstract: Chiara Lubich (1920–2008), founder and president of the international lay ecclesial organization called the Focolare Movement, was hailed by the *New York Times* as "one of the most influential women in the Catholic Church."[1] In a speech to communication professionals in 2000, Lubich proposed guidelines that they might adopt in service of unity. This chapter outlines those communication principles that educe from her spirituality and that serve as fitting responses to our contemporary technologized times.

Introduction

In 1943–1944, World War II raged in Trent, Italy, where Chiara Lubich and her companions took shelter in a cellar. During one bomb raid, they gathered and read Jesus' prayer to the Father "that all may be one" (Jn 17: 21 NJB). "Unity" galvanized their imagination. Nevertheless, Lubich and her companions continued to face the ravages of the war, and, one by one, they saw their respective dreams shattered. In the midst of such loss, the group asked themselves if there existed any ideal that no bomb could destroy, and with the question came the answer, "Yes, God, and He is Love. We decided to make God-Love our ideal in life."[2]

Lubich's understanding of unity and the love of God goes hand-in-hand with the origins and development of the Focolare Movement, a lay ecclesial community, now present in 182 nations. "Focolare" is an Italian term, meaning "family fireside" or "hearth," and the term describes the movement that took shape beginning in the 1940s and continued throughout the life of Chiara Lubich, its founder, and beyond. That movement has spawned additional movements within specific sectors as well as more than a thousand social projects and activities. In recognition of her movement's achievements in the promotion of dialogue, peace, ecumenism, and unity, she was awarded international, national, ecumenical, and interreligious awards, honorary citizenships, awards from civic administrations, local churches, and cultural boards as well as nineteen honorary doctorates.

While the cellar in Trent is a world away from our contemporary mediated context, Lubich's reflections on media and technology open up space to counter some of the limitations of *technological determinism*, or "the notion that the role that technology plays in shaping human consciousness and culture is deterministic, or causal."[3] The birth of Lubich's spirituality of unity and love takes place in the context of war, where Lubich and her followers trusted God to provide for the needy and poor. It is within this context that Lubich offered specific reflections on spiritual principles or "guidelines" for media professionals. While she did not take up technological determinism directly, her work serves as a unique calming presence to such thinking, providing a specifically spiritual agency for those immersed in a media-saturated world.

The Beginnings of a Spirituality of Unity

The Focolare spirituality lies at the basis of Lubich's advice to communication students, scholars, and professionals. Understanding Lubich's rather simple sketching of its primary tenets warrants a word on the birth of the movement. Although Lubich's experiences in war-torn Trent served as an important beginning to the movement, Lubich wanted a way to put God-Love—which arose as the first point of Lubich's unfolding spirituality—into practice, realizing, in some way, the unity that captured their imaginations. For example, they read in the Gospels, "It is not anyone who says to me, 'Lord, Lord,' who *will* enter the kingdom of Heaven, but the *person* who does the *will* of my Father in heaven" (Mt 7:21). Doing the will of God therefore became a second point of the Focolare spirituality.[4]

Lubich searched for more precise direction on living the will of God. They continued to read Scripture together, and they came upon Jesus' command to "love your neighbor as yourself" (Mt 19:19). In a time of war, they found many opportunities to love their neighbor: an old lady who needed help in returning to the shelter each time a bomb fell, the five frightened children, and the sick person confined at home. Lubich continued to engage the Scriptures intimately and read, "In so far as you did this to one of the least of these brothers of mine, you did it to me" (Mt 25:40). The Gospels showed Lubich and her companions a means of loving their neighbors: "Ask, and it will be given to you" (Mt 7:7; Lk 11:9). Lubich frequently recalled a particular episode in which a person they met needed a pair of shoes size 8½. One of Lubich's group went before the tabernacle at church and asked, "Lord, give me a pair of shoes size 8½ for you in that poor person."[5] As the person who needed the shoes was leaving church, a friend of hers handed her a package containing a pair of shoes size 8½.

Reading the Gospels and serving others, they came to form additional tenets of the Focolare spirituality: mutual love, Jesus in the midst, Jesus Forsaken, the Holy Spirit, Church, Mary, and the Eucharist. Together these tenets worked in service of the one overarching aim that Lubich saw as the principal mission of the movement: unity. By aiming at putting the Gospels into practice, with a particular focus on trying to contribute to Jesus' prayer for unity, Lubich and her companions began to attract people. By 1945, five hundred people from all walks of life came to share and participate in the same spiritual longings as the young women gathered around Lubich. In an effort to love God in a spirit of unity, they decided to place all their possessions in common as recorded in the book of Acts (Acts 2:44). Lubich's movement began to extend beyond the Catholic Church and even beyond the religious realm to exert influence on various social spheres: economics, politics, sociology, family life, art, and communication.

A Charism of Unity and the Media

In an address to media professionals at Castel Gandolfo on June 2, 2000, titled "A Charism of Unity and the Media," Lubich offered four moral guidelines that would promote unity and love.[6] But before turning to the principles, Lubich first sketched "intuitions" that she said might prompt further "research in communications . . . still to be done, or better, still to be lived."[7]

After reminding the audience that she was not an expert in communication nor in many other fields, she aligned herself with the apostle Paul in saying, "I decided to know nothing among you except Jesus Christ, and him crucified" (1 Cor 2:2). She added to this "crucified *and forsaken*" to indicate a particular aspect of Jesus' suffering that her spirituality reveals. Instead of relying on her own expertise, she pointed to Jesus' expertise as a "great communicator," citing the Gospels of John and Luke: "Never has anyone spoken like this!" (Jn 7:46) and "All the people were spellbound by what they heard" (Lk 19:48).

Additionally, Lubich found "shadows" in the great communicator's life. She pointed to the betrayal by Peter and to the moment of abandonment on the cross when, in Jesus crying out, "My God, my God, why have you forsaken me?" (Mt 27:46), the Father "seems to break off all communication."[8] Lubich described Jesus in the moment of his abandonment as "the mediator (the medium) between humanity and God." She described Jesus in that moment as "an infinite void, almost the pupil of God's eye, [a] window through which God can look at humanity and humanity in a certain way can see God."[9]

With these intuitions established, Lubich enumerated four "guiding principles of communication." A first principle is that "*communication is essential.*"[10] Here, her point was not merely a philosophical one on the communicative nature of human beings but an admonition that experiences of living the Gospels should be relayed. Her focus—as was always the case in her speeches and writings—was on the lived word that would, in turn, be communicated. "What is not communicated," she stated, "is lost."[11] Members of the movement, accustomed as they have been to sharing their experiences, "have almost a vocation for communication."[12] Her continuous relaying of the beginnings of her movement and the ongoing experiences of her adherents in living the Gospels attest to the essentiality of the communication that she sees. Lubich thus emphasized the communitarian (versus individualistic) nature of living the Gospels that her spirituality proposes in all endeavors.

A second principle is the need her members feel *"to make ourselves one."*[13] In this 2000 address, she described the communication process as consisting of more than possessing command of material or of our own thoughts; it necessarily entails "the need to know who we have before us, to know the listener or the audience, their needs, desires, problems." The process is not passive. In turn, members also "make ourselves known, explaining why we want to give this talk, what has led us to do it, its effects on ourselves, thus creating mutuality."[14] We see her applying this guideline in this speech itself in her opening remarks, when she identified the "affinity" between her movement and the media, which she located in shared goals and methodologies, before offering her thoughts and proposing her guidelines.

A third thought she offered was to *"emphasize the positive."*[15] Having described contemporary communication practices as a "panorama of lights and shadows" and acknowledging the need to point out "errors, shortcoming and failures" for those in a position of responsibility, she nonetheless affirmed her movement's way of highlighting the good, of emphasizing good and positive aspects.[16] Recognizing the "shadows" of globalization, ethical relativism, life as spectacle, excessive competition, and invasion of public space, as well as the horror of a crucified and forsaken Christ, she nonetheless found "light" in Jesus in presenting his "cry" as "his fullest expression as the Word . . . the height of his communication."[17] She stated, "Precisely in giving himself without limit he reveals himself as Word, infinitely communicating himself and introducing us into the mystery of redemption and of the life of God, into the vortex of love among Father, Son and Holy Spirit."[18] The reason for such emphasis, Lubich asserted, is love: "Because this is how love is: it is aware of reality, but it knows how to transfigure it in order to make good triumph in others."[19] Lubich implored communicators to do likewise in their various communication practices.

Finally, Lubich submitted that *"the person matters, not the media."*[20] She returned to the idea that media are merely instruments. She recalled that Jesus' suffering was out of love for persons, construed as "children of God."[21] She also invoked the role of a mother, who is "capable of believing all things, of hoping all things for her child, even the most wild, of understanding, of putting up with all the trouble involved."[22] Lubich reminded her audience that these principles are turned in the service of promoting unity; media, she said, should be used "as *instruments for achieving a more united world.*"[23]

Media, Culture, and Technological Determinism

In our increasingly hyper-mediated culture, many have lamented the deification of three so-called values of media culture. The value of efficiency gained salience as new technologies made it possible for information, stimulation, and weaponry to be achieved or deployed in breakneck time. Utility has also arisen as a metric of social systems; "outcomes," for example, has entered the lexicon of higher education, where it seems settled in for the long haul. Progress similarly stands as a measure of whether something is rendered good or bad, but "progress" is often reduced only to "change," as if change for its own sake is a worthwhile pursuit.

A growing intellectual community within the emerging field of media ecology has laid the blame for such developments at the feet of technological "advances." Technology, these critics warn, is turning the promised "global village" into new forms of tribalism, new strands of nationalism. Even as people across the continents become more and more connected and each of us amasses hundreds of "friends" through social media, the extremes of electronic connection are transforming us into people who are "alone together."[24] In assigning blame, this growing intellectual community endorses a theory of technology called "technological determinism." Adopting such a perspective would mean that people feel the effects of technology are inevitable and there is little recourse apart from a radical resistance to technological advances—for example, by completely abstaining from social media or getting rid of the television.

In the face of these problems, Lubich's insights can offer various, constructive responses. First, by saying "communication is essential," she is privileging a mutual self-giving, an authentic exchange of selves and ideas, over the efficiency of the transmission. For Lubich, communication presents an opportunity for the communicating partners to live out the commandment that Jesus called "new" and "his": "love one another as I have loved you" (Jn 13:34). Whether in the everyday communication episodes of answering the phone or in the globally distributed reporting of the news, Lubich counsels all of us to think of what is essential about communication: something distinctly more than the unclad stimulus-response transmission model of communication. Communication in light of the other guidelines she proposes and the larger spirituality from which they arise, entails something more akin to the model of communication-as-ritual by American communication theorist and media critic James Carey, which involves mutual participation of one communicator in the "person" of the other.[25] As French sociologist and lay theologian Jacques Ellul has written, "Communication transcends technics because it can only take place where two human beings are fully engaged in a real conversation."[26] Such a guideline works to promote dialogue, as Lubich's spirituality does, and stands in stark contrast to the self-serving communication model that unfortunately plagues individuals and nations and arouses rivalries that can lead to mutual destruction.

Second, her guideline of "making ourselves one" can serve as a corrective to the runaway value that "progress" has been accorded in our society. Technology exists as a means toward achieving a particular end. The "end" that Lubich holds ever before herself and that she proposes to all communication practitioners is that for which Jesus prayed: "That all may be one." People make progress in proportion to their fostering of unity, and even failures in that effort can be accounted as a participation in Jesus' own cry, which Lubich described (above), as Jesus' "fullest expression as the Word . . . the height of his communication."[27]

Third, Lubich's observation that "shadows" do exist offers a response to the problem of utility. Her insight recalls a comment that Mother Teresa made when visiting a New York studio to be interviewed. She noticed on a color monitor the man who would be interviewing her as well as the television commercials featuring nonfattening food, and she remarked, "I see that Christ is needed in television studios."[28] This is the sentiment that Lubich expresses, yet her acknowledgment of the "shadows" often comes off as passing acknowledgment. In her speeches, she tends to mention disasters, tragedies, errors, and other problems but moves quickly toward affirming positive societal developments. Her emphasis typically rests with activities that tend toward unity. Such a move from darkness to light is typical of Lubich's spirituality, where the "utility" of love works its transformation. Utility, in other words, matters insofar as it gives way to what is positive, particularly with respect to what builds up the family of God.

Finally, Lubich's insistence that the person, rather than the media, matters appears to reject the theory of technological determinism. Because Marshall McLuhan is often associated with this theory, Lubich's guideline can appear to reject McLuhan's dictum that "the medium is the message." At the other end of the spectrum, Lubich also appears to reject the notion that social and economic factors, not technology, set the course of how technology is used, unlike cultural studies scholar Raymond Williams, who argues that technology is indeed largely a symptom of these social and economic factors.[29] Lubich's guideline directs attention elsewhere. She restores the centrality of the persons who are the subjects of a communicated message or its receivers. The person remains always for her as a neighbor to be loved, and the media serve primarily as a tool to be used in that endeavor.

Lubich seeks to restore salience to the person, often obscured as a demographic (e.g., according to race, education, or gender) or masked in virtual worlds (e.g., in Second Life avatars or in social media profiles). Lubich counsels communication professionals to "love your neighbor," which in this case means to be aware of the individual(s) at the other end of the communication channel. Poignant cases abound. Focolare members would be familiar with the journalist in Ireland who, in covering a story on gypsies, continued to visit a gypsy family long after her story on them had run. In another instance, a photographer in the Middle East put down her camera while she was shooting to have a conversation with a man rendered homeless by the war.

Lubich's spirituality, based as it is on the Gospels, teaches people to see Jesus in every neighbor, whether the person be a member of an audience, someone being interviewed, a student sitting in a communication class, or the technician assisting someone with a satellite transmission. Lubich's counsel is to love one's neighbor until love becomes mutual, at which point unity is achieved. Even when one's neighbor acts as one's enemy, Lubich applies the same guidance derived from the Gospels as that derived for her other imperatives to "love your neighbor" and "love one another." As this applies to the communication world, it means to view communication technology or equipment as an instrument in service of love that can lead to unity.

Conclusion

While not ignoring the deleterious effects of media, Lubich pointed to positive potentialities media might have in promoting the transcendent purpose of Jesus' prayer. Indeed, she chronicled her movement's use of the technological advances of media. But her focus was to empower people as agents of media with the autonomy to direct the use of media toward the concept of *ut omnes unum sint* ("that they may be one").[30]

Lubich's guidelines to media professionals provide a blueprint for a return of agency for human persons against the assumptions of technological determinism. In both her statement of guidelines and her communicative practice of them, she offered an antidote to the evils ascribed to media. Lubich prophesied that adherence to these guidelines would lead to transformative results: media would not be invasive but attentive to the socialization of people; production structures would not be torn down by competition but guided by a sincere regard for the public; information would respect God in all creatures and not take advantage of suffering; true values would be shared in helping people in their search for truth; globalization would lead to communion among people and not suffocate people. She concluded her 2000 speech by addressing "my dear workers and experts in the world of communication" as people "whose heart became a space for communication where Love could speak its Word, to make each of you . . . a new person able to begin and make grow a communication in keeping with the heart of God."[31]

CHAPTER 39

Desmond Tutu: Communicating Forgiveness through *Ubuntu*

Kathleen Osbeck Sindorf

Abstract: Archbishop Desmond Tutu (1931–) argued that forgiveness is a fourfold process in which survivors must tell their story, name their hurt, grant forgiveness to the one who hurt them, and renew or release the relationship. His insights offer constructive ways of expanding the way western communication scholars engage in forgiveness research.

Introduction

During the South African apartheid, young teacher and Anglican priest Desmond Tutu witnessed incredible atrocities in which white South Africans systematically oppressed those who were black. Tutu sometimes felt powerless, and he was feeling especially powerless on the day he was asked to speak at a protest meeting in Cape Town. Just days prior, police had brutally killed two young boys in that township. Tutu says that despite the understandable tension, the audience surprised him. In the midst of trauma and anger, his audience had not lost their capacity to laugh.[1] It seemed extraordinary to him—this gift of joy in the midst of so much anguish. This experience caused Tutu to think more deeply about the healing power of forgiveness, and forgiveness was central to any hope of national healing in the post-apartheid era.

This chapter suggests that Tutu's years of work and reflection on forgiveness can serve as a constructive dialogue partner for the manner in which communication studies theorizes and researches forgiveness. At the end of apartheid, the newly elected Nelson Mandela appointed Tutu to head the Truth and Reconciliation Commission (TRC), a task force charged with investigating apartheid-era crimes against humanity. The commission based their work on the concept of *ubuntu*, an African anthropological framework that underscores the interdependence of humanity. Through *ubuntu*, the TRC engaged in restorative justice, offering reparations to survivors and amnesty to criminals.

In reflecting on the years of work of the TRC in their book *The Forgiving Book: The Fourfold Path for Healing Ourselves and Our World*, Tutu and his daughter Mpho Andrea Tutu argue that forgiveness is a process in which survivors must tell their story, name their hurt, grant forgiveness to the one who hurt them, and renew or release the relationship. In Western culture, forgiveness studies reflect an individualism and narrowness that has a limiting effect on our understanding of forgiveness. Communication studies may be able to overcome an individualistic approach to forgiveness through an understanding and application of *ubuntu*. *Ubuntu* suggests that the entire world is at stake in even the smallest act of forgiveness. Similarly, Tutu's emphasis on storytelling offers the possibility of understanding forgiveness as an artistic act of the imagination.

Ubuntu, Truth, and Reconciliation

In the mid-1980s, apartheid plunged South African into a time of significant turmoil, and it was at this moment that Desmond Tutu became the first black archbishop of Cape Town, the highest position in the Anglican Church in South Africa. Tutu spoke out about the injustices of the apartheid regime, for which he garnered international attention. In the early 1990s, apartheid ended. When blacks were finally given the right to vote in 1994, there was some anxiety that the election might become violent.[2] However, the election was peaceful and nonviolent. Nelson Mandela, after three decades behind bars, became South Africa's first president elected after apartheid, and he asked Tutu to lead the TRC to investigate apartheid-era crimes.

The TRC chose a model of conflict resolution informed by the African concept of *ubuntu*. Tutu uses the term to describe both the qualities of a person and a larger anthropological affirmation. A person with *ubuntu* is said to be generous, hospitable, friendly, sharing, and compassionate. However, that person's *ubuntu* emerges out of a conviction about herself and the rest of humanity. Unlike a Western, individualistic conception of humanity, *ubuntu* affirms that a "person is a person through other persons."[3] One person's humanity "is caught up, is inextricably bound up," with others in a "bundle of life."[4] A person with *ubuntu* "does not feel threatened that others are able and good, for he or she has a proper self-assurance that comes from knowing that he or she belongs in a greater whole and is diminished when others are humiliated or diminished, when others are tortured or oppressed."[5]

Ubuntu meant that the TRC would not hold a trial that delivered retributive justice or punishment; instead, the TRC would hear stories of both victims and perpetrators. To victims, the TRC granted reparations and rehabilitations. To the perpetuators, the TRC had the power to grant amnesty to those who were willing to make a full confession of their crimes. Tutu decided to personally hear each story of atrocity—both from survivors as well as from those who had committed what the TRC called "gross violations of human rights" or a "crime against humanity."[6] These actions meant that the TRC was concerned with "the healing of breaches, the redressing of imbalances, the restoration of broken relationships, a seeking to rehabilitate both the victim and the perpetrator."[7]

Throughout the TRC hearings, over seven thousand perpetrators applied for amnesty and confessed to unbelievably gruesome stories of torture and cruelty that they had inflicted during the years of apartheid. Because amnesty demanded full disclosure of one's crime, not all perpetrators who came forward received it.[8] The criminals applying for amnesty had all their hearings in public, and citizens could hear the stories of victims and criminals over radio and television.[9] Except in a few cases where victims feared reprisals, the TRC aimed to keep these stories as public as possible.

From these experiences, Tutu argues that true reconciliation cannot happen on the cheap; it is costly to heal the breach between victim and wrongdoer. People rarely rush to expose their vulnerability and sinfulness, but for the breach to be healed, the truth of wrongdoing must be faced. "Forgiving and being reconciled," claims Tutu, "are not about pretending that things are other than they are. It is not about patting one another on the back and turning a blind eye to the wrong. True reconciliation exposes the awfulness, the abuse, the pain, the degradation, and the truth. It could even sometimes make things worse. It is a risky undertaking, but in the end it is worthwhile."[10]

The Fourfold Path of Forgiving

In *The Forgiving Book*, Desmond Tutu and Mpho Andrea Tutu describe the path that those who are hurt must walk to forgive those who hurt them. The one who is hurt must (1) tell the story, (2) name the hurt, (3) grant forgiveness, and (4) renew or release the relationship.

In telling the story of hurt, all of us must face the reality that every day of our lives those we encounter may hurt us.[11] Many may not have a choice about when and how they are hurt, but after a hurt takes place they can choose either a path of forgiveness or a path of revenge.[12] For those who choose forgiveness, they must first tell their story. "This is what we did in South Africa," says Tutu and Tutu; storytellers let "the truth be heard in all its rawness, in all its ugliness, and in all its messiness."[13] This means that storytellers must begin with the facts of their experience. When black South Africans told their stories, they started to escape the indignity and isolation of their pain,[14] and they gained a deeper understanding of the hurt and the ones who caused the pain. As a result of this deeper understanding, stories changed as their understanding changed.[15]

Next, when tempted to dismiss, rationalize, or deny pain, the survivor of the hurt must name the hurt as hurt. A hurt causes the survivor to experience shame, silence, the loss of dignity, or isolation. Therefore, naming a hurt demands courage and bravery because it demands that the one who is hurt admit her own vulnerability.[16] Those who deny the existence of their hurt "end up seeking destruction,"[17] either through self-destruction (like substance abuse) or through cycles of revenge (perhaps against those closest to them). As painful as naming the hurt might be, the act disrupts cycles of destruction because, in and through the naming, the storyteller can learn to accept her own vulnerability.[18] Over time, the pain "loses its stranglehold on our lives and our identities. It stops being the central character in our stories."[19]

Third, the one who was hurt must grant forgiveness to those who caused harm, and it is only through forgiveness that a new story can be told. As Desmond Tutu reflects, "I know that, were I born a member of the white ruling class at the time in South Africa's past, I might easily have treated someone with the same dismissive disdain with which I was treated."[20] This means that, like the survivor, the perpetrator has her own story. Therefore, forgiveness can become a possibility only when the one who is hurt realizes that she shares something with her abuser. Both inhabit a "shared humanity," a shared fragility, vulnerability, and capacity for "thoughtlessness and cruelty."[21] In discovering a shared humanity, storytellers can tell a new story and thereby escape the "endless loop of telling stories and naming hurts."[22] The new story does not deny the hurt of the victim or the injustice of the perpetrator. Instead, storytellers use the new story to become "richer, deeper, more empathetic people," sometimes working "to prevent such harm from happening to others."[23] In short, this new story enables the storyteller to "move from victim to hero" of her own story.[24]

Finally, storytellers must renew or release the relationship with the one who caused the harm, which involves both a realization of responsibility and asking for what the storyteller needs from the one who caused harm. Tutu and Tutu admit that it is sometimes easier to renew relationships with a spouse, parent, sibling, close friend, or anyone else with whom the storyteller has shared intimacy. Similarly, it is easier to release a relationship with an acquaintance, neighbor, or stranger. The stranger might not simply "hold as much of your heart" as someone who is dear.[25] Releasing or renewing a relationship is easier when the storyteller can accept responsibility for her part in the conflict.[26] Of course, there are times when the survivor did absolutely nothing wrong. Rather, accepting responsibility draws on the *ubuntu* understanding of society.

Ubuntu says that we all have a part in creating a society that created a perpetrator; therefore, I have a part not only in every conflict I find myself personally, but in every conflict happening right now in my family, in my community, in my nation, and around the globe. This thought may seem overwhelming. The gift hidden in the challenge of *ubuntu* is that we don't need to walk in the corridors of power to build peace. Each of us can create a more peaceful world from wherever in the world we each stand.[27]

The storyteller must also ask for what she needs from the perpetrator. Sometimes the one who was hurt needs to know the truth about why that perpetrator caused the hurt or needs to claim restitution or recompense for what was lost or taken.[28] In the end, a renewed relationship is an act of new life, because it keeps "anger, resentment, hatred, and despair from ever having the last word."[29]

Individualism, Narrowness, and *Ubuntu*

While there is a growing number of communication scholars interested in the study of forgiveness, Vincent R. Waldron and Douglas L. Kelley's book *Communicating Forgiveness* is a clear and important introduction into this burgeoning area of research. While Waldron and Kelley's work shares with Tutu many of the same steps or stages of forgiveness, they have at least one important difference, an anthropological one.

The anthropological difference between Waldron and Kelley and Tutu can be categorized as the West's individualistic and narrowing anthropology over and against the holistic anthropology of *ubuntu*. By individualistic and narrow, I mean to say something similar to what philosopher Charles Taylor says about it. Individualism, according to Taylor, "was won by our breaking loose from older moral horizons. People used to see themselves as part of a larger order."[30] However, dislodged from that larger moral horizon, the West underwent a "narrowing. People lost the broader vision because they focused on their individual lives."[31] Waldron and Kelley's work records the individualism and narrowness that Taylor describes as it applies to the communicative act of forgiveness. The people they interviewed tend to localize the impact of forgiveness such that it ends at the boundaries of the relationship. For example, while Waldron and Kelley do mention forgiveness with reference to hope and an imagined future,[32] their interviewees only provide a small gesture toward the role groups play in a relationship and give virtually no account of the effect interpersonal forgiveness can have on a larger group.[33]

Narrowness also has a relational quality. For their interviewees, forgiveness in many cases seems to function as a means to preserve the status quo. Individuals often forgive another person so that the relationship can "return to normal"[34] or in order to "keep the peace."[35] Within such a framework, forgiveness can be experienced as an "obligation,"[36] a way to "get over it [i.e., a transgression],"[37] or the means by which a wounded person can "take the good with the bad."[38] Furthermore, Waldron and Kelley deploy the language of "management" to describe the forgiveness process. These scholars draw heavily on the frameworks of Uncertainty Management[39] and Identity Management theories.[40] In addition, emotions are realities that must also be managed. The wounded individual manages her emotions by "expressing" and "labeling" them.[41] Finally, forgiveness as a managing device is also present when Waldron and Kelley "assume that that *the desire to preserve moral codes is what motivates forgiving (and unforgiving) behavior.*"[42] Preservation in this case functions similarly to managing a status quo.

Tutu does not deny the importance of the act of forgiveness to the individual; however, his use of *ubuntu* goes beyond the individualism and narrowness Waldron and Kelley describe. As a holistic and broad rendering of anthropology, *ubuntu* resists narrowness because it holds together individuals with the rest of the world. Both are connected and implied in each other. Put differently, very few in the West think that the world hangs together in such a way that the wider world is affected in the forgiveness of one person. But Tutu's work begs the question: What if such an anthropology were accurate? Or put more directly, what gain might occur if Western notions of forgiveness moved away from individualism and narrowness? What if communication scholars started to theorize and research forgiveness with *ubuntu* in mind?

I want to suggest that at least two gains might emerge if communication scholars approached forgiveness from an *ubuntu* perspective. First, *ubuntu* might allow us to imagine a moral order in which the world is at stake in even the smallest act of forgiveness and enact research out of such an imagination. *Ubuntu* does not equate a gross crime against humanity to, for example, the interruption of a female student by a male professor during class. Nevertheless, in a real and serious way, *ubuntu* raise the stakes of the kind of issues Waldron and Kelley address. If one person's humanity "is caught up, is inextricably bound up" with others such that an individual has her own part "in every conflict happening right now in [her] family, in [her] community, in [her] nation, and around the globe," then even mundane offenses and forgiveness matter because the entire world is affected. Grounded in *ubuntu*, communication scholars might perform research in such a way, for instance, that would equip the interrupted female student with the skills and resources necessary to tell her story, name her hurt, grant forgiveness, and renew or release her relationship with the male professor. If such forgiveness took place, it would not, of course, necessarily mean the entire world would change in that moment. However, unless that one moment is repeated and ritualized, the world will likely continue to remain a hostile place for women. Like Tutu says, *ubuntu* does not apply only to the corridors of power. Rather, such research might very well acknowledge the real power of anyone who pursues forgiveness because, as *ubuntu* reminds us, the world is at stake in every act of forgiveness.

Second, if communication studies theorized forgiveness with Tutu's use of *ubuntu* in mind, forgiveness might avoid the narrowness of management and be best understood as an artistic act of the imagination that can serve as a means of healing the survivor, the perpetrator, and the world. Hurt creates a reality, a reality where one human is transformed into a victim and the other into a perpetrator. To bring into existence a new reality, the survivor must first be able to imagine that new reality. The first fruits of that new reality come into being when the survivor engages in an artistic, imaginative act—the act of telling her story. However, for a new reality to emerge, the survivor's story must change. The survivor needs to tell her story in such a way that she embraces a humanity shared with the perpetrator. The ability to perform this reversal demands an imaginative act of creation.

If communication research on forgiveness understood it as an artistic act, then it might conduct research in such a way as to equip survivors with creative and interpretive skills necessary for forgiveness. If forgiveness is an act of the imagination, then the language of management might not be adequate to the task of forgiveness. The same might be true for the tendency to accept forgiveness as the means to return a relationship to the status quo. For example, when a male professor interrupts a female student, it is likely not an isolated incident. That female student likely faces a lifetime of such small wounds that can compound into deep and difficult wounding. In reality, the female student does not need research that will help her manage her emotions or return to some relational status quo. She needs forgiveness to be that way to imagine and create a new reality in which she and her professor can be healed.

Conclusion

Not every wounded person can be like that crowd of protestors to whom Tutu spoke—able to experience joy in the midst of anguish. However, communication research on forgiveness can move beyond the strictures of individualism and narrowness. Scholars and researchers have the potential to equip students of communication to affirm that, in a real way, the world is at stake in even the smallest act of forgiveness and that forgiveness is an artistic and imaginative act. If we in the West can learn from Tutu's use of *ubuntu*, then perhaps those small gains might make it possible for us in the West to have the emotional dexterity in the midst of sorrow, be it for mundane transgressions or national tragedies, to take hold of joy.

CHAPTER 40

WALTER BRUEGGEMANN: CONFRONTING THE DOMINANT CULTURE THROUGH PROPHETIC IMAGINATION

Terri Lynn Cornwell

Abstract: In *The Prophetic Imagination*, Walter Brueggemann (1933–) chronicles biblical prophets who brought public expression to the evils of the empires under which they lived, criticized them incessantly, and brought hope to the people through visions of amazement at God's power of renewal. Similarly, the process of "prophetic imagination" can be used by Christian communicators to confront the failures of today's dominant culture and awaken people from their numbness restoring their amazement and hope.

Introduction

Walter Brueggemann remembers when one day in 1954 his undergraduate sociology professor, Theophil W. Mueller, arrived in class and proceeded to dance. He remembers Mueller as "a contrarian figure"[1] and "a crotchety, unaccommodating teacher."[2] Nevertheless, Brueggemann recalls, "we adored him."[3] That adoration was, in part, a result of Mueller's fervent attention to the pressing matters of injustice facing the United States at the time. Mueller had been working on race issues, and, on that day in 1954, the U.S. Supreme Court handed down the *Brown v. Board of Education* decision declaring separate schools for black and white children unconstitutional. The witness of Mueller's teaching and life, including his dance of celebration, represented to the young Brueggemann "the passion of a Christian prophet for justice."[4] By Brueggemann's own account, this teacher served as an important formational influence shaping his vision of what he considered to be social justice and public theology.[5]

While honing his vision, Brueggemann earned divinity degrees from Eden and Union Theological Seminaries, was ordained in the United Church of Christ, and settled into his life as "a scholar for the church."[6] Brueggemann outlined his concept of how theology can be applied to public discourse to provoke social change in his seminal publication, *The Prophetic Imagination*

(1978), which explored how Old Testament prophets criticized each successive ruling empire and energized their communities to work toward alternatives.

Today's Christian communicators can use Brueggemann's insights to challenge the dominant cultural consciousness of technological, consumerist militarism permeating every dimension of common life.[7] Brueggemann contends that it is the work of prophetic imagination to proclaim a counterscript. Many individuals today see the church as being co-opted by the dominant cultural script, and people have stated this as one of the reasons they have left the church or claim no religious affiliation. Christian communicators can apply the tools of prophetic imagination to create a counterscript that resonates with these unaffiliated individuals or "nones." This chapter outlines the tools of prophetic imagination, discusses Brueggemann's theses of script/counterscript, and provides an application of his concepts designed to resonate with the nones.

The Prophetic Imagination

In *The Prophetic Imagination,* Brueggemann offers three examples of the prophetic imagination, and in each case, the prophet faces the injustices of empire and expresses grief and hope.

First, Moses confronted the social reality of Pharaoh's Egypt, a reality that oppressed Israelites in slavery. Moses did not simply engage in a social action against Egypt's status quo. Rather, Moses displayed God's desire for counter-consciousness that led to a counter-community, the counter-community of Israel.[8]

The prophetic utterance in this story began with words of grief. Expressions of grief at the dominant consciousness is the first task of prophetic ministry.[9] True criticism begins with grieving. People under oppression must break away from the dominant culture that says everything is fine, and they must "live into" their cry of misery and recognize that their lament is the beginning of criticism. Once the people were awakened and gave full voice to their grief, Moses urged them to actions that disrupted Pharaoh's stable society. Following grief and God's great deliverance of Israel from oppression, Moses deploys the language of amazement (Exodus 15, The Song of Moses) to outline a new reality of freedom under the rule of God, language that points to hope.[10] This is not just social change; it is a profound altering of public consciousness to create a culture counter to the dominant ideology.

Brueggemann's second example of an oppressive society involves the royal consciousness of Israel in King Solomon's wake. Solomon's reign had created an affluent lifestyle and, in that condition, Israel fell prey to a royal consciousness. In the shadow of Solomon's empire, Israel did not pay attention to those who were suffering in their midst. They grew comfortably numb to the reality they lived in. Because they were numb, the prophet then expressed for them the grief that they had denied. For the people living under this royal consciousness, the ultimate language of grief is the book of Lamentations, the prophetic expressions of what some people believe was the prophet Jeremiah. Living through a period of grief brought the people to despair, but despair prepared the way for the energy that flows with the promise of newness. With this energy, an alternative consciousness becomes possible. The expressed grief was a necessary precursor to the uplifting words of Isaiah (Is 40:1–2). Isaiah expresses amazement with glorious poetry of nourishment, birth, and hope.

Third, turning to the New Testament, Brueggemann considers the entire life and actions of Jesus as the ultimate criticism to the dominant consciousness of the first-century Roman Empire. In the Gospels, the lowly birth of Jesus is far removed from the experiences of those occupying the palaces of the reigning authorities. Throughout his life, Jesus announced the coming of a kingdom so different from the reality of the times. That kingdom criticizes both the civil and religious powers. Jesus offered a forgiveness that Rome refused to grant to the lowly and oppressed; in Jesus' kingdom the Sabbath could be violated to heal the sick, meals could be shared with outcasts, and women were an important part of the kingdom. In describing his kingdom, Jesus was often moved to compassion—a radical form of criticism against the dominant consciousness. One of the clearest expressions of Jesus' compassion for the people, whom Brueggemann called "nonpersons consigned to nonhistory,"[11] is the Beatitudes (Lk 6:20–26). These sayings of Jesus not only express criticism, they also engender energy, giving hope to those most oppressed by the dominant culture.

But the ultimate act of prophetic criticism was the crucifixion of Jesus. Brueggeman argues that "there is no more radical criticism" of the dominant consciousness of empire than Jesus' announcement of his death. The statement the "Son of Man must suffer" means that "the power of God takes the form of death and that real well-being and victory only appear via death."[12] Jesus' announcements of his death, says Brueggeman, "are the decisive dismissal of every self-serving form of power upon which the royal consciousness is based."[13] The resurrection, however, is that reality that brings amazement and energy to God's people, leading them to a new beginning.

Script and Counterscript in the Twenty-First Century

Brueggemann wrote *The Prophetic Imagination* during the 1970s, a period of worldwide oil shortages leading to long gas lines, a time when the Vietnam War finally ended, when the scandal known as Watergate caused a presidential resignation, and when *Roe v. Wade* legalized abortion. The 1970s for Brueggemann was a time for "serious consideration of prophecy as a crucial element in ministry."[14] He summarized what a prophetic ministry would be with the statements of Jesus: "Blessed are you who weep now, for you shall laugh" (Lk 6:21 ESV) and "Blessed are those who mourn, for they shall be comforted" (Mt 5:4 ESV). This was Brueggemann's hope while writing in the 1970s. However, the need for a prophetic ministry has become increasingly urgent in the aftermath of 9/11, an event that Brueggemann compares to the destruction of the temple in ancient Jerusalem. This catastrophic event added an element of fear to the dominant consciousness and consequently strengthened the perceived need for safety and security.

In his 2005 essay for the *Christian Century*, Brueggemann outlined the dominant scripts of the post-9/11 United States and how the church should be using the tools of prophetic imagination to provide a counterscript.[15] Underlying Brueggemann's assertions is the fact that all people have scripts by which they live. These scripts are metanarratives or worldviews.[16] Scripts often provide a sense of security, and when a script is employed by the majority in a culture, that culture is strengthened and stabilized. Individuals are scripted or socialized within families; parents model appropriate beliefs and behavior, and the institutions of society, including the media, reinforce these scripts. Brueggemann describes the dominant contemporary script as one of "therapeutic, technological, and consumerist militarism."[17] The script says that all ills can be treated so that life can be lived without inconvenience; everything can be fixed through human ingenuity; more of everything is better; and the system is protected by an overt militarism. Underlying this script is the brand of American exceptionalism that Brueggemann expanded upon in his 2014 publication *Reality, Grief, Hope*.[18] Ubiquitous advertising and propaganda reinforce the dominant cultural script throughout public life. The people live in a "bubble that is absent of critical reflection,"[19] and they have become numb to the effects of the script that permeate the culture.

Brueggemann's contention is that this script has failed. All people have not had their basic needs met, they are not happier with more and better consumer goods readily available, and the American military has often destabilized the world order. The dominant script seems only to produce more insecurity and unhappiness.

Brueggemann's solution is to disengage from this failed script and relinquish the dominant ideology—a formidable task when some Americans are comfortable and numb to the suffering of most of the world's population. Here is where the church comes in. The prophets make the case for a change in the dominant script, the first to awaken the people from their numbness to the status quo. That is the work of prophetic imagination, and it is up to the church and its ministry today to take up that challenge.

An alternative script—a counterscript—must be presented steadily, patiently, and powerfully to convince the people of its assurance of safety and true joy. Too often the church has only echoed the dominant culture's script in which support for the U.S. Military, while not inherently bad, is given preference over the greater security offered by God's "truth [that] will set you free" (Jn 8:32 ESV). And, too often, the church has been complicit in support of a consumerist culture that tells everyone that comfort and happiness is just an online click away, or, as a billboard for Amazon Prime Now in California asserts, "From zero to happiness in one hour."

The counterscript that the church is called to proclaim is rooted in a biblical worldview, and it is enacted through the tradition of the church, especially the sacrament of baptism. But the church has been reluctant or even embarrassed, says Brueggemann, to speak about this counterscript. Christians have not done the hard work to discover "the strange new world within the Bible," a world that subverts the false world the dominant scripts claim exists.[20] But this alternative to the dominant script of today's culture is difficult to proclaim, especially when the various factions of the church become insistent on elevating their visions over others. Conservatives emphasize what the Bible says about sexuality and ignore its radical teachings on economics. Liberals proclaim the opposite. These arguments will not awaken the people to the fact that the therapeutic, technological, consumerist, exceptionalist militarism of the twenty-first century is a path to death.

To enact this vision of an alternative reality, the church must recover the power of baptism, which asks the new believer, "Do you renounce evil and its power in this world?" The question that the church should be asking, by inference, is, "Do you renounce the dominant script?" It is the prophetic ministry of the church to nurture and socialize each baptized individual into the counterscript of the kingdom of God, especially since many Christians have confused the dominant, comfortable, secular script with the counterscript of the God Brueggemann describes as "elusive, irascible."[21]

With such a formidable goal for pastors, they often become either red or blue ministers serving the side of the political spectrum that is most comfortable for them and their congregations. But the church must resist aligning with either side because both sides are representative of the dominant culture. Ministry must accept the challenge to use the gifts of prophetic imagination to describe the human predicament, renounce the old scripts of death, and enter into new scripts of life. And this work of ministry, according to Brueggemann, is indispensable.

Reaching the "Nones" through Prophetic Imagination

Many functions of the twenty-first-century church have been coopted by the culture of the day, and they support rather than criticize what is wrong with society. Brueggemann's term for pastors who fail to point out the harm done by the culture's dominant script is "chaplains for the old order."[22] This acquiescence to the dominant script by many churches has been, I believe, a factor in the increase in the percentage of individuals claiming no religious affiliation. These individuals, a mixture of Christians and non-Christians, commonly called "nones,"[23] were 16 percent of the U.S. adult population in 2007, but they now number 23 percent overall.[24] Furthermore, the percentage of nones is higher in each subsequent generation beginning with the Silent Generation and the Boomers to Gen-X and the Millennials.

As these percentages continue to grow, skilled Christian communicators must face the challenge of accepting and articulating what has gone wrong with the way the church has been functioning in society. But the prophetic voice is much harder to make credible today, especially when engaging nones. Whatever discourse is prophetic must be "more cunning and more nuanced and perhaps more ironic."[25] Below is an overview of how prophetic imagination can be applied to the communication challenges of today followed by a specific example.

The first task of prophetic imagination is public declaration of the clash of the dominant culture with the alternative culture. The nones are often the first to see that the dominant culture has already coopted the church; they say that the church is too concerned with money and power, too divisive, or has caused too much harm (e.g., clergy sex abuse scandals).[26] Pastors face a challenge reaching these individuals, but the great "fissure"[27] that the Christian church faces with the growing population of nones is not hopeless. Brueggemann's term "fissure" describes the reality that Enlightenment tenets are in jeopardy; that anxiety, fear, and anger are being evoked by that loss; and that all institutions, including the church, are under assault. Furthermore, these current institutional structures are not sustainable. Brueggemann says that the church must walk people into the fissure with honesty and walk them out with hope. The prophets of the Old Testament and the ministry of Jesus point the way to confront and repair the fissure.

Reaching nones, though, is exceptionally challenging. While younger generations may not be familiar with the Old Testament prophets discussed by Brueggemann, they most likely have heard of Martin Luther King Jr.'s "I Have a Dream" speech, a moving example of twentieth-century prophetic imagination that energized the Civil Rights Movement. Calling Martin Luther King Jr. a prophet in the long line of prophets beginning with Moses can serve to catch the attention of individuals immersed in the dominant culture but still separated from Jesus' alternative consciousness. Many of the nones are familiar with King's glorious words, in which he skillfully tied contemporary cultural institutions to his dream of racial equality by evoking the metaphor of the exchange of money. King said, "In a sense, we've come to our nation's capital to cash a check," promised by the "magnificent words of the Constitution and the Declaration of Independence," but "America has given the Negro people a bad check, a check which has come back marked 'insufficient funds.' "[28]

One example of a way that today's prophets can nudge people into counter-cultural behavior, into relinquishing the tendencies of the consumerist culture, would be to remind them of keeping the Sabbath.[29] Brueggemann explored this topic in his book *Sabbath as Resistance: Saying NO to the CULTURE OF NOW* (2014). In this text, Brueggemann reminds readers of the negative consequences of the market economy in which advertising, "the liturgy of consumerism,"[30] is pervasive and demonstrates the deep need for the alternative behavior of "non-consuming" on the Sabbath. This action would lessen the anxiety of needing to buy the latest consumer item, which might lead to lowering the anxiety of needing to control more, know more, give the children more, be more beautiful, be thinner, etc.—the draw of coercive competition. This rhetoric would appeal to nones who are so closely aligned with the fast-paced, anxious, career-driven society from which they desperately need respite. Brueggemann reminds his readers, "People who keep Sabbath live all seven days differently."[31] Thus individuals might begin to imagine a society with less competition and more neighborliness.

Conclusion

Many people today express the pain of extreme stress and anxiety caused by the pressures of their dominant culture, a culture that says they must get more and more, do more and more, be more and more, and still they are not satisfied. It is the church that must confront this reality, express grief at its injustices, and offer hope for a better future. It is the effective prophet, employing the knowledge and skills of communication augmented with the tools of prophetic imagination, that can begin to energize individuals to imagine an alternative reality.

For Brueggemann the greatest challenge is to confront cultural dominance with truth. Sometimes truth must use a "sneaky whisper," like the gentle but firm action of Rosa Parks during the civil rights struggle or the steadfast witness of Desmond Tutu during South Africa's apartheid movement. Twenty-first-century North American society needs that "sneaky whisper," not the shout from the dominant culture that says money, power, or military might can fix society. Prophetic imagination can open the eyes of those today who are numb to the failures of the dominant culture and present to them the alternative that strives for steadfast love, justice, and righteousness and that expresses amazement at God's everlasting power of renewal.

CHAPTER 41

Peter Kreeft: Perspective-Taking to Promote Religious Dialogue

Timothy M. Muehlhoff

Abstract: Peter Kreeft (1937–) promotes perspective-taking with Muslims. In *Between Allah & Jesus: What Christians Can Learn from Muslims*, Kreeft advocates the value of narrative and dialogue in facilitating perspective-taking with those who are often deemed threatening. The result is Kreeft's most relevant book helping foster two-way communication and connectivity between individuals from diverse religious groups in a time characterized by isolation and fear.

Introduction

Since joining the philosophy faculty at Boston College in 1965, Catholic philosopher Peter Kreeft has taught many students; however, one particular student haunted him. At their first meeting, Kreeft was immediately impressed by the student's spiritual toughness, which he describes as the "spiritual power of moral conviction in a person's soul."[1] Teaching at a Catholic university, Kreeft regularly encountered students who are religious. However, this student gave off such a clear sense of what the psalmist describes as the "fear of the Lord" (Ps 111:10) that it made a lasting impression. This student had something that most of his other students had lost—a sense of awe toward God. In an attempt to be more tolerant, most of Kreeft's students pulled back from overt expressions of religious passion or dogma. This student regularly chided fellow classmates for their lack of zeal. Kreeft would later comment that in some ways this student was the best Christian he had ever encountered in a classroom. Ironically, the student was Muslim.

In our contemporary moment, Kreeft encourages suspicious Christians to push past stereotypes and fear to engage in perspective-taking with Muslim neighbors. But how? His answer is to introduce readers to his Muslim student. He records his interactions and attempts of perspective-taking in a book that is part autobiographical and part fiction. *Between Allah & Jesus: What Christians Can Learn from Muslims* is Kreeft's attempt to cultivate an alliance between

Muslims and Christians via the communication theory known as perspective-taking. For Christian communicators, Kreeft's call for perspective-taking suggests a new way to form a sense of understanding and comradery (without compromising the security of one's own view) with a religious view that is not only seen as different, but threatening.

Learn from Whom?

In his long academic career, Peter Kreeft has written over seventy-five books covering diverse genres such as philosophy, poetry, fiction, children stories, cultural criticism, Christian apologetics, and fictive dialogues between historical characters such as John F. Kennedy, Aldous Huxley, and C. S. Lewis. In the mid-1990s Kreeft, as a Catholic philosopher, became concerned with a form of secularism that devalued and threatened religious thought. Such fears fostered an idea that would dominate his thinking and writing: an ecumenical alliance.

Subsequently, Kreeft calls on all major religions to put aside theological differences and focus on common ground rooted in transcendent morality and ethics. He asserts that today's religious community is marked by deep divisions and mistrust not only between Eastern and Western religions but particularly between Christians and Muslims. What is needed is a common enemy or crisis that will bring these religions together. "Nothing unites like a common enemy and a common emergency. A blizzard makes neighbors into friends,"[2] says Kreeft. He asserts that the common enemy is a form of secularism that views morality as a social construct untethered from transcendent truth.

Essential to this alliance between Christians and Muslims is each group's ability to overcome fear of each other and engage in embodied perspective-taking in order to renew an appreciation of the depth of each other's tradition and areas of commonality resulting in cooperation. Such an alliance is possible for the "simple and strong reason that Muslims and Christians preach and practice the same First Commandment: *islam*, total surrender, submission of the human will to the divine will."[3] However, terrorist attacks—past and present—have created a deep-seated aversion to Islam inhibiting many attempts at an ecumenical alliance. Kreeft is not blind to the concerns and fears of many Christians toward Muslims. "They have reasons: over three thousand of them after 9/11,"[4] he observes.

However, North American fear has created a context in which many Muslims are targeted unjustly. Nine years after the 2001 terrorist attacks on the World Trade Center and Pentagon, the Civil Rights Division of the U.S. Department of Justice has sought to monitor and prosecute incidents of discrimination and violence toward Muslims, Sikhs, and persons of Arab descent. Subsequently, evidence has been uncovered of discrimination toward Muslims in the areas of education, employment, fair housing, and religious land use. Most concerning is the rise in hate crimes. The Civil Rights Division has investigated over eight hundred incidents involving violence, vandalism, threats, and arson toward the Muslim community post-9/11.[5]

Furthermore, in light of the 2015 terrorist attack in Paris leaving 129 people dead and the shootings in San Bernardino, California, where a radicalized couple took the lives of fourteen people, there were fears of a renewed Muslim backlash in 2016. Playing off these fears, one prominent U.S. political voice proposed a ban on all Muslims seeking to enter the United States.[6] While this politician's suggestion has received mixed reviews, prominent evangelist Franklin Graham publicly supported the ban stating that he has proposed similar restrictions in the past.[7] Such fears, prejudice, and division put into jeopardy the project of ecumenical alliance Kreeft advocates.

In the context of abuse against Muslims, increasing fear of Muslims, and a world where Muslims will eventually outnumber Christians, Christians must find a way to alleviate their fear and make peace with the followers of Islam. For all of our differences, Kreeft claims that every Christian can learn from Muslims a deep-seated awe of the divine and a type of spiritual toughness, which he defines as the "spiritual power of moral conviction in a person's soul."[8] He asserts that Christians could learn from devout Muslims faithfulness in prayer and fasting, sacredness of the family, absoluteness of moral laws that govern daily life, and the need to submit to God (the heart of Islam).[9] "As a Christian," explains Kreeft, "I say Islam crucially lacks the cross, and Christ, and his radical love. But as a Christian I also say Islam has great and deep resources of morality and sanctity that should inspire and shame us and prod us to admiration and imitation."[10]

Perspective-Taking in *Between Allah & Jesus*

The central goal of *Between Allah & Jesus* is to introduce readers to the spirit of Islam—a type of spiritual toughness—that characterizes the Muslims that Kreeft has encountered. "Rather than *telling* you what it is, by definition, like a philosopher, or selling it, like a motivational speaker," says Kreeft, "I want to *show* you what it is, by exemplifying it, in a fictional character, like a novelist."[11] Kreeft engages in imaginative dialogues between himself and a fictive character, Isa, who represents the Muslim student Kreeft encountered, a dialogue that encourages his audience to engage in an act of perspective-taking with the Muslim Isa.

The central area that Christians need to engage in perspective-taking with Muslims, asserts Kreeft, is a reclaiming of the fear of the Lord. In essence, explains Kreeft, "We need to preserve this 'fear of the Lord' because for any living thing (like a plant), its end is deformed and doomed to death if it is cut off from its beginning."[12] Kreeft notes that a Christian's goal is not simply to transition from a fear of God to a love of God, eschewing the former as we embrace the latter. According to Kreeft, "Our progress is not simply from fear to love, but from servile fear to loving fear; from naked fear to fear clothed in love. . . . It is the progress from the awe of terror to the awe of adoration."[13] He adds that Muslims will not be impressed by Christians who only want to focus on the end of wisdom (love of God via Christ) if that wisdom is cut off from the beginning of wisdom (fear of God). In order for modern Christians—fixated on the love of their Abba Father—to embrace godly fear we will need a guide. As Kreeft notes, "Isa Ben Adam can show us *that* beginning. Even if it is we who can show him the end of wisdom, still he can show us the beginning."[14]

For Muslims, the starting point in reclaiming a fear of God is acknowledging the wildness of God that molds our sense of prayer. In a chapter titled "On Prayer and the Wildness of God," Kreeft models what it means to courageously learn from a Muslim how to view God and our communication with him. The chapter begins with a character named Father Heerema humbly admitting to Isa that he feels deficient in his soul. "I think my soul is too skinny. My body is fat enough, God knows, but my soul is too skinny. It needs to eat all the food that it can, to strengthen it for this business of becoming a saint and saving the world."[15] He then shows courage by coming to Isa for advice. "And if that's the business you are in too, we can help each other by telling each other whatever we know about that. To be specific, things about prayer."[16]

Isa's input comes in the form of an analogy of how to view God. "To me," begins Isa, "Allah is like the sea."[17] Isa is not advocating a type of pantheism where God is in everything such as oceans or coral reefs, but rather how we experience and approach the sea is how we should approach God. He explains, "The sea does not wait upon your consent. It is there. For another thing, its waves cleanse you only when you step into them and submit to them. It's like soul-surfing: surrendering to the wave."[18] Isa's observing of the sea also helps him understand how Allah makes contact with humans. He notes that there are three ways waves make contact with the shore. On a calm day, little waves come and go every few seconds. In contrast, two slow major tides come every day. There's also a third type of wave that comes during winter storms or nor'easters. These massive waves are unpredictable and rare but change the entire shoreline through their power. For Isa, these three types of waves are similar to three different types of prayers.

After describing the awesomeness of God, Isa offers to take Kreeft to a prayer meeting at his mosque so he can physically experience a small slice of the wildness of God. Isa's suggestion to engage the body moves perspective-taking from merely an intellectual exercise to being something that engages us emotionally, intellectually, and physically.

In the only chapter the author appears in as a character, Kreeft writes that the impact of bodily attending the prayer service was profound. As he recalls, "I understood only a few words of Arabic, but the palpable sincerity, devotion and single-mindedness of the worshipers impressed me."[19] What Kreeft most remembers is how people act when worshipers believe they are in the presence of the wildness of God: "There was no whispering, no gossiping, no *relaxing*, even."[20]

What difference did it make for Kreeft to physically enter a mosque to engage in perspective-taking? Could he not merely have Isa describe what a Muslim prayer service entails? One of the limitations of the definition of perspective-taking is an "intellectual's error" which consists of "believing that one can know without understanding and even more *without feeling*."[21] What Kreeft wants to avoid is an overly cognitive approach to the narratives of others that is stripped of emotions. Embodied perspective-taking is facilitated by physically placing oneself in situations that foster emotional and intellectual insight.

Communicators in a Pluralistic Setting

Regardless of how a reader feels about Kreeft's openness to Islam, there are several applications Christian communicators can glean from his approach when engaging those outside the Christian community. First, Christians need to address a deep-seated aversion to engaging in perspective-taking and learning from those outside our faith community. The subtitle of Kreeft's book presumes there is much to learn from Muslims. Yet are we teachable? If "all truth is God's truth" as Augustine argued, then we have the freedom to consult and explore the truths uncovered by communities and traditions outside our own. However, not all Christians may agree. If Christians have the Truth, why do we need to consult other faith traditions? Kreeft's response is that Muslims like Isa can help us understand and appreciate Christian truths—such as the awe of God—in new and fresh ways, without compromising biblical truths.

Being open to engaging in perspective-taking and learning from other faith traditions is supported throughout the Bible. Repeatedly, Scripture acknowledges the wisdom of cultures outside Israel: for example, Egypt (Is 19:11–13), the Edomites (Jer 49:7), the Phoenicians (Zech 9:2), and many others. The remarkable achievements produced by human wisdom are acknowledged in Job 28:1–11. The wisdom of Solomon is compared to that of the "men of the east" and of Egypt in order to show that it surpassed that of people with a longstanding, well-deserved reputation for wisdom (1 Kings 4:29–34). Paul approvingly quotes pagan philosophers (Acts 17:28). For John Wesley, the study of extra-biblical information and the writings of those outside the Christian community was of critical value for growth and maturity. To neglect such knowledge was a "very great and dangerous mistake."[22]

Second, for Christian readers to be open to learning from a Muslim perspective, they need to first set aside preconceived notions of Muslim theology and practices. Heading into a conversation with a person of a different worldview, we are often convinced we already know his or her position and decide he or she is wrong. Through Father Heerema's interaction with Isa, Kreeft chides Christian readers, "I wish more Christians read the Qur'an and got an accurate idea of your religion, instead of believing the secular media."[23] Kreeft implores Christian readers to turn aside radical stereotypes of Muslims fostered by sensational headlines vividly describing the latest terrorist attack. How much have we as a community of believers preferred mediated generalities and avoided "direct encounters with the human" being who calls herself Muslim?[24] Put differently, how might our conversations improve if we allow fellow Muslim students or neighbors to speak for themselves? The first step in perspective-taking is to enter into a conversation with an openness and willingness to listen and take the perspective of the other.

Third, what is the best way to communicate with those who are resistant or fearful? Eugene Peterson, award-winning Christian author of *The Message: The Bible in Contemporary Language*, notes that Jesus' communication style, as reported by Matthew, Mark, Luke, and John, was adaptable to diverse circumstances. Often, Scripture presents Jesus preaching to masses or formally and informally teaching. However, when Jesus enters Samaria—unfriendly territory—he exclusively speaks through stories and parables. A parable or story, explains Peterson, "slants" the message, or "keeps the message at a distance, slows down comprehension, blocks automatic prejudicial reactions, dismantles stereotypes."[25] In other words, Jesus "told it slant." Kreeft understands that his call to learn from Muslims in an age of terrorism situates him in a Samaria-like context sure to produce knee-jerk prejudicial reactions by those fearful of Muslim radicals. By situating his call to perspective-taking in narrative he hopes, like Jesus, to dismantle stereotypes and bypass prejudices. As our culture steadily moves away from a biblical worldview, Christian communicators will need to become proficient in utilizing stories to present the Christian worldview indirectly.

Fourth, Christians should engage in perspective-taking with each other. While it is imperative that we engage the perspectives of those outside the Christian community, we must afford each other the same respect. Peter writes to fellow believers that we should "live in harmony with one another, be sympathetic, love as brothers, be compassionate and humble" (1 Pet 3:8 NIV). As divisions within the church grow concerning differing views of immigration, sexual identity, the nature of marriage, embracing of homosexuality, supporting specific political parties, the trustworthiness of the Bible, and so on, the need for sympathetic perspective-taking will increase. How can we engage the views of others before we engage those sitting next to us on Sunday mornings?

Fifth, the call to perspective-taking follows a tradition established by Jesus. For Christians, embodied perspective-taking has as its clear biblical precedent the incarnation. Could it not be argued that the essence of the incarnation was atonement mixed with God's perspective-taking? We do not have a High Priest immune to our feelings and thoughts, but One who traveled into our world and observed it through our own eyes (see Heb 4:15). Christ's perspective-taking was not limited merely to those who would become his followers. Rather, he engaged in perspective-taking with everyone—collective humanity. Our decision to engage in perspective-taking with Muslim neighbors, those made in God's image, is honoring the example left to us by Christ.

It should be noted that Christ's desire to engage the perspectives of others did not come without cost. Religious leaders witnessing his table fellowship with outsiders and the ritually unclean caused them to describe Jesus as being a glutton and drunkard. To them, his decision to have table fellowship with the unsavory was synonymous with sharing in their sin. The same negative reaction could be experienced by Christians deciding not only to engage in perspective-taking with Muslims but also to learn from them. Just as it did not deter Christ, it should not deter us from engaging others.

Conclusion

The central goal of Kreeft's *Between Allah & Jesus* is to call Christians to a deeper fidelity to God that recaptures both awe and intimacy. His concern is that our familiarity with God has blinded us to the need to reclaim an appropriate fear. How can we learn to balance the two? What is needed today is a new Paul who can balance intimacy and awe. Perhaps the "new St. Paul is a Christian lacking only the passion of a Muslim to energize him, needing to be prodded to jealousy by a Muslim."[26] The first step in reenergizing the church is to push past the fear of radical Islam to engage in perspective-taking with devout Muslim followers who can guide us back to a wild God. "If this book can help provoke that reaction," Kreeft suggests, then "its existence is justified."[27]

CHAPTER 42

James H. Cone: Analyzing Public Symbols to Expose Social Injustices

Kevin D. Miller

Abstract: In his book *The Cross and the Lynching Tree,* James Cone (1938–2018) raises uncomfortable questions about how the white church missed the connection between the cross Jesus died upon and the trees African Americans hung from during the first half of the twentieth century. His analysis reveals a theology that generated blindness to seeing Jesus as "the first lynchee." Interpreting the cross through the lynching tree and the lynching tree through the cross, Cone presents a model of contextualized communication analysis that can be replicated to help us recognize injustices beneath the surface of stereotyping terms in our society today.

Introduction

As a young boy growing up in the 1940s in Bearden, Arkansas, James Cone would sit at the front window of his home each evening to study the headlights coming down the road. With each approaching vehicle, James prayed that it would be his father's pickup truck bringing his father home from work. Cone recalls his mother's voice over his shoulder as she reminded him that God would protect "Daddy" from "any harm that whites could do to him."[1] He wanted to believe her, but he had also overheard the stories grownups told of the lynching of black men like his father.

By the time Cone entered college, he realized that many of the white people condoning—even conducting—these terrorist lynchings were Christians and members of the white churches. Cone came close to rejecting the Christian faith. But he also knew it was his parents' faith and hope in God that sustained them through those dark days. His driving ambition was to untangle the Jesus of his parents' faith from that of the lynchers.

As a distinguished professor of theology at Union Seminary in New York and the author of the 2011 book *The Cross and the Lynching Tree,* Cone asks two questions in his project: How could the white church have missed the similarities between the Roman cross and the American tree of lynching when they read Scripture passages like Acts 10:39 (ESV), where it states about Jesus that "they put him to death by hanging him on a tree"? And how does one reconcile the enormity of the extralegal lynching of nearly five thousand black Americans between 1890 and 1940 with the biblical assertion that God is a God of sovereign love and power?[2] He concludes that "while the lynching tree symbolized white power and 'black death,' the cross symbolized divine power and 'black life'—God overcoming the power of sin and death."[3]

Communication is commonly defined as the systematic process by which symbols are used to create and interpret meanings. Given the central role symbols play in all public communication events, Cone provides a model for how we should critique cultural symbols around us for their often implicit messages, including labels like "thug" and "illegals" and political narratives of "law and order" that lead to the disproportionate incarceration of minorities. *The Cross and the Lynching Tree* teaches us that the meanings connected to our public symbols are not ethically neutral labels but that they enable groups of people to be excluded, marginalized, and dehumanized.

The Cross as the Lynching Tree

In the same way that Jesus was horribly tortured, shamed, and done so in public, so were black Americans who were lynched. There is nothing quite so public, violent, and dehumanizing in modern American history. The same is true for the political and governmental injustices surrounding Jesus' crucifixion and the similar injustice and misuse of power in the lynching events. These similarities led Cone to read both public executions as demonic acts, the works of Satan.

Cone reframes the symbolic meaning of the lynching tree in much the same way the New Testament writers reframe and transform the meaning of the Roman cross from one of shame and humiliation into one of honor and glory (e.g., Phil 2:9–11). Cone reminds us that the first-century cross was an execution method reserved for slaves, criminals, and rebels. A passage from the Roman lawyer Cicero, in the century before the crucifixion of Jesus, underscores the absolute repulsion and abomination of crucifixions in the ancient world. He claims that "the very word 'cross' should be far removed not only from the person of a Roman citizen but from his thoughts, his eyes and his ears. For it is not only the actual occurrence of these things or the endurance of them, but liability to them, the expectation, nay, the mere mention of them, that is unworthy of a Roman citizen and a free man."[4]

Reframed by the early church, Cone writes, the cross became "a paradoxical religious symbol because it *inverts* the world's value system with the news that hope comes by way of defeat, that suffering and death do not have the last word."[5] For African Americans in the Jim Crow era, the belief that "God could 'make a way out of no way' in Jesus' cross was truly absurd to the intellect, yet profoundly real in the souls of black folk."[6]

It is easy to nod in intellectual agreement with such points yet not *feel* the horrific nature of these lynchings, much less grasp the central role white Christians played in these acts of terror. In order to encourage his audience to feel the horror of these scenes, Cone describes the lynching of a young black man named Sam Hose who was accused of killing a white employer and then raping his wife. Research into the case shows that the rape accusation was a fabrication and that the killing was done in self-defense when Hose's life was threatened by the employer. Historical accounts also demonstrate the central role large numbers of white Christians played in such lynchings.

The lynching was held on a Sunday morning just as church let out. When news of Hose's planned lynching reached Atlanta, some twenty-five miles north of rural Palmetto where the lynching was to take place, so many people rushed to the train station that "the railroad added two special excursions to Palmetto."[7] By early afternoon about five thousand white individuals and entire families—with children of all ages—assembled, forming the mob. A *New York Times* story reported how "a line of buggies and vehicles of all kinds, their drivers fighting for positions in line, followed the procession, at the head of which, closely guarded, marched the negro."[8] Hose was tied to a pine tree, and then

> a hand grasping a knife shot out and one of the negro's ears dropped into a hand ready to receive it. Hose pleaded pitifully for mercy and begged his tormentors to let him die. . . . The second ear went the way of the other. Hardly had he been deprived of his organs of hearing than his fingers, one by one, were taken from his hands and passed among the members of the yelling and now thoroughly maddened crowd.[9]

The torture of Hose lasted for another half hour as the mob roasted him alive over a fire. The only words Hose could manage at the end were, "Oh, my God! Oh, Jesus!" When Hose had breathed his last, "the crowd cut his heart and liver from his body, sharing the pieces among themselves, selling fragments of bone and tissue to those unable to attend. No one wore a disguise, no one was punished."[10]

The parallels between the American lynchings and the Roman crucifixion of Jesus are pronounced. "Both Jesus and blacks were publicly humiliated, subjected to the utmost indignity and cruelty. They were stripped, in order to be deprived of dignity, then paraded, mocked and whipped, pierced, derided and spat upon, tortured for hours in the presence of jeering crowds for popular entertainment."[11] Cone notes that the white lynchers of black individuals were not considered criminal. Rather, the victims—like Jesus—were labeled the criminals and insurrectionists. "The lynchers were the 'good citizens' who often did not even bother to hide their identities. They claimed to be acting as citizens and Christians as they crucified blacks."[12]

Cone puts the theological question to us squarely: "If God loves black people, why then do we suffer so much?" He adds, "That was my question as a child; that is still my question."[13] The insight Cone offers is this: We may want a God who eliminates suffering. Instead, we have a God in Christ who, in and through his crucifixion, is present with those who suffer and stands in solidarity with the least of these. Cone calls Jesus "the first lynchee" because he "foreshadowed all the lynched black bodies on American soil. He was crucified by the same principalities and powers that lynched black people in America. Because God was present with Jesus on the cross and thereby refused to let Satan and death have the last word about his meaning, God was also present at every lynching in the United States."[14] This means, Cone concludes, that "every time a white mob lynched a black person, they lynched Jesus. The lynching tree is the cross in America."[15]

A Blinding Whiteness

White Christians were blind to these injustices, because they failed to relate the message of the cross to their social context and time, which, according to Cone, is the pressing challenge for the church in each generation. Unless this hermeneutical practice of contextualized interpretation of Scripture is used, it is hard to recognize the instances in society where "they are again crucifying the Son of God" (Heb 6:6 GNT). Avoiding contextualization, white American theology contributed to the interpretive blindness of the first half of the twentieth century in several ways.

First, it regarded the cross as an abstraction, avoiding any link to the contemporary context of Jim Crow America. As a result, white theologians interpreted the gospel in ways that made it easy to avoid acknowledging the sin of white supremacy, or the ideological basis for the systems of slavery, segregation, and white mob lynchings. Second, white theology defined salvation as exclusively personal and not social, allowing the white church to miss seeing Jesus among the African Americans they lynched. Third, white theology led Christian preaching and piety to become hyper-individualized and focused on personal morality while ignoring the scriptural teaching that God loves and sides with the poor and the oppressed. Cone writes, "Without concrete signs of divine presence in the lives of the poor, the gospel becomes simply an opiate; rather than liberating the powerless from humiliation and suffering, the gospel becomes a drug that helps them."[16]

Cone argues that American Christianity needs to keep the cross and the lynching tree together to form a holistic, contextualized theology for the church, given its heritage and history of racism. The lynching tree needs the cross to redeem it from the stigma of shame surrounding it. Cone writes that when African Americans would learn of a lynching, they would retreat to their homes, pull the shades, and pray that the mercurial mob violence would not touch their friends or family members. Cone argues that the cross can transform the stigma surrounding the lynching tree, thereby allowing black Americans to openly embrace a part of African American history they have instinctively covered in silence. "God's loving solidarity can transform ugliness—whether Jesus on the cross or a lynched black victim—into beauty, into God's liberating presence."[17]

Just as Germans today must acknowledge and remember the Holocaust, Cone continues, Americans today need to acknowledge and remember the lynching tree. "Whites today cannot separate themselves from the culture that lynched blacks, unless they confront their history and expose the sin of white supremacy."[18] Doing so, Cone argues, begins the process of breaking down the us/them binary that white supremacy depends upon. Through the process of corporate repentance, we begin to realize that what happened to blacks also happened to whites and that the healing of the one is the healing of the other. "When whites lynched blacks, they were literally and symbolically lynching themselves—their sons, daughters, cousins, mothers and fathers, and a host of other relatives."[19]

The cross also needs the lynching tree to liberate the cross from its Americanized distortions. Cone writes, "The cross has been transformed into a harmless, non-offensive ornament that Christians wear around their necks."[20] The seemingly benign piety of bejeweled crosses can keep Americans from full repentance. The lynching tree, therefore, is needed to strip the cross of sentimentality, reminding us that it operated as a blood-soaked instrument of social and political control in the Roman Empire even as the lynching tree did in America. As Cone notes, "Until we can see the cross and the lynching tree together, until we can identify Christ with a 'recrucified' black body hanging from a lynching tree, there can be no genuine understanding of Christian identity in America, and no deliverance from the brutal legacy of slavery and white supremacy."[21]

Recognizing the Symbols of Oppression Today

Cone's analysis of the lynching tree demonstrates a powerful and practical way to attune our ethical sensitivities so that we might see more clearly what it is to do justice (see Mic 6:8) and to love God with all our minds (see Mt 22:37). It contains four approaches.

The first is to practice historical-analogical reasoning. Thinking in analogies means focusing on the profound similarities between two historical events that are, in some ways, different from one another. It is precisely in the tension of those similarities and differences that the analogical comparisons can jolt Christians out of their ideological complacency. When Cone calls Jesus' crucifixion a lynching, the statement has the potential to help contemporary white Christians recover the abject horror and terrible scandal of Jesus' death. When he calls a lynching a crucifixion, the statement has the potential to help contemporary white Christians see how much Jesus loves those who suffer such horrors, because, quite literally, Jesus has numbered himself among the lynchees. Students of communication can learn from Cone's historical-analogical reasoning how to recognize and resist the banality of evil, be they holocausts or slavery or World War II internment camps or lynchings, and the like.

The second approach is to practice a healthy skepticism toward smug claims of moral progress. We should instead recognize that past evils can resurface in new forms that, because they are not replicas or straightforward recapitulations of past injustices, are hard to recognize. The Jim Crow era acknowledged chattel slavery of the bygone era as a moral evil even as it erected racial lynchings to "keep the Negro in his place." Cone would have us ask if the evil of white supremacy has, in fact, been eradicated or if it has morphed into a new form today. Near the end of *The Cross and the Lynching Tree*, Cone warns us not to congratulate ourselves too readily for having put lynchings behind us. He points to the practice of the mass incarceration of young black men in our society as a new permutation of the same/reborn control mechanisms that gave rise to black lynchings. The era of slavery defined a black person as *slave*, the Jim Crow era defined a black person as *second-class citizen*, and today's era of mass incarceration identifies a black person as *criminal* or felon.[22] "'Felony' is the new N-word. They don't call you a nigger anymore. They just say you're a felon. In every ghetto you see alarming numbers of young men with felony convictions. . . . Today's lynching is a felony charge. Today's lynch mobs are professionals. They have a badge; they have a law degree."[23]

Putting indexing into practice, Cone would surely have us interrogate the power that the index "illegals" has on our perception of Latin American immigrants. For example, at church one Sunday, I was playing a game of catch with a class of eight-year-olds. While most of the children were white, one child's family had recently immigrated from Guatemala. When the ball slipped through the Guatemalan child's fingers, another child remarked, "Oh man, just like a silly Mexican!" Taken aback and rather confused, I asked him what he could possibly mean by such a statement. He noted that, at a local Mexican restaurant that employs "illegals," a waiter had recently dropped a bowl of soup near his table. Some of the soup splashed on him and his family. The immigrant boy with whom he was playing catch was "clearly" a Mexican just like the wait staff at the restaurant. Despite the fact that I have seen this white child's parents model a respectful, friendly attitude with the Hispanic workers there, their son seems to have absorbed a lower view of those who serve him food and the occasional Hispanic child whom he encounters at church. In a political climate in which the adjective "illegal" has been turned into a noun, it is not surprising to see a young child articulate the prevailing attitude. In fact, it was only recently that the Associated Press revised its style book guide on how journalists refer to unauthorized immigrants in the United States to avoid this totalization—even though in other parts of the very same style manual it reminded journalists that in the United States people are considered innocent until proven guilty by a court of law.

Fourth, and most foundational for people of faith, is to read Scripture over and against ourselves, or put differently, to read Scripture as though we are the villains of the story. To continue the example above, Cone would have us read the contemporary usage of the "illegal" epithet in light of the Scriptures—and read Scripture anew in light of these sojourners and strangers among us (such as Lev 19:33–34; Deut 27:19; Mt 25:35). This is no truer for the sojourner and stranger than it was for Jesus. Under the threat of King Herod's organized massacre of infants, Jesus' family fled his country for safer space. If we can see Jesus' flight as analogous to the flight of other immigrants,[24] then we might hesitate to call them "illegal," because it would mean that we must also call Jesus "illegal." In fact, we might very well see our temptation to use the term as analogous to Herod's murdering desire. If, as Jesus claims in the Sermon on the Mount, an angry word is not that different from murder, then perhaps our use of the term "illegal" does not make us that different from Herod.

Conclusion

In thinking about the cross through the lynching tree and the lynching tree through the cross, Cone enables students of communication to use the tools of historical-analogical reasoning, skepticism of moral progress, indexing, and seeing oneself as the villain as productive means to understand how communicative messages can distort us and our world. In the same way that Cone's book can help us see the fear lynching produced in his life, thinking after Cone can help us imagine the pain the Guatemalan boy in my church lives with today. Rather than convince ourselves that sin and wrongdoing are mainly individual affairs, Cone's work reminds us how abuses are also communal, systemic, and societal, and, when thought through Jesus' body, they are also ultimately bound up with God's own life. Because, in Christ, God was lynched on that cross and because, in Christ, God becomes an "illegal," our communal sins may be aimed at people with black skin and people with brown skin. But in the end, such sins end up landing as lashes on Jesus' back. Cone's work suggests that if Christians can see this reality more clearly, they might become different people. They might become God's people.

CHAPTER 43

Stanley Hauerwas: Using Narrative as the Catalyst and Context for Moral Reasoning in Faith Communities

Richard K. Olsen and Julie W. Morgan

Abstract: Theologian Stanley Hauerwas's (1940–) reflections on narratives and skills necessary for a distinctly Christian ethic can help shed light on how one Christian community, Eastern University, dealt with the issue of discrimination as it relates to same-sex attraction. This chapter focuses on three of Hauerwas's ten theses to critique Eastern University's process of dealing with same-sex attraction, and offers guidance for other Christian communities dealing with similar moral issues.

Introduction

During Stanley Hauerwas's second year at Yale Divinity School in July 1940 he called home to talk with his father, a working-class bricklayer, a "good but simple man."[1] On one of these calls the topic of conversation landed on a deer rifle his father was making. Hauerwas did not give the gun much thought. That summer, his father surprised him by giving him that deer rifle. "Flushed with the theories about the importance of truthfulness and the irrationality of our [American] society's gun policy," Hauerwas responded to his father's gift saying, "Of course you realize that it will not be long before we as a society are going to have to take all these things away from you people."[2] Although Hauerwas notes that as a moral position he believes what he said was correct, he counts this interchange as "one of lowest points of my 'moral development.' "[3] It was not because he had failed "to grasp some moral principle."[4] Rather, he did not have the "moral skills to know that [he] had been given a gift," and he lacked a story that could hold together his past with the person he was becoming.[5]

Christians always face the temptation, as Hauerwas did with his father, to forget our central story—the Jesus story. That story allows us the skills to live in community with people who are not like us, a community that is an alternative to the world, because the world typically uses authority to control people and sees others, especially strangers, as problems to be solved. That Christians have forgotten this story is nothing new. There are "Christians" who engage in violent behaviors, who cheer for dead enemies, who foster hate and fear that in no way resembles good news. To simply challenge that behavior does not get at the root cause of such beliefs and behaviors. Communities must steward their narratives as carefully as they steward other more obvious resources. In his book *A Community of Character*, Hauerwas describes an alternative Christian process of ethical reflection. It aims to convince readers that their most important social act is to "be a community capable of hearing the story of God we find in the scripture and living in a manner that is faithful to that story."[6]

Focused on how communities should process divisive issues, Hauerwas's reflections on stewarding narratives help illuminate how one Christian community, Eastern University, dealt with the issue of same-sex attraction. He makes his claims as a Christian formed by various Christian traditions and against the backdrop of the irrelevance of Christian ethics to the secular world. By way of application, this chapter uses three of Hauerwas's ten proposed theses— specifically, the necessity of narrative (Thesis Two), welcoming the unexpected as a gift (Thesis Four), and living "out of control" (Thesis Six)—to critique Eastern University's process of dealing with same-sex attraction.

A Community of Character

In Thesis Two, Hauerwas claims, "Every social ethic involves a narrative."[7] In claiming the centrality of narrative for ethical reflection, he simply acknowledges that our stories shape what we do and how we communicate. Narratives not only shape ethical (or unethical) actions or acts of communication, but disagreements that communities have about particular courses of action are often disagreements about how to interpret or make sense of that story. Because contested interpretations are inevitable and because a community can never know what or who it might encounter, communities need particular skills to navigate these inevitabilities.

"Communities," Hauerwas writes in Thesis Four, "must provide the skills to transform fate into destiny so that the unexpected, especially as it comes in the form of strangers, can be welcomed as gift."[8] As Christians, we affirm that God delivers us from our past sins through a figure not like us, through the stranger Jesus Christ. Like all strangers, Jesus threatens and disrupts our lives. Part of Hauerwas's point is that there are events and forces that we cannot change. For example, Christians can never change their past sins. In Jesus, God does not erase this past. However, God gives Jesus to the sinner as a gift, and in accepting the gift, Christians receive a life in which that past no longer dictates their future. Jesus, therefore, is not something we possess. Jesus, as an interruption in our old lives of sin, is a gift. Christians may often be tempted to forget that Jesus is not our possession. Jesus is a gift we continually receive, because God is still transforming us into the people God wants us to be. As a result, Hauerwas claims that a community shaped by this story must be an "interruptible" people, particularly attentive to strangers we encounter. Because the stranger Jesus has interrupted our lives with the gift of God's truth, we must "be willing to face both the possibilities and the threats a stranger represents."[9] When Christian communities accept these disruptions as gifts, they act as though their past does not dictate their future.

Building from Thesis Four, Thesis Six underscores the contingency communities inhabit and their need to rely on gifts God gives the entire community. "Christian social ethics," on this account, "can only be done from the perspective of those who do not seek to control national or world history but who are content to live 'out of control.'"[10] It is the habit of many leaders to deny that the cross of Jesus determines the meaning of human history. This denial takes the shape of control. Leaders often aim to control the actions of those in their charge and control how others perceive their weaknesses. Liberated from the need to control, leaders of a Jesus community need not deny their failures or the contingency of the situations they face. Rather than trust in their ability to control, leaders can trust in the gifts that God has gifted to diverse members of the community. In and through those gifts, God will work his will. To accept that we are not in control is to accept that Christian communities are always in a process—in this life, at least—always becoming, always being sanctified, always journeying, and always leaning on the gifts God gives the community in order to survive. All Christians have various motives for joining a Christian community; however, this process is part of the means God uses to form them into a people. To be a Christian is, in part, to be committed to this alternative way of living.

The Place of Christianity and Church

Hauerwas the theologian experienced a diverse range of faith traditions. At the time he wrote *A Community of Character*, he described his formation as a strange Christian mix: "I am, after all, a (Southern) Methodist of doubtful theological background; . . . who teaches and worships with and is sustained morally and financially by Roman Catholics; who believes that the most nearly faith form of Christian witness is best exemplified by the often unjustly ignored people called Anabaptists or Mennonites."[11] While at Notre Dame, Hauerwas encountered many Catholics who would shape him and his view of ethics. One such person was Charlie Sheedy, a priest and then acting chair of the theology department. Sheedy defied all stereotypes. In the years surrounding Vatican II,

Hauerwas notes that many men entering the priesthood "assumed that priests needed to have all the answers worked out. Charlie never assumed he had any answers worked out," but he knew who he was—"he knew he was a priest."[12] He also encountered Catholic philosopher Alasdair MacIntyre, whose emphasis on tradition and virtues shaped Hauerwas's work. It is likely that this eclectic exposure to Christian traditions explains part of Hauerwas's emphasis on the Christian community as committed to an alternative way of doing ethics.

In addition, in the early 1980s, the time in which Hauerwas wrote *A Community of Character*, the secular world all but ignored Christian reflection on pressing ethical concerns. For Hauerwas, this unfortunate reality had several causes. The West grew increasingly secular and by and large simply ignored or dismissed religious voices as having anything substantial to say. Trying to stay relevant to a world that ignored them, Christian ethicists made two decisions. First, they assumed that doing ethics meant doing the difficult work of reflecting on principles to solve moral quandaries. Second, having discerned principles from Christian sources, they translated their reflection into secular language. In an increasingly secular world, Christian ethicists assumed these two choices could provide the means to positively contribute to the larger social good.[13]

For Hauerwas, however, these two decisions only exacerbated the problem of Christian irrelevance. In focusing on moral quandaries and principles, Christian ethics became detached from Christian life. Christian people formed by a Christian way of life were, in fact, not needed to perform Christian ethics. Furthermore, having translated Christian sources into principles and then into secular language, such writings only reinforced the secular assumption that the particulars of a Christian way of life were not necessary to do ethics. When Christian reflection on medical ethics was indistinguishable from non-Christian medical ethics, it only "substantiate[d] the view that theology has little of importance to say in the area of ethics."[14]

In a context where Christian ethics was indistinguishable from secular ethics, Hauerwas changed the rules of the game. In turning to a narrative account of how the church performs ethical deliberation, he put the emphasis of Christian ethics squarely in social processes of Christian communities. Christian ethics is, in short, what the church does when it attempts, fails, revises, deliberates, and yearns to live faithfully the story of Jesus Christ. Certainly *what* conclusions churches reach are important. But the coup Hauerwas performs is in the *how* of Christian ethics. The *how* or process of ethical reflection becomes internal to whatever term "Christian ethics" means. That Hauerwas has his critics is without question. What is also without question is how successful his insight proved. As one of the most public of all public theologians, Hauerwas has certainly made Christian ethics relevant to a secular world. Scholars from many fields read and debate his work. In 2001 he delivered the prestigious

Gifford Lectures, and *Time Magazine* named him "America's Best Theologian." *Christianity Today* also counted *A Community of Character* as one of the top 100 works of the twentieth century. And if all these accolades were not public enough, he also appeared as a guest on *The Oprah Winfrey Show*.

Narrative and Practical Action

By way of application, this section turns to the way Eastern University, a small, private, Christian liberal arts university, processed the issue of same-sex attraction on campus. Hauerwas's three theses highlighted above (Two, Four, and Six) help to bring understanding to the unfolding events as they occurred in the 2014–2015 academic year.

Eastern University is located about twenty minutes from Philadelphia, Pennsylvania, with an enrollment of forty-five hundred diverse and multi-cultural students. The core of Eastern's mission is embodied in its motto, "Faith, Reason, and Justice," and the community has internalized this commitment. In fact, a 2012 self-report noted that the majority of students and faculty claim the mission shapes their daily lives at Eastern.

In June 2014, the president of Eastern, Dr. Robert Duffett, was one of one hundred fifty leaders who signed a letter petitioning President Barak Obama concerning an Executive Order that would ban federal contractors from hiring discrimination against gays and lesbians. The petition asked for a religious exemption from the order saying, "The expansion of hiring rights will come at an unreasonable cost to the common good, national unity and religious freedom."[15] When Duffett's signing became public, the act caused considerable outcry and brought divisions already latent in Eastern's community into full view.

Thesis Two: Narratives Are Vital and Narratives Are Contestable

Thesis Two reminds us that even while celebrating diversity, communities should also provide coherence. It also highlights the power that narrative has on relations and actions. Duffett faced a great deal of criticism for his actions. While some in the Eastern community supported his decision to sign the letter, many were deeply offended and hurt, reasoning that the stand to discriminate against a marginalized group was not in keeping with the university's narrative built around the biblical commitment to faith, reason, and justice. Close to one thousand alumni and current faculty, students, and staff signed a petition asking for Duffett to rescind his support of the letter. Many of the comments explaining why Duffett should rescind focused on the university's mission. Hauerwas notes in Thesis Two that "what counts as 'social ethics' is a correlative of the content of that narrative."[16] Many in Eastern's community seemed to believe that signing the letter was not in keeping with the institution's commitment to faith, reason, and justice.[17] Alongside those who expressed outrage were also those who supported Duffett's letter. Discerning Christians, therefore, must be aware of how the community's narrative, which includes its core values and mission, informs the interpretation of specific actions community members and leaders take.

Thesis Four: Welcoming the Unexpected and Stranger as Gift

Thesis Four insists that our community narrative must help us make sense of our past but not allow our past to dictate our future. We must be "interruptible" as a community and welcome that interruption as a gift. Within Eastern's narrative the question then arises: How does a university with a commitment to faith, reason, and justice remain interruptible?

Duffett used his State of the University Address in August to respond head-on to his signing of the letter. In giving the background, Duffett explains that his intention was to advocate for religious freedom but acknowledged that there were unintended consequences. He said, "Not only that I have heard your concerns and pain but I have sought out many of you for conversation. Not only do I feel your pain but am sorrowful that I caused it."[18] His response also included a request for forgiveness and action, with a commitment to set up a task force.

It is likely that Duffett did not expect the amount or intensity of backlash his action received from the Eastern community. However, this unexpected reaction—the contested interpretation of Eastern's story—is precisely the kind of interruption to which Christians should remain open in light of Hauerwas's Thesis Four. Duffett received the "interruption" as a gift. But his response put another question to Eastern's story: Would Eastern see LGBT desire as faithful or unfaithful to the Christian story?

Thesis Six: Living "Out of Control" and Trusting Others' Gifts

Thesis Six affirms that trust, control, and fear operate in close association with one another and that communities must welcome and trust the diversity of gifts that each member brings to the group.

In responding to the outcry, Duffett chose not to control or mandate a particular dialogue. Rather, he appointed a Task Force on Dialogue on Human Sexuality. On the task force, Duffett appointed two of the most respected faculty leaders, each representing a different theological understanding to co-chair an institutional exploration of the issues.

The task force chose to structure the dialogue with community involvement. They invited proposals from the entire community with the promise to fund those events. In all, about twenty different departments and student

groups hosted events, including departments such as English, Christian Studies, and Psychology, and student clubs such as the Philosophy Club and Refuge
(an LGBT support club). Each event included a moderator, a guest speaker,
and an opportunity for questions and answers. Opening dialogue around such
an explosive topic required the community to engage with one another in an
attempt to live truthfully.

The process and emergent programming summarized above demonstrates
how the task force chose not to control the process but to trust the gifts of the
community. This commitment not to dictate an agenda honored disciplinary
diversity, theological diversity, and diversity of perspectives within the university and the community.

In the case of Eastern and the volatility of the topic, engaging in the dialogue came with significant fear. At the beginning of the process, members of
the community were fearful that one side would win, rather than trusting in a
process of exploration. Students expressed that they were afraid to voice their
opinions, in case their opinion did not match the opinion of their professor—in
which case, their grade might suffer. Untenured faculty members expressed fear
that expressing their opinion could put their career in jeopardy. Staff worried
that they would be fired. Fear was a common thread.

In an effort to model the process and the trust it required, the task force
planned a Dialogue event at the biannual faculty workshop. Five full-time, ten-
ured faculty members were asked to share their perspectives on LGBT issues
and how they arrived at those conclusions. The five represented a diversity of
opinion, with two faculty expressing a more traditional/conservative approach,
two expressing a more progressive approach, and one who was "wishy washy"
(his words). The second conservative to speak started by reading his prepared
comments. In the opening, he noted that he came with a heavy burden knowing that some of his opinions would cause harm to community members for
whom he cares deeply. As he read his comments, he became sadder and sadder,
with tears streaming down his face. He turned to his colleague and asked if she
could continue reading for him until he regained composure. She (a progressive) began reading and also teared up. In gestures of care, colleagues on either
side of the speakers reached to put their hand on their backs. Kindness and
friendship was expressed even as truth was pursued.

This scene manifests the themes within Hauerwas's project. First, we see
the value of diversity in perspectives. Diversity can clarify, not obscure our own
positions. Second, we see the importance of committing to a God-honoring
process that fosters civility among competing viewpoints. Hauerwas notes, "For
to be out of control means Christians can risk trusting in gifts as they have no
reason to deny the contingent character of our existence."[19] To be a Christian
means admitting that we are contingent creatures and, as such, our positions
on a wide variety of matters are contingent as well. As a result, all we can do

is seek truth and offer our current understandings as a gift to others. It is the process of sharing that makes this example so compelling.

To be honest with gentleness in that moment lifted the entire faculty community. After the event, some colleagues reported that the panel discussion represented the ideal when it comes to what it means to be a faculty member at Eastern. The takeaway for discerning Christians is to make sure that they have a God-honoring process, and that an inevitable part of that process is uncertainty not control. It is this "out of control" dimension that leads Christians to trust in God rather a certainty that replaces the need for such trust.

Conclusion

Hauerwas fully embraces the distinctives of a community of faith and is not dismissive of orthodoxy. He also asserts that "the first social task of the church is to provide space and time necessary for developing skills of interpretation and discrimination sufficient to help us recognize the possibilities and limits of our society."[20] Notice the focus on the activities of interpretation and discernment. That call continues. What Hauerwas offers is a process that commits us to the process of redemption. This process is no easy task. Hauerwas helps us in this challenge by illuminating the characteristics of good narratives and by providing a helpful lens through which discerning followers of Christ can assess their beliefs and behaviors and the narratives that inform and give meaning to each.

NOTES

Foreword

1. Thomas Kuhn, *The Structure of Scientific Revolutions*, 3rd ed. (Chicago: University of Chicago Press, 1996).
2. Herbert Blumer, "What Is Wrong with Social Theory?" *American Sociological Review* 19, no. 1 (February 1954): 3–10.
3. Robert Miner, *Truth in the Making: Creative Knowledge in Theology and Philosophy* (London: Routledge, 2004).
4. Hans-Georg Gadamer, *Truth and Method*, 2nd ed., trans. Joel Weinsheimer and Donald G. Marshall (New York: Seabury Press, 1989), 443.
5. Susanne K. Langer, *Philosophy in a New Key* (Cambridge, MA: Harvard University Press, 1942).
6. Paul Tillich, *The Theology of Culture*, ed. Robert C. Kimball (New York: Oxford University Press, 1959).

Introduction

1. We would like to acknowledge Robert E. Webber's significant influence on the study of communication and theology. His book *God Still Speaks: A Biblical View of Christian Communication* (Nashville, TN: Thomas Nelson, 1980) was one of the earliest attempts to provide a systematic theology of communication. Among Webber's later books are his "ancient-future" line, for instance, *Ancient-Future Worship: Proclaiming and Enacting God's Narrative* (Grand Rapids, MI: Baker Books, 2008).
2. For example, see Thomas Farrell and Paul Soukup, eds., *Of Ong and Media Ecology: Essays in Communication, Composition, and Literacy Studies* (New York: Hampton Press, 2012), and Ronald C. Arnett, *Dialogic Confession: Bonhoeffer's Rhetoric of Responsibility* (Carbondale: Southern Illinois University Press, 2005).
3. For example, see Quentin J. Schultze and Diane M. Badzinski, *An Essential Guide to Interpersonal Communication: Building Great Relationships with Faith, Skill, and Virtue in the Age of Social Media* (Grand Rapids, MI: Baker Academic, 2015); Quentin J. Schultze, *An Essential Guide to Public Speaking: Serving Your Audience with Faith, Skill, and Virtue* (Grand Rapids, MI: Baker Academic, 2006).
4. Neil Postman, *Technopoly: The Surrender of Culture to Technology* (New York: Knopf, 1992).
5. Quentin J. Schultze, *Habits of the High-Tech Heart: Living Virtuously in the Information Age* (Grand Rapids, MI: Baker Academic, 2002), 75. See also G. K. Chesterton, *Orthodoxy: The Romance of Faith* (New York: Image Books, 1990), 48.
6. Kevin Healey, "Contemplative Media Studies," *Religions* 6, no. 1 (2015): 948–68.
7. Schultze, *Habits of the High-Tech Heart*, 21.

8. See Mark A. Noll, *Jesus Christ and the Life of the Mind* (Grand Rapids, MI: Eerdmans, 2011), 151; and Mark A. Noll, *The Scandal of the Evangelical Mind* (Grand Rapids, MI: Eerdmans, 1994), 10–11.

9. James K. A. Smith, *Who's Afraid of Postmodernism?* (Grand Rapids, MI: Baker Academic, 2006), 74.

10. Ibid., 29.

11. Alister E. McGrath, *Historical Theology: An Introduction to the History of Christian Thought*, 2nd ed. (Oxford: Wiley-Blackwell, 2013), 201. The recovery of the Christian tradition is sometimes called *resourcement*. This term, apart from describing a certain movement within Catholic theology, can also be used to describe, more broadly, particular theologies concurrent in Protestant theology that aim to critique modernity and Protestant Liberalism, like the so-called postliberal theology of the Yale School and Radical Orthodoxy. Both turn to a recovery of historic theologies and church practices. See McGrath, 207 and 209.

12. Walter Brueggemann, *The Prophetic Imagination*, 2nd ed. (Minneapolis, MN: Fortress, 2001), 43.

Chapter 1

1. Gerald L. Sittser, *Water from a Deep Well: Christian Spirituality from Early Martyrs to Modern Missionaries* (Downers Grove, IL: InterVarsity Press, 2007), 33.

2. W. H. C. Frend, *The Rise of Christianity* (Philadelphia: Fortress, 1984), 174.

3. Leslie W. Barnard, *Justin Martyr: His Life and Thought* (Cambridge: Cambridge University Press, 1967), 4.

4. By "faithful witness," I mean a broad and prescriptive framework—informed by the theology and religious traditions of evangelical Christianity broadly speaking—by which to approach public and cultural engagement in a pluralistic and democratic polity such as the United States. See Mark Allan Steiner, "Reconceptualizing Christian Public Engagement: 'Faithful Witness' and the American Evangelical Tradition," *Journal of Communication and Religion* 32 (2009): 289–318.

5. Frend, *The Rise of Christianity*, 120.

6. These themes are discussed more extensively in Robert L. Wilken, *The Christians as the Romans Saw Them* (New Haven, CT: Yale University Press, 1984).

7. Leslie William Barnard, "Introduction," in *St. Justin Martyr: The First and Second Apologies*, ed. and trans. Leslie William Barnard (Mahwah, NJ: Paulist Press, 1997), 2.

8. Ibid., 7.

9. Erwin Ramsdell Goodenough, *The Theology of Justin Martyr: An Investigation into the Conceptions of Early Christian Literature and Its Hellenistic and Judaistic Influences* (1923; repr., Amsterdam: Philo Press, 1968), 82.

10. See ibid., 84–87.

11. See, for instance, Barnard, "Introduction." For discussion of the theory that the *Second Apology* is essentially a fragmented collection of material intended for different purposes, see Paul Parvis, "Justin, Philosopher and Martyr: The Posthumous Creation of the *Second Apology*," in *Justin Martyr and His Worlds*, ed. Sara Parvis and Paul Foster (Minneapolis, MN: Fortress, 2007), 22–37.

12. Eva Brann, *The Logos of Heraclitus: The First Philosopher of the West on Its Most Interesting Term* (Philadelphia: Paul Dry Books, 2011), 19–20.

13. C. Jan Swearingen, *Rhetoric and Irony: Western Literacy and Western Lies* (New York: Oxford University Press, 1991), 26–39.

14. In taking this position—on which he elaborates as well in the *Dialogue with Trypho*—Justin articulates a broader theological stance known as "supersessionism," also known as "replacement theology" or "fulfillment theology." While doing throughout history some important and edifying theological and rhetorical work for Christians in sorting out their epistemological and ontological stances, this approach has given rise to some disturbing consequences, most notably the centuries-long persecution of Jews at the hands of Christians and others acting on behalf of the Christian faith tradition broadly speaking. Martin Luther's rhetoric on Jews is a particularly noteworthy and disturbing example of how this broad theological stance can go wrong.

15. Justin Martyr, *1 Apology*, 46. This and all subsequent citations to Justin's *First Apology* and *Second Apology* are to Leslie William Barnard's translation. See *St. Justin Martyr: The First and Second Apologies*, ed. and trans. Leslie William Barnard (Mahwah, NJ: Paulist Press, 1997).

16. Justin Martyr, *2 Apology*, 10.

17. Ibid.

18. Ibid.

19. Ibid.

20. Vincent E. Bacote, *The Political Disciple: A Theology of Public Life* (Grand Rapids, MI: Zondervan, 2015), 14.

21. Cornel West, *Democracy Matters: Winning the Fight against Imperialism* (New York: Penguin Books, 2004), 145–72.

22. Rod Dreher, *The Benedict Option: A Strategy for Christians in a Post-Christian Nation* (New York: Sentinel, 2017).

23. For more elaborate arguments making the case for this phenomenon, see Stephen L. Carter, *God's Name in Vain: The Wrongs and Rights of Religion in Politics* (New York: Basic Books, 2000); Alan Wolfe, *The Transformation of American Religion: How We Actually Live Our Faith* (Chicago: University of Chicago Press, 2003).

24. Steve Wilkens and Mark L. Sanford, *Hidden Worldviews: Eight Cultural Stories That Shape Our Lives* (Downers Grove, IL: InterVarsity Press, 2009), 139–59.

25. James Traub, "The United States of America Is Decadent and Depraved," *Foreign Policy* (December 19, 2017), http://foreignpolicy.com/2017/12/19/the-united-states-of-america-is-decadent-and-depraved/#.

26. Susan J. Wendel, *Scriptural Interpretation and Community Self-Definition in Luke-Acts and the Writings of Justin Martyr* (Boston: Brill, 2011), 3.

27. "Coalition Against Poverty in Suffolk," accessed December 29, 2017, https://capsuffolk.org.

28. Wayne C. Booth, *The Rhetoric of Rhetoric: The Quest for Effective Communication* (Malden, MA: Blackwell, 2004), 10.

29. See Eugene Garver, *Aristotle's Rhetoric: An Art of Character* (Chicago: University of Chicago Press, 1994).

Chapter 2

1. *Contra omnes haereses libri quinque*, 1.31.4. The English translations of this work (*Against Heresies*) are based on the text in *The Ante-Nicene Fathers*, 10 vols., ed. Alexander Roberts and James Donaldson (Edinburgh: T&T Clark, 1883–1884; repr., Grand Rapids, MI: Eerdmans, 1986–1990), 1:315–567; future references will be indicated as *Haer.*

2. *Haer*, 1.8.1.

3. Ibid., 1.13.1–3.

4. Frederik Wisse, "The Apocryphon of John (II, 1, III, 1, IV, 1, and BG 8502, 2)," in *The Nag Hammadi Library in English*, 4th ed. rev., ed. James M. Robinson (New York: E. J. Brill, 1996), 106.

5. Douglas Farrow, "St. Irenaeus of Lyons: The Church and the World," *Pro Ecclesia* 4 (1995): 336 (italics added).

6. *Haer*, 3.16.6–7.

7. Ibid., 2.22.4–5.

8. Ibid., 3.18.7.

9. Ibid., 2.30.7; see 1 Cor 12:2.

10. Ibid., 3.1.1; see 1 Tim 3:15.

11. Ibid., 1.10.2.

12. Ibid., 3.24.2; see 2.11.1.

13. Ibid., 1.8.1.

14. See ibid., 4.39.1.

15. See ibid., 4.37.

16. Ibid., 4.38.1.

17. Ibid.

18. *Haer*, 4.38.3 (italics added).

19. Ibid., 4.12.2.

20. Ibid., 1.10.2–3.

21. "Motorola Droid 2 for Verizon Commercial (HD)," last modified August 14, 2010, https://www.youtube.com/watch?v=q8bSLMcerCc.

22. Jacques Ellul, *The Technological Society* (New York: Knopf, 1967), xxv, 24.

23. "The Chicago Statement on Biblical Inerrancy," last modified January 6, 2009, http://library.dts.edu/Pages/TL/Special/ICBI_1.pdf.

24. Ibid.

25. "Living Life Happy . . . Joel Osteen," last modified February 26, 2016, https://www
.youtube.com/watch?v=ISQuKHNBkZ4&index=2&list=PLF39384EF9F105157.

Chapter 3

1. Socrates Scholasticus, *Ecclesiastical History, Book 1, Chapter 27*, in *Nicene and Post-Nicene Fathers* [*NPNF*], vol. 2, 2nd series, ed. Philip Schaff and Henry Wace (repr., Grand Rapids, MI: Eerdmans, 1955), 29–30. See also R. P. C. Hanson, *The Search for the Christian Doctrine of God: The Arian Controversy, 318–381* (Grand Rapids, MI: Baker Academic, 2005), 256–57.

2. Socrates Scholasticus, *Ecclesiastical History*, 32. See also Peter J. Leithart, *Defending Constantine: The Twilight of an Empire and the Dawn of Christendom* (Downers Grove, IL: IVP Academic, 2010), 174; Gerald McDermott, *The Great Theologians: A Brief Guide* (Downers Grove, IL: IVP Academic, 2010), 32. See also Philip Schaff and Henry Wace, *Prolegomena, Chapter 2*, in *Nicene and Post-Nicene Fathers* (*NPNF*), vol. 4, 2nd series, ed. Philip Schaff and Henry Wace (repr., Grand Rapids, MI: Eerdmans, 1955), xl.

3. See Quentin J. Schultze and Robert H. Woods Jr., eds., *Understanding Evangelical Media: The Changing Face of Christian Communication* (Downers Grove: IL, IVP Academic, 2008), 20–22; Robert H. Woods Jr. and Paul D. Patton, *Prophetically Incorrect: A Christian Introduction to Media Criticism* (Grand Rapids, MI: Brazos Press, 2010), 8–9.

4. Athanasius, *A Defense of the Nicene Definition* (*De Decretis*), trans. John Henry Newman (San Bernardino, CA: Assumption Press, 2014). Quoted passages are taken from this translation.

5. Rowan Williams, *Arius: Heresy and Tradition* (Grand Rapids, MI: Eerdmans, 1987), 100.

6. Schaff and Wace, *NPNF*, 4: xvi.

7. Williams, *Arius*, 74–75.

8. Samuel N. C. Lieu, "Constantine in Legendary Literature," in *The Cambridge Companion to the Age of Constantine* (Cambridge: Cambridge University Press, 2012), 299.

9. Hanson, *Search for the Christian Doctrine*, 329–34.

10. McDermott, *Great Theologians*, 33; Hanson, *Search for the Christian Doctrine*, 342.

11. Hanson, *Search for the Christian Doctrine*, 419, notes the work likely was authored in 356.

12. Williams, *Arius*, 86–88, 237; Leithart, *Defending Constantine*, 176.

13. Hans Von Campenhausen, *The Fathers of the Church* (repr., Peabody, MA: Hendrickson, 1998), 81.

14. William Rusch, *The Trinitarian Controversy* (Philadelphia: Fortress, 1980), 20, considers Eusebius of Caesarea "not an Arian" but rather one whose ideas were greatly opposed to Alexander of Alexandria, and thus Athanasius.

15. Bruce Shelley, *Church History in Plain Language*, 2nd ed. (Nashville: Thomas Nelson, 1995), 104.

16. John Anthony McGuckin, "The Road to Nicaea," *Christian History and Biography* 85 (2005): 22.

17. *De Decretis*, Sec. 1.

18. John Piper, *Contending for Our All: Defending Truth and Treasuring Christ in the Lives of Athanasius, John Owen, and J. Gresham Machen* (Wheaton, IL: Crossway, 2006), 65.

19. *De Decretis*, Sec. 27.

20. Williams, *Arius*, 95.

21. *De Decretis*, Sec. 9.

22. Ibid., Sec. 10.

23. Ibid.

24. Lewis Ayers, "Athanasius's Initial Defense of the Term 'homoousios': Rereading the *De Decretis*," *Journal of Early Christian Studies* 12, no. 3 (2004): 348.

25. *De Decretis*, Sec. 16.

26. Ibid., Sec. 17.

27. Ibid., Sec. 18.

28. McDermott, *Great Theologians*, 41.

29. *De Decretis*, Sec. 18.

30. Rusch, *Trinitarian Controversy*, 10. "Trinity" is a word not found in Scripture.

31. *De Decretis*, Sec. 20.

32. Ibid., Sec. 19.

33. McDermott, *Great Theologians*, 45.

34. Piper, *Contending for Our All*, 63–64.

35. Woods and Patton, *Prophetically Incorrect*, 21.

36. *De Decretis*, Sec. 2.

37. Ibid., Sec. 14.

38. Piper, *Contending for Our All*, 41.

39. McDermott, *Great Theologians*, 30.

40. Rusch, *Trinitarian Controversy*, 22.

41. Campenhausen, *Fathers of the Early Church*, 81.

42. Ibid., 70, 73.

43. Robert Gregg, foreword to *"The Life of Antony" and "The Letter to Marcellinus"* (New York: Paulist Press, 1980), xi. See also Von Campenhausen, *Fathers of the Early Church*, 77, and Hanson, *Search for the Christian Doctrine*, 239–73.

44. Woods and Patton, *Prophetically Incorrect*, 38–40, 91–94.

45. Ibid., 54.

46. Ibid.

Chapter 4

1. Gregory of Nyssa, *The Life of Saint Macrina*, trans., intro., and notes Kevin Corrigan (Eugene, OR: Wipf & Stock, 2005), 10.

2. Ibid., 39.

3. Jennifer A. Glancy, *Slavery in Early Christianity* (Oxford: Oxford University Press, 2002), 24, 16, 137.

4. Ibid., 142.

5. See Keith Bradley, "Slavery in the Roman Republic," in *The Cambridge World History of Slavery*, vol. 1, The Ancient Mediterranean World, ed. K. R. Bradley (New York: Cambridge University Press, 2011), 242.

6. Glancy, *Slavery*, 10.

7. Ibid.

8. Ibid., 240.

9. James H. Cone, *The Cross and the Lynching Tree* (Maryknoll, NY: Orbis Books, 2011), 30.

10. Gregory of Nyssa, *Homilies on Ecclesiastes: An English Version with Supporting Studies*, ed. Stuart George Hall (New York: Walter de Gruyter, 1993), 60.

11. Ibid., 73.

12. Ibid., 72.

13. Ibid., 74 (italics added).

14. Ibid. (italics added).

15. Hans Boersma, *Embodiment and Virtue in Gregory of Nyssa: An Anagogical Approach* (Oxford: Oxford University Press, 2013), 156–57, accessed November 11, 2017, doi: 10.1093/acprof:oso/9780199641123.001.0001.

16. Gregory of Nyssa, *Homilies*, 74.

17. Gregory of Nyssa, "On the Making of Man," 722–24.

18. Gregory of Nyssa, *Homilies*, 75.

19. Ibid., 74.

20. Ibid.

21. Ibid.

22. Ibid., 75.

23. Douglas Wilson and Steve Wilkins, *Southern Slavery: As It Was* (Moscow, ID: Canon Press, 1996), 14. Douglas Wilson, *Black & Tan: A Collection of Essays and Excursions on Slavery, Culture War, and Scripture in America* (Moscow, ID: Canon Press, 2005), 102.

24. John Piper, "My Story: From Greenville to Bethlehem," *Bloodlines: Race, Cross, and the Christian* (Wheaton, IL: Crossway, 2011).

25. Piper, "The Creation of One New Humanity by the Blood of Christ," *Bloodlines*.

26. Mark Mulder, "Right Diagnosis, Wrong Cure," *Comment* (January 18, 2012), accessed December 19, 2017, https://www.cardus.ca/comment/article/3038/right -diagnosis-wrong-cure/.

27. John Jefferson Davis, *Evangelical Ethics: Issues Facing the Church Today*, 4th ed. (Phillipsburg, NJ: P&R Publishing, 2015), 309, 311.

28. Ibid., 304.

29. Mark Charles, "Race, Trauma, and the Doctrine of Discovery," *The January Series of Calvin College*, accessed November 19, 2017, https://www.youtube.com /watch?v=fYZ2rj2Jooc.

30. "Declaration of Independence: A Transcription," *National Archives*, accessed November 19, 2017, https://www.archives.gov/founding-docs/declaration-transcript.

31. Ibid.

32. "The Constitution of the United States: A Transcription," *National Archives*, accessed November 19, 2017, https://www.archives.gov/founding-docs/constitution-transcript.

33. Mark Charles and Mike Hogeterp, "Icebergs in Our History—The Doctrine of Discovery," *Christian Reformed Church*, accessed November 19, 2017, https://vimeo .com/118735770.

34. Charles, "Race," *The January Series*.

Chapter 5

1. Augustine, *Confessions*, trans. John K. Ryan (New York: Image Books, 1960), II.ii.2.

2. Ibid., II.iii.6.

3. Ibid., II.iii.7.

4. Ibid.

5. Ibid., I.i.1.

6. Ibid.

7. Ibid., II.i.1; II.x.18.

8. Ibid.

9. Ibid., II.4–10.

10. Ibid., IV.iv.4–6.

11. Ibid., IV.vi.11.

12. Ibid., IV.iv.9.

13. Augustine, *On Christian Doctrine*, trans. D. W. Robertson Jr. (Upper Saddle River, NJ: Prentice-Hall, 1958), I.xxvi.27; I.xxix.30.

14. Augustine, *Confessions*, XI.x.12.

15. Calvin L. Troup, *Temporality, Eternity, and Wisdom* (Columbia: University of South Carolina Press, 1999), 172–78.

16. C. S. Lewis, *Mere Christianity* (1952; repr., New York: HarperCollins, 2001), 77.

17. Augustine, *Confessions*, X.xxxxiii.69.

18. Augustine, *On Christian Doctrine*, II.xvi.24.

19. Ibid., II.xviii.28.

20. Augustine, *Confessions*, VII.ix.15.

21. Ibid.

22. Ibid., X.iv.6.

23. Ibid., XI.ii.4–XI.ix.11.

24. Ibid., XII.xxix.40.

25. Ibid., XIII.xxi.

Chapter 6

1. Carmen Acevedo Butcher, *A Life of St. Benedict: Man of Blessing* (Brewster, MA: Paraclete Press, 2006) 48.

2. Benedict, *The Rule of Saint Benedict in English,* ed. Timothy Fry (Collegeville, MN: Liturgical Press, 1982), xxvii.

3. Dom Justin McCann, *Saint Benedict* (London: Sheed and Ward, 1937), 37.

4. Leslie A. Baxter and Dawn O. Braithwaite, "Relational Dialectical Theory: Crafting Meaning from Competing Discourses," in *Engaging Theories in Interpersonal Communication,* ed. Leslie A. Baxter and Dawn O. Braithwaite (Thousand Oaks, CA: Sage, 2008), 359.

5. Esther de Waal, *Living with Contradiction: An Introduction to Benedictine Spirituality* (Harrisburg, PA: Morehouse, 1997), 69–70.

6. Benedict, *The Rule,* 5.

7. Quentin R. Skrabec, *St. Benedict's Rule for Business Success* (West Lafayette, IN: Purdue University Press, 2003), 1.

8. McCann, *Saint Benedict,* 131.

9. Esther de Waal, *Seeking God: The Way of Saint Benedict* (Collegeville, MN: Liturgical Press, 2001), 15.

10. McCann, *Saint Benedict,* 54.

11. De Waal, *Seeking God,* 146–47.

12. McCann, *Saint Benedict,* 82–83.

13. Esther de Waal, *A Life-Giving Way: A Commentary on the Rule of St. Benedict* (Collegeville, MN: Liturgical Press, 1995), xiv.

14. Parker J. Palmer, *The Promise of Paradox: A Celebration of Contradictions in the Christian Life* (San Francisco: Jossey-Bass, 2008), xxix.

15. Benedict, *The Rule,* 43.

16. Joan Chittister, *Wisdom Distilled from the Daily: Living the Rule of St. Benedict Today* (New York: HarperCollins, 1990), 42.

17. McCann, *Saint Benedict,* 142.

18. Benedict, *The Rule,* 44.

19. Ibid., 16–20.

20. Chittister, *Wisdom Distilled from the Daily,* 55.

21. Benedict, *The Rule,* 13.

22. Ibid., 12.

23. Thomas Moore, foreword, in ibid., xix.

24. Benedict, *The Rule,* 3.

25. De Waal, *Seeking God,* 43.

26. Leslie A. Baxter and Barbara M. Montgomery, *Relating: Dialogues and Dialectics* (New York: Guilford, 1996). See also Leslie A. Baxter and Kristen M. Norwood, "Relational Dialectics Theory: Navigating Meaning from Competing Discourses," in *Engaging Theories in Interpersonal Communication: Multiple Perspectives,* 2nd ed., ed. Dawn O. Braithwaite and Paul Schrodt (Thousand Oaks, CA: Sage, 2015).

27. Donna R. Pawlowski, "Dialectical Tensions in Marital Partners' Accounts of Their Relationships," *Communication Quarterly* 46, no. 4 (1998): 396–416.

28. Donna R. Pawlowski, "Dialectical Tensions in Families Experiencing Acute Health Issues: Stroke Survivors' Perceptions," in *The Family Communication Sourcebook,* ed. Lynn H. Turner and Richard West (Thousand Oaks, CA: Sage, 2008), 474.

29. Baxter and Norwood, "Relational Dialectics Theory," 287.

30. Ibid.

31. Palmer, *The Promise of Paradox*, 8 (italics original).

32. Julie L. Semlak and Judy C. Pearson, "Big Macs/Peanut Butter and Jelly: An Exploration of Dialectical Contradictions Experienced by the Sandwich Generation," *Communication Research Reports* 28, no. 4 (2011): 296–307.

33. Ibid., 304.

34. Ibid., 298.

35. Rod Dreher, *The Benedict Option: A Strategy for Christians in a Post-Christian Nation* (New York: Penguin Random House, 2017).

Chapter 7

1. Eadmer, *The Life of St. Anselm, Archbishop of Canterbury, by Eadmer*, ed. R. W. Southern (London: Thomas Nelson and Sons, 1962), 65.

2. Ibid., 64–65; see also 65n1.

3. Ibid., 66–67.

4. Anselm, *Monologion*, 10; Francis S. Schmitt, ed., *Anselmi Opera Omnia* (Edinburgh: Thomas Nelson and Sons, 1946), 1.24.29–30. Citations to the *Monologion* are given by title and chapter, followed by the location (volume, page, lines) of the relevant passage in Schmitt, who remains the authoritative edited version of Anselm's Latin manuscripts.

5. *Monologion*, 10; Schmitt, 1.24.30–25.1.

6. Ibid.; Schmitt, 1.25.1–2.

7. Ibid.; Schmitt, 1.25.4–9.

8. Ibid.; Schmitt, 1.25.22.

9. Gillian R. Evans, *Anselm and Talking about God* (Oxford: Clarendon Press, 1978), 20.

10. See *Monologion*, 65; Schmitt, 1.77.1–3. See also *Monologion* 15; Schmitt, 1.28.5–7.

11. *Monologion*, 74; Schmitt, 1.83.7–8.

12. *Monologion*, 28; Schmitt, 1.45.24. See also *Monologion*, 4; Schmitt, 1.16.31–17.01.

13. *Monologion*, 31; Schmitt, 1.48.18–19.

14. *Monologion*, 9; Schmitt, 1.24.10–20.

15. *Monologion*, 36; Schmitt, 1.55.4–6.

16. R. W. Southern, *Saint Anselm: A Portrait in a Landscape* (Cambridge: Cambridge University Press, 1990), 190–93.

17. M. J. Charlesworth, *St. Anselm's "Proslogion"* (South Bend, IN: University of Notre Dame Press, 1979), 10; *Proslogion*, prologue. Citations to the *Proslogion* are given by reference to the relevant page number in Charlesworth, followed by the location in *Proslogion*.

18. Charlesworth, 111; *Proslogion*, 1.

19. *Monologion*, 65; Schmitt, 1.77.1–3.

20. Charlesworth, 117; *Proslogion, 2*.

21. David Brody, "Exclusive: Michele Bachmann: 'God Raised Up' Trump to be GOP Nominee" (August 30, 2016), http://www1.cbn.com/thebrodyfile/archive/2016/08/30/only-on-the-brody-file-michele-bachmann-says-god-raised-up-trump-to-be-gop-presidential-nominee.

22. Pat Robertson, "700 Club" (August 2, 2016). See esp. 3:51–5:30 time signature, http://www1.cbn.com/video/700club/2016/08/02/the-700-club-august-2-2016.

23. See Austin L. Hughes, "The Folly of Scientism," in *The New Atlantis* (Fall 2012), http://www.thenewatlantis.com/publications/the-folly-of-scientism.

24. Jan Markell, "Understanding the Times Radio" (July 9, 2016), esp. 4:38–6:50.

25. For example, Hrafnkell Haraldsson, "Unhinged Michele Bachmann Says God 'Lifted Up' Trump to Defeat Hillary" (July 13, 2016), http://www.politicususa.com/2016/07/13 /unhinged-michele-bachmann-god-lifted-up-trump-defeat-hillary.html.

Chapter 8

1. Clement C. J. Webb, *John of Salisbury* (London: Methuen, 1932), 4.

2. Jan Van Laarhoven, introduction to *John of Salisbury's Entheticus Maior and Minor,* vol. 1, ed. Jan Van Laarhoven (Leiden: E. J. Brill, 1987), 3–100.

3. Edward Grant, *God and Reason in the Middle Ages* (Cambridge: Cambridge University Press, 2001), 106.

4. John of Salisbury, *Metalogicon*, trans. Daniel D. McGarry (Philadelphia: Paul Dry, 2009), 189.

5. Walter J. Ong, *The Presence of the Word* (New Haven, CT: Yale University Press, 1967), 59; John of Salisbury, *Metalogicon*, 189.

6. John of Salisbury, *Metalogicon*, 190–91.

7. Ibid., 191, 193, 196.

8. Ibid., 199.

9. Ibid., 67.

10. Ibid., 103.

11. Ibid., 108.

12. Ibid., 143.

13. Ibid., 64.

14. Ibid., 94.

15. Brad S. Gregory, *The Unintended Reformation: How a Religious Revolution Secularized Society* (Cambridge: Harvard University Press, 2012), 179.

16. "The Real Presence of Jesus Christ in the Sacrament of the Eucharist: Basic Questions and Answers," *United States Conferences of Catholic Bishops,* accessed May 30, 2017, http://www.usccb.org/prayer-and-worship/the-mass/order-of-mass/liturgy-of -the-eucharist/the-real-presence-of-jesus-christ-in-the-sacrament-of-the-eucharist -basic-questions-and-answers.cfm.

17. Eamon Duffy, *The Stripping of the Altars: Traditional Religion in England c. 1400– 1580* (New Haven, CT: Yale University Press, 1992), 91.

18. Ibid., 98.

19. Ann W. Astell, *Eating Beauty: The Eucharist and the Spiritual Arts of the Middle Ages* (Ithaca, NY: Cornell University Press, 2006).

20. Jacques Le Goff, *Medieval Civilization: 400–1500*, trans. Julia Barrow (Oxford: Basil Blackwell, 1990), 255.

21. Ibid., 258.

22. Ibid.

23. See David C. Lindberg, *The Beginnings of Western Science: The European Scientific Tradition in Philosophical, Religious, and Institutional Context, Prehistory to A.D. 1450,* 9th ed. (Chicago: University of Chicago Press, 2007), 220.

24. Brian Gilchrist, "The Smartphone as Permanent Substitute Teacher," in *Communication Theory and Millennial Popular Culture: Essays and Applications*, ed. Kathleen Glenister Roberts (New York: Peter Lang, 2016), 150.

25. Deborah Eicher-Catt and Isaac E. Catt, "Peirce and Cassirer, 'Life' and 'Spirit': A Communicology of Religion," *Journal of Communication and Religion* 36, no. 2 (2013): 98.

26. Corey Anton, "On Communicology (Richard Lanigan)," www.youtube.com, accessed February 6, 2016, https://www.youtube.com/watch?v=HQsv2Jg1K-U.

27. Gilchrist, "The Smartphone as Permanent Substitute Teacher," 151.

28. See Charles Taylor, *A Secular Age* (Cambridge, MA: Harvard University Press, 2007).

29. Martin Luther King Jr., "'Loving Your Enemies,' Sermon Delivered at Dexter Avenue Baptist Church," in *Martin Luther King, Jr., and the Global Freedom Struggle*, accessed September 24, 2016, http://kingencyclopedia.stanford.edu/encyclopedia /documentsentry/doc_loving_your_enemies/index.html.

Chapter 9

1. Angela of Foligno, *Complete Works*, trans. and comm. Paul Lachance (New York: Paulist Press, 1993), 136.

2. Paul Lachance, "The Mystical Journey of Angela of Foligno," *Vox Benedictina: A Journal of Translations from Monastic Sources* 4, no. 1 (1987): 9–39.

3. Angela of Foligno, *Complete Works*, 147.

4. Verna Harrison, "The Relationship between Apophatic and Kataphatic Theology," *Pro Ecclesia* 4, no. 3 (1995): 319.

5. Michael Glazier and Monika Hellwig, ed., *The Modern Catholic Encyclopedia* (Collegeville, MN: The Liturgical Press, 1994), 477.

6. Brian McGrath Davis, "Apophatic Theology and Masculinities," *Cross Currents* 61, no. 4 (December 2011): 504.

7. William Short, *Poverty and Joy: The Franciscan Tradition* (Maryknoll, NY: Orbis Books, 1999), 48.

8. Lachance, in *Angela of Foligno: Complete Works,* 48.

9. Angela of Foligno, *Complete Works*, 144–48.

10. Ibid., 149.

11. Ibid., 150.

12. Ibid., 225.

13. Ibid., 234.

14. Ibid.

15. Ibid., 263.

16. Ibid., 126.

17. Paul Lachance, *Angela of Foligno: Passionate Mystic of the Double Abyss* (Hyde Park, NY: New City Press, 2006), 10.

18. Becky Johns, "Hidden Strategies of Resistance in Female Mormon Missionary Narratives: Two Case Studies," *Journal of Communication and Religion* 31, no. 1 (March 2008): 61.

19. Lachance, in *Angela of Foligno*, 15.

20. Darleen Pryds, *Women of the Streets: Early Franciscan Women and Their Mendicant Vocation* (St. Bonaventure, NY: Franciscan Institute Publications, 2010), ix–x, 35–36.

21. Lachance, *Passionate Mystic of the Double Abyss*, 31.

22. Don Miller, OFM, "Saint Angela of Foligno," *Franciscan Media*, accessed October 2, 2017, https://www.franciscanmedia.org/saint-angela-of-foligno/.

23. Ibid.

24. Lk 24:11 (NIV).

25. Bert Roest, "Female Preaching in the Late Medieval Franciscan Tradition," *Franciscan Studies* 62 (2004): 119; Ryan Murphy, "Promises Unfulfilled: American Religious Sisters and Gender in Equality in the Post-Vatican II Catholic Church," *Social Compass* 61, no. 4 (2014): 608.

26. Clare Malone, "Holy Rollers: The Nuns on the Bus Are Just One Example of Progressive Dissidents Challenging the Hierarchy of the Catholic Church," *The American Prospect*, no. 7 (2012): 7.

27. LaVonne Neff, "A Nun on a Bus: How All of Us Can Create Hope, Change, and Community," *The Christian Century* 131, no. 14 (2014): 37. Neff notes that although the sisters were questioned on their stance on abortion, Campbell's focus on the lives of the poor never meant she did not care for the lives of the unborn.

28. Ibid.

29. David Gibson, "Leader of Nuns on the Bus Calls GOP Budget Immoral," *The Christian Century* 129, no. 20 (2012): 16.

30. Rosemary Carbine, "Creating Communities of Justice and Peace: Sacramentality and Public Catholicism in the United States," *Journal for the Academic Study of Religion* 29, no. 2 (2016): 196.

31. Denys Turner, *The Darkness of God: Negativity in Christian Mysticism* (Cambridge: Cambridge University Press, 1998), 20.

32. Sister Simone Campbell, "Sister Simone Campbell: Finally, Affirmation for Nuns," www.time.com (April 20, 2015): n.p.

33. Barbara Brown Taylor, *Learning to Walk in the Dark* (New York: Harper One, 2014), 34.

34. Ibid.

35. Ibid., 45.

Chapter 10

1. Karl Jaspers, *The Great Philosophers* (New York: Harcourt, Brace, and World, 1966), 116.

2. Nicholas of Cusa, *Complete Philosophical and Theological Treatises of Nicholas of Cusa*, vol. 1, trans. Jasper Hopkins (Minneapolis, MN: Banning, 2001), 538.

3. Ibid., 540.

4. Ibid., 141.

5. Nicholas of Cusa, *Complete Philosophical and Theological Treatises*, vol. 2, trans. Jasper Hopkins (Minneapolis, MN: Banning, 2001), 681.

6. Nicholas of Cusa, *De possest (On Actualized-Possibility)*, in *Complete Philosophical and Theological Treatises*, vol. 2, 923–24.

7. Nicholas of Cusa, *Complete Philosophical and Theological Treatises*, vol. 1, 151.

8. Harvey J. Graff, *The Legacies of Literacy* (Bloomington: Indiana University Press, 1987).

9. P. J. Tichenor, G. A. Donohue, and C. N. Olien, "Mass Media Flow and Differential Growth in Knowledge," *Public Opinion Quarterly* 34, no. 2 (1970): 159–70.

10. Nicholas of Cusa, *Complete Philosophical and Theological Treatises*, vol. 1, 42.

11. Nicholas of Cusa, *De ludo globi (The Bowling Game)* and *De beryllo (On Eyeglasses)*, in *Complete Philosophical and Theological Treatises*, vol. 2, 1179–1274, 791–838.

12. Nicholas of Cusa, *Complete Philosophical and Theological Treatises*, vol. 1, 537.

13. Jaspers, *The Great Philosophers*, 119.

14. Christine K. Cassel and David B. Reuben, "Specialization, Subspecialization, and Subsubspecialization in Internal Medicine," *New England Journal of Medicine* 364, no. 12 (2011): 1169–73.

15. Pierre Levy, *Collective Intelligence* (New York: Basic Books, 1999), 213.

Chapter 11

1. Quoted in Christopher J. Probst, *Demonizing the Jews: Luther and the Protestant Church in Nazi Germany* (Bloomington: Indiana University Press, 2012), 129.

2. Martin Luther, *On the Jews and Their Lies*, ed. Domenico d'Abrruzo (Princeton, NJ: Eulenspiegel, 2015), passim.

3. Ibid.

4. Ibid., viii.

5. Ibid., 10.

6. Ibid., 9.

7. Ibid., 30–31.

8. Ibid., 30.

9. Ibid., 40.

10. Ibid., 42.

11. Ibid., 165–70.

12. Ibid., 188.

13. Eric W. Gritsch, *Martin Luther's Anti-Semitism: Against His Better Judgment* (Grand Rapids: Eerdmans, 2012), 35.

14. Martin Luther, "Lectures on the Psalms," in *Luther's Works, I–LV*, ed. Jaroslav Pelikan and Helmut Lehmann, vol. 10 (Philadelphia, PA: Fortress; St. Louis, MO: Concordia, 1955–1986), 30.

15. Ibid., 88.

16. Martin Luther, "Lectures on Galatians," in *Luther's Works, I–LV*, ed. Jaroslav Pelikan and Helmut Lehmann, vol. 27 (Philadelphia, PA: Fortress; St. Louis, MO: Concordia, 1955–1986), 265.

17. Martin Luther, "Treatise on Good Works," in *Luther's Works, I–LV*, ed. Jaroslav Pelikan and Helmut Lehmann, vol. 44 (Philadelphia, PA: Fortress; St. Louis, MO: Concordia, 1955–1986), 96.

18. Martin Luther, "Lectures on Deuteronomy," in Jaroslav Pelikan and Helmut Lehmann, ed., *Luther's Works, I–LV*, ed. Jaroslav Pelikan and Helmut Lehmann, vol. 9 (Philadelphia, PA: Fortress; St. Louis, MO: Concordia, 1955–1986), 146.

19. Martin Luther, "Four Psalms of Comfort for the Queen of Hungary," in *Luther's Works, I–LV*, ed. Jaroslav Pelikan and Helmut Lehmann, vol. 14 (Philadelphia, PA: Fortress; St. Louis, MO: Concordia, 1955–1986), 267–68.

20. Martin Luther, "Against the Sabbatarians," in *Luther's Works, I–LV*, ed. Jaroslav Pelikan and Helmut Lehmann, vol. 47 (Philadelphia, PA: Fortress; St. Louis, MO: Concordia, 1955–1986), 96–97.

21. Quoted in Gritsch, *Martin Luther's Anti-Semitism*, 96.

22. Charles Horton Cooley, Human Nature and the Social Order (New York: Scribner, 1922); George Herbert Mead, Mind, Self, and Society (Chicago: University of Chicago Press, 1934).

23. Henri Tajfel and John Turner, "An Integrative Theory of Intergroup Conflict," in *The Social Psychology of Intergroup Relations*, ed. William G. Austin and Stephen Worchel (Monterey, CA: Brooks / Cole, 1979), 38–43.

24. Peter Berger, *The Sacred Canopy: Elements of a Sociological Theory of Religion* (New York: Anchor, 1967).

25. Peter Berger, *The Desecularization of the World: Resurgent Religion and World Politics* (Grand Rapids, MI: Eerdmans, 1999).

26. Christian Smith, *Moral, Believing Animals: Human Personhood and Culture* (Oxford: Oxford University Press, 2003).

27. James K. Wellman, *Evangelical vs. Liberal: The Clash of Christian Cultures in the Pacific Northwest* (New York: Oxford University Press, 2008), 193.

28. Christian Smith, *American Evangelicalism: Embattled and Thriving* (Chicago: University of Chicago Press, 1998), 121.

29. Pew Research Center, *America's Changing Religious Landscape* (Washington, DC: Pew Research Center, 2015), accessed June 22, 2017, http://assets.pewresearch.org/wp-content/uploads/sites/11/2015/05/RLS-08–26-full-report.pdf.

30. Randall Balmer, *Blessed Assurance: A History of Evangelicalism in America* (Boston: Beacon Press, 1999), 109.

31. Franklin Graham, "From Franklin Graham: The Most Important Election of Our Lifetime," Billy Graham Evangelistic Association, accessed June 22, 2017, https://billygraham.org/decision-magazine/september-2016/from-franklin-graham-the-most-important-election-of-our-lifetime/?utm_source=DecisionElectionGuide+LP+Post+Event&utm_medium=link&utm_campaign=Decision+Election+Guide&utm_content=Post+Event+BD160YDEG&SOURCE=BD160YDEG.

32. Charles Chandler, "Tony Perkins: 'This Is Not a Time to Stand on the Sidelines,'" Billy Graham Evangelistic Association, accessed June 22, 2017, https://billygraham.org/decision-magazine/september-2016/tony-perkins-this-is-not-a-time-to-stand-on-the-sidelines/?utm_source=DecisionElectionGuide+LP+Post+Event&utm_medium=link&utm_campaign=Decision+Election+Guide&utm_content=Post+Event+BD160YDEG&SOURCE=BD160YDEG.

33. Jerry Pierce, "Two Visions, Two Americas," Billy Graham Evangelistic Association, accessed June 22, 2017, https://billygraham.org/decision-magazine/september-2016/two-visions-two-americas/?utm_source=DecisionElectionGuide+LP+Post+Event&utm_medium=link&utm_campaign=Decision+Election+Guide&utm_content=Post+Event+BD160YDEG&SOURCE=BD160YDEG.

34. William B. Gudykunst, "Anxiety/Uncertainty Management (AUM) Theory of Effective Communication: Making the Mesh of the Net Finer," in *Theorizing about Intercultural Communication*, ed. William B. Gudykunst (Thousand Oaks, CA: Sage, 2005): 281–322.

35. Mark Ward Sr., "Managing the Anxiety and Uncertainty of Religious Otherness: Interfaith Dialogue as a Problem of Intercultural Communication," in *A Communication Perspective on Interfaith Dialogue: Living within the Abrahamic Traditions*, ed. Daniel S. Brown Jr. (Lanham, MD: Lexington, 2013), 36.

36. James A. Keaten and Charles Soukup, "Dialogue and Religious Otherness: Toward a Model of Pluralistic Interfaith Dialogue," *Journal of International and Intercultural Communication* 2, no. 2 (2009): 168–87.

37. Ibid., 180–81.

38. Charles Soukup and James Keaten, "Humanizing and Dehumanizing across Four Orientations to Religious Others," in *A Communication Perspective on Interfaith Dialogue: Living within the Abrahamic Traditions*, ed. Daniel S. Brown Jr. (Lanham, MD: Lexington, 2013), 50.

Chapter 12

1. John W. O'Malley, *Jesuits: A History from Ignatius to the Present* (New York: Roman and Littlefield, 2014), 7.

2. Ibid., 11.

3. Jaroslav Pelikan, *The Christian Tradition: A History of the Development of Doctrine, Volume 4: Reformation of Church and Dogma (1300–1700)* (Chicago: University of Chicago Press, 1985), 275.

4. Robert E. McNally, "The Council of Trent, the *Spiritual Exercises*, and the Catholic Reform," *Church History: Studies in Christianity and Culture* 34 (1965): 36.

5. Pelikan, *The Christian Tradition*, 275–76.

6. Ibid., 7.

7. Ignatius Loyola, "Dealing with Others," first section of "Instructions for the Sojourn at Trent," in *Selected Letters and Instructions of Saint Ignatius Loyola*, ed. Joseph N. Tylenda (Chicago: Loyola University Press, 1985), 19.

8. Ibid.

9. Ibid.

10. Ibid.

11. Ibid., "Helping Souls," second section of "Instructions for the Sojourn at Trent," 20.

12. Ibid.

13. Ibid.

14. Ibid., "Some Self-Helps," third section of "Instructions for the Sojourn at Trent," 20.

15. Ibid.

16. Ibid.

17. Andrea Leskes, "A Plea for Civil Discourse: Needed, the Academy's Leadership," *Liberal Education* 99, no. 4 (Fall 2013): 44.

18. Ray Williams, "The Rise of Incivility and Bullying in America," *Psychology Today*, accessed August 5, 2016, https://www.psychologytoday.com/blog/wired-success/201207/the-rise-incivility-and-bullying-in-america.

19. Kate Shuster, "Toward a More Civil Discourse," *Teaching Tolerance* 37 (Spring 2013), accessed June 21, 2017, http://www.tolerance.org/publication/civil-discourse-classroom.

20. Leskes, "A Plea for Civil Discourse," 46.

21. Stephen I. Carter, *Civility: Manners, Morals, and the Etiquette of Democracy* (New York: Basic Books, 1998), 19.

22. Weber Shandwick and Powell Tate, "Civility in America 2013," *Weber Shandwick: Engaging Always*, accessed January 27, 2016, http://www.webershandwick.com.

23. Alleen Pace Nilsen, "Civility: The Right Thing to Teach in Contentious Times," *English Journal* 97 (2008): 65.

24. Peter Levine, "Teaching and Learning Civility," *New Directions for Higher Education* 152 (Winter 2010): 16.

25. Leskes, "A Plea for Civil Discourse," 48.

26. Ignatius Loyola, "Dealing with Others," 19.

27. Nilsen, "Civility: The Right Thing," 65.

28. Sharon Crowley, *Towards a Civil Discourse: Rhetoric and Fundamentalism* (Pittsburgh: University of Pittsburgh Press, 2006), 32.

Chapter 13

1. Diarmaid MacCulloch, *Thomas Cranmer: A Life* (New Haven, CT: Yale University Press, 1996), 599–605.

2. Albert Fredrick Pollard, *Thomas Cranmer and the English Reformation (1489–1556)* (New York: Putnam's Sons, 1906), 380–84.

3. Theodore Maynard, *The Life of Thomas Cranmer* (Chicago: Henry Regnery, 1956), 234.

4. Ashley Null, *Thomas Cranmer's Doctrine of Repentance* (New York: Oxford University Press, 2000), n7.

5. MacCulloch, *Thomas Cranmer: A Life*, 41–78.

6. Ibid., 41–42.

7. Ibid., 129.

8. Ashley Null and John W. Yates III, eds., *Reformation Anglicanism: A Vision for Today's Global Communion* (Wheaton, IL: Crossway, 2017), 72–74.

9. Ibid., 74–76.

10. *The Oxford Guide to "The Book of Common Prayer": A Worldwide Survey*, ed. Charles Hefling and Cynthia Shattuck (Oxford: Oxford University Press, 2006), 3.

11. Simon Chan, *Liturgical Theology: The Church as a Worshiping Community* (Downers Grove, IL: InterVarsity Press), 91.

12. *The First and Second Prayer Books of Edward VI*, Everyman's Library ed. (London: J. M. Dent and Sons, 1960), 348.

13. Evan Daniel, *The Prayer Book: Its History, Language and Contents*, 22nd ed. (London: Wells Gardner, Darton, 1909), 100.

14. Ashley Null, *Divine Allurement: Cranmer's Comfortable Words* (London: The Latimer Trust, 2014).

15. *The First and Second Prayer Books of Edward VI*, 225.

16. *The Oxford Guide to "The Book of Common Prayer,"* 1.

17. *The Book of Common Prayer: The Texts of 1549, 1559, and 1662*, xii.

18. The word "catholic" is defined in traditional Anglican theology as "universal," referring to the Christian church throughout the world.

19. Null, *Thomas Cranmer's Doctrine of Repentance*, 4.

20. The Book of Common Prayer is not a panacea for all disputes in society or even in the church. The Anglican Communion itself has become fractured over the last fifteen years. One reason for the fracturing may be that the Prayer Book is no longer the standard for Anglican worship in parts of the Communion.

Chapter 14

1. See Rom 16:17 and Mt 18:17, respectively.

2. Menno Simons, "Instruction on Excommunication," in *The Complete Writings of Menno Simons*, trans. Leonard Verduin, ed. J. C. Wenger (Scottdale, PA: Herald Press, 1984), 959–98. His other writings include "A Clear Account of Excommunication," and "Final Instruction on Marital Avoidance," in *The Complete Writings of Menno Simons*, 455–585 and 1058–61, respectively.

3. Simons, "A Kind Admonition on Church Discipline," in *The Complete Writings of Menno Simons*, 412.

4. Simons, "Reply to Gellius Faber," in *The Complete Writings of Menno Simons*, 729.

5. Simons, "Instruction on Excommunication," 975–76.

6. Ibid., 976.

7. Ibid., 984.

8. Simons, "A Kind Admonition on Church Discipline," 413.

9. Simons, "Instruction on Excommunication," 974.

10. Simons, "Foundation of Christian Doctrine," in *The Complete Writings of Menno Simons*, 140.

11. Simons, "Why I Do Not Cease Teaching and Writing," in *The Complete Writings of Menno Simons*, 313.

12. Ibid.

13. Simons, "Instruction on Excommunication," 969.

14. Simons, "A Clear Account," 471–72.

15. Simons, "Instruction on Excommunication," 970–71.

16. Ibid., 970.

17. Ibid., 972.

18. "Yoder, Howard John (1927–1997)," *Global Anabaptist Mennonite Encyclopedia* online, accessed June 22, 2017, http://gameo.org/index.php?title=Yoder,_John_Howard_(1927–1997).

19. See Michelle Sokol, "Mennonite Seminary Apologizes to Victims of Famed Theologian John Howard Yoder," *National Catholic Reporter*, https://www.ncronline.org/news/accountability/mennonite-seminary-apologizes-victims-famed-theologian-john-howard-yoder, and Rich Preheim, "Mennonites Apologize for History of Sex Abuse Following Theologian John Howard Yoder Scandal, *The Washington Post* (July 7, 2015), accessed June 22, 2017, https://www.washingtonpost.com/pb/national/religion/mennonites-apologize-for-history-of-sex-abuse-following-theologian-john-howard-yoder-scandal/2015/07/07/9fdb2092–24b7–11e5-b621-b55e495e9b78_story.html.

20. Council of Christian Colleges and Universities, "Our Work and Mission," accessed June 23, 2017, http://cccu.org/about.

21. TWU Community Covenant, Preamble and "The TWU Community Covenant" overview, accessed March 2016, https://twu.ca/studenthandbook/twu-community-covenant-agreement.pdf.

22. Ibid.

23. Chapter B, 2.0, Employment Policies, 2.09 Termination of Employment, Trinity Western University, Langley, B.C., Canada, and Student Accountability Policy, "Emergency Temporary Suspension," accessed March 2016, https://twu.ca/studenthandbook/university-policies/student-accountability-policy.html.

24. Student Handbook, "The Goal of the Accountability Process," accessed March 2016, https://twu.ca/studenthandbook/university-policies/student-accountability-policy.html.

25. Ibid.

26. Simons, "Instruction on Excommunication," 968.

Chapter 15

1. John Calvin, qtd. in Frans Pieter Van Stam, "Radical Church Reformation," in *The Calvin Handbook*, ed. Herman J. Selderhuis, trans. Henry J. Baron et al. (Grand Rapids, MI: Eerdmans, 2009), 31.

2. Guillaume Farel, qtd. in ibid., 31.

3. *Calvin's New Testament Commentaries: The Gospel According to St John 11–21 and The First Epistle of John*, ed. David W. Torrance and Thomas F. Torrance, trans. T. H. L. Parker (Grand Rapids, MI: Eerdmans, 1961).

4. *Institutes of the Christian Religion*, ed. John T. McNeill, trans. Ford Lewis Battles, 2 vols., Library of Christian Classics, nos. 20–21 (Philadelphia: Westminster Press, 1960), II.2.1; II.6.4.

5. Raymond A. Blacketer, *The School of God: Pedagogy and Rhetoric in Calvin's Interpretation of Deuteronomy* (Dordrecht, The Netherlands: Springer, 2006).

6. William J. Bouwsma, *John Calvin: A Sixteenth-Century Portrait* (New York: Oxford University Press, 1988), 5.

7. Thomas M. Conley, *Rhetoric in the European Tradition* (Chicago: University of Chicago Press, 1990), 109–33.

8. Ford Lewis Battles, "God Was Accommodating Himself to Human Capacity," *Interpretation* 31 (1997): 19–38.

9. *Institutes* I.12.1.

10. For concerns about accommodation, see Arnold Huijgen, *Divine Accommodation: Analysis and Assessment* (Göttingen: Vandenhoeck & Ruprecht, 2011), 282–88, 294, et passim, and Vern S. Poythress, "Rethinking Accommodation in Revelation," *Westminster Theological Journal* 76 (2014): 143–56.

11. This example reflects an actual experience from summer 2017; the name and some details have been altered to preserve the anonymity of this ministry volunteer.

12. On the similarity between evangelism and marketing, see Jonathan K. Dodson, *The Unbelievable Gospel: Say Something Worth Believing* (Grand Rapids, MI: Zondervan, 2014), 35–40.

13. Calvin's commentary on Is 40:11, qtd. in Jon Balserak, *Divinity Compromised: A Study of Divine Accommodation in the Thought of John Calvin* (Dordrecht, The Netherlands: Springer, 2006), 43.

14. Chrysostom (d. 407), the church father most influential in advancing accommodation (*sunkatabasis*), emphasized that God's communication is characterized by love; see Robert C. Hill, "On Looking Again at *Sunkatabasis*," *Prudentia* 13 (1981): 3–11.

Chapter 16

1. James Herbert Midgley, *Margaret Fell: The Mother of the Early Quaker Church* (Newberg, OR: Historical Quaker Books, 1916), 21, http://digitalcommons.georgefox.edu/cgi/viewcontent.cgi?article=1002&context=quakerbooks.

2. Ibid., 23.

3. Ibid.

4. Ibid.

5. The pamphlet is fully titled *Women's Speaking Justified, Proved, and Allowed by the Scriptures, All Such as Speak by the Spirit and Power of the Lord Jesus and How Women Were the First That Preached the Tidings of the Resurrection of Jesus, and Were Sent by Christ's Own Command Before He Ascended to the Father.*

6. See also Mary Anne Schofield, "*Women's Speaking Justified*: The Feminine Quaker Voice, 1662–1797," *Tulsa Studies in Women's Literature* 6, no. 1 (1987): 61–77.

7. Margaret Fell, *Women's Speaking Justified, Proved, and Allowed by the Scriptures* (Ann Arbor, MI: Text Creation Partnership, 1666, 2008), title page, accessed November 23, 2017, http://name.umdl.umich.edu/A41072.0001.001ell.

8. Ibid., 10.

9. Ibid., 13–16.

10. Jacqueline Broad, "Margaret Fell," *The Stanford Encyclopedia of Philosophy*, ed. Edward N. Zalta (Spring 2012), accessed November 17, 2017, https://stanford.library .sydney.edu.au/archives/spr2012/entries/margaret-fell/.

11. Margaret Fell, *The Life of Margaret Fox, Wife of George Fox: Compiled from Her Own Narrative, and Other Sources with a Selection from Her Epistles, Etc.* (Philadelphia: Association of Friends, 1859).

12. Schofield, "*Women's Speaking Justified.*"

13. Ibid.

14. Phyllis Mack, *Visionary Women: Ecstatic Prophecy in Seventeenth-Century England* (Berkeley: University of California Press, 1992), 216.

15. Bruce Ware, "Summaries of Egalitarian and Complementarian Positions," *The Center for Biblical Manhood and Womanhood*, accessed November 17, 2017, https://cbmw .org/uncategorized/summaries-of-the-egalitarian-and-complementarian-positions/.

16. John Piper, "Should Women Be Police Officers?," *Desiring God*, accessed November 17, 2017, https://www.desiringgod.org/interviews/should-women-be-police-officers.

17. John Piper, "Do You Use Bible Commentaries Written by Women?," *Desiring God*, accessed November 17, 2017, https://www.desiringgod.org/interviews/do-you -use-bible-commentaries-written-by-women.

18. Ibid.

19. Rachel Pietka, "Hey John Piper, Is My Femininity Showing?," *Christianity Today* (April 2017), accessed November 27, 2017, https://www.christianitytoday.com/women /2013/april/hey-john-piper-is-my-femininity-showing.htmlc.

20. Rachel Held Evans, "The Absurd Legalism of Gender Roles: Exhibit C—'As long as I can't see her . . . ,'" *Rachel Held Evans* (April 5, 2013), accessed November 27, 2017, https://rachelheldevans.com/blog/legalism-gender-roles-exhibit-c-piper-commentary.

Chapter 17

1. Nancy Carol James, "Madame Jeanne Guyon: The Accused Witch Who Defied King Louis XIV," *Culture & Stuff* (April 11, 2012), accessed October 1, 2017, http:// cultureandstuff.com/2012/04/11/madame-jeanne-guyon-the-accused-witch-who -defied-king-louis-xiv/.

2. Ibid.

3. Jeanne Guyon, *Experiencing the Depths of Jesus Christ*, ed. Gene Edwards (Sargent, GA: SeedSowers, 1975), 15.

4. Jeanne Guyon, *Union with God* (Sargent, GA: SeedSowers, 1981), 48.

5. Guyon, *Experiencing the Depths of Jesus Christ*, 97.

6. Ibid., 24.

7. Ibid., 107.

8. Ibid.

9. Ibid.

10. Ibid.

11. Jeanne Guyon, *Autobiography of Jeanne Guyon,* etext in public domain, scanned from Moody Press by Harry Plantinga (1995), accessed October 22, 2017, http://www .ntslibrary.com/PDF%20Books/Madame%20Guyon%20Autobiography.pdf.

12. Ronney Mourad and Dianne Guenin-Lelle, *The Prison Narratives of Jeanne Guyon* (Oxford: Oxford University Press, 2011), 110.

13. Ibid., 114.

14. Aaron Smith, "Record Shares of Americans Now Own SmartPhones, Now Have Broadband," *Pew Research Center* (January 12, 2017), accessed May 27, 2017, http://www.pewresearch.org/fact-tank/2017/01/12/evolution-of-technology/.

15. Aaron Smith, "Americans and Their Cell Phones," *Pew Research Center* (August 15, 2017), accessed October 1, 2017, http://www.pewinternet.org/2011/08/15/americans-and-their-cell-phones/.

16. Jack Cafferty, "Technology Replaces Social Interaction at What Cost?" (January 4, 2011), *Cable Network News*, accessed September 4, 2017, http://caffertyfile.blogs.cnn.com/2011/01/03/technology-replacing-personal-interactions-at-what-cost/.

17. Lisa Eadicicco, "Americans Check Their Phones 8 Billion Times a Day," *Time Magazine* (December 15, 2015), accessed September 4, 2017, http://time.com/4147614/smartphone-usage-us-2015/.

18. Chuck Hadad, "Why Some 13-Year-Olds Check Social Media 100 Times a Day," *CNN* (October 13, 2015), accessed May 30, 2017, http://www.cnn.com/2015/10/05/health/being-13-teens-social-media-study/.

19. Hilarie Casha, Cosette D. Raea, Ann H. Steela, and Alexander Winkler, "Internet Addiction: A Brief Summary of Research and Practice," *Current Psychiatry Reviews* 8, no. 4 (2012): 296, accessed August 30, 2017, https://www.ncbi.nlm.nih.gov/pmc/articles/PMC3480687/.

20. Ibid., 293.

21. Michelle Drouin, Daren H. Kaiser, and Daniel A. Miller, "Phantom Vibrations among Undergraduates: Prevalence and Associated Psychological Characteristics," *Computers in Human Behavior* 28, no. 4 (2012): 1490.

22. Eric Barker, "This Is the Best Way to Overcome Fear of Missing Out," *Time* (June 07, 2016), accessed October 1, 2017, http://time.com/4358140/overcome-fomo/.

23. John Wesley, qtd. in Bo Karen Lee, "Madame Jeanne Guyon (1648–1717): *A Short and Very Easy Method of Prayer*," in *Christian Spirituality: The Classics,* ed. Arthur Holder (New York: Routledge, 2009), 263.

24. Guyon, *Union*, 37.

Chapter 18

1. John Wesley, "Dramatic Scenes at Falmouth, Entry March 4, 1745," *Journal of John Wesley*, Christian Classics Ethereal Library (Chicago: Moody Press, 1951), 83.

2. Ibid.

3. Ibid.

4. Ibid.

5. Ibid.

6. Ibid.

7. Charles Taylor, "The Great Awakening of the Eighteenth Century," Charles Taylor Ministries, accessed August 21, 2016, www.charlestaylorministries.com.

8. Ibid.

9. John Wesley, "Dispute with Whitefield, Entry March 28, 1741," *Journal of John Wesley*, Christian Classics Ethereal Library (Chicago: Moody Press, 1951), 52, http://www.ccel.org/ccel/wesley/journal.html.

10. "*The Arminian Magazine*" (2013), *18th Century Religion, Literature, and Culture: Explorations of Cultural Intersections*, https://18thcenturyculture.wordpress.com/primary-sources/the-armenian-magazine/.

11. John Wesley, "On Working Out Our Own Salvation," Sermon 85," in *John Wesley's Sermons: An Anthology*, ed. Albert C. Outler and Richard P. Heitzenrater (Nashville, TN: Abingdon Press, 1991), 486–92.

12. Ibid., 487.

13. Ibid., 488.

14. Ibid.

15. Ibid.

16. Ibid., 489.

17. Ibid., 489–90.

18. Ibid., 490.

19. Ibid., 491.

20. David Kinnaman and Gabe Lyons, *unChristian: What a New Generation Really Thinks About Christianity . . . And Why It Matters* (Grand Rapids, MI: Baker Books, 2007), 26.

21. Munk Debates, *Religion* (November 26, 2010), http://www.munkdebates.com /debates/religion.

22. Ibid.

23. "Choosing a New Church or House of Worship," *Pew Research Center Religion and Public Life* (August 23, 2016), http://www.pewforum.org/2016/08/23/2-religious -attendance-fluid-for-many-americans/#religious-nones-give-variety-of-reasons-for -disaffiliation-from-religion.

24. Charles W. Colson, *Born Again* (Lincoln, VA: Chosen Books, 1976), 93.

25. Ibid., 112.

26. Ibid., 114.

27. Ibid., 130.

28. Ibid., 284 (italics original).

29. Charles W. Colson, *Life Sentence* (Lincoln, VA: Chosen Books, 1979), 150–52.

30. Ibid., 150.

31. "Who We Are," https://pfi.org/who-we-are/Prison Fellowship Ministries.org.

32. J. D. Walsh, "Wesley vs. Whitefield," *Christian History Institute*, http://www .christianitytoday.com/history/issues/issue-38/wesley-vs-whitefield.html, para. 30.

33. Ibid.

Chapter 19

1. Wilhelm Pettersen, *The Light in the Prison Window* (Minneapolis, MN: K. C. Holter, 1921), 98–99.

2. Ibid.

3. Eric Hobsbawm, *The Age of Revolution 1789–1848* (1962; repr., New York: Random House, 1996).

4. Jacob Bull, *Hans Nielsen Hauge: The Thrilling Story of a Great Christian Hero*," trans. N. N. Rönning (Minneapolis, MN: The Friend Publishing, 1950), 10–11.

5. Anton Christian Bang, *Hans Nielsen Hauge og hans samtid: Et tidsbillede fraomkringaar 1800* [*Hans Nielsen Hauge and His Contemporary: A Time Image from around the Year 1800*], 3rd ed. (Christiania [Oslo]: Gyldendal, 1910), 110.

6. Hans Nielsen Hauge, *Om religiøse følelser og deres værd* [*On Religious Feelings and Their Worth*] (Norway: S. A. Stein, 1840).

7. Alison Heather Stibbe, *Hans Nielsen Hauge and the Prophetic Imagination* (PhD diss., University of London, London, 2007), 45–46.

8. Trygve Riiser Gundersen, *Om å ta Ordet: Retorikk og utsigelse i den unge Hans Nielsen Hauges forfatterskap* [*To Take the Word: Rhetoric and Expression in the Young Hans Nielsen Hauge's Authorship*], Sakprosa, 3 (Oslo: Norsk Sakprosa, 2001), 38.

9. Hans Nielsen Hauge, *Betragtning over Verdens Daarlighed* [*Consideration of the World's Folly*] (Christiania [Oslo]: Jens Ørbeck Berg, 1796), 9.

10. Bull, *Hans Nielsen Hauge*, 9.

11. Knut Tveit, "The Development of Popular Literacy in the Nordic Countries: A Comparative Historical Study," *Scandinavian Journal of Educational Research* 35, no. 4 (1991): 241–52; Ragnar Anker Nilsen, "Hva fikk nordmennene å lese in 1814?" [*"What Did the Norwegians Have to Read in 1814?"*] (Oslo: Oslo University Library, 1997).

12. Stibbe, *Hans Nielsen Hauge*, 18.

13. See Arne Bugge Amundsen, "Books, Letters and Communication: Hans Nielsen Hauge and the Haugean Movement in Norway, 1796–1840," in *Revival and Communication. Studies in the History of Scandinavian Revivals 1700–2000*, ed. Arne Bugge Amundsen (Lund: Lund University, 2007), 45–64.

14. Hans Nielsen Hauge, *Infogalactic*, accessed July 5, 2017, https://infogalactic.com /info/ Hans_Nielsen_Hauge.

15. Ann Garborg, qtd. in Vegard Tafjord Rødel and Andreas Kiplesund, *Hans Nielsen Hauge: Entrepreneur, Banker, and Industrialist* (MA thesis, Norwegian School of Economics, Bergen, 2009), 8, accessed July 26, 2017, https://brage.bibsys.no/xmlui /bitstream/handle/11250/168811/Rodal%202009.pdf?sequence=1.

16. Ibid., 8.

17. Linda Haukland, "Hans Nielsen Hauge: A Catalyst of Literacy in Norway," *Scandanavian Journal of History* 39, no. 5 (2014): 539–59.

18. Finn Wiig Sjursen, "Fra Hans Nielsen Hauge til Norsk Lærerakademi," speech given at the Norsk Lærerakademi 25th jubilee in Bergen, September 4, 1993.

19. Haukland, "Hans Nielsen Hauge," 542.

20. Ibid., 542. See also Elisabeth S. Eide, "Reading Societies and Lending Libraries in Nineteenth-Century Norway," *Library & Information History* 26, no. 2 (2010): 121–38.

21. Haukland, "Hans Nielsen Hauge," 543.

22. Evenlien A. Schilder, Barbara B. Lockee, and D. Patrick Saxon, "The Issues and Challenges of Assessing Media Literacy Education," *Journal of Media Literacy Education* 8, no. 1 (2016): 32–48.

23. Dan Stout, "Religious Media Literacy: Toward a Research Agenda," *Journal of Media and Religion* 1, no. 1 (2002): 49–60.

24. Stephanie Iaquinto and John Keeler, "Faith-based Media Literacy Education: A Look at the Past with an Eye toward the Future," *Journal of Media Literacy Education* 4, no. 1 (2012): 31.

25. Sjursen, *Den haugianske Periode (III).*

Chapter 20

1. William Carey, qtd. in John Clark Marshman, *The Life and Labours of Carey Marshman & Ward: The Serampore Missionaries* (New York: U. D. Ward, 1867), 8.

2. John Ryland Sr., qtd. in ibid.

3. William Carey, *An Enquiry into the Obligations of Christians, to Use Means for the Conversion of the Heathens. In Which the Religious State of the Different Nations of the*

World, the Success of Former Undertakings, and the Practicability of Further Undertakings, Are Considered (Leicester: Printed and Sold by Ann Ireland, 1792).

4. Ibid., 28.

5. Ibid., 67.

6. Ibid., 78–79.

7. Ernest A. Payne, introduction to William Carey and Ernest A. Payne, *An Enquiry into the Obligations of Christians to Use Means for the Conversion of the Heathens* (London: Carey Kingsgate Press, 1961), ii.

8. James Ainsworth, *Sociology of Education: An A-to-Z Guide*, vol. 1 (Los Angeles: Sage, 2013), 324.

9. Eli Daniel Potts, *British Baptist Missionaries in India; 1793–1837* (Cambridge: Cambridge University Press, 1967), 119.

10. Sisir Kumar Das, *A History of Indian Literature: 1800–1910: Western Impact, Indian Response* (New Dehli: Sahitya Akademi, 1991), 419.

11. B. S. Kesavan, *History of Printing and Publishing in India: A Story of Cultural Reawakening*, vol. 1 (New Delhi: National Book Trust, 1985), 254.

12. Sunil Kumar Chatterjee, *William Carey and Serampore* (Calcutta: Ghosh Pub. Concern, 1984), vi.

13. Ibid., vii.

14. Ibid., viii.

15. Kesavan, *History of Printing and Publishing in India*, 298.

16. See Potts, *British Baptist Missionaries in India*, 92, 96. See also Sushil Kumar De, *History of Bengali Literature in the Nineteenth Century, 1800–1825* (Calcutta: University of Calcutta, 1919), 250.

17. Marshman, *The Life and Labours of Carey Marshman & Ward*, 466.

18. "On the Progress and Present State of the Native Press in India," *The Friend of India* (Serampore: The Mission Press, May 1825), 143.

19. Marshman, *The Life and Labours of Carey Marshman & Ward*, 187.

20. Michael F. Suarez and H. R. Woudhuysen, *The Book: A Global History* (Oxford: Oxford University Press, 2013), 109.

21. Jim A. Kuypers, *Rhetorical Criticism: Perspectives in Action* (Lanham, MD: Lexington Books, 2009), 4.

Chapter 21

1. Søren Kierkegaard, *Concluding Unscientific Postscript to Philosophical Fragments, Vol. I,* trans. and ed. Howard V. Hong and Edna H. Hong (Princeton, NJ: Princeton University Press, 1846/1992), 186.

2. Ibid.

3. Ibid.

4. Stephen Backhouse, *Kierkegaard: A Single Life* (Grand Rapids, MI: Zondervan, 2016), 23.

5. Robert Inchausti, *Subversive Orthodoxy: Outlaws, Revolutionaries, and Other Christians* (Grand Rapids, MI: Brazos Press, 2005), 34.

6. Kyle Roberts, *Emerging Prophet: Kierkegaard and the Postmodern People of God* (Eugene, OR: Cascade Books, 2013).

7. Ibid., 15.

8. Ibid., 14.

9. Ibid., 15.

10. Bruce Kirmmse, "'Out with It!': The Modern Breakthrough, Kierkegaard and Denmark," in *The Cambridge Companion to Kierkegaard*, ed. Alastair Hannay and Gordon D. Marino (Cambridge: Cambridge University Press, 1998), 17.

11. Ibid.

12. Ibid.

13. Roberts, *Emerging Prophet*, 13 (italics original).

14. Mark A. Tietjen, *Kierkegaard: A Christian Missionary to Christians* (Downers Grove, IL: IVP Academic, 2016).

15. Ibid.

16. Søren Kierkegaard, *The Point of View for My Work as an Author: A Report to History*, ed. Benjamin Nelson (1848-9; repr., New York: Harper & Row, 1962), 40 (italics original).

17. Kierkegaard, *Concluding Unscientific Postscript*, 236-39.

18. Alison Milbank, "Apologetics and the Imagination: Making Strange," in *Imaginative Apologetics: Theology, Philosophy and the Catholic Tradition*, ed. Andrew Davison (Grand Rapids, MI: Baker Academic, 2011), 31-45.

19. Paul Muench, "The Socratic Method of Kierkegaard's Pseudonym Johannes Climacus: Indirect Communication and the Art of 'Taking Away,'" in *Søren Kierkegaard and the Word(s): Essays on Hermeneutics and Communication*, ed. Poul Houe and Gordon D. Marino (Copenhagen: C. A. Reitzel), 139.

20. Kierkegaard, *Concluding Unscientific Postscript*, 236-39.

21. Roberts, *Emerging Prophet*, 2.

22. Timothy Keller, *Making Sense of God: An Invitation to the Skeptical* (New York: Viking, 2016), 11-12.

23. Ibid., 14.

24. Ibid., 52. See also John Hughes, "Proofs and Arguments," in *Imaginative Apologetics: Theology, Philosophy and the Catholic Tradition*, ed. Andrew Davison (Grand Rapids, MI: Baker Academic, 2011), 7.

25. Andrew Davison, "Christian Reason and Christian Community," in *Imaginative Apologetics: Theology, Philosophy and the Catholic Tradition*, ed. Andrew Davison (Grand Rapids, MI: Baker Academic, 2011), 16.

26. C. S. Lewis, *The Collected Letters of C. S. Lewis, Volume 3: Narnia, Cambridge, and Joy, 1950-1963*, ed. Walter Hooper (San Francisco: HarperSanFrancisco, 2009), 651.

27. Quoted in James Como, *Branches to Heaven: The Geniuses of C. S. Lewis* (Dallas: Spence Publishing, 1994), 114.

28. Austin Farrer, qtd. in Alan Jacobs, *The Narnian: The Life and Imagination of C. S. Lewis* (New York: HarperCollins 2006), 312.

29. Milbank, "Apologetics and the Imagination: Making Strange," 35.

30. Paul E. Little, *Know Why You Believe* (Wheaton, IL: Victor Books 1975), 16.

31. Ibid.

32. Ibid.

33. Ibid.

34. Ibid.

Chapter 22

1. James Madison, qtd. in Robert Richardson, *Memoirs of Alexander Campbell: Embracing A View of the Origin, Progress and Principles of the Religious Reformation Which He Advocated, Vol. 2* (Nashville, TN: Gospel Advocate, 1956), 313.

2. Alexander Campbell, "The Christian Religion," *Christian Baptist* (August 3, 1823), 7.

3. Ibid.

4. Ibid.

5. Ibid.

6. Ibid.

7. Alexander Campbell, "The Third Epistle of Peter, to the Preachers and the Rulers of Congregations," *Christian Baptist* (July 4, 1825), 167.

8. Ibid.

9. Ibid., 167–68.

10. Ibid., 168.

11. Alexander Campbell, "The Crisis," *Millennial Harbinger* (February 6, 1832), 86.

12. Alexander Campbell, "Address on War," *Popular Lectures and Addresses* (Philadelphia: James Challen & Son, 1863), 358.

13. Gary Holloway, "Alexander Campbell as a Publisher," *Restoration Quarterly* 37 (1995): 29.

14. James De Forest Murch, *Christians Only: A History of the Restoration Movement* (Cincinnati, OH: Standard Publishing, 1962), 70.

15. Campbell, qtd. in Richardson, *Memoirs of Alexander Campbell*, 50.

16. Ibid.

17. Ibid., 53.

18. Thomas Chalmers, *Alexander Campbell's Tour in Scotland: How He Is Remembered by Those Who Saw Him Then* (Louisville, KY: Guide Printing & Publishing, 1892), 21.

19. See David Paul Nord, *The Evangelical Origins of Mass Media in America, 1815–1835*, Journalism Monographs 88 (N.p.: Association for Education in Journalism and Mass Communication, 1984).

20. See Nathan O. Hatch, *The Democratization of American Christianity* (New Haven, CT: Yale University Press, 1991), 4.

21. Ibid.

22. See Craig M. Watts, *Disciple of Peace: Alexander Campbell on Pacifism, Violence and the State* (Indianapolis, IN: Doulos Christou Press, 2005), 48–52.

23. Alexander Campbell, "Tracts for the People: An Address on War," *Millennial Harbinger* (July 1848), 363–65; 377.

24. Michael Casey, "The Ethics of War: Pacifism and Militarism in the American Restoration Movement," *Leaven* 7, no. 4 (1999): 6.

25. See John Rawls, *A Theory of Justice*, 2nd ed. (Cambridge, MA: Belknap Press, 1999).

26. See Clifford G. Christians, et al., *Media Ethics: Cases and Moral Reasoning*, 10th ed. (New York: Routledge, 2017), 21–23.

27. See Ruth Graham, "How Sex Trafficking Became a Christian Cause Célèbre," *Slate* (March 2015), http://www.slate.com/articles/double_x/faithbased/2015/03/christians_and_sex_trafficking_how_evangelicals_made_it_a_cause_celebre.html.

28. Clifford G. Christians, "Universalism versus Communitarianism in Media Ethics," in *The Handbook of Global Communication and Media Ethics*, vol. 1, ed. Robert S. Fortner and P. Mark Fackler (Malden, MA: Wiley-Blackwell, 2007), 393–414.

Chapter 23

1. C. Stephen Dessain, "Cardinal Newman on the Theory and Practice of Knowledge," *Downside Review* 75 (January 1957): 5.

2. Richard Cimino and Christopher Smith, "The New Atheism and the Formation of the Imagined Secularist Community," *Journal of Media and Religion* 10, no. 1 (2011): 24–38.

3. Edward P. J. Corbett, "Some Rhetorical Lessons from John Henry Newman," *College Composition and Communication* 31, no. 4 (December 1980): 403, http://www.jstor.org/stable/356590.

4. Walter Jost, "What Newman Knew," *Renascence* 49, no. 4 (1997): 251.

5. Dessain, "Cardinal Newman," 3.

6. John Henry Cardinal Newman, *An Essay in Aid of a Grammar of Assent* (New York: Longmans, Green, 1939), 94.

7. Ibid., 92–93.

8. Dessain, "Cardinal Newman," 3.

9. Corbett, "Some Rhetorical Lessons," 405–6.

10. Newman, *Grammar*, e.g., 167, 189–90.

11. Ibid., 294–95.

12. Ibid., 323.

13. Ibid., 195.

14. Ibid., 190.

15. Ibid., 192.

16. Dessain, "Cardinal Newman," 3.

17. Jost, "What Newman Knew," 241.

18. James M. Tallmon, "Newman's Contribution to Conceptualizing Rhetorical Reason," *Rhetoric Society Quarterly* 25 (1995): 199, http://www.jstor.org/stable/3886284.

19. Walter Jost, *Rhetorical Thought in John Henry Newman* (Columbia: University of South Carolina Press, 1989), 76.

20. Ibid., 72–73.

21. Ibid., 76.

22. Newman, *Grammar*, 410, 413, 418.

23. David Berlinski, *The Devil's Delusion*, 2nd ed. (New York: Basic Books, 2009).

24. Cimino and Smith, "The New Atheism," 26.

25. Newman, *Grammar*, 179, 269–70.

26. Corbett, "Some Rhetorical Lessons," 405.

27. Newman, *Grammar*, 323.

28. Ibid., 179, 269–70.

29. Charles Taylor, *A Secular Age* (Cambridge, MA: Belknap Press, 2007).

Chapter 24

1. Frederick St. George De Latour Booth-Tucker, *The Life of Catherine Booth: The Mother of the Salvation Army, Vol. 1* (London: Salvation Army International Headquarters, 1892), 417.

2. Catherine Mumford Booth, "Adaptation of Measures," in *Papers on Aggressive Christianity* (London: Salvation Army, 1888), 8.

3. Roger J. Green, *Catherine Booth: A Biography of the Cofounder of the Salvation Army* (Grand Rapids, MI: Baker Books, 1996), 159.

4. Catherine Mumford Booth, *Female Ministry; Or, Woman's Right to Preach the Gospel* (London: Morgan & Chase, 1870).

5. Ibid., 3.

6. Catherine Booth, *Female Teaching: Or, the Rev. A.A. Rees versus Mrs. Palmer, Being a Reply to a Pamphlet by the Above Gentleman on the Sunderland Revival* (London: G. J. Stevenson, 1861), 4.

7. Booth, *Female Ministry*, 3.

8. Ibid. (italics original).

9. Ibid.

10. Booth, *Female Ministry*, 3.

11. Judith Newton, "Engendering History for the Middle Class: Sex and Political Economy in the *Edinburgh Review*," in *Rewriting the Victorians: Theory, History, and the Politics of Gender*, ed. Linda M. Shires (New York: Routledge, 1992), 7.

12. Booth, *Female Ministry*, 4–5.

13. Ibid., 5.

14. Ibid., 7.

15. Ibid., 9.

16. Ibid., 16.

17. Ibid., 10 (italics original).

18. Ibid. (italics original).

19. Ibid., 22.

20. Barbara Welter, "The Cult of True Womanhood 1820–1860," *American Quarterly* 18, no. 2, part 1 (Summer 1966): 1.

21. Booth, *Female Ministry*, 4.

22. Alexander Welsh, *Strong Representations: Narrative and Circumstantial Evidence in England* (Baltimore: Johns Hopkins University Press, 1992), ix.

23. Harold Begbie, *Life of William Booth: The Founder of the Salvation Army, Vol. 2* (London: Macmillan, 1920), 28–29.

24. Joad Raymond, *Pamphlets and Pamphleteering in Early Modern Britain* (Cambridge: Cambridge University Press, 2003), 6–7.

25. Ibid., 10, 26.

26. Ibid., 297.

27. Catherine Bramwell-Booth, *Catherine Booth: The Story of Her Loves* (London: Hodder and Stoughton, 1970), 186.

28. Booth-Tucker, *The Life of Catherine Booth*, 417.

29. Ibid., 259.

30. Ibid., 251.

31. Norman H. Murdoch, *Origins of the Salvation Army* (Knoxville: University of Tennessee Press, 1994), 136.

32. John Read, *Catherine Booth: Laying the Theological Foundations of a Radical Movement* (Eugene, OR: Pickwick Publications, 2013), 24.

33. Sandall, *The History of the Salvation Army, Vol. 1*, 184.

34. Norman H. Murdoch, "Female Ministry in the Thought and Work of Catherine Booth," *Church History* 53, no. 3 (1984): 348–62.

35. Pamela Jane Walker, "Pulling the Devil's Kingdom Down: Gender and Popular Culture in the Salvation Army, 1865–1895" (PhD diss., Rutgers, the State University of New Jersey, 1992), 19.

36. Arch Wiggins, *The History of The Salvation Army, Vol. 4* (London: Thomas Nelson & Sons, 1964), 256.

37. Roy Hattersley, *Blood & Fire: William and Catherine Booth and Their Salvation Army* (London: Little Brown, 1999), 228.

38. Nicholas Carr, *The Shallows: What the Internet Is Doing to Our Brains* (New York: W. W. Norton, 2010), 115–16.

39. John M. Culkin, "A Schoolman's Guide to Marshall McLuhan," *Saturday Review* (March 18, 1967), 70.

40. Rachel Held Evans, *A Year of Biblical Womanhood* (Nashville, TN: Thomas Nelson, 2012).

41. See Andrew Mark Eason, *Women in God's Army: Gender and Equality in the Early Salvation Army* (Waterloo, ON: Wilfred Laurier University Press, 2003), especially chs. 4 and 6.

42. Donald W. Dayton, *Discovering an Evangelical Heritage* (Peabody, MA: Hendrickson, 1976), 94.

43. Col. Chris Webb (Secretary for Spiritual Life Development), e-mail message to author Kenneth Baillie, September 21, 2015. Percentage is as of 2012.

44. Munn, *Theory and Practice of Gender Equality in The Salvation Army*, 61.

45. Janette Hassey, *No Time for Silence* (Grand Rapids, MI: Zondervan, 1986).

46. Ibid., 31–45.

47. Gilbert Bilezikian, *Beyond Sex Roles* (Grand Rapids, MI: Baker Book House, 1985), 11.

48. Nancy Beach, *Gifted to Lead: The Art of Leading as a Woman in the Church* (Grand Rapids, MI: Zondervan, 2008), 201–4. The "Willow Creek Community Church Elders' Statement on Women and Men in Ministry" is found in Appendix 3.

49. Booth, *Female Ministry*, 23.

50. Booth, "Adaptation of Measures," 8.

Chapter 25

1. Thérèse of Lisieux, *Story of a Soul: The Autobiography of St. Thérèse of Lisieux*, trans. John Clarke, 3rd ed. (Washington, DC: ICS Publications, 1996), 222 (italics original).

2. Ibid., 223.

3. Ibid.

4. Ibid.

5. Ibid., ch. X, 203ff.

6. Ibid., 192–93.

7. Ibid., 194 (capitalization original).

8. Ibid., 220.

9. Ibid., 249.

10. Ibid.

11. Ibid., 247.

12. Ibid., 248.

13. "Our Charism," *Order of Carmelites*, accessed July 6, 2017, http://ocarm.org/en/content/ocarm/charism.

14. "The Charism of the Order," *Order of Carmelites*, accessed July 6, 2017, http://ocarm.org/en/content/ocarm/charism-order.

15. John Clarke, introduction to *Story*, xix.

16. Thérèse of Lisieux, *Story*, 263.

17. Ibid.

18. Michael Welch, "Anti-Immigrant Policies," in *Encyclopedia of Activism and Social Justice*, ed. Gary L. Anderson and Kathryn G. Herr (London: Sage, 2007), 159.

19. "Here's Donald Trump's Presidential Announcement Speech," *Time* (June 16, 2015), accessed July 7, 2017, http://time.com/3923128/donald-trump-announcement-speech/.

20. Simone de Beauvoir, *The Second Sex*, trans. Constance Borde and Sheila Malovany-Chevallier (1949; repr., New York: Vintage, 2009), 6.

21. Sarah Pulliam Bailey, "'God Is Not Against Building Walls!' The Sermon Trump Heard from Robert Jeffress before His Inauguration," *The Washington Post* (January 20, 2017), accessed July 7, 2017, https://www.washingtonpost.com/news/acts-of-faith/wp/2017/01/20/god-is-not-against-building-walls-the-sermon-donald-trump-heard-before-his-inauguration/?utm_term=.c2a1aa6cba6f.

22. Gregory A. Smith, "Most White Evangelicals Approve of Trump Travel Prohibition and Express Concerns about Extremism," *Pew Center Research* (February 27, 2017), accessed July 7, 2017, http://www.pewresearch.org/fact-tank/2017/02/27/most-white-evangelicals-approve-of-trump-travel-prohibition-and-express-concerns-about-extremism/.

23. Bailey, "'God Is Not Against,'" *The Washington Post*.

24. Thérèse of Lisieux, *Story*, 220–21.

25. Dustin Weber (lead pastor, Dearborn Free Methodist Church), phone conversation with author, June 15, 2017.

26. "ESL English Day Camp for Refugee Children," NEWSFeed Dearborn Free Methodist Church, posted May 18, 2017, accessed July 7, 2017, http://www.dearbornfmchurch.org/category/announcement/.

27. Ibid.

28. Weber, phone conversation with author, June 15, 2017.

29. Megan Weber, "Partnering with Muslims," *Spring Arbor Free Methodist Church Blog*, posted November 7, 2016, accessed July 7, 2017, http://springarborfm.org/blog/view/partnering_with_muslims.

30. "Dinners with Refugees," *Free Methodist Church USA Blog*, accessed July 7, 2017, http://fmcusa.org/blog/2017/02/22/dinners-with-refugees/.

Chapter 26

1. See Judith Serrin and William Serrin, *Muckraking! The Journalism That Changed America* (New York: New Press, 2002).

2. Josiah Strong, "The Problem of 'Tainted' Money," *The Homiletic Review* 49 (January–June 1905): 422–25.

3. See, for example, Walter Rauschenbusch, *Christianizing the Social Order* (New York: Macmillan, 1919), 337–50.

4. For instance, see Walter Rauschenbusch, *Christianity and the Social Crisis: The Classic That Woke Up the Church* (New York: HarperOne, 2007), 190.

5. See, for example, Paul M. Minus, *Walter Rauschenbusch* (New York: Macmillan, 1988), 60.

6. Walter Rauschenbusch, *A Theology for the Social Gospel* (New York: Macmillan, 1917).

7. Walter Brueggemann, *The Prophetic Imagination*, 2nd ed. (Minneapolis, MN: Fortress, 2001).

8. Rauschenbusch, *A Theology for a Social Gospel*, 47.

9. Ibid., 48.

10. Ibid., 60.

11. Ibid., 80–81.

12. Ibid., 182.

13. Ibid., 248–59.

14. Ibid., 142.

15. Ibid., 265.

16. Ibid., 196.

17. Ibid., 137.

18. Ibid., 139.

19. Janette Thomas Greenwood, *The Gilded Age: A History in Documents* (New York: Oxford University Press, 2003), 21.

20. Charles Howard Hopkins, *The Rise of the Social Gospel in American Protestantism* (New Haven, CT: Yale University Press, 1940), 67–69.

21. Rauschenbusch marriage rosters (American Baptist Historical Archive, Rauschenbusch Family Archives, box 97).

22. Cleveland Kingdom of God Reminiscence, January 2, 1913 (American Baptist Historical Archive, Rauschenbusch Family Archives, box 39).

23. Minus, *Walter Rauschenbusch*, 51.

24. Rauschenbusch, *Christianizing the Social Order*, 27.

25. George Marsden, *Fundamentalism and American Culture* (Oxford: Oxford University Press, 2006).

26. Rauschenbusch, *Christianity and the Social Crisis*, xxi; and *Christianizing the Social Order*, 14–15.

27. Rauschenbusch, *A Theology for the Social Gospel*, 33.

28. Ibid., 36.

29. Ibid., 92.

30. Ibid., 37.

31. Rauschenbusch, YMCA investigation (American Baptist Historical Society, Rauschenbusch Family Archives, box 49); and School Board (American Baptist Historical Society, Rauschenbusch Family Archives, box 49).

32. Rauschenbusch, *A Theology for the Social Gospel*, 54.

33. See Supreme Court of the United States blog for specifics: http://www.scotusblog.com/case-files/cases/citizens-united-v-federal-election-commission/.

34. Paul Rauschenbush, introduction to Rauschenbusch, *Christianity and the Social Crisis*.

35. Rauschenbusch, *A Theology for the Social Gospel*, 227.

Chapter 27

1. James D. Bratt, introduction to Abraham Kuyper, *Abraham Kuyper: A Centennial Reader*, ed. James D. Bratt (Grand Rapids, MI: Eerdmans, 1998), 9.

2. George Harinck, "A Historian's Comment on the Use of Abraham Kuyper's Idea of Sphere Sovereignty," *Journal of Markets & Morality* 5, no. 1 (Spring, 2002): 277–84.

3. Abraham Kuyper, "Sphere Sovereignty," in *Abraham Kuyper: A Centennial Reader*, 488 (italics original). I will cite Kuyper as the author when I reference his two speeches ("Sphere Sovereignty" and "The Blurring of the Boundaries") found in Bratt's 1998 text, but I will cite Bratt to reference his comments about Kuyper's speeches.

4. Bratt, *Centennial Reader*, 363.

5. Kuyper, "Blurring the Boundaries," 368 (italics original).

6. Bratt, *Centennial Reader*, 363.

7. Kuyper, "Blurring the Boundaries," 373.

8. Ibid. (italics original).

9. Cornelius P. Venema, "The Worldview of Abraham Kuyper," *Christian Library* (2013), 1–10, www.ChristianStudyLibrary.org, 3 (italics original).

10. Kuyper, "Blurring the Boundaries," 368.

11. Guillaume Groen van Prinsterer, *Christian Political Action in an Age of Revolution*, trans. Colin Wright (1860; repr., Aalten, Netherlands: Wordbridge, 2015).

12. Guillaume Groen van Prinsterer, *Unbelief and Revolution Lectures VIII and IX: A Series of Lectures in History*, ed. and trans. Harry Van Dyke (Amsterdam: Groen Van Prinsterer Fund, 1975).

13. Abraham Kuyper, *Lectures on Calvinism* (1898; repr., Grand Rapids, MI: Eerdmans, 1999).

14. See for example the issue of *Argumentation and Advocacy* 35, no. 1 (Summer 1998).

15. Richard A. Cherwitz and James W. Hikins, "Communication and Knowledge: An Investigation in Rhetorical Epistemology," in *Studies in Rhetoric/Communication*, ed. Carroll C. Arnold (Columbia: University of South Carolina Press, 1986).

16. Jan L. Souman, Ilja Frissen, Manish N. Sreenivasa, and Marc O. Ernst, "Walking Straight into Circles," *Current Biology* 19, no. 18 (September 29, 2009): 1538–42.

17. Kuyper, "Sphere Sovereignty," 488.

Chapter 28

1. Charles M. Sheldon, "*The Topeka Capital* This Week," *The Topeka Daily Capital* (March 13, 1900), 2.

2. Ibid.

3. Michael Ray Smith, *The Jesus Newspaper* (Lanham, MD: University Press of America, 2002), 96.

4. Charles M. Sheldon, "Starving India," *The Topeka Daily Capital* (March 13, 1900), 1.

5. Smith, *The Jesus Newspaper*, 97.

6. Ibid., 143–48.

7. Hector Leroy Cordova, "Charles M. Sheldon" (MA thesis, San Jose State College, 1967), 8.

8. Billie Barnes Jensen, "A Social Gospel Experiment in Newspaper Reform," *Church History* 23, no. 1 (1964): 74–83.

9. Ibid.

10. Ibid., 79.

11. Ibid.

12. Smith, *The Jesus Newspaper*, 123.

13. Ralph Woodworth, "The Life and Writings of Charles M. Sheldon (1857–1946), with Special Reference to His Relations with the Press" (MA thesis, Southern Illinois University at Carbondale, 1983), 8–9.

14. Smith, *The Jesus Newspaper*, 136.

15. Charles M. Sheldon, "Speech," *The Topeka Daily Capital* (May 17, 1941), 1.

16. Charles M. Sheldon, *The Topeka Daily Capital* (March 13, 1900), 2.

17. Lynn Vavreck, "A Superhero Power for Our Time: How to Handle the Truth," *New York Times* (June 20, 2017), https://www.nytimes.com/2017/06/20/upshot/a-superhero-power-for-our-time-how-to-handle-the-truth.html?em_pos=small&emc=edit_up_20170621&nl=upshot&nl_art=2&nlid=71882947&ref=headline&te=1.

18. Ibid.

19. Council for Christian Colleges & Universities, "Our History" (September 9, 2017), https://www.cccu.org/about/#heading-our-history-3.

20. J. I. Balderas, journalism professor, personal communication with the author, June 17, 2017.

21. J. I. Balderas, personal communication with the author, September 8, 2017.

22. *The Pulse*, Spring Arbor University Journal (Spring Arbor, MI: Spring Arbor University, 2017), 4.

23. Chris Carroll, *The New Advisor Handbook: A Guide to Advising Student Media at the College or University Level*, 2nd ed. (New York: College Media Advisers, 2001).

24. Timothy Miller, *Following in His Steps: A Biography of Charles M. Sheldon* (Knoxville: University of Tennessee Press, 1987), 118.

Chapter 29

1. John Lawlor, *C. S. Lewis: Memories and Reflections* (Dallas: Spence, 1998), 30.

2. Ibid., 119.

3. *Christianity Today*, "Books of the Century" (April 24, 2000), www.christianitytoday .com/ct/2000/april24/5.92html.

4. See *U. S. Public Becoming Less Religious*, Pew Research Center: Religion & Public Life (November 3, 2015), accessed July 11, 2016, http://www.pewforum.org/2015/11/03 /u-s-public-becoming-less-religious/.

5. Richard Baxter, *Church History of the Government of Bishops*, 1680.

6. C. S. Lewis, *Mere Christianity* (London: Geoffrey Bles, 1952), xi.

7. Ibid.

8. Ibid., viii.

9. C. S. Lewis, *Broadcast Talks* (London: Geoffrey Bles, 1942).

10. C. S. Lewis, *Christian Behavior* (London: Geoffrey Bles, 1943).

11. C. S. Lewis, *Beyond Personality* (London: Geoffrey Bles, 1944).

12. Lewis, *Mere Christianity*, 29.

13. Ibid., 69.

14. Ibid., 121.

15. Welch, qtd. in Roger Lancelyn Green and Walter Hooper, *C. S. Lewis: A Biography* (London: HarperCollins, 2002), 202.

16. Lewis, qtd. in ibid.

17. Ibid.

18. Ibid.

19. Bruce R. Johnson, "C. S. Lewis and the BBC's Brains Trust: A Study in Resiliency," *VII: An Anglo-American Literary Review* 30 (2013): 67–92.

20. Justin Phillips, *C. S. Lewis in A Time of War* (New York: HarperCollins, 2002), 275.

21. Ibid.

22. C. S. Lewis, "The Language of Religion," *Christian Reflections*, ed. Walter Hooper (London: Geoffrey Bles), 136.

23. Lewis, *Mere Christianity*, 3–7.

24. Phillips, *C. S. Lewis in a Time of War*, 117–18.

25. Lewis, *Mere Christianity*, 54–55.

26. *Religion and the Unaffiliated*, Pew Research Center: Religion & Public Life (October 9, 2012), accessed July 11, 2016, http://www.perforum.org/2012/10/09/nones-on -the-rise-religion/.

27. See *U. S. Public Becoming Less Religious*, Pew Research Center: Religion & Public Life (November 3, 2015), accessed July 11, 2016, http://www.pewforum.org/2015/11/03 /u-s-public-becoming-less-religious/.

28. C. S. Lewis, "Sometimes Fairy Stories May Say Best What's to Be Said," *Of Other Worlds: Essays and Stories*, ed. Walter Hooper (London: Geoffrey Bles, 1966), 37.

29. Ibid.

30. For an extended discussion about the definition and nature of communication, see F. E. X. Dance and Carl Larson, *Speech Communication: Concepts and Behavior* (New York: Holt, Rinehart and Winston, 1972).

31. C. S. Lewis, "Christian Apologetics," in *God in the Dock: Essays on Theology and Ethics* (Grand Rapids, MI: Eerdmans, 1970), 96.

32. C. S. Lewis, "Letter to Patricia Thomson," December 8, 1941, in *The Collected Letters of C. S. Lewis, Vol. II*, ed. Walter Hooper (New York: HarperCollins, 2004), 499–500.

33. Lewis, *Mere Christianity*, vii.

34. C. S. Lewis, transcript of BBC Broadcasts, BBC Archives, Reading, England, "Materialism or Religion," delivered Wednesday, August, 20, 1941.

35. Ibid.

36. Lewis, *Mere Christianity*, vii.

37. Walter Hooper, ed., *The Collected Letters of C. S. Lewis, Vol. I* (New York: HarperCollins, 2000), x.

38. C. S. Lewis, "Myth Became Fact," in *God in the Dock*, 63.

Chapter 30

1. William H. Shannon, preface in *Thomas Merton: The Hidden Ground of Love: Letters on Religions Experience and Social Concerns*, ed. William H. Shannon (London: Collins, 1985), v.

2. Thomas Merton, *The Seven Storey Mountain: An Autobiography of Faith* (New York: Harcourt, 1948).

3. Aurelius Augustine, *Confessions*, trans. R. F. Pine-Coffin (London: Penguin Classics, 1961).

4. William H. Shannon, "A Note to the Reader," in *The Seven Storey Mountain*, xix.

5. See Ursula King, *Christian Mystics: The Spiritual Heart of the Christian Tradition* (New York: Simon & Schuster, 1998).

6. Thomas Merton, "Symbolism: Communication or Communion," in *Love and Living*, ed. Naomi Burton Stone and Brother Patrick Hart (San Diego: Harcourt, 1979), 54.

7. Yann Martel, *Life of Pi: A Novel* (New York, Mariner, 2003).

8. Augustine, *Confessions*, 315.

9. Thomas Merton, *Love and Living*, ed. Naomi Burton Stone and Brother Patrick Hart (San Diego: Harcourt, 1979), 64 (italics original).

10. Ibid., 56.

11. Gray Matthews, "The Healing Silence: Thomas Merton's Contemplative Approach to Communication," *Merton Annual* 15 (2002): 61.

12. Ibid., 58.

13. Ibid., 60.

14. Ibid.

15. Jen Jones, "Simple Guide to a Complex Design," review of *Simply Merton: Wisdom from His Journals*, ed. Linus Mundy, *The Merton Seasonal* 40, no. 2 (2015): 39.

16. Merton, *Love and Living*, 69.

17. Ibid., 34.

18. Ibid., 35.

19. Ibid., 36.

20. Ibid., 28.

21. Ibid., 34.

22. Ibid., 30–31.

23. Ibid., 32.

24. Ibid., 33.

25. Ibid., 34.

26. Ibid., 27 (italics original).

27. "Who We Are," last modified 2015, http://www.narrative4.com/mission-vision/.

28. Merton, *Love and Living*, 34.

29. Ibid., 35.

30. Ibid., 57.

31. Merton's ideas are at odds with a self-centered approach in the best-selling self-help book by Dale Carnegie, *How to Win Friends and Influence People* (1936; repr., New York: Simon & Schuster, 1981).

32. Linus Mundy, *Simply Merton: Wisdom from His Journals* (Cincinnati: Franciscan Media, 2014), 129.

33. Merton, *Love and Living*, 55 (italics original).

34. Shannon, preface to Thomas Merton, *The Hidden Ground of Love*, vii.

35. Patrick F. O'Connell, "From Communication to Communion: Thomas Merton on the Use and Abuse, the Functions and Possibilities of Language," *Journal of Communication & Religion* 37, no. 4 (2014): 5.

Chapter 31

1. Coretta Scott King, *My Life with Martin Luther King, Jr.* (New York: Holt, Rhinehart, and Winston, 1969), 126–30.

2. Martin Luther King Jr., qtd. in King, *My Life with Martin Luther King, Jr.*, 130.

3. Alan Noble, "Is Evangelical Morality Still Acceptable in America?," *The Atlantic* (July 23, 2014), http://www.theatlantic.com/national/archive/2014/07/is-evangelical-morality-still-acceptable-in-america/374341/.

4. Martin Luther King Jr., "Loving Your Enemies," sermon delivered at Dexter Avenue Baptist Church, November 17, 1957, http://kingencyclopedia.stanford.edu/encyclopedia/ documentsentry/doc_loving_your_enemies/index.html, para. 8.

5. Ibid., para. 10.

6. Ibid.

7. Ibid.

8. Ibid., para. 13.

9. Ibid., para. 14.

10. Ibid., para. 20.

11. Ibid., para. 25.

12. Ibid., para. 37.

13. Sondra Gordy, "Lost Year," http://www.encyclopediaofarkansas.net/encyclopedia/entry-detail.aspx?entryID=737.

14. See http://kingencyclopedia.stanford.edu/encyclopedia/chronologyentry/1955_12_01/ index.html.

15. For an excellent chronology of the events in Martin Luther King's life, see the King Encyclopedia hosted and developed as part of the Resources of the Martin Luther King, Jr., Research and Education Institute at Stanford University, http://kingencyclopedia.stanford.edu/encyclopedia/chronologyentry/1956_12_23/index.html.

16. Ibid.

17. Renee Romano, *Racial Reckoning: Prosecuting America's Civil Rights Murders* (Cambridge, MA: Harvard University Press, 2014), 18–19.

18. Ibid., 19.

19. The Charles Chestnutt Digital Archive, "Lynching Statistics," accessed December 30, 2016, http://bereafaculty.wpengine.com/faculty/browners/chesnutt/classroom /lynchingstat.html.

20. Phillip C. Kolin, "On the Record: The Emmett Till Murder Trial and the Southern Press," *Southern Quarterly* 50, no. 3 (2013): 28–31; Romano, *Racial Reckoning*, 18–19.

21. Martin Shapiro, "Where Is the World Christian Outcry?," *Huffington Post* (June 9, 2015), http://www.huffingtonpost.com/martin-shapiro/where-is-the-world-christ_b _7545896.html.

22. Greg Palkot, "Attacker Who Murdered Catholic Priest under Police Supervision Wore Monitoring Bracelet," *Fox News* (July 26, 2016), http://www.foxnews.com/world /2016/07/26/ french-police-kill-2-attackers-who-took-several-hostages-at-church.html.

23. Evan Perez and Shimon Prokupecz, "Feds Warn of ISIS Threats to Churches, Holiday Events," *CNN*, http://www.cnn.com/2016/12/23/politics/feds-warn-of-isis-threats -to-churches-holiday-events/, para. 1.

24. King, "Loving Your Enemies," para. 14.

25. Carey Lodge, "Meet the Christians Who Love Their Enemies, Even When It's ISIS," *Christian Today* (September 14, 2016), http://www.christiantoday.com/article/meet.the .christians.who.love.their.enemies.even.when.its.isis/95436.htm, para. 35.

26. Ibid., para. 10.

27. King, "Loving Your Enemies," para. 24.

28. King, "Loving Your Enemies," para. 38.

Chapter 32

1. *Time* (March 8, 1948).

2. Langdon Gilkey, *On Niebuhr: A Theological Study* (Chicago: University of Chicago Press, 2001), 11.

3. Ibid., 10.

4. Martin Halliwell, *The Constant Dialogue: Reinhold Niebuhr and American Intellectual Culture* (Lanham, MD: Rowman & Littlefield, 2005).

5. Larry Rasmussen, *Reinhold Niebuhr: Theologian of Public Life* (London: Collins Theological Publications, 1988), 1–2.

6. Reinhold Niebuhr, *The Nature and Destiny of Man*, vol. 1, *Human Nature* (New York: Scribner's, 1941), 5.

7. Ibid., 7.

8. Ibid., 16.

9. Ibid., 18.

10. Ibid., 10.

11. Ibid., 11.

12. Ibid., 15.

13. Ibid., 16.

14. Rasmussen, *Reinhold Niebuhr*, 6.

15. Halliwell, *Constant Dialogue*, 12–19.

16. See Aristotle, *Rhetoric*, I.1, 1354a1.

17. Halliwell, *Constant Dialogue*, 29–78.

18. Reinhold Niebuhr, "On Academic Vagabondage," in *Young Reinhold Niebuhr*, ed. William C. Crystal (St. Louis, MO: Eden, 1977), 145.

19. Reinhold Niebuhr, *Does Civilization Need Religion?* (New York: Macmillan, 1927), 39.

20. Reinhold Niebuhr, *Christian Realism and Political Problems* (New York: Scribner's, 1954).

21. Halliwell, *Constant Dialogue*, 4.

22. See, for instance, Pat Arneson and Ronald C. Arnett, *Dialogic Civility in a Cynical Age: Community, Hope, and Interpersonal Relationships* (Albany, NY: SUNY Press, 1999); Clifford G. Christians and John Merrill, eds., *Ethical Communication: Moral Stances in Human Dialogue* (Columbia: University of Missouri Press, 2009).

23. See C. S. Lewis, *God in the Dock: Essays on Theology and Ethics* (Grand Rapids, MI: Eerdmans, 1970), 263–68.

Chapter 33

1. Maisie Ward, *Unfinished Business* (New York: Sheed & Ward, 1964), 88.

2. Ibid.

3. See, for instance, Alan Cooperman, "Many Americans Don't Argue about Religion—Or Even Talk about It," Pew Research Center (April 15, 2016).

4. Ronald C. Arnett, Janie Harden Fritz, and Leeanne M. Bell, *Communication Ethics Literacy: Dialogue and Difference* (Thousand Oaks, CA: Sage, 2009), 90.

5. Frank J. Sheed, *God and the Human Condition Vol I: God and the Human Mind* (New York: Sheed & Ward, 1966).

6. Frank J. Sheed, *To Know Christ Jesus* (New York: Sheed & Ward, 1962).

7. Frank J. Sheed, *Theology for Beginners* (New York: Sheed & Ward, 1958), 6.

8. Sheed, *God and the Human Condition*, ix.

9. Ibid., 192.

10. Ibid., 190.

11. Ibid., 273.

12. Ibid., 192.

13. Ibid., 200.

14. Ibid., 69.

15. Ibid., 67.

16. Ibid., x.

17. Ibid., 196.

18. Ibid., 193.

19. Ibid., 68.

20. Ibid., 17.

21. The Catholic Evidence Guild, founded in 1918, was a guild of lay Catholics committed to understanding and speaking about the Catholic faith.

22. See Frank J. Sheed, "My Life on the Street Corner," *Saturday Review* 52 (1969): 22–23.

23. Ibid., 22.

24. Ibid.

25. Ibid.

26. Mary Jo Weaver, "Sheed and Ward," *U.S. Catholic Historian* 21, no. 3 (2003): 1–18.

27. Frank J. Sheed, *Theology and Sanity* (London: Sheed & Ward, 1946), 387.

28. Sheed, "My Life," 22–23.

29. Ibid., 22.

30. See David Meconi, introduction to *Frank Sheed & Maisie Ward, Spiritual Writings*, ed. David Meconi (Maryknoll, NY: Orbis Book, 2011), 13–41.

31. Sheed, *God and the Human Condition*, 67.

32. Cooperman, "Americans Don't Argue."

33. "Religion among Millennials," Pew Research Center (2010).

34. Heidi A. Campbell, "Understanding the Relationship between Religion Online and Offline in a Networked Society," *Journal of the American Academy of Religion* 80, no. 1 (March 1, 2012): 82.

35. Sheed, *God and the Human Condition*, 190.

36. Hans-Georg Gadamer, *Truth and Method*, 2nd. ed., trans. and rev. Joel Weinsheimer and Donald G. Marshall (New York: Continuum, 1989), 362.

37. Sheed, *God and the Human Condition*, 38.

38. Ibid., 190.

39. Ibid., ix.

40. Arnett, Fritz, and Bell, *Communication Ethics*, 90.

41. Sheed, "My Life," 22.

42. Ibid.

43. Sheed, *God and the Human Condition*, 3.

44. Sheed, "My Life," 22.

45. Ibid.

46. In his writing and speaking, Sheed frequently referred to Jesus' promise, "If you believe, you will receive whatever you ask" (Mt 21:22 NIV). Believers who voice a question believe they will eventually receive an answer.

Chapter 34

1. Hans Urs von Balthasar, *My Work: In Retrospect* (San Francisco: Communio Books, 1993), 15.

2. Hans Urs von Balthasar, "Theology and Sanctity," in *The Word Made Flesh*, vol. 1 of *Explorations in Theology*, trans. A. V. Littledale and Alexander Dru (San Francisco: Ignatius Press, 1989), 206.

3. Hans Urs von Balthasar, *Seeing the Form*, vol. 1 of *The Glory of the Lord: A Theological Aesthetics*, ed. John Riches, trans. Erasmo Leiva-Merikakis (San Francisco: Ignatius Press, 2009), 10.

4. Ibid., 19–20.

5. Ibid., 75.

6. Ibid., 19.

7. Ibid., 34.

8. Hans Urs von Balthasar, *Studies in Theological Style: Clerical Styles*, vol. 2 of *The Glory of the Lord: A Theological Aesthetics*, ed. John Riches, trans. Andrew Louth, Francis McDonagh, and Brian McNeil (San Francisco: Ignatius Press, 1984), 12.

9. Balthasar, *Seeing the Form*, 121.

10. Balthasar, *Studies in Theological Style: Clerical Styles*, 15.

11. Hans Urs von Balthasar, *The Realm of Metaphysics in Antiquity*, vol. 4 of *The Glory of the Lord: A Theological Aesthetics*, ed. John Riches, trans. Oliver Davies, Andrew Louth, Brian McNeil, John Saward, and Rowan Williams (San Francisco: Ignatius Press, 1991), 216.

12. Hans Urs von Balthasar, *The Realm of Metaphysics in the Modern Age*, vol. 5 of *The Glory of the Lord: A Theological Aesthetics*, ed. Brian McNeil and John Riches, trans. Andrew Louth, John Saward, Rowan Williams, and Oliver Davies (San Francisco: Ignatius Press, 1989), 614–15, 646–48.

13. Hans Urs von Balthasar, *Theology: The Old Covenant*, vol. 6 of *The Glory of the Lord: A Theological Aesthetics*, ed. John Riches, trans. Brian McNeil and Erasmo Leiva-Merikakis (San Francisco: Ignatius Press, 1991), 302.

14. Ibid., 374.

15. Ibid., 391.

16. Hans Urs von Balthasar, *Theology: The New Covenant*, vol. 7 of *The Glory of the Lord: A Theological Aesthetics*, ed. John Riches, trans. Brian McNeil (San Francisco: Ignatius Press, 1990), 498.

17. Jaroslav Pelikan, *Christian Doctrine and Modern Culture (Since 1700)*, vol. 5 of *The Christian Tradition: A History of the Development of Christian Doctrine* (Chicago: University of Chicago Press, 1989), 5.

18. Ibid., 175–77.

19. David Moss and Edward T. Oakes, introduction to *The Cambridge Companion to Hans Urs von Balthasar*, ed. Edward T. Oakes and David Moss (New York: Cambridge University Press, 2004), 2.

20. Hans Urs von Balthasar, *Truth of the World*, vol. 1 of *Theo-Logic: Theological Logical Theory*, trans. Adrian J. Walker (San Francisco: Ignatius Press, 2000), 28–29.

21. Hannah Arendt, *Men in Dark Times* (New York: Harcourt, Brace, and World, 1968), viii.

22. Hans Urs von Balthasar, *Epilogue*, trans. Edward T. Oakes (San Francisco: Ignatius Press, 2004), 10–11.

23. Arendt, *Men in Dark Times*, ix.

24. Augustine, *On Christian Doctrine* 4.32, trans. D. W. Robertson Jr. (New York: Macmillan, 1958), 140.

25. Robin P. Clair, *Organizing Silence: A World of Possibilities* (Albany, NY: SUNY Press), 1998.

26. Plato, *Phaedrus*, trans. Alexander Nehamas and Paul Woodruff (Indianapolis, IN: Hackett, 1995), 251c–251d.

27. William G. Kelley Jr., "Rhetoric as Seduction," *Philosophy and Rhetoric* 6 (1973): 69.

28. C. S. Lewis, preface to *Essays Presented to Charles Williams*, ed. C. S. Lewis (Grand Rapids, MI: Eerdmans, 1966), vi.

29. Balthasar, *Epilogue*, 11.

Chapter 35

1. Jacques Ellul, *Jacques Ellul on Religion, Technology, and Politics: Conversations with Patrick Troude-Chastenet*, trans. Joan Mendès France (Atlanta, GA: Scholars Press, 1998), 52.

2. Jacques Ellul, *Perspectives on Our Age: Jacques Ellul Speaks on His Life and Work*, ed. William H. Vanderburg (Toronto: Anansi, 1981), 11–12.

3. Jacques Ellul, *The Presence of the Kingdom*, trans. Olive Wyon, 2nd ed. (Colorado Springs: Helmers & Howard, 1989), xiv.

4. Ibid., ix.

5. John Durham Peters and Peter Simonson, *Introduction to Mass Communication and America Social Thought*, ed. John Durham Peters and Peter Simonson (Lanham, MD: Rowman and Littlefield, 2004), 88.

6. Ellul, *Presence*, 118.

7. Ibid., 9.

8. Ibid.

9. Ibid., 71–77.

10. Ibid., 119.

11. Ibid., 71–77.

12. Ibid., 13.

13. Ibid., 51.

14. Ibid.

15. Ibid., 54.

16. Ibid., 82.

17. Ibid.

18. Ibid., 83.

19. Ibid.

20. Ibid., 85.

21. Ibid.

22. Ibid.

23. Ibid., 63.

24. Ibid., 94.

25. Ibid., 120.

26. Ibid.

27. Ibid., 121–23.

28. James Emery White, *The Rise of the Nones: Understanding and Reaching the Religiously Unaffiliated* (Grand Rapids, MI: Baker, 2014), 20.

29. See Christine D. Pohl, *Making Room: Recovering Hospitality as a Christian Tradition* (Grand Rapids, MI: Eerdmans, 1993).

30. Ellul, *Presence*, 106.

31. Ibid., 107.

32. See Walter J. Ong, SJ, "Voice and the Opening of Closed Systems," in *Faith and Contexts, Vol. 2, Supplemental Studies 1946–1989*, ed. Thomas J. Farrell and Paul A. Soukup (Atlanta: Scholars Press, 1992), 162–90.

33. Ellul, *Presence*, 124.

34. Ibid., 118.

Chapter 36

1. Karl Barth and John Howard Yoder, qtd. in Gerald J. Mast, "Pacifism as a Way of Knowing," in *John Howard Yoder: Radical Theologian*, ed. J. Denny Weaver (Eugene, OR: Cascade Books, 2014), 243.

2. Mark Thiessen Nation, *John Howard Yoder: Mennonite Patience, Evangelical Witness, Catholic Convictions* (Grand Rapids, MI: Eerdmans, 2006), 1–16.

3. Ibid., 17–29.

4. Earl Zimmerman, *Practicing the Politics of Jesus: The Origin and Significance of John Howard Yoder's Social Ethics* (Telford, PA: Cascadia, 2007), 32–69.

5. Rachel Waltner Goosen, "Defanging the Beast: Mennonite Responses to John Howard Yoder's Sexual Abuse," *The Mennonite Quarterly Review* 89 (January 2015): 7–80.

6. For more discussion of Yoder's sexual abuse of women, see Gerald J. Mast, "Sin and Failure in Anabaptist Theology," in *John Howard Yoder: Radical Theologian*, ed. J. Denny Weaver (Eugene, OR: Cascade Books, 2014), 351–70.

7. Branson Parler, *Things Hold Together: John Howard Yoder's Trinitarian Theology of Culture* (Harrisonburg, VA: Herald Press, 2012), 25.

8. John Howard Yoder, "Armaments and Eschatology," *Studies in Christian Ethics* 1 (1988): 58.

9. John Howard Yoder, *The Christian Witness to the State* (Newton, KS: Faith and Life, 1964), 33n3.

10. Ibid., 13.

11. John Howard Yoder, *Body Politics: Five Practices of the Christian Community before the Watching World* (Scottdale, PA: Herald Press, 2001), ix.

12. Ibid., 20.

13. Ibid., 2–4.

14. Ibid., 32–34.

15. Ibid., 49.

16. Ibid., 70.

17. Ibid., 10.

18. For a recent study of how Yoder's work on body politics interacts helpfully with theories of media and technology, see Paul C. Heidebrecht, *Beyond the Cutting Edge?: Yoder, Technology, and the Practices of the Church* (Eugene, OR: Pickwick, 2014).

19. John Howard Yoder, *The Christian and Capital Punishment* (Newton, KS: Faith and Life), 1961.

20. See John L. Ruth, *Forgiveness: A Legacy of the West Nickel Mines Amish School* (Scottdale, PA: Herald Press, 2007).

21. Yoder, *Christian and Capital Punishment*, 4–5.

22. Ibid.

23. Ibid., 7.

24. Ibid., 5–6.

25. Ibid., 6.

26. Ibid., 17.

27. Ibid.

28. Ibid., 19.

29. Ibid., 20.

30. John Howard Yoder, "On Not Being Ashamed of the Gospel," *A Pacifist Way of Knowing: John Howard Yoder's Nonviolent Epistemology*, ed. Christian E. Early and Ted G. Grimsrud (Eugene, OR: Cascade Books, 2010), 51.

31. Ibid., 52.

32. According to Yoder, good news "cannot be imposed by authority, or coercively. It is rendered null when assent is imposed." Ibid., 50. Yoder points out that the particulars of the gospel story include the rejection and crucifixion of Jesus Christ. This rejection is "part of the validation" of the gospel, such that "readiness to bear hostility is part of the message." Ibid., 51–52.

Chapter 37

1. Carl F. H. Henry, *The Uneasy Conscience of Modern Fundamentalism* (Grand Rapids, MI: Eerdmans, 1947), 18.

2. Ibid.

3. Ibid.

4. See Martin E. Marty, *Pilgrims in Their Own Land: 500 Years of Religion in America* (New York: Penguin Books, 1984), 379.

5. Henry, *Uneasy Conscience*, 20, 28.

6. Ibid., 32.

7. Ibid., 65.

8. Ibid., 70.

9. Ibid.

10. Ibid.

11. Ibid., 71.

12. Ibid., 72.

13. Ibid., 86.

14. Ibid.

15. Ibid.

16. Ibid., 52.

17. He would earn the second of his two doctorates at Boston University, which in 1839 had been founded as a Methodist Bible institute. "Boston University Timeline," accessed January 9, 2016, www.bu.edu/timeline/.

18. George Marsden and Bradley J. Longfield, eds., *The Secularization of the Academy* (New York: Oxford University Press, 1990), 3–4.

19. "About the CCCU," accessed January 10, 2015, www.cccu.org/about.

20. See L. Nelson Bell, "Should We Ever Be Intolerant?" *The Preacher's Magazine* 34, no. 3 (March 1959): 1; Marshall McLuhan, *Understanding Media: The Extension of Man* (New York: McGraw-Hill), 9.

21. David Paul Nord, "Religious Publishing and the Marketplace," in *Communication and Change in American Religious History*, ed. Leonard I. Sweet (Grand Rapids, MI: Eerdmans, 1993), 241.

22. *The Fundamentals: A Testimony to the Truth* was published by what was then the Bible Institute of Los Angeles (later Biola University) between 1910 and 1915. See B. M. Pietsch, "Lyman Stewart and Early Fundamentalism," *Church History* 82, no. 3 (September 2013): 618.

23. See Mark Noll, *A History of Christianity in the United States and Canada* (Grand Rapids, MI: Eerdmans, 1992), 383.

24. Henry, *Uneasy Conscience*, 34.

25. "Education and Training: History and Timeline," U.S. Department of Veterans Affairs, accessed June 30, 2016, http://www.benefits.va.gov/gibill/history.asp.

26. "Poverty Rate 1947–2012," The Heritage Foundation, accessed May 5, 2016, http://www.heritage.org/multimedia/infographic/2014/09/poverty-rate-1947-2012.

27. "Hoover Report Defines a Difficulty," *Congressional Digest* 28, no. 12 (December 1, 1949): 301.

28. Thomas E. Bergler, "Youth, Christianity and the Crisis of Civilization," *Religion & American Culture* 24, no. 2 (Summer 2014): 260–61.

29. See John Paul Hill, "Commissioner A. B. 'Happy' Chandler and the Integration of Major League Baseball," *Nine: A Journal of Baseball, History & Culture* 19, no. 1 (2010): 28.

30. Eileen Boris, "'You Wouldn't Want One of 'Em Dancing with Your Wife': Racialized Bodies on the Job in World War II," *American Quarterly* 50, no. 1 (1998): 77–108; see also, George Lipsitz, *Rainbow at Midnight: Labor and Culture in the 1940s* (Urbana: University of Illinois Press, 1994).

31. Mark Hearn, "Color-Blind Racism, Color-Blind Theology, and Church Practices," *Religious Education* 104, no. 3 (May–June 2009): 279–80.

32. Andrew Preston, "Peripheral Visions: American Mainline Protestants and the Global Cold War," *Cold War History* 13, no. 1 (February 2013): 112.

33. Barna Research Group, "Black Lives Matter and Racial Tension in America" (May 5, 2016), accessed June 5, 2017, https://www.barna.com/research/black-lives-matter -and-racial-tension-in-america/.

34. David French, "The Ferocious Religious Faith of the Campus Social-Justice Warrior," *The National Review* (November 23, 2015), accessed June 9, 2017, http://www .nationalreview.com/article/427523/ferocious-religious-faith-campus-social-justice -warrior-david-french.

35. See Peter Catron, "Made in America? Immigrant Occupational Mobility in the First Half of the Twentieth Century," *Journal of Sociology* 122, no. 2 (2016): 325; Edwin Ackerman, "'What Part of Illegal Don't You Understand?': Bureaucracy and Civil Society in the Shaping of Illegality," *Ethnic & Rural Studies* 37, no. 2 (2014): 183–203.

36. Henry, *Uneasy Conscience*, 68.

37. John Dewey, *Democracy and Education* (1916; repr., New York: Macmillan, 1944), 357.

38. Henry, *Uneasy Conscience*, 68.

39. Ibid., 77.

40. Ibid., 71.

41. Ibid., 70.

42. See Bertrall L. Ross II, "Administering Suspect Classes," *Duke Law Journal* 66, no. 8 (2017): 1807–46. For discussion of the Free Exercise-Establishment debate, see Richard H. Fallon Jr., "Constitutionally Forbidden Legislative Intent," *Harvard Law Review* 130, no. 2 (2016): 523–89; and David Cinotti, "The Incoherence of Neutrality: A Case for Eliminating Neutrality from Religion Clause Jurisprudence," *Journal of Church & State* 45, no. 3 (2003): 499–533.

Chapter 38

1. Ian Fisher, "Chiara Lubich, Who Founded Catholic Lay Group, Dies at 88," *New York Times* (March 15, 2008), http://www.nytimes.com/2008/03/15/world/europe /15lubich.html.

2. Lubich has recounted the origins of the Focalare Movement in many formats and on many occasions. The version here comes from two sources. Chiara Lubich, "The Beginnings," in *Essential Writings: Spirituality, Dialogue, Culture*, ed. Michel Vandeleene, trans. Bob Cummings et al. (Hyde Park, NY: New City Press, 2007), 3–11. Another version is found at *Focolare Movement*, accessed August 31, 2017, http://www.focolare.org /en/chiara-lubich/chi-e-chiara/gli-inizi/.

3. Dennis D. Cali, *Mapping Media Ecology: Introduction to the Field* (New York: Peter Lang, 2017), 25.

4. Scripture quotations in this chapter are taken from the New International Version (NIV).

5. Lubich, "The Beginnings," 5–6.

6. Chiara Lubich, "The Charism of Unity and the Media," in *Essential Writings: Spirituality, Dialogue, Culture,* ed. Michel Vandeleene (Hyde Park, NY: New City Press, 2007), 290–97. This address was given at a conference called "Communication and Media." Lubich gave another noteworthy speech about communication in receiving

an honorary doctorate in Social Communications by St. John's University in Bangkok, Thailand, January 25, 1997. Transcripts unavailable.

7. Lubich, "The Charism," 295.

8. Ibid, 294.

9. Ibid., 295.

10. Ibid., 296 (italics original).

11. Ibid.

12. Ibid.

13. Ibid. (italics original).

14. Ibid.

15. Ibid. (italics original).

16. Ibid., 293.

17. Ibid., 295.

18. Ibid.

19. Ibid., 296.

20. Ibid. (italics original).

21. Ibid.

22. Ibid.

23. Ibid., 297 (italics original).

24. Sherry Turkle, *Alone Together: Why We Expect More from Technology and Less from Each Other* (New York: Basic Books, 2011).

25. James Carey, *Communication as Culture: Essays on Media and Society* (London: Routledge, 1988).

26. Jacques Ellul, *The Presence of the Kingdom* (Colorado Springs: Helmers & Howard), 49.

27. Lubich, "The Charism," 295.

28. Mother Teresa, qtd. in Malcolm Muggeridge, *The Very Best of Malcolm Muggeridge*, ed. Ian Hunter (Vancouver: Regent College Publishing, 2003), 68.

29. Raymond Williams, *Television: Technology and Cultural Form* (London: Fontana, 1974), 1–23.

30. This has become the motto for many groups because it is the Latin Vulgate rendering for Jn 17:21.

31. Lubich, "The Charism," 295.

Chapter 39

1. Mary Benson, *Nelson Mandela: The Man and the Movement,* foreword by Desmond Tutu (New York: W. W. Norton, 1986), 5.

2. Desmond Tutu, *No Future Without Forgiveness* (New York: Image, 1999), 3–4.

3. Desmond Tutu, *Where Is Now Thy God?* audiotapes of lectures presented at Trinity Institute Conference (New York: Parish of Trinity Church, 1989).

4. Tutu, *No Future*, 31.

5. Ibid., 31.

6. Ibid., 105, 107.

7. Ibid., 54–5.

8. Ibid., 54.

9. "Amnesty Hearings and Decisions," *Department of Justice and Constitutional Development of the Republic of South Africa*, accessed October 12, 2017, http://www.justice .gov.za/.

10. Tutu, *No Future*, 270.

11. Desmond Tutu and Mpho Tutu, *The Forgiving Book: The Fourfold Path for Healing Ourselves and Our World* (New York: HarperOne, 2014), 70.

12. Ibid., 71.

13. Ibid., 74.

14. Ibid., 78.

15. Ibid.

16. Ibid.

17. Ibid., 104.

18. Ibid., 115.

19. Ibid., 110.

20. Ibid., 127.

21. Ibid., 125.

22. Ibid., 121.

23. Ibid., 134.

24. Ibid., 121.

25. Ibid., 148.

26. Ibid., 150.

27. Ibid., 151.

28. Ibid., 152.

29. Ibid., 157.

30. Charles Taylor, *The Ethics of Authenticity* (Cambridge, MA: Harvard University Press, 1991), 3.

31. Ibid., 4.

32. Ibid., 87.

33. Vincent R. Waldron and Douglas L. Kelley, *Communicating Forgiveness* (Thousand Oaks, CA: Sage, 2007), 77, 80.

34. Ibid., 122.

35. Ibid., 109.

36. Ibid.

37. Ibid., 59.

38. Ibid., 131.

39. Ibid., 67–72.

40. Ibid., 73–78.

41. Ibid., 137.

42. Ibid., 80 (italics original).

Chapter 40

1. Walter Brueggemann with Carolyn J. Sharp, *Living Countertestimony: Conversations with Walter Brueggemann* (Louisville, KY: Westminster John Knox Press, 2012), 44.

2. Walter Brueggemann, qtd. in Andrew Santella, "Renowned Scholar: Walter Brueggemann '55 Brings the Bible to Life as a Leading Authority on the Old Testament," accessed January 26, 2016, http://www.elmhurst.edu/magazine/alumnistories/7499737.html.

3. Ibid., para. 23.

4. Brueggemann, qtd. in Sharp, *Countertestimony*, 44.

5. Ibid.

6. Brueggemann, qtd. in Santella, para. 14.

7. Walter Brueggemann, "Counterscript: Living with the Elusive God," accessed June 23, 2017, http://christiancentury.org/article/2005–11/counterscript.

8. Walter Brueggemann, *The Prophetic Imagination*, 2nd ed. (Philadelphia: Fortress, 2001), 28.

9. Ibid., 12.

10. Ibid.

11. Ibid., 104.

12. Ibid., 95.

13. Ibid.

14. Ibid., 9.

15. Ibid., 23.

16. See Steve Wilkens and Mark L. Sanford, *Hidden Worldviews: Eight Cultural Stories That Shape Our Lives* (Downers Grove, IL: IVP Academic, 2009).

17. Brueggemann, "Counterscript," 22.

18. Brueggemann, *Reality, Grief, Hope: Three Urgent Prophetic Tasks* (Grand Rapids, MI: Eerdmans, 2014).

19. Brueggemann, "Counterscript," 22.

20. Karl Barth, qtd. by Brueggemann, "Counterscript," 24.

21. Ibid., 26–27.

22. Walter Brueggemann, "Relinquishment and Reception: Ministry in the Fissure," lecture, 2017 Festival of Homiletics, May 16, 2017.

23. Michael Lipka, "Religious 'Nones' Are Not Only Growing, They're Becoming More Secular" (November 11, 2015), Pew Research Center, accessed January 29, 2016, http://www.pewresearch.org/fact-tank/2015/11/11/religious-nones-are-not-only-growing-theyre-becoming-more-secular/, para. 2.

24. Ibid.

25. Brueggemann, *The Prophetic Imagination*, xii.

26. Michael Lipka, "Why America's 'Nones' Left Religion Behind" (August 24, 2016), Pew Research Center, accessed August 18, 2017, http://www.pewresearch.org/fact-tank/2016/08/24/why-americas-nones-left-religion-behind/.

27. Brueggemann, "Relinquishment and Reception."

28. Martin Luther King Jr., "I Have a Dream," speech delivered August 23, 1963, Washington, DC, accessed August 24, 2017, http://www.americanrhetoric.com/speeches/mlkihaveadream.htm, para. 4.

29. In the second edition of *The Prophetic Imagination* (2001), Brueggemann provides other examples in which prophetic imagination permeates ministry: a church-run day-care facility for elderly patients with dementia or Alzheimer's disease, former president Jimmy Carter's work for Habitat for Humanity, a church pastor beginning services not with praise but with lament as "public processing of pain" (121–23).

30. Walter Brueggemann, *Sabbath as Resistance: Saying NO to the CULTURE OF NOW* (Louisville, KY: Westminster John Knox Press, 2014), 13.

31. Ibid., 43.

Chapter 41

1. Peter Kreeft, *Between Allah & Jesus: What Christians Can Learn from Muslims* (Downers Grove, IL: InterVarsity Press, 2010), 14.

2. Ibid., 27.

3. Ibid., 30.

4. Ibid., 10.

5. "Combating Post-9/11 Discriminatory Backlash," *The United States Department of Justice* (August 6, 2015), accessed January 1, 2016, http://www.justice.gov/crt/combating-post-911-discriminatory-backlash-6.

6. Eugene Scott, "Trump: My Muslim Friends Don't Support My Immigration Ban," *CNN Politics* (December 13, 2015), accessed January 5, 2016, http://www.cnn.com/2015/12/13/politics/donald-trump-muslim-ban-state-of-the-union/.

7. Sarah Larimer, "Why Franklin Graham Says Donald Trump Is Right about Stopping Muslim Immigration," *The Washington Post* (December 10, 2015), accessed January 5, 2016, washingtonpost.com/news/acts-of-faith/wp/2015/12/10/why-franklin-graham-says-donald-trump-is-right-about-stopping-muslim-immigration/.

8. Kreeft, *Between Allah & Jesus*, 14.

9. Ibid., 12.

10. Ibid., 9.

11. Ibid., 12 (italics original).

12. Ibid., 17.

13. Ibid.

14. Ibid.

15. Ibid., 117.

16. Ibid.

17. Ibid., 118.

18. Ibid.

19. Ibid., 26.

20. Ibid.

21. Antonio Gramsci, *Selections from the Prison Notebooks*, trans. Quintin Hoare and Geoffrey Smith (New York: International Publishers, 1971), 418 (italics added).

22. John Wesley, *A Plain Account of Christian Perfection* (London: Epworth, 1952), 87.

23. Kreeft, *Between Allah & Jesus*, 89.

24. Edward Said, *Orientalism* (New York: Vintage, 1979), 93.

25. Eugene Peterson, *Tell It Slant: A Conversation on the Language of Jesus in His Stories and Prayers* (Grand Rapids, MI: Eerdmans, 2008), 20.

26. Kreeft, *Between Allah & Jesus*, 17–18.

27. Ibid., 18.

Chapter 42

1. James H. Cone, *The Cross and the Lynching Tree* (New York: Orbis Books, 2011).

2. Ibid., 31.

3. Ibid., 18.

4. Quintus Tullius Cicero, *Pro Rabirio [The Speech in Defence of Gaius Rabirius Postumus Charged with High Treason]*, 467, in *Cicero: The Speeches: Pro Lege Manilia. Pro Caecina. Pro Cluentio. Pro Rabirio Perduellionis Reo*, trans. H. Grose Hodge (New York: G. P. Putnam's Sons, 1927).

5. Cone, *The Cross*, 2.

6. Ibid.

7. James Goodman, "'At the Hands of Persons Unknown': Peculiar Institution," review of *At the Hands of Persons Unknown: The Lynching of Black America,* by Philip Dray, *New York Times* (May 26, 2002), para. 3.

8. "Negro Dies at the Stake," *New York Times* (1899), accessed February 11, 2016, http://query.nytimes.com/mem/archive-free/pdf?res=9B03E4DA1530EE32A25757C 2A9629C94689ED7CF.

9. Ibid.

10. As cited by Edward L. Ayers in "An American Nightmare," review of *Trouble in the Mind: Black Southerners in the Age of Jim Crow,* by Leon F. Litwack, *New York Times* (May 3, 1998), para. 2.

11. Ibid., 31.

12. Ibid., 159.

13. Cone, *The Cross,* 154.

14. Ibid., 158.

15. Ibid.

16. Ibid., 155.

17. Ibid., 162.

18. Ibid., 165.

19. Ibid.

20. Ibid., xiv.

21. Ibid., xv.

22. Michelle Alexander, *The New Jim Crow: Mass Incarceration in an Age of Colorblindness* (New York: New Press, 2010), 192.

23. Quoted in Alexander, *The New Jim Crow,* 159.

24. Christine Wicker, "Refusing Sanctuary to Children in Need," *The Dallas Morning News Online* (June 29, 2014).

Chapter 43

1. Stanley Hauerwas, *A Community of Character: Toward a Constructive Christian Social Ethic* (South Bend, IN: University of Notre Dame, 1981), 145.

2. Ibid., 146.

3. Ibid.

4. Ibid.

5. Ibid.

6. Ibid., 1.

7. Ibid., 9.

8. Ibid., 10

9. Ibid.

10. Ibid., 11.

11. Ibid., 6.

12. Stanley Hauerwas, *Hannah's Child: A Theologian's Memoir* (Grand Rapids, MI: Eerdmans, 2010), 96.

13. Stanley Hauerwas, "On Keeping Theological Ethics Theological," in *The Hauerwas Reader,* ed. John Berkman and Michael G. Cartwright (Durham, NC: Duke University Press, 2001), 64–69.

14. Ibid., 69.

15. See http://apps.washingtonpost.com/g/documents/local/letter-to-obama-from -faith-leaders/1072/.

16. Hauerwas, *A Community of Character*, 10.

17. See http://www.oneeastern.com/2014/07/17/president-duffett-seeks-right-to-discriminate-against-lgbt-individuals/.

18. See http://waltonian.eastern.edu/news/state-of-the-university-address-by-president-duffett/.

19. Hauerwas, *A Community of Character*, 11.

20. Ibid., 74.

INDEX